Palgrave Series in Islamic Theology, Law, and History

Series Editor
Khaled Abou El Fadl
School of Law
University of California, Los Angeles
Los Angeles, CA, USA

This ground-breaking series, edited by one of the most influential scholars of Islamic law, presents a cumulative and progressive set of original studies that substantially raise the bar for rigorous scholarship in the field of Islamic Studies. By relying on original sources and challenging common scholarly stereotypes and inherited wisdoms, the volumes of the series attest to the exacting and demanding methodological and pedagogical standards necessary for contemporary studies of Islam. These volumes are chosen not only for their disciplined methodology, exhaustive research, or academic authoritativeness, but for their ability to make critical interventions in the process of understanding the world of Islam as it was, is, and is likely to become. They make central and even pivotal contributions to understanding the experience of the lived and living Islam, and the ways that this rich and creative Islamic tradition has been created and uncreated, or constructed, deconstructed, and reconstructed. In short, the volumes of this series are chosen for their great relevance to the many realities that shaped the ways that Muslims understand, represent, and practice their religion, and ultimately, to understanding the worlds that Muslims helped to shape, and in turn, the worlds that helped shaped Muslims.

Abbas Panakkal • Nasr M Arif
Editors

Matrilineal, Matriarchal, and Matrifocal Islam

The World of Women-Centric Islam

Editors
Abbas Panakkal
School of History
University of St Andrews
St Andrews, UK

Nasr M Arif
University of St Andrews
St Andrews, UK

University of Cairo
Giza, Egypt

ISSN 2945-669X   ISSN 2945-6703   (electronic)
Palgrave Series in Islamic Theology, Law, and History
ISBN 978-3-031-51748-8   ISBN 978-3-031-51749-5   (eBook)
https://doi.org/10.1007/978-3-031-51749-5

© The Editor(s) (if applicable) and The Author(s), under exclusive licence to Springer Nature Switzerland AG 2024
This work is subject to copyright. All rights are solely and exclusively licensed by the Publisher, whether the whole or part of the material is concerned, specifically the rights of translation, reprinting, reuse of illustrations, recitation, broadcasting, reproduction on microfilms or in any other physical way, and transmission or information storage and retrieval, electronic adaptation, computer software, or by similar or dissimilar methodology now known or hereafter developed.
The use of general descriptive names, registered names, trademarks, service marks, etc. in this publication does not imply, even in the absence of a specific statement, that such names are exempt from the relevant protective laws and regulations and therefore free for general use. The publisher, the authors, and the editors are safe to assume that the advice and information in this book are believed to be true and accurate at the date of publication. Neither the publisher nor the authors or the editors give a warranty, expressed or implied, with respect to the material contained herein or for any errors or omissions that may have been made. The publisher remains neutral with regard to jurisdictional claims in published maps and institutional affiliations.

This Palgrave Macmillan imprint is published by the registered company Springer Nature Switzerland AG.
The registered company address is: Gewerbestrasse 11, 6330 Cham, Switzerland

Paper in this product is recyclable.

CONTENTS

Part I South and Southeast Asia 1

Matrifocal, Matrilineal, or Matriarchal? Cultural Resilience
and Vulnerability Among the Matrilineal and Muslim
Minangkabau in Indonesia 3
Lyn Parker

Adat Perpatih in Malaysia: Nature, History, Practice, and
Contemporary Issues 43
Alexander Wain and Norliza Saleh

Cultural and Social Integrations in Matrilineal, Matriarchal,
Matrifocal Muslim Communities of South India 77
Abbas Panakkal

Part II Northeast Asia 111

Affective Matrivocality and Women's Voices: A History of
Muslim Women Writers in China 113
Jing Wang

v

vi   CONTENTS

Matriarchal Family Structure in Korea's Jeju Island and its
Implications for the Muslim Community in Korea   145
Hee Soo Lee

The Maternal Initiative Role in the Japanese Muslim
Community: Japanese Muslim Wives as Mediators Between
Muslim Immigrants and Japanese Society   169
Yuki Shiozaki

Part III   Africa   191

Muslim Family Under Portuguese Rule: *Sharī ʿa* and
Matrilineal Custom in Colonial Coastal Northern
Mozambique (ca. 1900–1974)   193
Liazzat J. K. Bonate

Asante Nkramo and Fantse Nkramo: Unravelling the Paradox
of Islam and Matriliny in Ghana   221
Mustapha Abdul Hamid

Part IV   Andalusia and Americas   245

The Tuareg, from Arabia to Americas   247
Samira Benturki Saïdi

The Origins of Andalusian Muslim Matrilineal Systems   273
Alfred G. Kavanagh

Index   315

Notes on Contributors

Mustapha Abdul Hamid is the former minister for information and professor at the Department of Religion and Human Values of the University of Cape Coast. In September 2017, he completed and was awarded a PhD in Religious Studies by the University of Cape Coast. Mustapha Abdul-Hamid's research interests are in the areas of Islamic mysticism, political thought in Islam, Islam and gender, and Islam in Ghana. He has published extensively in reputable journals around the world. Some of his publications include "Religious Language and the Charge of Blasphemy: In Defense of Al-Hallaj" and "Christian-Muslim Relations in Ghana: A Model for World Dialogue and Peace."

Nasr M. Arif is a visiting professor at St. Andrews University, UK, and Professor of Political Science at Cairo University, Egypt. He served as Professor of Islamic Studies and founding Executive Director of the Institute for Islamic World Studies at Zayed University, UAE. He is the editor of the Routledge series on Global Islamic Cultures. Arif's works have been published in Arabic and translated into English, Spanish, Hungarian, Kurdish, Persian, and Urdu. His research focuses on Islamic traditions and political thought, the history of Islamic cultures, political development, and comparative political systems. He received a Ph.D. degree in Political Science in 1995 from Cairo University, Egypt, and the University of Maryland, College Park, USA.

Liazzat J. K. Bonate is an associate professor at Chr. Michelsen Institute Bergen, Norway, and was Lecturer in African History at the University of

viii   NOTES ON CONTRIBUTORS

the West Indies (UWI), St Augustine in Trinidad and Tobago. She has researched Islam in northern Mozambique in colonial and post-colonial periods by focusing on Islamic law, ajami, gender relations, land and matriliny, Islamic education, Islamic NGOs, Salafism, Sufi Orders, Muslim relationships with colonial and post-colonial states, governments and institutions, Indian Ocean and Swahili networks, Muslims and liberation movements, and Muslim women's access to resources and power. Previously she taught at Seoul National University in South Korea (2011–2015) and at the Centre for African Studies and the Department of History at the Eduardo Mondlane University in Mozambique (1993–2016, on and off).

Alfred G. Kavanagh is a distinguished academic serving as the Professor of Globalization Trends in the Middle East at the University of Comillas in Madrid. With a European PhD in Fine Arts, his research has centred on the symbolism of power in the Modern Age, earning recognition for its depth and insight. Gutiérrez-Kavanagh's educational journey is marked by excellence, encompassing a Law degree, an MBA from the Instituto de Empresa in Madrid, and an MA in Arts from the University Complutense. His linguistic prowess includes a post-graduate degree in Indo-European Languages (Avestic-Pahlevi-Sanskrit) from the University of Salamanca. Moreover, his commitment to continuous learning is evident through the acquisition of various diplomas awarded by the University of Cambridge and the prestigious Chambre de Commerce of Paris. Gutiérrez-Kavanagh's multifaceted background and dedication have made a profound impact on fields such as globalization, international relations, fine arts, and legal translation, inspiring the academic community and shaping future generations of scholars and thinkers.

Hee Soo Lee is Emeritus Professor of Cultural Anthropology at Hanyang University and the Director of the Institute of Islamic Culture at SungKongHoe University, Seoul. A well-known anthropologist of Islamic studies in Korea, he holds BA and MA degrees from Hankuk University of Foreign Studies, Seoul, and PhD from Istanbul University. He has conducted extensive anthropological field works in such Muslim countries as Saudi Arabia, Tunisia, Egypt, Iran, Malaysia, and Uzbekistan since 1979. He served as the President of the Korean Association of Middle East Studies for 2008–2009. He continued his research on Islamic-Middle East issues at such institutes as Center for Economic and Social Studies and Research (CERES) (Tunisia), Research Centre For Islamic History, Art and Culture

(IRCICA) (Istanbul), and Marmara University (Turkey). He also pursued research at the University of Washington in 2002 and 2012 and the University of Vienna in 2014 where he was a visiting professor. In addition, he serves as the advisor of Ministry of Foreign Affairs (MOFA), Prime Ministry National Counterterrorism Center of Korea. His book entitled *ISLAM: 9.11 and Changes of the Muslim World* sold out more than 230,000 copies. He is also the author of 95 books including *Korea and Muslim World: A Historical Encounter, Islam for Children*, and *History of Turkey*.

Abbas Panakkal is a historian currently affiliated to the School of History, University of St Andrews, UK. Panakkal is a member of the advisory board of the Religious Life and Belief Centre at the University of Surrey, UK. He is working on a research project focused on the diverse nature of the integration and indigenization of vernacular communities. He edited *South Asian Islam: A Spectrum of Integration and Indigenisation* (Routledge 2023) and *Southeast Asian Islam: Integration and Indigenisation* (Routledge 2024). Panakkal is the Director of the International Interfaith Harmony Initiative, which has been organizing international interfaith conferences in collaboration with the United Nations Interfaith Initiatives, the Malaysian Prime Minister's Department for Unity and Integration, and the International Islamic University Malaysia for a decade. He was awarded a research fellowship by Griffith University in Australia. He was also the project coordinator of the G20 Interfaith Summit in Australia (2014), Turkey (2015), and Germany (2017).

Lyn Parker is a sociocultural anthropologist and researcher specializing in contemporary Indonesian culture and society, environmental problems, and gender issues at the School of Social Sciences at the University of Western Australia (UWA). Her main research interests are the anthropology of Indonesia, women and gender relations, education, and the environment. Her interest in Indonesia flourished during her high school years when she enrolled in an Indonesian language class, the first Indonesian class taught in schools in New South Wales. She acknowledges that if Hindi, Urdu, or Sanskrit had been offered, her career could have taken a different trajectory, studying and researching in India. Parker did not foresee that she would combine her love for the Indonesian language with the culture and become an anthropologist, until she had finished her honours year at Australian National University (ANU). Following her tertiary education, Parker conducted doctoral fieldwork in east Bali in

1980–1981, studying the integration of a pre-colonial kingdom into the Indonesian nation-state.

Samira Benturki Saïdi is an independent Algerian historian, researcher, author, and editor. Working in the field of publishing and audiovisual production, she is an author, illustrator, and translator of historical works edited by publishers in Europe and the Middle East. She specializes in the field of maritime research on ancient peoples, particularly Arab and Muslim and African navigators and explorers. For several decades, she has specialized in the pre-Columbian history of America, highlighting the contribution of pre-Islamic Arab seafarers and discoverers to its discovery and settlement, and the continuity of its occupation by expeditions launched from West and North Africa at the advent of Islam. Her most recent works, published or in progress, are the following: "Archaelogy Under the Light of Qur'anic Verses" (2009), Dictionary of Muslim Names (2015) by Éditions Universel, France; *The Arab and Muslim Identity of Peoples & Native American Tribes* (United Kingdom, The Fountain of E-Knowledge, 2018); *The Teaching of History: Background and Premises to Globalism* (Éditions Sydney Laurent, June 2021); *Arab, Muslim, and Black African America Before 1492, a Mathematical Equation?* (France, December 2021); *The Algerian Regency and the Founding of the US Navy?* (France, February 2022).

Norliza Saleh has served the International Institute of Advanced Islamic Studies (IAIS) Malaysia as the Head of Publications since 2009. Prior to that, she dealt with historical manuscripts and academic journals during her stint as a Graduate Research Assistant (GRA) at the International Institute of Islamic Thought and Civilization (ISTAC), under International Islamic University of Malaysia from 2005 to 2009. She is passionate about Muslim historiography, Malay history, and the development of Islamic thought throughout the Muslim world.

Yuki Shiozaki is an associate professor at the School of International Relations/Graduate School of International Relations, University of Shizuoka, Japan. He was formerly an assistant professor (August 2017– March 2019) in the Faculty of Language and Management, International Islamic University Malaysia. His important publications are *Islam Facing the State: The Development of Islamic Law in Malaysia and Fatwas* (Japanese) (Tokyo: Sakuhinsha) and *Fiqh for Minority Muslims* (Japanese)

(Tokyo: Saudi Arabia-Japan Society; Shiozaki Yuki (ed.)). He also received academic award from the International Institute for the Study of Religions (Japan) in the year 2013.

Alexander Wain joined the School of Divinity in 2021. A specialist in the eastern Islamic world, his interests lie primarily in the theological, historical, and literary traditions of the Malay Muslim world (modern-day Indonesia, Malaysia, Brunei, and Singapore), with an ancillary focus on China's hui-hui Muslim ethnic grouping. After obtaining his DPhil in Theology from the University of Oxford in 2015 with a thesis focused on the role Sino-Muslims played in the conversion of Maritime Southeast Asia to Islam between the thirteenth and sixteenth centuries, he joined the International Institute of Advanced Islamic Studies (IAIS) in Kuala Lumpur, where he stayed as a research fellow for six years. In addition to his work on the St Andrews Encyclopaedia of Theology, he is engaged in a major research project exploring and re-evaluating the early history and Muslim culture of Melaka, Southeast Asia's first great sultanate. A practising Muslim, he has been involved in numerous community outreach programmes, both in the UK and in Malaysia

Jing Wang is the senior research manager at the Center for Advanced Research in Global Communication (CARGC) at the Annenberg School for Communication at the University of Pennsylvania. Wang studies the anthropology of Islam and Muslim societies, race and ethnicity, media and global studies, and digital religion studies. She holds a PhD degree in Sociocultural Anthropology from Rice University (2019). From September 2019 to 2020, she was a "Global Perspectives on Society" Postdoctoral Fellow at NYU Shanghai. She is working on a book manuscript that critically examines the history of Islamophobia in China and Sinophone Muslims' media practices in everyday life. Wang has published in *Asian Anthropology, Journal of Contemporary East Asia, Terrain: Anthropologie & Sciences Humaines, Journal of Transformative Learning*, and other journals and edited books. In 2020, she co-founded TyingKnots, an independent, non-profit, volunteer-based group committed to breaking down walls between academia, media, and the public through translation projects and the promotion of public-facing scholarship

LIST OF TABLES

The Maternal Initiative Role in the Japanese Muslim Community: Japanese Muslim Wives as Mediators Between Muslim Immigrants and Japanese Society

Table 1	Foreign residents in Japan from Muslim-majority countries at the end of December 2019	177
Table 2	Responses from four respondents from Muslim families in Japan on the family name, livelihood, and local community activities, including school activities	180

Introduction: Women-Centric Islam

Nasr M. Arif and Abbas Panakkal

Around the world, some Islamic cultures have developed distinctive matrilineal, matrifocal, matrilocal, or matriarchal natures as a result of how they have been practised by integrated and indigenised Muslim communities. In matrilineal descent systems, in contrast to the more common mosaic of patrilineal patterns, children belong to the mother's ancestry group. Matrilineal Muslims therefore follow a social system in which people are identified with their mother's lineage, and the inheritance of property as well as succession are transferred through the matriline. There are a number of such Muslim communities found throughout the world, in regions as diverse as Indonesia, Malaysia, the Philippines, India, Mozambique, Ghana, Spain, Japan, China, and Korea. All these integrated communities have unique forms of women-centred social systems. This volume focuses on matrilineal, matrifocal, and matriarchal Muslims and their unique folk natures, integrated social structures, adopted legal systems, and so on.

Nasr M. Arif
University of St Andrews, St Andrews, UK

University of Cairo, Giza, Egypt
e-mail: na90@st-andrews.ac.uk; nasrarif@gmail.com

Abbas Panakkal
School of History, University of St Andrews, St Andrews, UK
e-mail: ap399@st-andrews.ac.uk

The focus on matrilineal Muslim communities is a discovery in itself, since it goes against the dominant paradigm in Islamic studies and legal treatises. In the history of Islamic jurisprudence, women, slavery, and the people of the *dhimma* (Jews and Christians) have constituted three major issues; in response to these issues, inherited customs and traditions were adapted to fit religious texts as a means of restructuring and to resolve any conflicts. Islam preaches equality between women and men based on justice and the balance between rights and duties, but jurisprudence has preserved the dominance of men and their absolute control over the family. Islam also introduced the principle of eliminating human enslavement and liberating slaves, while jurisprudence aligned itself with society and created contexts for perpetuating enslavement. Islam set the rules for a society of citizenship; Islamic jurisprudence, however, created a *dhimmi* system to distinguish between citizens.

This book engages with the first of these three issues and challenges the stagnant paradigm on Muslim women by presenting cases of Muslim societies with matrilineal and matriarchal cultures, in which women took the roles of leaders and guardians. Paradoxically, it is almost impossible to imagine the existence of such societies, as traditional Islamic jurisprudence is based on the central role of the man, and the Muslim community in general considers the man to be the leader and protector of the family. Guardianship in the Muslim family is entrusted to the man, and marriage is solemnised by a man, who takes care of official procedures. All these well-established ideas and judgements have created serious issues around the role of women and gender dynamics. Since the mid-twentieth century, the issue of gender has been one of the most problematic dilemmas for Muslim thought.

Contemporary studies on women and gender in Islamic jurisprudence, both current and historical, have started from the position that Islam is in essence patriarchal and that Muslim societies throughout history have exalted the role of men while—in many cases—oppressing women. This vision finds the source of its legitimacy in the identification between Arabs and Muslims and between Arab historical traditions that stem from inherited tribal customs and Islam in general. Arabs are usually treated as the source and permanent representatives of Islam, even though they do not represent more than one-sixth of contemporary Muslims. Despite the numerous patriarchal Islamic traditions regarding the issue of women within the Arab World, and countries in the surrounding area such as Pakistan and Afghanistan, historical practices in Southeast Asia, Africa,

China, and other regions exist that are both contrary to Arab traditions and also compatible with the spirit of Islam and its higher values. The identification between Arabs and Muslims is the first problem facing gender studies in Muslim societies, and here the question arises as to why Islamic jurisprudence was unable to change Arab perceptions of women, and why so many of their pre-Islamic practices have continued to exist in their societies to this day.

This situation has created a historical problem for women in Muslim societies that differs from the issues facing women in European civilisations, both in essence and in its manifestations. The ontological nature of women and their basic human rights was not a subject of much discussion in Muslim contexts. The question of whether women have souls, for example, never arose in a Muslim culture, although it dominated European thought until the middle of the nineteenth century. Likewise, in Islamic history there was no concept of an inherent curse passed down through women, as was the case in European traditions. Instead, Islamic history has witnessed many cases of injustice towards women because Muslim jurists have been influenced by regional patriarchal traditions more than the spirit of Islamic law (*sharīʿa*). As a result, opinions, legal rulings (*fatwas*), and jurisprudence as a whole have undermined the role of women and made them completely subservient to men. Yet this is not a true reflection of the position of women according to the main Islamic sources of the Qurʾān and Sunna. The influence of traditions and social norms wielded more power over many jurists than religion itself.

The predicament of women in Islam is not, therefore, comparable to that of women in the West; this does not seek to imply that there are no problems for women in Muslim societies, but rather that the issues affecting them are essentially different in nature, meaning that the questions around them must also be formulated differently. In addition, the problem and its internal questions must be expressed in a manner consistent with the lexis of Islamic customs and not become a mere repetition of the ideas existing in the Western arena. The problem of women in the Islamic world is not an issue of freedom but rather a matter of justice, since the supreme value in Islam is justice while freedom is the absolute value in Western civilisation.

The Islamic civilisational system understands the family to be the basic unit of human society rather than the individual, as in the Western perspective. Considering the family as the primary social unit, Islam gives rights to its followers through their roles as part of a whole system rather than as independent beings. It is therefore impossible to look at either a man or a woman as simply a being living in a vacuum: they are a mother, sister, wife, daughter, and grandmother or a father, brother, husband, son, and grandfather. Every human being has a social as well as a biological identity. He or she is a man or woman, but there is also a social role that makes the biological being a mother or father, a daughter or son. Hence, it is not possible to look at the issue of women in isolation from women's status and social context, which is the family. The issue cannot be addressed without taking into consideration the mutual and interdependent interests of women, men, and their kinship groups. The place of each individual is determined by a delicate process of balancing individual identity and identity as a member of the family, the basic social unit. This membership gives him or her a function beyond that of the individual, for example as a husband or wife.

Any consideration of the role of men or women should therefore be in the context of the set of values that determine the functions of the family, how its members interact, and how matters are conducted within it. These values are:

- Justice: This is the supreme value of the various Islamic systems—social, economic, and political—and numerous verses in the Qurʾān deal with justice in the family.
- Consultation and compromise: Consultation is the basic value that controls the decision-making process within the family, ensuring that one of its members does not dominate the others and that the family does not turn into an institution that manufactures tyrants or slaves. The family is, in fact, a political institution that may be either democratic or authoritarian. In Sūrat al-Baqara, for example, the Qurʾān emphasises the value of consultation and mutual consent when deciding when to wean a child: "If they want to wean by mutual consent and consultation, there is no sin on them" (Al-Baqarah 233).
- The balance of rights and duties or rather the assurance that each member of the family enjoys both rights and duties in equal measure. It is not possible to look at Islamic legislation on women's issues except from this angle. The issue of inheritance, for example, is a clear manifestation of the value of this balance of rights and duties. The Qurʾān allots the woman half of the man's share because a married woman has no financial duties within the family; this responsibility falls to men. If we look at this matter from a socio-economic

perspective, it therefore appears that women benefit more than men according to this system. Endowments in Islamic history thus became an area where civilised women could be particularly effective, as we find that most endowments were established by women from their own money.

The matrilineal and matriarchal societies that embraced Islam did not experience any problem with the new religion except the issue of distributing inheritance. These societies came up with an innovative idea that accords with the principles of Islamic jurisprudence: to transform the inheritance into a *waqf* (endowment) under the mother's guardianship. Thus matrilineal societies succeeded in preserving their inherited traditions on the one hand and adhering to all the rules and principles of the new religion on the other.

This book introduces many cases of matrilineal, matrifocal, matrilocal, and matriarchal Islam from different geographical locations and historical eras that prove the diversity and pluralism of Muslim cultures and traditions. Chapters on various matrilineal and matriarchal communities highlight diverse cultural scenarios connected with distinctive social practices, particularly related to ownership of property and the transfer of inheritance from mother to daughter. The power, freedom, and comfort enjoyed by women in their ancestral homes and communities are also matter for discussion, alongside the comparison of practices in otherwise similar patriarchal Muslim communities.

Taking into consideration the geographical locations of these studies, this volume has been divided into four parts: "South and Southeast Asia"; "Northeast Asia"; "Africa"; and "Andalusia and Americas." The first part, which covers the region of South and Southeast Asia, comprises three chapters. Lyn Parker, in the first chapter, discusses vulnerability and resilience among the matrilineal Muslim Minangkabau in Indonesia, which is considered to be the largest matrilineal group in the world. This chapter explores how various integrations and adaptations contributed to the cultural resilience of the Minangkabau and surveys studies from different historical periods which variously claimed that Minangkabau society was matrifocal, matrilineal, or matriarchal. The author illustrates how *adat* (custom) has been both remarkably resistant to change and capable of adaptability, addressing the core question of its vulnerability or resilience. *Adat* provides many women with cultural, political, and practical resources that enable them to be comparatively powerful, not only in family life but also in village life and the village economy. The Minangkabau integrated traditional law and indigenised Islam in the region, and as a result it received greater societal acceptance. Muslims in the region succeeded in integrating their women-centred traditions with the Islamic religion, facilitating the cultural, economic, and social resources that sustain their distinctive way of life. The practical power of matrilineal *adat* might recede, but the rich and flexible intermeshing of Islamic devotion and matrilineal ethnic identity survives.

In Chap. 2, titled "*Adat Perpatih* in Malaysia: Nature, History, Practices, and Contemporary Issues," Alexander Wain and Norliza Saleh explore the evolution of *adat perpatih*, the traditional matrilineal system found primarily across Negeri Sembilan, Malaysia. The authors outline the early history of *adat perpatih* and investigate how the practice relates to concerns around community leadership, marriage, property ownership, inheritance, and so on. The chapter also highlights how *adat perpatih* protects the fundamentals of the matricentric community, in which tradition upholds the status of women as mothers of society and shelters the women-centred social structure with vernacular Islam. Marriage customs in *adat perpatih* endorse the principle of exogamy, in which marriage within the same *suku* (matriclan) is strictly forbidden; all members of the same clan are considered siblings, between whom marriage is unacceptable for the sake of the *suku*'s long-term health and prosperity. The chapter also illustrates *adat perpatih*'s degeneration from the mid-nineteenth century onwards as societal changes linked to colonialism began to manifest across Southeast Asia.

Abbas Panakkal discusses cultural and social integrations in matrilineal, matriarchal, and matrifocal Muslim communities in South India in Chap. 3. This chapter sheds light on the early traces of matrilineal Islam in the Indian subcontinent by studying the manuscript of *Futūḥāt al-Jazāʾir*, which describes the early history of Islam on the Lakshadweep Islands. The essential work of society in the region—including everything from economic production to property rights to policymaking—was seldom carried out solely by men and usually involved much consultation with women. The author explores the long-existing legal traditions that supported the continuation of Malabar Muslim matrilineal practices and the impact of colonial laws aiming to curb matrilineal customs, which the British government considered "un-Islamic." This study redefines matrilineal Muslim identity, which was solely connected to the Nair communities by early researchers, citing the existence of matrilineal traditions even in tribal communities. Matrilineal societies have succeeded in preserving their cultural moorings in the face of external attacks, and there are many examples of men sacrificing the status accorded them by colonial and neo-colonial legislation to uphold integrated family traditions.

The second part of this volume focuses on matricentric Muslim cultural stories from Northeast Asian countries—China, Japan, and South Korea—that do not reflect the specific features of earlier matrilineal communities but have nevertheless become home to forms of integrated women-centric Islam. In Chap. 4, Jing Wang discusses matrivocality among Hui Muslim women in China, where women's voices have created a female space extending from women's mosques to the public sphere. The chapter illustrates the unique heritage of women's mosques among Hui Muslim women, despite the long tradition of Han Chinese patriarchy, and highlights Hui Muslim women's work, which significantly expanded the scope of women's influence beyond the home, into workplaces and women's mosques. The author introduces the term "matrivocality," which refers to a historically changing cluster of features that define Chinese Muslim women's roles and voices in a predominantly patrilineal society under both the Islamic and Confucian patriarchal systems. The chapter argues that Hui Muslim women have cultivated a moderate, non-factional image of Islam in China through cultural representations in public spheres. The changing gender consciousness manifested through Huo Da, Ma Jinlian, and other Hui women writers' works reflects the affective dimension of matrivocality within the heterogeneous Hui communities in China, challenging the stereotypical misconception of Muslim women as passive, submissive, and voiceless.

Hee Soo Lee, in Chap. 5, explores the matriarchal family structure on Korea's Jeju Island and its implications for the wider Muslim community. Traditionally, in early Korean society, women had an important role and social function, and matrilocal marriages—when a man moved to live in his wife's house—were quite common. Women could inherit property and dispose of it as they wished. From the fifteenth century onwards, however, the influence of neo-Confucianism led to a decline in women's position. On Jeju Island, however, a women-centred social system thrived as a result of women's important role in the economy; women are the heads of their households and responsible for the family economy and inherit property as well as their mother's occupation. Under the influence of the matriarchal traditions of Jeju, newly converted Muslim women on the island continue to be part of local women-centred life, combining their traditions

xxii   INTRODUCTION: WOMEN-CENTRIC ISLAM

with their religion. This case study serves as an example of a matriarchal society that challenges stereotypes of both patriarchal Islam and traditional Korean Confucianism, analysing how this phenomenon may impact the wider Muslim community in Korea. In an atmosphere of rapidly rising gender equality in the country overall, the Muslim community in Korea as a whole seems likely to become increasingly women-centred.

In Chap. 6, Yuki Shiozaki explores the importance of mothers and maternal initiative in the Japanese Muslim community through the results of recent research. This study analysed the family dynamics of Muslim families living in Japan in cases where Japanese Muslim women were married to foreign Muslim husbands with permanent resident status. Although these permanent residents are a minority among Muslims living in Japan, they are core actors in the formation of Muslim communities. One of the characteristics of the Japanese household system is frequent inheritance by an adopted son—usually a paternal or maternal relative, but sometimes a non-relative—who marries a daughter of the household and becomes part of the family lineage, taking the family name. In the Muslim families in the case study, most children took the mother's Japanese family name—the key point for succession to the homestead-line, resembling the tradition of inheritance by the adopted son. Japanese Muslim women, as wives and mothers, play the key role in integrating the Muslim community with Japanese society, taking on the responsibility of acting as mediators, negotiators, and translators between their families and wider society while at the same time translating Islamic knowledge into the Japanese context for their children. Muslim society in Japan relies on this maternal initiative of Japanese Muslim women to integrate families and indigenise the community.

Part III discusses two prominent case studies from African models of matrilineal and matriarchal Islam, which provide an explicitly indigenised and historically integrated model similar to those of South and Southeast Asia. Liazzat J. K. Bonate, in Chap. 7, describes the Muslim family under Portuguese rule in northern Mozambique, based on *sharīʿa* and matrilineal custom. The author sheds light on this issue by exploring Portuguese colonial approaches and perceptions of the family relations and personal status of coastal Muslims, with evidence from historical, ethnographic, and legal records. Portuguese approaches to *sharīʿa* and *fiqh*, as well as customary norms, are examined and compared to those of the British, French, and Dutch. The chapter analyses how the colonial regime understood Islamic marriage, gender relations within the Muslim family, property rights, divorce, inheritance, and custody of children and illustrates how the Portuguese dealt with matriliny and its interaction with Islamic tradition. The concrete legal steps taken by the Portuguese in relation to the Muslim family and their consequences are also discussed, and the author concludes that throughout the colonial period the family relations and personal status of coastal African Muslims continued to be regulated by a combination of matrilineal norms and the rules of the Shāfiʿī *madhhab*.

In Chap. 8, Mustapha Abdul Hamid discusses the historic matrilineal kinship traditions of the Asante and Fantse groups of Akan Muslims in Ghana. For the Akans, these matrilineal kinship and legal traditions are the most distinguishing features of their culture and law. In this context the Mālikī

legal tradition played a remarkable role in the indigenisation of customs and traditions, unlike other Muslim matrilineal communities from South and Southeast Asia—or even Mozambique—that followed the Shāfiʿī tradition. Asante and Fantse culture makes it possible to bequeath property acquired through personal efforts to people outside the matrilineal order of inheritance. Such flexibility in both the Islamic and Asante/Fantse worldviews makes the management of these apparently contradictory systems possible and enables Asante and Fantse Muslims to live comfortably with an integrated system. This chapter narrates how the old tribal matrilineal and matriarchal tradition was steadily integrated into Islam and how Muslim culture was indigenised in line with the women-centric customary law and cultural traditions of the tribal group.

Part IV of this volume unearths matrilineal Islamic traditions from Andalusia and Americas. Samira Benturki Saïdi, in Chap. 9, discusses the matrilineal tradition of the Tuareg and their expansion to the Americas. The author showcases Tuareg and pre-Islamic migrations which brought the structures of whole societies from Arabia to North Africa—including culture, language, and arts—to the other side of the Atlantic. The Tuareg do not form a homogeneous ethnic group and trace their origin through different paths following their beginnings in ancient Arabia. Samira Benturki Saïdi traces these paths of the Tuareg through space and time, critically analysing their identity and language before reconstructing the matrilineal route of the Tuareg from Arabia to Africa and then to Americas. The chapter tries to answer fundamental questions regarding their provenance and the stopovers that they made through their journeys to Africa and beyond to reach their destination on the American continent.

In Chap. 10, Alfred Gutiérrez-Kavanagh discusses the influence of Germanic and Roman law on matrilineal institutions in al-Andalus, which was a bridge between Europe and Africa and a meeting point of different cultures, civilisations, and linguistic families. Matrilineal heritage and matrifocal institutions existed in different forms almost from the dawn of history in the Iberian Peninsula. A high record of maternal African lineages is detected in western Andalusia, evidence of the contact between the Iberian Peninsula and Africa throughout thousands of years of trade relations. The author points to the traditions of matrilineal kinship systems that correlate with other cultural traits, including bride price, residence after marriage, jurisdictional hierarchy, plough use, and the presence of animal husbandry. The Iberians settled in the north of Spain provide another clear example of cultures with a strong presence of women in both public and private life, and the author discusses four potential sources that have contributed to the matrilineal and matrifocal heritage through interaction between Indo-European and Semitic groups, giving rise to kinship structures, traditions, rites, and institutions which attest to the diversity of Spanish cultural and historical interaction. The study of the evolution of certain legal institutions in the Iberian Peninsula reveals the presence of earlier matrilineal institutions, for example, pre-Roman dowry systems that interacted with Germanic law and were later assimilated by Islamic law, influenced by the customs of the Mozarabs living in territories under Muslim rule.

These ten chapters on various matrilineal, matriarchal, matrifocal, and matrilocal communities highlight the multi-layered matricentric cultural scenarios that are linked with distinctive social practices related to ownership of property and the transfer of inheritance from mother to daughter. These remarkable communities around the globe have ensured economic and social stability for women, giving them the upper hand in fiscal and personal choices. This volume provides a unique perspective for understanding global Muslim communities that have succeeded in integrating the matrilineal tenets of local practices with religion, adhering to essential Islamic values in a way that makes traditional women-centred cultures acceptable to mainstream Islam.

PART I

South and Southeast Asia

Matrifocal, Matrilineal, or Matriarchal? Cultural Resilience and Vulnerability Among the Matrilineal and Muslim Minangkabau in Indonesia

Lyn Parker

The Minangkabau are reputed to be the largest matrilineal group in the world. At the 2010 census in Indonesia, they numbered around 6.5 million.[1] Of these, 4.2 million live in their homeland of West Sumatra, one of the most ethnically homogeneous provinces in Indonesia.[2] The remainder

[1] BPS (Badan Pusat Statistik), Sensus Penduduk 2010 (2010 Census).
[2] PCGN (The Permanent Committee on Geographical Names), Indonesia: population and administrative divisions, 2003, 6, table 3.

L. Parker (✉)
School of Social Sciences, The University of Western Australia,
Crawley, WA, Australia

School of Culture, History and Language, College of Asia and the Pacific,
The Australian National University, Canberra, ACT, Australia
e-mail: lyn.parker@uwa.edu.au

© The Author(s), under exclusive license to Springer Nature
Switzerland AG 2024
A. Panakkal, N. M. Arif (eds.), *Matrilineal, Matriarchal, and Matrifocal Islam*, Palgrave Series in Islamic Theology, Law, and History, https://doi.org/10.1007/978-3-031-51749-5_1

4   L. PARKER

live primarily in the neighbouring provinces of Riau and North Sumatra, and in Jakarta—the capital city—and the surrounding urban areas that make up the megalopolis of Jabodatabek.[3] Others live in Negeri Sembilan, in Malaysia, or scattered around the archipelago.

The equatorial homeland of the Minangkabau (*alam Minangkabau*) experiences frequent natural disasters such as volcanic eruptions, earthquakes, and tsunamis. Running through and beyond the province of West Sumatra, parallel to the west coast, is the Bukit Barisan—a spectacular, jungle-clad mountain range consisting of several active volcanoes—that divides the coastal plain from the beautiful upland. This fertile volcanic upland is the original homeland of the Minangkabau, the *darek*, and roughly consists of the contemporary administrative districts of Agam, Limapuluh Kota, and Tanah Datar, marked by Mount Singgalang to the west and Lake Singkarak to the south. To the north, south, and east, as well as the western coastal plain, including the provincial capital city, Padang, is the *rantau*, the traditional frontier region.

At different times, scholars have variously claimed that Minangkabau society is "matrifocal,"[4] "matrilineal,"[5] and "matriarchal".[6] Minangkabau *adat* (social organisation, tradition, and custom) is distinctive:

> The core of Minangkabau social organisation was the *adat pusako*, the *adat* of matrilineal heritage that regulated kinship, group affiliation, inheritance of property and succession to office within the *nagari* [village].[7]

It is often seen as a paradox that the Minangkabau, while enjoying this matrilineal heritage, are also fervently Muslim, and known for being

---

[3] BPS (Badan Pusat Statistik), Kewarganegaraan, Suku Bangsa, Agama dan Bahasa Sehari-hari Penduduk Indonesia Hasil Sensus Penduduk 2011, 36.

[4] For example, Nancy Tanner, "Matrifocality in Indonesia and Africa and Among Black Americans," in Michelle Z. Rosaldo and Louise Lamphere (eds.), *Woman, Culture and Society* (Stanford: University of Stanford Press, 1974), 129–56.

[5] For example, Joke van Reenen, *Central Pillars of the House: Sisters, Wives and Mothers in a rural community in Minangkabau, West Sumatra*, Leiden: Research School CNWS, Leiden University, 1996, and Evelyn Blackwood, *Webs of power: Women, kin and community in a Sumatran village*, Lanham, MD: Rowman and Littlefield, 2000.

[6] For example, Peggy Reeves Sanday, *Women at the Center: Life in a Modern Matriarchy*, Ithaca: Cornell University Press, 2002.

[7] Franz and Kebeet von Benda-Beckmann, *Political and Legal Transformations of an Indonesian Polity: The Nagari from Colonisation to Decentralisation* (New York: Cambridge University Press, 2013), 11.

among Indonesia's most pious. This chapter surveys some distinctive features of Minangkabau society—their descent, residence, and inheritance patterns; their social life; their propensity to move away from their homeland (*merantau*); their education, livelihoods, and economy; their mode of governance; and their Islamic identity—in order to assess the claims of matrifocality, matrilineality, and matriarchy, and concludes that Minangkabau social organisation is both matrifocal and matrilineal, but not matriarchal. The chapter also has a second aim: to note how these features, and recent changes, contribute to both the vulnerability and the resilience of the Minangkabau.

I begin with some definitional discussion of the terms under examination: first matrifocality, matrilineality, and matriarchy, and then resilience and vulnerability. I next introduce the distinctive melding of Islam and *adat* practised by the Minangkabau through a brief historical survey. The chapter then shifts to a more ethnographic mode, examining social organisation—the structure of families and households, the position of men, matrilocal and neolocal residence, sibling bonds, the practice of *merantau* (migration)—followed by education, ancestral inheritance (*harto pusako*), work and the village economy, the larger economy, *merantau* and remittances, and governance, arguing for the continuing vitality of matrilineal *adat* in this strongly Muslim society.

KEY CONCEPTS

Matrifocality

Nancy Tanner's excellent 1974 paper on "Matrifocality in Indonesia, Africa and Among Black Americans" was not the first to use this term, but was the clearest exposition of the concept and the first to identify the Acehnese, Minangkabau, and Javanese societies in Indonesia as "matrifocal". She provided a useful summary of matrifocality as referring to "the *cultural elaboration and valuation*, as well as the *structured centrality, of mother roles within a kinship system*".[8] For the Minangkabau, she identified the following features as constituting its matrifocality: "[T]he woman, as mother, is focal in terms both of affect and of effective power within the minor lineage, the matrilineally extended family, and the nuclear family. ... [Other] structural features include women's important economic roles,

---

[8] Tanner, "Matrifocality in Indonesia," 154 (italics in original).

women's extensive participation in decision making, and a residential pattern that enhances ties among kinswomen."[9] To my knowledge, the aptness of the term for the Minangkabau has never been challenged. Ng makes the argument that Minangkabau society is matrifocal the central argument of her thesis, and I would also subscribe to its validity.[10] It is worth noting, though, that matrifocal societies do not have to be matrilineal: indeed, the Javanese kinship system is bilateral, not matrilineal.

Matrilineality

Matrilineality among the Minangkabau is assumed by Tanner, and their matrilineality is generally accepted as fact in Indonesia—in anthropology textbooks, for example. Matrilineality refers to a kinship system where descent is traced through the female line. For the Minangkabau it is associated with matrilocal residence (newly married couples live with the bride's mother) and matrilineally traced descent groups (*suku*), with descent traced to an apical ancestress, as well as with exogamy of descent groups, inheritance from mother to daughter of descent group-owned assets such as land and multi-generational longhouses—and an important role for the mother's brother (*mamak*).

The place of men in matrilineal societies has often been problematised by anthropologists, because a man's loyalties are seen to be divided between responsibilities to his mother, sister, and larger matrilineage, on the one hand, and to his wife and children on the other. Upon marriage, a man typically leaves his mother's house for his wife's house. Schneider claims that in matrilineal kinship systems,

> the role of men as men is defined as … having authority over women and children (except perhaps for specially qualifying conditions applicable to a very few women of the society). Positions of highest authority within the matrilineal descent group will, therefore, ordinarily be vested in statuses occupied by men.[11]

---

[9] Tanner, "Matrifocality in Indonesia," 143.

[10] Cecilia Ng, The Weaving of prestige: Village women's representations of the social categories of Minangkabau society, Ph.D. dissertation: The Australian National University, 1987.

[11] David M. Schneider, "Introduction: The Distinctive Features of Matrilineal Descent Groups," in David M. Schneider and Kathleen Gough (eds.), *Matrilineal Kinship* (Berkeley and Los Angeles: University of California Press, 1961), 6.

Feminist scholars have challenged the patriarchal assumptions of Schneider and others—for example that it is a problem for men to be exchanged in marriage and for men not to have authority over women; that men are "missing" in matrilineal societies; and that men have no place in matrilineal societies and so are pushed "out" to migrate or wander.[12] Such scholars have also convincingly shown that Minang women command respect and have considerable authority in Minang society[13] and that they wield "practical power",[14] even if they do not always appear in public to be the decision-makers.

Scholars of the *alam* Minangkabau—the Minangkabau world—have long predicted the demise of matrilineality due to the incursions of a patriarchal national gender ideology, a revitalised Islam in Indonesia, and global capitalism, which entails private property. Neolocal residence has become common in towns and cities in West Sumatra, and many multi-generational longhouses are no longer maintained and are now defunct. The role of men in families is changing, with fathers and husbands becoming more important and the nuclear family emerging as a significant social unit. However, Minangkabau society is still based on matriliny, and I agree with Simon that the matrilineal kinship system is "thriving" and basically uncontested today.[15] I am interested to see how matriliny provides resources to sustain people, especially women and girls, and, in turn, to see if it somehow makes men vulnerable.

Matriarchy

Matriarchy is a contested concept in anthropology, and the designation of Minangkabau society as matriarchal is also contested. Etymologically, the word means "rule by mothers," and more generally refers to "domination

---

[12] See also Evelyn Blackwood, "Wedding Bell Blues: Marriage, Missing Men, and Matrifocal Follies," *American Ethnologist* 32:1 (2005), 3–19, and Jennifer Krier, "The Marital Project: Beyond the Exchange of Men in Minangkabau Marriage," *American Ethnologist* 27:4 (2000), 877–97.

[13] Blackwood, *Webs of Power*; van Reenen, *Central Pillars of the House*; Sanday, *Women at the Center*; Ng, *The Weaving of Prestige*; Lucy A. Whalley, *Virtuous Women, Productive Citizens: Negotiating Tradition, Islam and Modernity in Minangkabau, Indonesia*, Ph.D. dissertation: University of Illinois, 1993.

[14] Gregory M. Simon, *Caged in on the Outside: Moral Subjectivity, Selfhood, and Islam in Minangkabau, Indonesia* (Honolulu: University of Hawaii Press, 2014), 36.

[15] Simon, *Caged in on the Outside*, 8.

by female members of society".[16] However, some feminist anthropologists have advocated for a different view of matriarchy that aims to avoid what they see as a sexist focus on power and substitute a socio-cultural definition:

> [I]n terms not of power but of the cultural roles of mothers in knitting together the social ties of daily life in their various activities including the ritual exchange of gifts in the life cycle. [...] [M]atriarchy [is] applicable to archetypically mother-centered societies [and is] reflected in life-cycle and daily activities based on maternal–fraternal values, consensus decision making, peace building, and negotiating controversy toward peaceful ends.[17]

The two main meanings might be understood as relating to different domains, so the definition that refers to dominance and "rule" focuses on the politico-jural domain while the other refers to the social or perhaps only the domestic domain.[18] Nevertheless, Sanday, a prominent feminist anthropologist of the Minangkabau, is one of the principal advocates of this socio-cultural view of matriarchy,[19] and sees the Minangkabau as a clear example. On the other hand, some anthropologists, myself included, do not:

> Whether these societies [such as the Minangkabau] are not only matrilineal but also matriarchal is a matter of debate. Most anthropologists sharply distinguish matrilineal descent from matriarchy and refuse the term *matriarchy* for these societies. They point to studies showing that matrilineal descent and the distribution of power, though interrelated, are separate.[20]

I find that one can only describe the Minangkabau as matriarchal if one accepts Sanday's definition of matriarchy, and to me it is not significantly different from Tanner's matrifocality. In my estimation, Minangkabau society is both matrilineal and matrifocal—but not matriarchal. This section has flagged some of the issues inherent to these matri-kinship terms,

[16] Anne Siegetsleitner, "Matriarchy," in H. James Birx (ed.) *Encyclopedia of Anthropology* (Thousand Oaks, CA: SAGE Publications, 2006), 1554–5.

[17] Peggy Reeves Sanday, "Matriarchy," in Hilary Callan (ed.) *The International Encyclopedia of Anthropology*, Hoboken, NJ: John Wiley, 2018.

[18] André Béteille, "Inequality and Equality," in Tim Ingold (ed.) *Companion Encyclopedia of Anthropology: Humanity, Culture and Social Life*, London: Taylor & Francis Group, 1993.

[19] Sanday, *Women at the Center.*

[20] Siegetsleitner, "Matriarchy," 1555.

which will be teased out for the Muslim Minangkabau in the main body of the chapter.

This introductory section now moves to two other key words that shape this chapter: resilience and vulnerability. Why discuss the resilience and vulnerability of the Minangkabau? One obvious answer might be because scholars—and the Minangkabau themselves—have been engaged in a long debate about the fate of their ethnic identity. While this debate is interesting and important to many Minangkabau, my purpose in addressing Minangkabau resilience and vulnerability is not to join this debate. I do not see Minangkabau culture and society as being in danger of moral decay, dysfunction, or extinction, and have discussed what I see as a moral panic elsewhere.[21] Rather, here I am interested in examining the resources that matrifocality, matrilineality, and Islamic religiosity offer the Minangkabau, and, conversely, if and how these social arrangements and ideologies are sources of vulnerability.

The research underpinning this chapter is part of a larger team project on economic, social, and health vulnerabilities in Indonesia, and the Minangkabau site is one of several around the archipelago.[22] That project is about the conditions that make people vulnerable as individuals and as sub-populations. We are particularly interested in the resources that cultures offer to those who are disadvantaged or suffer mishaps, and the ways that people adapt to misfortune. This investigation is multi-scalar: while cultural resources apply more or less to groups, and indeed can be negotiated and adapted in group decision-making, they also apply to individuals who are differently positioned within these groups, and individuals have to cope with disadvantage and change on a daily basis.

Vulnerability

Vulnerability involves a precarious balance between risks and resources.[23] Risks can be sudden events, such as health shocks, environmental disasters,

---

[21] Lyn Parker, "The Moral Panic About the Socializing of Young People in Minangkabau," *Wacana: Journal of the Humanities in Indonesia* 15:1 (2014), 19–40.

[22] This chapter is part of a large team project on Social, Economic and Health Vulnerabilities in Indonesia, funded by the Australia Research Council, DP160101559. Fieldwork in villages and the town of Bukittinggi in West Sumatra has been conducted intermittently since 2004.

[23] Elisabeth Schröder-Butterfill and Ruly Marianti, "Understanding Vulnerabilities in Old Age," *Ageing and Society* 26:1 (2006), 3–8.

or sudden unemployment; gradual social change, such as changing family structures; or longer-term social and individual conditions such as intergenerational poverty, persistent food scarcity, lack of education, or individual disability. Resources can include material capital (income, assets), social capital (social networks, social welfare), cultural capital (such as education, religious expertise), and natural resources (reliable rainfall, fertile soils, accessible forest or sea, access to arable land), as well as human capital (health, resourcefulness) and symbolic capital (status, reputation). When the risks outweigh the resources, people are made vulnerable. I take it as axiomatic that vulnerability will be culturally mediated—that is, that people's perceptions of risks, threats, vulnerability, and resources to pre-empt or ameliorate the worst possible outcomes will be shaped by the cultural context. Here, I place agency centre-stage, examining how individuals and networks negotiate challenges, mobilise resources, and engage in diverse strategies to avoid bad outcomes.[24]

Resilience

Resilience has become a key word in several fields—including poverty reduction/development studies, disaster risk reduction, climate change adaptability, and social protection—and is now ubiquitous in public discourse, such as media reportage of natural disasters, COVID-19, and so on. A simple definition is that resilience is the "ability to resist, recover from, or adapt to the effects of a shock or a change";[25] a more substantial one incorporates three dimensions of resilience: absorptive capacity or persistence (the various strategies by which individuals and/or households resist, moderate, or buffer the impacts of shocks on their livelihoods and basic needs); adaptive capacity (the ability of a system to adjust to change to moderate potential damage, take advantage of opportunities, and/or to cope with the consequences); and transformability (the "capacity to create a fundamentally new system when ecological, economic or social structures make the existing system untenable").[26] It is these three dimensions that will be referenced in the body of this chapter.

---

[24] Lyn Parker (ed.), *The agency of women in Asia*, Singapore: Marshall Cavendish Academic, 2005; Schröder-Butterfill and Marianti, "Understanding Vulnerabilities in Old Age."

[25] Tom Mitchell and Katie Harris, "Resilience: A risk management approach," ODI Background Note, London: Overseas Development Institute, 2012.

[26] Walker et al. 2004, 5, cited in Christophe Béné et al., "Resilience: new utopia or new tyranny? Reflection about the potentials and limits of the concept of resilience in relation to vulnerability reduction programmes," *IDS Working Papers* 2012 (405), 21.

The Minangkabau

Most discussions about the vulnerability and resilience of the Minangkabau have centred on the possibility that the distinctive Minangkabau *adat* was under threat and that the continued existence of Minangkabau ethnicity was therefore open to question. The conclusion of most recent scholars has been that the matrilineal *adat* is alive and well, having resisted or adapted to various incursions over the last two centuries. This may be called "cultural resilience".[27] A second, related question has been the reason for the decline in the influence of the Minangkabau in the Indonesian public sphere—in politics, education, literature, and intellectual life. This question is not addressed here, but has been discussed by various authors.[28] A third question is, "[W]hether Minangkabau society is properly Islamic?"[29] Today, the formulaic response to this last question would be "ABS-SBK", an acronym from *"adat basandi syarak, syarak basandi kitabullah"* meaning that *adat* is based on Islamic law and Islamic law is based on the Qur'ān. ABS-SBK is patently ahistorical, but to the Minangkabau it "conveys the notion that Islam, as Truth, is the eternal and immutable source of *adat*".[30] However, there is another, earlier version of this saying, which gives *adat* more authority: *"adat* is based on *syarak* (Islamic law), *syarak* is based on *adat"* (ABS-SBA). This version is no longer in use. History provides some answers as to how ABS-SBK came to be the answer to the apparent paradox posed by the co-existence of *adat* and Islam.

The History of *Adat* and Islam in the *Alam Minangkabau*

Central Sumatra, which includes the contemporary province of West Sumatra, became secure in its Islamic identity during the seventeenth and

---

[27] Jeffrey Hadler, *Muslims and Matriarchs: Cultural Resilience in Indonesia Through Jihad and Colonialism*, Ithaca and London: Cornell University Press, 2008.

[28] See Hadler, *Muslims and Matriarchs;* Franz and Kebeet von Benda-Beckmann, *Political and Legal Transformations of an Indonesian Polity;* Franz and Kebeet von Benda-Beckmann, "Ambivalent Identities: Decentralization and Minangkabau Political Communities," in H. Schulte-Nordholt and G. van Klinken (eds.) *Renegotiating Boundaries: Local Politics in Post-Suharto Indonesia* (Leiden: KITLV Press, 2007), 417–42; Audrey Kahin, *Rebellion to Integration: West Sumatra and the Indonesian polity 1926–1998*, Amsterdam: Amsterdam University Press, 1999.

[29] Simon, *Caged in on the Outside*, 50.

[30] Simon, *Caged in on the Outside*, 51.

eighteenth centuries.[31] Much of what is now called *adat*, or custom, predates Islamisation and is a complex mix of animistic beliefs; belief in the divinity of the ruler, lore enshrined in Minangkabau myths, folk stories (*carito*), and chronicles (*tambo*); and a distinctive, hierarchical, matrilineal social organisation.[32] Islamisation occurred via the west coast entrepôts and east coast rivers, with rulers and important brokering families leading the way. Three Sufi orders (*tarekat*) were well established in Minangkabau by the eighteenth century; Islam was attractive to local rulers and traders; and there was an easy accommodation between Sufi Islam and pre-existing animistic traditions.[33]

The Padri Wars of 1821–1837 had a decisive influence on the construction of Minangkabau identity. Sometimes presented as a civil war, sometimes as a war of independence between local people and the Dutch, this intermittent conflict was both. At the beginning there were two opposed local Minangkabau sides, both nominally professing Islam. One side, the traditionalists or *adat* followers saw much value in their pre-Islamic traditions. They were opposed by the Padris: Wahhabi Muslim reformers or "modernists", some of whom had gone to the Middle East to perform the *hajj* and to study, then returned, inspired to cleanse their homeland of what they saw as local accretions. This was the conflict that triggered, or presented itself as an excuse for, Dutch intervention in the Sumatran highlands from 1821 to 1837, and so began the colonial period.[34] The challenge posed by the returning Padri forced the Minangkabau to articulate a defence of their matrilineal society and to evaluate their own response to the impositions of the colonial state. Matriliny survived in Minang, not in spite of the violent Islamic revival but because of it.[35]

---

[31] Christine Dobbin, *Islamic revivalism in a changing peasant economy: Central Sumatra, 1784–1847*, London and Malmo: Curzon Press, 1983.

[32] von Benda-Beckmann, *Political and Legal Transformations of an Indonesian Polity*, chapter two.

[33] Dobbin, *Islamic revivalism in a changing peasant economy*, 117–21.

[34] Dobbin, *Islamic revivalism in a changing peasant economy;* Taufik Abdullah, *Schools and politics: The Kaum Muda movement in West Sumatra*, Ithaca, NY: Cornell University Modern Indonesia Project, 1971; Elizabeth E. Graves, *The Minangkabau response to Dutch colonial rule in the nineteenth century*, Ithaca, NY: Cornell University, 1981; Joel Kahn, *Constituting the Minangkabau: peasants, culture and modernity in colonial Indonesia*, Oxford: Berg Publishers, 1993.

[35] Hadler, *Muslims and Matriarchs*, 180.

MATRIFOCAL, MATRILINEAL, OR MATRIARCHAL? CULTURAL RESILIENCE... 13

Nearly a century later, in the 1910s and 1920s, another unequivocally "modern" nationalist movement rocked the *alam* Minangkabau.[36] The first aim of the modernist reformists (the Kaum Muda, literally the "Young Group") was a re-run of the Padri efforts almost a century before, but it was the second of their aims that really revolutionised Minangkabau society:

> The religious and educational activities of the Kaum Muda ulama and their students and followers brought about an expansion and modernization of religious schools. By using Islam as the basis of their programs, the Islamic modernists could claim religious sanction for their activities.[37]

Their antagonists were the Kaum Tua, literally the "Old Group", who were committed either to matrilineal *adat* or to *tarekat*-based (Sufi) Islam.

I will return to education in more detail later, but the Kaum Muda movement and the new, politicised Islamic schools—particularly the Sumatra Thawalib School in Padang Panjang—were a significant force, producing "a peculiar form of intellectualized Islamic communism".[38] The new movement introduced schools for girls, promoted the growth of government schools, fostered a vibrant new journalism, and heralded a strong women's movement, which encouraged women to be active in politics, social welfare, and media.[39] A devastating earthquake in 1926 was followed by the 1927 "Communist" uprising by tin and coal miners. The Dutch quelled the uprising with considerable force. The Kaum Muda movement was over, but once again the Minangkabau had been forced to defend their *adat*, rationalise it, write it down, and justify it. The opposition the Kaum Muda protagonists had provoked had shown that Minangkabau matrilineal *adat* was both strong and adaptable.

The history of the Minangkabau through the twentieth century is interesting, but here my focus must be on matriliny and Islam, so I will only mention the nationwide movements of Islamisation since the 1980s, and democratisation and decentralisation post-1998.

---

[36] Abdullah, *Schools and Politics*; Kahin, *Rebellion to Integration*.
[37] Abdullah, *Schools and Politics*, 1.
[38] Hadler, *Muslims and Matriarchs*, 139.
[39] Hadler, *Muslims and Matriarchs*.

14 L. PARKER

Islamisation is a global process, and has been active in Indonesia since the 1980s.[40] It has created a more Islamic public space in Indonesia, and a much more public expression of piety. Perhaps the most noticeable change has been the widespread wearing of the Islamic headscarf (*jilbab*). While Islam is extremely diverse in Indonesia, there has been an obvious shift from an open, tolerant Islam that was "inclined to compromise" to a more conservative and fundamentalist expression of religion.[41] Fundamentalism has emerged as an important force in Indonesian society, encouraged by the presence of transnational Islamic movements such as Wahhabism and the Muslim Brotherhood.

In West Sumatra, the widespread adoption of the *jilbab*, the building of many mosques, and the increased popularity of Islamic schooling are salient manifestations of Islamisation. There is a renewed interest in personal practices of faith and the cultivation of one's own identity as a moral and devout person. This project of personal morality occurs within a strengthened community commitment to Islamic values. People are constantly monitoring themselves and their friends and family through questions such as "Have you prayed yet?" or suggesting "Let's pray first before we do that!". Such reminders punctuate conversations in a remarkable effort of community piety. Exhortations to pray regularly pepper sermons and other religious talks, which are relayed over loud speakers—sometimes for entire days. The twin aims are to work on oneself, to become truly *ikhlas*, or sincere, with a "genuine devotion to fulfilling the moral and ethical teaching of Islam",[42] and to implement *dakwah* (the call to Muslims to obey Allāh and model the life of the Prophet). It is apposite to describe Islamisation as a project of personal morality.

In Minangkabau, the long history of reconciling *adat* with Islam has no doubt left a legacy of some insecurity about the extent to which their version of Islam is adequate, yet people are loathe to discuss "versions" of Islam and are much happier to see it as the objective Truth—hence the way that the aphoristic acronym ABS-SBK (*Adat* is based on Islamic law;

---

[40] Greg Fealy and Sally White (eds.), *Expressing Islam: Religious Life and Politics in Indonesia*. Singapore: Institute of Southeast Asian Studies, 2008.

[41] Martin van Bruinessen, "Introduction: Contemporary Developments in Indonesian Islam and the 'Conservative Turn' of the early twenty-first century," in Martin van Bruinessen (ed.), *Contemporary Development in Indonesian Islam: Explaining the "Conservative Turn"* (Singapore: Institute of Southeast Asian Studies, 2013), 3.

[42] Mitsuo Nakamura, *The crescent arises over the banyan tree: a study of the Muhammadijah movement in a Central Javanese town*, Ph.D. dissertation: Cornell University, 1976.

Islamic law is based on the Qur'ān) is used as a way to rhetorically but definitively end any questioning. Islamisation in Minangkabau has not been directed at changing the basic structures of society but rather at cultivating sincere and pious Muslim subjects.[43] People do not always agree on what being a good Muslim means—there is disagreement on whether or not young people are allowed by Islam to have boy- and girlfriends, for instance—but the desirability of being a good Muslim is unquestionable.

A feature of rejuvenated Islam is that behaviour is thought to reveal the inner self. The regular performance of prayers indicates a person who will not steal, gamble, or defraud others. Learning to recite the Qur'ān will automatically lead to piety and good behaviour.

> [T]he person is evident on the surface, and the moral person is one who is apparent conforming to accepted standards of sociality. The intense focus on socializing (*bagaua*), on conforming (being *biaso*), and on situating oneself within the social body (*awak*) rather than separating oneself from it as an individual (being *sombong*) all fit well into this moral and epistemological framework in which the value of persons lies in their realization of integration with others. ... Minangkabau people tend to understand etiquette as realizing a genuine part of self. Social appearances, as part of the lived fabric of human life, are themselves morally significant.[44]

Islamisation was already underway in Indonesia when the 1998 downfall of long-term authoritarian ruler President Suharto ushered in an era of democracy and decentralisation. It was the notion of local, community participation that articulated democratisation and decentralisation in Indonesia.[45] Decentralisation connoted the devolution of finances, power, and control of local affairs to local authorities, made local constituencies accountable for local authorities, and made each region responsible for the equitable distribution of its own wealth.[46] Local institutions were revived

---

[43] Simon, *Caged in on the Outside.*

[44] Simon, *Caged in on the Outside*, 79.

[45] M. Turner, O. Podger, M. Sumardjono, and W.K. Tirthayasa (eds.), *Decentralisation in Indonesia: Redesigning the State* (Canberra: Asia Pacific Press, 2003), 6.

[46] E. Aspinall and G. Fealy (eds.) *Local power and politics in Indonesia: Decentralisation & democratisation* (Singapore: Institute of Southeast Asian Studies, 2003), 2.

16   L. PARKER

and reformed, and there was a great rediscovery (and sometimes invention) of *adat* and tradition.[47]

In West Sumatra, the original form of the village, the *nagari*, was revived, and there was a great movement, *baliak ka nagari* (return to the *nagari*), which became provincial policy in 1998.[48] The (re-)establishment of the *nagari* in West Sumatra as the lowest level of government became the example *par excellence* of decentralisation in Indonesia. (Since the mid-1970s and especially since the 1979 Law on Village Government, villages in West Sumatra had to conform with the national model of a village [*desa*], basically following a Javanese model. This had caused the restructuring and splitting of *nagari*, which were seen by the Minangkabau to embody *adat* and traditional leadership structures.)

A further development after 1998 was the passing of multiple provincial and district regulations that attempted to implement aspects of *sharīʿa* and thereby create more moral Muslims. This movement was part of decentralisation—carried out under the Regional Autonomy Laws Nos. 22/1999 and 25/1999—but was also a response to nationwide unease and anxiety as the country moved to democracy, freeing the media from censorship and opening up to the incursions of global pop culture. The regulations mainly focused on restricting the mobility of women (especially at night) and imposing the wearing of the *jilbab* and modest dress, as well as requiring schoolchildren and people wanting to marry to recite certain passages of the Qurʾān.[49] All this activity focussed on conduct in public and led to increased levels of surveillance and monitoring, especially of women and young people. Those who were not much interested in religion, or who preferred a more free-and-easy lifestyle, found themselves subject to heightened social pressure to conform to an increasingly puritan way of life.

The essential and immutable ingredient of Minangkabau *adat* is the matrilineal kinship system. Matriliny and its economic base in addition to

---

[47] Henk Schulte Nordholt and Gerry van Klinken (eds.) *Renegotiating Boundaries: Local Politics in Post-Suharto Indonesia*, Leiden: Brill, 2007.

[48] von Benda-Beckmann, *Political and Legal Transformations of an Indonesian Polity*, 7.

[49] Lyn Parker and Pam Nilan, *Adolescents in Contemporary Indonesia* (New York: Routledge, 2013), 112–13; Edriana Noerdin, "Customary Institutions, Syariah Law and the Marginalisation of Indonesian Women" in Kathryn Robinson and Sharon Bessell (eds.), *Women in Indonesia: Gender, Equity and Development* (Singapore: Institute of Southeast Asian Studies, 2002), 179–86; M.B. Hooker, *Indonesian Syariah: defining a national school of Islamic law* (Singapore: ISEAS Publishing, 2008), 265–73.

matrilocal residence are the basis not only of the social structure and social life but also of the local governance system. The following sections examine these, with a view also to highlight the sources of vulnerability for different sub-populations and the different ways the Minangkabau have resisted and adapted to cope with, and embrace, changes.

Social Organisation

Minangkabau society is organised according to matrilineages or matri-clans (*suku*).[50] The most basic unit consists of a mother and her children (*samande*, meaning "of one mother"), who traditionally occupied one room (*bilik*) in a longhouse (*rumah gadang*), with a roof shaped like buffalo horns. A woman's husband (*sumando*) was not considered part of that unit: he was considered a visitor, who came at night and had a marginal place in the household. His primary duties and rights were as *mamak* (mother's brother) to his sister and her children, and they lived elsewhere. In the longhouse lived the grandmother, her daughters, and their children, in different *bilik*—usually three or four generations of women. They cooked and ate together, raised children communally, and, it should be mentioned, constituted a secure and stable female-dominated home. The longhouse was lively with sociality.

The *sumande* unit is not often spoken of these days and has largely been replaced by the nuclear family (*keluarga*) as the basic unit in society. Reasons for the shift are many and complex, but urbanisation, the rise of private property, and changing ideas of the family are clearly major factors. Women told me that life in the *rumah gadang* was dense with communal surveillance and afforded little privacy. The composition of families that constitute a household (i.e., those who live, sleep, and eat together) is now quite various and people come and go, but the augmented nuclear

---

[50] The clan system described here is a simplified version and there is considerable regional variation. In the village (*nagari*) of field research, there were more levels (or subdivisions) than are described here. Various authors provide descriptions (van Reenen, *Central Pillars of the House*; Ng, *The Weaving of Prestige*; Ok-Kyung Pak, *Lowering the High, Raising the Low: The Gender, Alliance and Property Relations in a Minangkabau Peasant Community of West Sumatra, Indonesia*, Ph.D. dissertation: University of Toronto, 1986; Franz von Benda-Beckman, *Property in social continuity: Continuity and change in the maintenance of property relationships through time in Minangkabau, West Sumatra*, The Hague: Martinus Nijhoff, 1979).

18   L. PARKER

family—the nuclear family with additional members such as the wife's mother, or her sisters and their children—is perhaps the most common.

Nowadays, the husband/father, along with the wife/mother, is responsible for the upkeep and education of the children. The Marriage Law of 1974 and the state gender ideology place the husband/father as the head of the household (*kepala keluarga*), and if asked who the head of the household is, in a formal context, people usually respond that it is the husband/father. This no doubt is due to the bureaucratisation of everyday life: for censuses, registration for social welfare, school enrolment, clinic attendance, and a host of other daily activities that involve interaction with the state, people have been trained to provide this answer. Yet there is no doubt that both men and women have claims to authority in the household. In villages, where a version of matrilocal residence prevails and women own the houses, it would be quite difficult for a man to have authority over his wife. In towns, my feeling is that this is changing. Certainly in the household where I lived, in Bukittinggi, the man, who was the sole breadwinner in the household, could wield power over his wife. On one occasion, for instance, he prohibited her from taking a desired trip to Jakarta to visit her family. Simon reports that one of his informants in Bukittinggi forbad his wife from working, but this is highly unusual.[51] Krier presents a memorable case of larger family conflict in which a woman's spirited self-defence worked against her, showing that this matrilineal system does not always work well for women.[52] But I would say that decisions within families are usually made by women; for broader kinship matters, men might appear publicly to be making a decision, but often women have already arranged matters beforehand.[53]

As Narny emphasises, "[T]he traditional context places women as the heads of families and the main decision-makers in the extended family".[54] The man is not a member of the matrilineage into which he has married and remains a member of his mother's lineage. Men are usually structurally marginal in houses. A Minangkabau man "does not really have a house or a place

---

[51] Simon, *Caged in on the Outside*, 35.

[52] Jennifer Krier, "Narrating Herself: Power and Gender in a Minangkabau Woman's Tale of Conflict," in Aihwa Ong and Michael G. Peletz (eds.) *Bewitching Women, Pious Men: Gender and Body Politics in Southeast Asia* (Berkeley, CA: University of California Press, 1995), 51–75.

[53] Blackwood, *Webs of Power*.

[54] Yenny Narny, *Resilience of West Sumatran women: historical, cultural and social impacts*, (Ph.D. dissertation: Deakin University, 2016), 150.

MATRIFOCAL, MATRILINEAL, OR MATRIARCHAL? CULTURAL RESILIENCE... 19

he can call his own. ... The house itself is for his mothers and sisters," according to Kato,[55] and Simon adds that "[b]eing a Minangkabau man thus means acknowledging that one's place is outside the household sphere".[56]

These days men usually live with their wives, but

> as domestic outsiders, are in a position of vulnerability in which they need to continually renew their social involvements. As guests in their wives' homes and *kampuang* [hamlets], men need to reach outside this sphere to form relationships. Both men and women emphasized to me that men who did not do this would be isolated.[57]

Younger men often sleep at a friend's place, having spent the evening with friends, at the local coffee-shop, snooker-hall, or *bengkel* (motorcycle repair garage). Young women do not stay over at friends' places: they should be home by *magrib* (sunset prayer-time), and stay there.

Often the nuclear family occupies its own house. Sometimes, when there are nuclear families, the husband builds a house for his wife and it becomes her house.[58] In the village, and also in towns where the house block surrounding a longhouse is large enough to accommodate more buildings, nuclear families of sisters occupy houses in a single block; in towns and the city of Padang, sisters typically try to buy next-door or nearby house blocks.[59] In the town of Bukittinggi, I lived in a house with a nuclear family, where the wife's mother would come to visit for two or three months, in rotation with visits to her other children in West Sumatra and Jakarta. The neighbouring house block contained four houses, one accommodating two elderly widows (sisters) and three accommodating the nuclear families of sisters, who were daughters of one of the elderly widows. There was no longer a longhouse. One family I knew well, who lived in a densely settled village that was not far from Bukittinggi, occupied a cramped and rickety wooden, three-storey house accommodating the elderly great-grandmother, her daughter (a primary school teacher)

---

[55] Tsuyoshi Kato, *Matriliny and Migration: Evolving Minangkabau Traditions in Indonesia* (Ithaca, NY: Cornell University Press, 1982), 61.

[56] Simon, *Caged in on the Outside*, 33.

[57] Simon, *Caged in on the Outside*, 67.

[58] Blackwood, "Wedding Bell Blues."

[59] Mina Elfira, *The Lived Experiences of Minangkabau Mothers and Daughters: Gender Relations, Adat, and Family in Padang, West Sumatra, Indonesia*, Ph.D. dissertation: The University of Melbourne, 2010.

and son-in-law (a butcher, listed formally as the head of the household), their seven adult children, one Javanese grandson-in-law, and the great-grandchildren. It was not a longhouse in design, but functioned much like one in everyday life. Such multi-generational households and house compounds, clustered around the matriline, are common; Blackwood calls them "matrihouses".[60] Thus matrilocal residence persists, alongside neolocal residence, albeit adapted to municipal town plans.

It has not been mentioned in the literature, to my knowledge, but since we now know that nuclear family houses are not necessarily safe spaces for women, it is worth mentioning that the matrilocal longhouse did provide safety for women: indeed, it is hard to imagine how intimate partner violence could be perpetrated in a longhouse. There are increasing reports of gender-based violence in West Sumatra, and newspapers now routinely report on women being injured and even killed by their partners or partners' male kin. It is easy to see that urbanisation and the rising prevalence of nuclear family households are contributing to the increasing vulnerability of women to the threat of gender-based violence.[61]

Matrilocal residence carries many advantages for women besides care of children, sharing of housework, and a safe, stable home environment. Women have authority in their own homes, and generally control the household economy. While they are usually the carers for the elderly, sick, and disabled, these burdens can be shared, especially among sisters; old age, a time of vulnerability for most, is not such a problem for the Minangkabau. Typically, widowed elderly men and women who can no longer work are looked after by their daughters. Unlike in some societies in Indonesia, this is not seen as shameful: rather, it is a source of pride that they have produced caring families. Childless elderly, however, can be vulnerable, as can those whose children have migrated away from the village. It can be difficult to find hands-on care for those who are bedridden and dependent.

[60] Blackwood, "Wedding Bell Blues."

[61] It is difficult to collect good data on domestic violence in Indonesia. Fatmariza and Febriani ("Domestic Violence and The Role of Women in Modern Minangkabau Society," 2019) present police statistics that show a rising incidence of domestic violence in West Sumatra, but the time span is short (2011–2013) and in any case the concept of domestic violence is still new, and many do not report it because of the stigma. Fatmariza and Febriani suggest that the incidence of domestic violence in West Sumatra is quite high because of patriarchal attitudes towards women, though "women who remain in their matrilineal relationship after marriage can prevent domestic violence."

While the most basic bond in Minang society is that between mother and daughter, the bond between siblings is also very strong. Brothers and sisters share a mother and therefore common goals: the strength of the matrilineage. Traditionally, a mother's brother (*mamak*) was the "sociological father" to his sister's children,[62] but a boy did not share his mother and sisters' living space once be began to approach puberty; around the age of ten he would move to sleep at the community *surau* (prayer house). Physical distance and a formal, polite relationship between brothers and sisters were required. This has changed recently, partly, no doubt, because brothers remain with their sisters in their natal home, so the physical distancing rule has relaxed. Moreover, Islamic law treats the brothers of women and girls as *muhrim*, close relatives, which means that, for instance, young women these days do not cover (wear the *jilbab*) in the company of their brothers. So the brother-sister relationship has become closer and less formal, even as the role of the *mamak* has declined to that of a benevolent and interested but distant uncle. Generally, the *mamak* is kept informed of plans regarding his nieces and nephews and their whereabouts, but does not take part in decision-making regarding education, employment, and marriage, and in my experience does not financially support his sister's children.

Ties between sisters are very strong. The oldest daughter in a family is respected and has authority; she, in turn, is responsible for younger siblings and for the care of their ageing mother. If a woman should die, her sister would almost automatically take over responsibility for her dead sister's children, even if she were not (yet) married. Older sisters these days frequently help with the schooling and university costs of their younger siblings.

This matrilineal social structure and matrilocal residence pattern, with its clan-based economic foundation (discussed below), is a source of security and power for women. It means that men have to "make themselves" in a way that women do not.

The tradition of *merantau* (wandering, migration) should be mentioned here, and I will say more below. The pattern was that young men would leave home for a period away, in order to seek wealth and experience and prove themselves as worthy husbands.[63] An older male informant

---

[62] Elfira, *The Lived Experiences of Minangkabau Mothers and Daughters*, 172.

[63] Kato, Matriliny and Migration; Mochtar Naim, *Merantau: Minangkabau voluntary migration*, Ph.D. dissertation: University of Singapore, 1974.

22   L. PARKER

told me that it used to be simply a seasonal search for work, with the destination and timing dependent upon the crops– for instance, when it was *gambir* season the young men would go to north Sumatra as seasonal day labourers. However, it was more usually presented as a product of the unique Minangkabau *adat*. Earlier writers on the Minangkabau always associated male out-migration with matrifocality and the practice of matriliny and matrilocal residence. There were various ways that this association was explained. Two explanations stress the ways in which men could have been perceived as vulnerable: they had "no place" at home, and matrilineal inheritance of land and other property meant that they had to seek their own fortune "away". Murad, for instance, stated that "the effect of this [matrilineal] system is often to *compel* men in disadvantaged kinship positions in their homeland to *merantau*".[64] Other scholars have put forward very different arguments: that men allowed women to make decisions and gave them land because husbands were unreliable and/or absent, and brothers had other resources. Blackwood calls this the "altruism" argument, a subset of the "missing man" phenomenon in those writings that see matrifocality and matrilineality as aberrant and as requiring explanation.[65] Another explanation assumes the inferiority of women:

> [W]omen are believed to require greater subsistence guarantees than men partly because they are held to be less flexible, resourceful, and adaptive than men, who can eke out a living wherever they find themselves, be it in the village in which they were born (or into which they married) or a … city.[66]

Today, one of the strongest discourses is what I call the "protection of women" or "women on a pedestal" discourse; according to female informants, it combines Islamic ideas about the place of women in Islam with concepts and practices of *adat*. In this narrative, Islam and Minangkabau *adat* both honour women; women are regarded as noble (*mulia*) and are so precious that they should be protected.[67] In Minang *adat*, women have a high position and are provided with economic resources through inheri-

---

[64] Auda Murad, *Merantau: Aspects of Outmigration of the Minangkabau People* (Master's dissertation: Australian National University, 1978), iii, emphasis added.

[65] Blackwood, "Wedding Bell Blues," 11.

[66] Michael G. Peletz, "Comparative Perspectives on Kinship and Cultural Identity in Negeri Sembilan," *Journal of Social Issues in Southeast Asia* 9:1 (1994), 23.

[67] This was advanced by some young female participants as a reason why Indonesia does not need feminism, which is viewed as a Western discourse.

tance to ensure their wellbeing. Sometimes, however, this discourse of protection is based less on the high position of women than on the idea of their inferiority, as previously discussed. The respected Minang scholar and *adat* expert, Datuk Rajo Penghulu, wrote:

> According to Minangkabau *adat*, economic resources (rice land and dry fields) are primarily for the benefit of women. … Because men are stronger physically and have greater capabilities than women, to them is given the responsibility and control of the rice land and dry fields. Men are the strong backbone for women; women always work within men's protection. As Islamic law says: Men are the backbone of women.[68]

There is no doubt that there is a connection between matriliny and matrifocality, on the one hand, and the practice of male *merantau*, on the other, but it is worth mentioning two points: first, there are other ethnic groups in Indonesia where the men are encouraged to seek fortune "away", such as the Bugis of South Sulawesi,[69] but their kinship systems are patrilineal or bilateral. Second, these days *merantau* is not gendered male. Young women are just as likely as young men to leave home for work or university, and nuclear families often migrate. Further, when young women migrate they do not simply follow a sibling or husband: they go on their own, to further their education or to see work, often in open-ended quests.[70] This "going away" is so common that the village where I carried out fieldwork often felt quite empty. There were literally empty houses everywhere. So while there may have been a stronger connection between matriliny and *merantau* in the past, I do not see that matrifocality, matriliny, or matrilocal residence is such a strong centrifugal force that it is a necessary or sufficient cause of *merantau*. Nevertheless, the association between matriliny and the perceived need for Minang men

---

[68] Rajo 1994, 65, cited in Blackwood, "Wedding Bell Blues," 11.

[69] G. Acciaioli, *Searching for Good Fortune: The Making of a Bugis Shore Community at Lake Lindu, Central Sulawesi*, Ph.D. dissertation: Australian National University, 1989; Kees van Dijk, Gregory Acciaioli, and Roger Tol (eds.), *Authority and Enterprise Among the Peoples of South Sulawesi*, Leiden: KITLV Press, 2000.

[70] See, for example, Diah Tjahaya Iman and A. Mani, "Motivations for migration among Minangkabau women in Indonesia," *Ritsumeikan Journal of Asia Pacific Studies* 32 (2013), 114–24; and Diah Tjahaya Iman and A. Mani, "The 'Positioning' of Identity Among Minangkabau Female Migrants in Indonesia," *Asia Pacific World* 6:1 (2015), 47–62.

24   L. PARKER

to prove themselves by successfully migrating has become entrenched in the literature.[71]

Education

With censuses in 1920 and 1930, then a gap until 1971, followed by a census in 1980 and every ten years thereafter, we have good evidence of high levels of education generally in West Sumatra and, more notably, consistently high levels of female education. While definitions of literacy and administrative boundaries have changed over time, the comparison of literacy in Minangkabau/West Sumatra with national levels always shows these high levels of female literacy and education. For instance, using 1980 census data, Oey-Gardiner showed that the Minangkabau female:male ratio of the school-attending population aged 16–18 was 99:100, while nationally it was 66:100. Much of the difference was probably due to the propensity of Minangkabau parents to send their daughters to religious schools.[72]

While large-scale statistics in Indonesia should always be examined critically, other data sets provide corroborating evidence. The Indonesia Demographic and Health Survey (DHS) for 2017 presents information on education for almost 50,000 women aged 15–49 in all provinces of Indonesia. Only 0.9% of women in this age range in West Sumatra had no education.[73] Looking at these women's median years of education completed, the province of West Sumatra (11.1 years) is only bettered by the university city of Yogyakarta and the capital, Jakarta (11.4 and 11.2 years, respectively); the national median years of education for these women was 8.9 years.[74] The Demographic and Health Survey 2017 also collected information on 10,000 currently married men aged 15–54. The figures

---

[71] Statements such as the following are common, for example: "Several ethnic groups are renowned for their long traditions of migration (Ind: *merantau*), which is, for example, a rite of passage for Minang men from West Sumatra." Ariane J. Utomo and Peter F. McDonald, "Internal migration, group size, and ethnic endogamy in Indonesia," *Geographical Research* (2020), 4.

[72] M. Oey-Gardiner, "Gender Differences in Schooling in Indonesia," *Bulletin of Indonesian Economic Studies* 27:1 (1991), 61, 64.

[73] BKKBN (National Population and Family Planning Board), Statistics Indonesia (BPS), Ministry of Health (Kemenkes), and ICF, *Indonesia Demographic and Health Survey 2017* (Jakarta: BKKBN, BPS, Kemenkes, and ICF, 2018), 259.

[74] BKKBN et al., *Indonesia Demographic and Health Survey 2017*, 259.

for West Sumatran men were as follows: 0.00% had no education at all, and there was a median of 8.7 years of education. Men in sixteen other provinces scored higher: the national median years of education for men were the same as for West Sumatra, at 8.7 years.[75] One can conjecture that parents consider that education is more important for girls than for boys; that the push, or urge, to *merantau* for work is stronger for boys than for girls; and/or that the range of occupations open to girls requires a higher level of education than those open to boys. I certainly know of married Minang couples where the woman is more highly educated than her husband. It is possible to conclude, then, that both men and women are well-educated, relative to the situation elsewhere in Indonesia, and suffer no disadvantage or vulnerability in the sphere of education.

Ancestral Inheritance *(harto pusako)*, Work, and the Village Economy

The economy of rural West Sumatra is based on agriculture: where landform and rainfall allow, wet rice dominates; elsewhere, dry agriculture of annual crops (mostly vegetables such as tomatoes, aubergine, onions and other alliums, cabbages, and corn) and perennials (such as coffee bushes, fruit trees, and cinnamon trees) prevail. In the village of fieldwork, which profits from the rich, fertile soil of the lower slopes of the active volcano Mt Merapi, nearly 90% of agricultural land is owned by clans and lineages. Some is devoted to wet rice—although conditions usually only allow one crop a year—and some to dry crops (annuals that alternate with wet rice, and large areas of fruit trees often inter-planted with coffee and cinnamon).

The economic importance of the matrilineal clans is striking. Theoretically, their land is collectively owned by their lineage (*harato pusako*) and inherited matrilineally, and can never be sold. *Harato pusako* is considered to have been inherited from the ancestors, who divided it among the various *rumah gadang*. However, most disputes in villages are about access to land, and it seems to me that disputed access to land is the main source of conflict in Minang society. Obviously, where land cannot be sold use rights are very important. The allocation of use rights can be simple—for example from a senior woman (*bundo kanduang*) to her daughters shared equally or in yearly rotation if the area is limited—but if the area of land is large and the "owner" a large clan, or there are no

[75] BKKBN et al., *Indonesia Demographic and Health Survey 2017*, 260.

26   L. PARKER

female descendants, it can become complicated and contested. The senior woman of one dominant clan in the fieldwork village had recently died; the *penghulu* was not actually living in the village, although he visited almost daily, and he had a male manager to organise the allocation of use rights. Lineage land is often managed by the *penghulu* and/or the senior woman. Land of smaller units is usually managed by the oldest woman in the sub-lineage. "The oldest woman in the *rumah* ... is in actual control: she holds the prime responsibility for the daily management, the modes of cultivation, and the distribution of the produce."[76]

Besides the *harato pusako* there is also *pancarian,* or individually acquired and owned private property. In the village of fieldwork, only a little over 10% of agricultural land was classified as *pancarian. Pancarian* can be owned by individual men or women, or by a married couple (in which case it is called *suarang*), but it is often considered to mean land that men have bought for themselves as private property. Some have seen this as a threat to *adat pusako,* and even as a conflict between men's and women's interests, but that would be an over-simplification. In earlier times, *pancarian* was added to the matrilineage of the person who bought it—so men were encouraged to acquire land for their mother's and sisters' lineage—but these days it is usually sold or passed on to the daughters, and often in the next generation becomes *pusako rendah* (low ancestral property). Thus, perhaps surprisingly, "*pusako*-isation" is still happening— an indicator of the continuing strength of matrilineal inheritance practices.[77] However, as van Reenen notes, in the past a man's *pancarian* would likely become the *pusako* of his mother's matrilineage; today it will likely become the *pusako* of his wife and daughters' matrilineage.[78] In recent times, the state has embarked upon a vigorous project of trying to register *adat* and privately owned land across the country, and *pusako* and *pancarian* land have been caught up in this process, producing a large number of court cases.

There is also *ulayat*—land that is not used for agriculture, usually uncleared forest. It used to be considered communal village land (*ulayat nagari*) under Dutch interpretations of *adat*, but under Suharto was classified as being owned by the state; since the downfall of Suharto, the state has been trying to regulate the status of communal land, culminating in

---

[76] van Reenen, *Central Pillars of the House*, 97.
[77] von Benda-Beckman, *Property in social continuity*.
[78] van Reenen, *Central Pillars of the House*, 103.

the Regulation on *Ulayat* Land (16/2008), which seemed to reinforce *adat* (matrilineal) rights.[79]

It is impossible to explore the intricacies of inheritance and property law here, but important to note that conflicts over land can be long and bitter, and often result in serious fissures within and between families and lineages. Court cases have to explore "usually long-lasting and complex histories of inheritance, registration and conversion",[80] involving negotiations under conditions of legal pluralism: *adat* law, state law, and Islamic law. Typically, property and inheritance issues are considered to be *adat* affairs; if the land is considered *pancarian*, state law might also be invoked; if gifts (*hibah*) are involved, conflicts might be seen as matters of both Islamic law and *adat* because they usually involve *pusako* land.[81] Despite all of the above, the von Benda-Beckmanns report that the matrilineal "inheritance consensus" of female inheritance rights has prevailed.[82]

Clearly, these matrilineal inheritance practices are not commensurate with Islamic inheritance laws. Islamic reformists during and since the Padri Wars have focused on this basic incompatibility, but *adat* persists and even thrives.[83] Most research participants understood Islamic inheritance laws to be that sons should inherit two-thirds and daughters one-third. They often argue that there is no real contradiction, since daughters do not inherit as individuals; and also maintain that sons are granted two-thirds on the assumption that they will care for their parents in old age, while in Minang this is the responsibility of daughters. More generally, many Islamic concepts in Islamic law are used and recognised in Minang *adat*, for example terms such as *hak* (right), *milik* (property, ownership), *hibah* (gift), and *warith* (heir), though with local understandings, so *warith* in Minang denotes matrilineal heirs. Often property disputes are settled (or pre-empted) through *hibah*—a gift of land—but in Minang this is

---

[79] von Benda-Beckmann, *Political and Legal Transformations of an Indonesian Polity*, 350–7.

[80] von Benda-Beckmann, *Political and Legal Transformations of an Indonesian Polity*, 373.

[81] von Benda-Beckmann, *Political and Legal Transformations of an Indonesian Polity*, 363.

[82] von Benda-Beckmann, *Political and Legal Transformations of an Indonesian Polity*.

[83] Hadler, *Muslims and Matriarchs*, 20, 56; Franz and Kebeet von Benda-Beckmann, "Transformation and Change in Minangkabau," in Lynn L. Thomas and Franz Von Benda-Beckmann (eds.), *Change and Continuity in Minangkabau: Local, Regional, and Historical Perspectives on West Sumatra* (Athens: Ohio University Center for International Studies, 1985), 235–78.

revocable and only effective at the time of the donor's death, and the amount of the gift is severely restricted.[84]

It should be noted that both men and women are considered farmers.[85] Women are more often landowners and have more secure access to land than men in the village of fieldwork, because their kin groups own the land. Men usually work their wives' land, while some also work that of their mother. They typically inherit nothing and have no rights, unless they are senior-titled men, such as the *penghulu*. Women do not usually inherit land individually: they are co-owners of kin group land, but often have exclusive use rights, or in rotation with sisters. In terms of property rights, there is no doubt that men are more vulnerable than women in Minangkabau society, though *penghulu* and other elite men (see below) are relatively privileged and secure.

In this rural society, access to land is the usual guarantee of livelihood. If one can farm wet rice land then subsistence is guaranteed, and sometimes a cash income after harvest as well—depending on the amount of land, the type of access granted, the share of harvest and crops, and various other factors. Dry land farming produces cash crops and, depending on the type of crop and the location, these are sold in local markets or to intermediaries. Sharecropping is the most common (and preferred) form of access to land; after that comes wage labour and pawning. Sharecropping is preferred because it entails an ongoing relationship, sometimes over decades, and is more guaranteed and less precarious. Wage labour, in a context where daily wages are low—about $2.50 a day—is not desirable because illness, lack of work, and weather and market conditions make it insecure. Pawning, when the owner is paid a lump sum for the right to use land, is not unpopular, but if it takes generations for the owner to pay back the pawn, then ill-feeling and suspicion of theft can arise. It is also worth noting that at any one time an individual woman may be (co-)landholder, sharecropper, and wage labourer. This means that villages are not usually clearly demarcated into wealthy landowners and a landless labouring "proletariat".

This is not an egalitarian society, however. Nor is it highly unequal. Matrilineal kinship still structures the society and the economy in rural

---

[84] von Benda-Beckmann, "Transformation and Change in Minangkabau."

[85] See below for a discussion of female occupations; also Evelyn Blackwood, "Not your average housewife: Minangkabau women rice farmers in West Sumatra," in M. Ford and L. Parker (eds.) *Women and Work in Indonesia*, London and New York: Routledge, 2008.

MATRIFOCAL, MATRILINEAL, OR MATRIARCHAL? CULTURAL RESILIENCE... 29

villages, in concert with the history of settlement and a largely kinship-based patron-client network. Some villages, such as that studied by Blackwood, have a clear stratification consisting of three layers:

> [E]lites (*orang asli*), who are members of the original founding lineages (*suku*); commoners or client kin (*orang datang*), newcomers or outsiders who arrived later and were adopted into the original lineages; and descendants of slaves, who were bought by and became subordinate members of the original lineages.[86]

The *nagari* studied in this fieldwork consisted of four *jorong* (hamlets), two of which were studied in detail. Jorong I is the centrally located, original village: it consists of four main lineage groups (*suku*), especially Bodi-Caniago. It is densely settled and consists of many *rumah gadang*; many houses are made of timber; there is a mosque built fairly recently, mainly financed by remittances from the many people who have moved away as *perantau*. Their houses have been left empty, but they come back to visit—often at Ramadan. People in this *jorong* are well-educated. There are many professional and middle-class members of this *jorong*; while many people own (or enjoy use rights to) *harato pusako*, most do not actually work the land. Jorong II is considered by inhabitants of Jorong I to be a village of newcomers (*pendatang*), many of whom are described as *anak buah* (clients) of patrons and lineages in Jorong I. Their status as newcomers (*pendatang*) is contested. Many people in Jorong II have moved around a lot; they used to be seen as poor, but many have been sharecroppers or wage labourers of *harto pusako* owned by lineages in the original village. Nowadays some have brick houses and cars, and some have bought dry land so they have some disposable property. The settlement pattern is dispersed, with no centre and no market; houses tend to be built on productive land, hidden amidst fruit trees. Jorong II has a "bushy," almost pioneering feel. There is a tendency for inhabitants of Jorong I to look down on those of Jorong II as "beyond the pale"—considering them coarse, irreligious, and even criminals.

Kin groups, kinship obligations, and patron-client relations (couched in terms of matrilineal kinship) shape village economies, and most of these

---

[86] Blackwood, "Not your average housewife," 22.

30 L. PARKER

are managed by women.[87] Women's control of land and labour—especially that of senior elite women who control considerable *harato pusako*—mean that women are powerful in the local economy. They are highly visible in public, as economic actors and managers—in the fields, in the market, and in negotiations with external traders. Elite women own rice mills, export coffee, and have professional jobs. In short, they are active in the public sphere and exert economic power and political influence.

The Larger Economy

The above view from inside the village is not really reflected in national statistics. For instance, the Demographic and Health Survey 2017 reports that 98.8% of men aged 15–54 in West Sumatra are currently employed, compared to only 57% of women aged 15–49.[88] The latter figure for all of Indonesia is 53%. One explanation for this reported low female labour force participation rate in Minang is that it does not reflect reality, because in surveys and censuses, women tend not to report that they work: instead, they often prefer to say that they are housewives (*ibu rumah tangga*). This status complies with the state gender ideology that idealises the nuclear middle-class family, with the man as the head of the household and breadwinner and the woman as housewife.[89] I have witnessed women saying that their occupation is housewife as they attend to customers at their *warung* (stall) at the front of their house or trade produce on the phone.[90] This would be even more likely for elite or wealthy women, for whom "not working" would mean high status—even though they manage a coffee export business or the labour arrangements for hectares of wet rice crops. Rural Minangkabau women usually work, though often in the informal sector, and often in such a way that they combine childcare, housework, and other domestic duties with income-generating work, usually as farmers, or in sales or trade.[91] For both men and women, it is

---

[87] Evelyn Blackwood, "Women, land, and labor: Negotiating clientage and kinship in a Minangkabau peasant community," *Ethnology* 36:4 (1997), 277–93.

[88] BKKBN et al., *Demographic and Health Survey 2017*, 267–8.

[89] Blackwood, "Not your average housewife."

[90] This is not unique to Minang women, however. The preference for stating that one is a housewife because of status was reported as long ago as 1982 by Valerie Hull, "Women in Java's Rural Middle Class: Progress or Regress?" in Penny Van Esterik (ed.), *Women of Southeast Asia* (De Kalb: Northern Illinois University Press, 1982), 78–95.

[91] Blackwood, "Not your average housewife."

praiseworthy to have a good work ethic; to be energetic, innovative, and pro-active in seeking work and in finding a new product to make or sell, or a new niche to occupy; and to be flexible in finding different kinds of work.

However, the national statistics better reflect reality—and in particular the high educational level of Minang women—when they examine women who report that they are employed. According to the Demographic and Health Survey data, women in West Sumatra are present in the professional/technical/managerial (PTM) field, sales, and agriculture at well above national averages, particularly in PTM occupations (17.6% of employed women in West Sumatra, compared to the national average of 11%), and are less well represented in clerical, industrial, and services occupations.[92]

Merantau and Remittances

As noted at the beginning, there are some 4.2 million inhabitants of the province of West Sumatra—and it is remarkably homogeneous ethnically—but around 6.5 million Minangkabau in Indonesia. This huge Minang diaspora is the result of both push and pull factors linked to culture and economic opportunity. The link between matriliny, matrifocality, and *merantau* has already been discussed. There are limited employment opportunities in West Sumatra. Many young people, of all genders, leave their village and even province after school for work or university. There are several universities in Padang, including Andalas University, which is well regarded, but top students aim for the better universities in Java. Once graduated, however, employment opportunities are extremely limited. For me, the symbol of this problem was the egg-seller in the market in Bukittinggi: a young man who had graduated from Andalas University, majoring in English literature.[93] An example of the alternative—*merantau*—was provided by my research assistant, whom I will call Debi. She is

[92] BKKBN et al., *Demographic and Health Survey 2017*, 269.

[93] The problem of graduate unemployment and underemployment is a national one—not at all unique to Minang or West Sumatra; the mis-match of qualifications and occupations is also part of a nationwide problem. Chris Manning, *The Political Economy of Reform: Labour After Soeharto*, Sydney: University of Sydney, 2008; Chris Manning and Sudarno Sumarto, "Employment, Living Standards and Poverty: Trends, Policies and Interactions," in Chris Manning and Sudarno Sumarto (eds.), *Employment, Living Standards and Poverty in Contemporary Indonesia* (Singapore: Institute of Southeast Asian Studies, 2011), 1–20.

the oldest of a three-child family; her mother is a widow, a primary school teacher. They lived in a rural village not far from Bukittinggi. Debi went to an Islamic high school and learnt to wear the *jilbab* there—she has worn it ever since. After graduating in anthropology from Andalas University, she worked for me for some years, intermittently, then obtained a job in Jakarta at an international bank. Her two brothers graduated in finance and engineering, and found jobs in their fields in Bandung and Banjarmasin. Some ten years later, all are married and living in Jabodatabek. The widowed mother has moved there too, to be with the children and grandchildren now that she is retired from teaching and has problems with her health.

Both men and women *merantau* these days; it is not at all gendered. The two *jorong* in the village of fieldwork present contrasting patterns. Jorong I is largely missing the generation aged between 20 and 49, due to their *merantau*. Unsurprisingly, it has few young children. There are a high proportion of elderly people, with many households being female-headed, and the issue of care for the elderly is a serious one. Jorong II has a much younger population, with many young children, and many women in their 20s and 30s reporting that they are housewives. Lack of childcare is an issue, especially as the extended family household is rarer here. There are few youth (15–24 years), even though there is a senior high school, and few elderly.

The *perantau* (out-migrants) are obviously a major source of revenue for Jorong I. The lineages and the *jorong* have organisations that exist in order to keep the lines of communication open between the folks at home and the *perantau*; leaders such as senior women and the *penghulu* some-times physically go to Jakarta or other migration sites, such as Pekanbaru, in order to solve disputes and seek funds for special projects; phone calls and WhatsApp groups are common.

Given the significant investment in education, especially in Jorong I, and the necessity then for young people to move away in order to capital-ise on the investment, the long-term cost for parents is considerable if they are neglected in old age. Apart from the now-established pattern symbol-ised by Debi's widowed mother—follow the children and migrate too—there is also the pattern followed by my host family in Bukittinggi: the grandmother rotated between her grown-up children who lived in various places, including Jakarta, spending two or three months with each.

Evidence from the village of research and from a limited number of other studies[94] shows not only that migrants are altruistically sending remittances to needy and also comfortable families but also that they are sponsoring a considerable amount of infrastructure improvement in home villages. Both men and women send money regularly, meaning that this external support has become expected, normal, and important.

> [T]he many long-distance migrations are the major source of wealth and prestige for the matriline, and elders are identified with, and receive the benefits of, successful family migration networks. Matrilines in the lowest strata are at a considerable disadvantage because they do not benefit to the same extent from such networks and the social and economic capital that they accumulate.[95]

Governance

In villages (*nagari*) in West Sumatra, local governance is shaped by kinship. It is not at all the case that matriliny rules in the private or domestic domain but is irrelevant in the public domain.

I agree with the position of van Reenan and Blackwood that the public-private split and its gendering (male = public, female = private) is not apposite in Minangkabau society, at least at village level.[96] The study of the *nagari* from the colonial period to today by the von Benda-Beckmanns is an excellent work on this subject, and they make it very clear that the village is a male institution, run by men, who are basically the *penghulu* of the major lineage groups.[97] Nevertheless, the source of their power and authority is the women behind them, in their lineages.

The status of the *nagari* today is quite different from what it once was. Virtually an autonomous unit in the past, it is now the lowest level of state governance and typically hosts a variety of state institutions including schools, clinics, agricultural extension offices, and its own administrative office, as well as the civil service personnel who provide the services. Thus

---

[94] See, for example, Ismawati Iis, Mustadjab Muslich, Hanani Nuhfil, and Syafria, "Factors Driving Remittances by Minangkabau's Migrants to Sending Households in Rural Areas," *Russian Journal of Agricultural and Socio-Economic Sciences* 80:8 (2018), 318–26.

[95] Philip Kreager, "Migration, social structure and old-age support networks: A comparison of three Indonesian communities," *Ageing & Society* 26:1 (2006), 49.

[96] van Reenan, *Central Pillars of the House*; Blackwood, *Webs of Power*.

[97] von Benda-Beckmann, *Political and Legal Transformations of an Indonesian Polity*.

34 L. PARKER

the *nagari* is both an *adat* law institution, representing matrilineages, administering matrilineal rights, and arbitrating disputes, and the lowest unit of the nation-state, administering state law, educating the younger generation, tending the sick and poor, and making decisions about large amounts of development funds. Here I quote at length from the major historical and legal study of the *nagari* by the von Benda-Beckmanns:

> The *nagari* is the embodiment of Minangkabau adat. With its adat council hall and mosque it stands for the unity of adat and Islam in Minangkabau society. It is in the *nagari* that the general principles of Minangkabau adat and adat law are concretised and specified. It is the *nagari* where matrilineal organisation was lived, and until the mid twentieth century matriliny was largely maintained through the rule of endogamy within the *nagari*. It is the *nagari*, as represented by its clan and lineage heads and the adat council, that held socio-political control over the village territory. It is through the *nagari* that people experience government. And it is the *nagari* with which people identify.
>
> In the course of our study we realised that we were dealing to an overwhelming degree with the views and experiences of men. To be sure, several female judges and female activists gave us their views on the political and legal developments in West Sumatra. And the only female elected mayor and some women in district and provincial offices or in village government discussed village government with us. But if women with an official function in village government talked about village government at all, they rarely discussed more than their particular tasks. Most women felt they had little to say about village government in general. Village government, whether in the sense of adat or of the state, turned out to be a predominantly male domain.[98]

And, to be sure, the higher levels of government, law, education, and religious authority are in the hands of men. When I arrived in West Sumatra, having read the work of late twentieth-century feminist scholars, I was surprised and disappointed to see that the governorship, district headships, and mayoral positions—indeed all major political positions— were held by men. Most judges, school principals, university rectors, and deans, as well as *ulama* and *adat* experts, were men. So the reach of matrilineal *adat* does not extend to the middle or higher levels of government and administration, and the term "matriarchy" is clearly inappropriate.

---

[98] von Benda-Beckmann, *Political and Legal Transformations of an Indonesian Polity*, 13.

Perhaps it should also be mentioned that women seemed to become more active in supra-village political life in West Sumatra after 1998, with democratisation and decentralisation, the precedent set by Megawati Sukarnoputri, Indonesia's first female President, and the introduction of a quota (at national level) specifying that at least 30% of candidates from each political party must be female. Local scholars have been researching this phenomenon and have found that actually women are comparatively absent from politics in West Sumatra. Scholars did find that extended family support helped Minang women to become politicians—but this is also a feature in many places where matriliny does not operate. One of the major findings in West Sumatra has been that the matrilineal arrangement of society did not seem to have made much difference to women's ability or success as politicians.[99]

Conclusion

The matrilineal organisation of Minangkabau society is uncontested today. While the adoption of Islam during the seventeenth and eighteenth centuries no doubt transformed society, Wahhabi-style incursions at the beginning of the nineteenth and twentieth centuries failed to dislodge matrilineality. Society remains matrifocal in fields such as family and village organisation, and the village economy. With reference to the question of its vulnerability or resilience, one can say that Minangkabau *adat* has been both remarkably resistant to change and capable of adaptability. It can therefore be labelled "culturally resilient". Larger structures—such as provincial government, the legal system, religious authority, and educational administration—are not noticeably different from such structures elsewhere in Indonesia when it comes to their patriarchal nature, so the labelling of Minang society as matriarchal seems a misnomer. While the matrilineal *adat* thrives today, so too does Islam. The relationship between the two has been worked out over centuries. While some unease remains with aspects of *adat,* such as inheritance practices—clearly at odds with parts of Islamic law—there is no doubt that for the Minangkabau, Islam is Truth, and the eternal and immutable source of *adat.*

---

[99] Jendrius, *Decentralization, Local Direct Elections and the Return to [the] Nagari: Women's Involvement and Leadership in West Sumatra*, Ph.D. dissertation: University of Malaya, 2014; Selinaswati, *Women in Politics in Matrilineal Society: A Case Study of West Sumatra, Indonesia*, Ph.D. dissertation: Deakin University, 2014.

Adat provides many women with cultural, political, and practical resources that make them comparatively powerful, not only in the domestic sphere but also in village life and the village economy. Further, their high level of education and mobility—at least before they have children—enables them to compete well in the modern economy beyond the village, and these days they are just as mobile as Minangkabau men. *Adat* practices do not guarantee security and prosperity for all women, however. Women who are not well embedded in matrilineages, who are members of small or insignificant matrilineages, or who are newcomers or in-marrying outsiders, struggle to attach themselves to patrons and thereby gain access to land and networks of support.

The position of men is changing. Although their traditional place in lineages was marginal, and their *adat* role as *mamak* (mother's brother) is almost defunct, as husbands and fathers they are finding a new importance, both within the household and family and in wider society, in a way that accords with both Islamic gender ideology and that of the Indonesian nation-state. Their *adat* role of *penghulu* (head of the *suku* or matrilineage) is of continuing and even increasing importance, due to the revitalisation of the *nagari* (village based on matrilineages). These senior men also often represent their village and district at higher levels of government. Nevertheless, men in this matrilineal society have to make their own way in ways that women do not, and so they are more vulnerable structurally than women. They have to exploit their individual abilities—for socialising and networking, for trade or other enterprises, for developing a range of skills, and for finding a livelihood—to a much greater extent than women, who tend to inherit their secure position. In this way, the usual disadvantages that women suffer—that they are ultimately responsible for their dependent children and bear the largest portion of the unpaid care burden, and yet are economically underpaid and under-resourced—are, to a large extent, mitigated in Minangkabau society.

Nevertheless, both male and female Minangkabau share some sources of vulnerability with Indonesians elsewhere: childlessness (either biological or because of social dysfunction) can lead to lack of care in old age or when ill or disabled; losing a spouse can leave a person alone or lonely, especially when daughters are absent. In this way, the Minangkabau propensity to migrate can be seen as both a successful adaptation that supports the vitality and longevity of villages in the homeland and a source of vulnerability for those "left behind." Two forms of adaptation by the older generation are apparent: moving away to join adult children and rotating among adult children who live away. Another successful adaptation is the institutionalisation of the maintenance of relationships with migrants: the *penghulu* and senior women are generally energetic in maintaining contact and soliciting funds for various causes in the village, and both remittances to family and donations to the village are generally an important source of support for rural villagers and villages.

Poor health infrastructure is ubiquitous in Indonesia (except, perhaps, in Jakarta) and the village of fieldwork was no exception. Babies and women were dying needlessly in childbirth; women were not treated for post-birth problems; people with some types of cancer were left untreated; diabetes, strokes, and heart attacks were becoming common. Most men smoked, creating huge vulnerabilities for their future. The problem of stunting among children was not apparent in Jorong I but is likely quite common in Jorong II. While the educational level of the Minangkabau has been historically high, there are weaknesses. Early childhood education was sadly lacking in the village. Nearly one quarter of household heads and spouses (23%) in Jorong I had graduated from senior high school, but in Jorong II only 9.7% had achieved this level of education. The problem of school-to-work transition is also ubiquitous throughout Indonesia and was a major reason for the emptying of young people from the village.

Looking to the future, one expects that matriliny and Islam will continue to provide the cultural, economic, and social resources that sustain the distinctive way of life of village Minangkabau. However, the flight from agriculture and the emptying of the villages raise questions about the ability of this way of life to migrate to the cities: matrilocal residence will be difficult to sustain, the inheritance of lineage land will become largely irrelevant, and livelihoods will be earned from outside the *alam Minangkabau*. The practical power of matrilineal *adat* may recede, but one suspects that the rich and flexible intermeshing of Islamic fervour and matrilineal ethnic identity will survive.

BIBLIOGRAPHY

Abdullah, Taufik, *Schools and politics: The Kaum Muda movement in West Sumatra*, Ithaca, NY: Cornell University Modern Indonesia Project, 1971.

Acciaioli, G., *Searching for Good Fortune: The Making of a Bugis Shore Community at Lake Lindu, Central Sulawesi*, Ph.D. dissertation: Australian National University, 1989.

Aspinall, E., and G. Fealy (eds.) *Local power and politics in Indonesia: Decentralisation & democratisation*, Singapore: Institute of Southeast Asian Studies, 2003.

Béné, Christophe, Rachel Godfrey Wood, Andrew Newsham, and Mark Davies, "Resilience: new utopia or new tyranny? Reflection about the potentials and limits of the concept of resilience in relation to vulnerability reduction programmes," *IDS Working Papers* 2012 (405), 1–61.

Béteille, André, "Inequality and Equality," in Tim Ingold (ed.) *Companion Encyclopedia of Anthropology: Humanity, Culture and Social Life*, London: Taylor & Francis Group, 1993.

BKKBN (National Population and Family Planning Board), Statistics Indonesia (BPS), Ministry of Health (Kemenkes), and ICF, *Indonesia Demographic and Health Survey 2017*, Jakarta: BKKBN, BPS, Kemenkes, and ICF, 2018.

Blackwood, Evelyn, "Women, land, and labor: Negotiating clientage and kinship in a Minangkabau peasant community," *Ethnology* 36:4 (1997), 277–93.

Blackwood, Evelyn, *Webs of power: Women, kin and community in a Sumatran village*, Lanham, MD: Rowman and Littlefield, 2000.

Blackwood, Evelyn, "Wedding Bell Blues: Marriage, Missing Men, and Matrifocal Follies," *American Ethnologist* 32:1 (2005), 3–19.

Blackwood, Evelyn, "Not your average housewife: Minangkabau women rice farmers in West Sumatra," in M. Ford and L. Parker (eds.) *Women and Work in Indonesia*, London and New York: Routledge, 2008.

BPS (Badan Pusat Statistik), Sensus Penduduk 2010 (2010 Census).

BPS (Badan Pusat Statistik), Kewarganegaraan, Suku Bangsa, Agama dan Bahasa Sehari-hari Penduduk Indonesia Hasil Sensus Penduduk 2011.

Dobbin, Christine, *Islamic revivalism in a changing peasant economy: Central Sumatra, 1784–1847*, London and Malmo: Curzon Press, 1983.

Elfira, Mina, *The Lived Experiences of Minangkabau Mothers and Daughters: Gender Relations, Adat, and Family in Padang, West Sumatra, Indonesia*, Ph.D. dissertation: The University of Melbourne, 2010.

Fatmariza, Fatmariza and R. Febriani, "Domestic Violence and The Role of Women in Modern Minangkabau Society," 2nd International Conference on Local Wisdom, Padang, 2019.

Fealy, Greg, and Sally White (eds.), *Expressing Islam: Religious Life and Politics in Indonesia*. Singapore: Institute of Southeast Asian Studies, 2008.

Graves, Elizabeth E., *The Minangkabau response to Dutch colonial rule in the nineteenth century*, Ithaca, NY: Cornell University, 1981.

Hadler, Jeffrey, *Muslims and Matriarchs: Cultural Resilience in Indonesia through Jihad and Colonialism*, Ithaca and London: Cornell University Press, 2008.

Hooker, M.B., *Indonesian Syariah: defining a national school of Islamic law*, Singapore: ISEAS Publishing, 2008.

Hull, Valerie, "Women in Java's Rural Middle Class: Progress or Regress?" in Penny Van Esterik (ed.), *Women of Southeast Asia* (De Kalb: Northern Illinois University Press, 1982), 78–95.

Iis, Ismawati, Mustadjab Muslich, Hanani Nuhfil, and Syafria, "Factors Driving Remittances by Minangkabau's Migrants to Sending Households in Rural Areas," *Russian Journal of Agricultural and Socio-Economic Sciences* 80:8 (2018), 318–26.

Iman, Diah Tjahaya, and A. Mani, "Motivations for migration among Minangkabau women in Indonesia," *Ritsumeikan Journal of Asia Pacific Studies* 32 (2013), 114–24.

Iman, Diah Tjahaya, and A. Mani, "The 'Positioning' of Identity among Minangkabau Female Migrants in Indonesia," *Asia Pacific World* 6:1 (2015), 47–62.

Jendrius, *Decentralization, Local Direct Elections and the Return to [the] Nagari: Women's Involvement and Leadership in West Sumatra*, Ph.D. dissertation: University of Malaya, 2014.

Kahin, Audrey, *Rebellion to Integration: West Sumatra and the Indonesian polity 1926–1998*, Amsterdam: Amsterdam University Press, 1999.

Kahn, Joel, *Constituting the Minangkabau: peasants, culture and modernity in colonial Indonesia*, Oxford: Berg Publishers, 1993.

Kato, Tsuyoshi, *Matriliny and Migration: Evolving Minangkabau Traditions in Indonesia*, Ithaca, NY: Cornell University Press, 1982.

Kreager, Philip, "Migration, social structure and old-age support networks: A comparison of three Indonesian communities," *Ageing & Society* 26:1 (2006), 37–60.

Krier, Jennifer, "Narrating Herself: Power and Gender in a Minangkabau Woman's Tale of Conflict," in Aihwa Ong and Michael G. Peletz (eds.) *Bewitching Women, Pious Men: Gender and Body Politics in Southeast Asia* (Berkeley, CA: University of California Press, 1995), 51–75.

Krier, Jennifer, "The Marital Project: Beyond the Exchange of Men in Minangkabau Marriage," *American Ethnologist* 27:4 (2000), 877–97.

Manning, Chris, *The Political Economy of Reform: Labour After Soeharto*, Sydney: University of Sydney, 2008.

Manning, Chris, and Sudarno Sumarto, "Employment, Living Standards and Poverty: Trends, Policies and Interactions," in Chris Manning and Sudarno Sumarto (eds.), *Employment, Living Standards and Poverty in Contemporary Indonesia*, (Singapore: Institute of Southeast Asian Studies, 2011), 1–20.

Mitchell, Tom, and Katie Harris, "Resilience: A risk management approach," ODI Background Note, London: Overseas Development Institute, 2012.

Murad, Auda, *Merantau: Aspects of Outmigration of the Minangkabau People*, Masters dissertation: Australian National University, 1978.

Naim, Mochtar, *Merantau: Minangkabau voluntary migration*, Ph.D. dissertation: University of Singapore, 1974.

Nakamura, Mitsuo, *The crescent arises over the banyan tree: a study of the Muhammadijah movement in a Central Javanese town*, Ph.D. dissertation: Cornell University, 1976.

Narny, Yenny, *Resilience of West Sumatran women: historical, cultural and social impacts*, Ph.D. dissertation: Deakin University, 2016.

Ng, Cecilia, *The Weaving of prestige: Village women's representations of the social categories of Minangkabau society*, Ph.D. dissertation: The Australian National University, 1987.

Noerdin, Edriana, "Customary Institutions, Syariah Law and the Marginalisation of Indonesian Women" in Kathryn Robinson and Sharon Bessell (eds.), *Women in Indonesia: Gender, Equity and Development* (Singapore: Institute of Southeast Asian Studies, 2002), 179–86.

Oey-Gardiner, M., "Gender Differences in Schooling in Indonesia," *Bulletin of Indonesian Economic Studies* 27:1 (1991), 57–79.

Pak, Ok-Kyung, *Lowering the High, Raising the Low: The Gender, Alliance and Property Relations in a Minangkabau Peasant Community of West Sumatra, Indonesia,* Ph.D. dissertation: University of Toronto, 1986.

Parker, Lyn (ed.), *The Agency of women in Asia*, Singapore: Marshall Cavendish Academic, 2005.

Parker, Lyn, "The Moral Panic about the Socializing of Young People in Minangkabau," *Wacana: Journal of the Humanities in Indonesia* 15:1 (2014), 19–40.

Parker, Lyn, and Pam Nilan, *Adolescents in Contemporary Indonesia*, New York: Routledge, 2013.

PCGN (The Permanent Committee on Geographical Names), Indonesia: population and administrative divisions, 2003.

Peletz, Michael G., "Comparative Perspectives on Kinship and Cultural Identity in Negeri Sembilan," *Journal of Social Issues in Southeast Asia* 9:1 (1994), 1–53.

Sanday, Peggy Reeves, *Women at the Center: Life in a Modern Matriarchy*, Ithaca: Cornell University Press, 2002.

Sanday, Peggy Reeves, "Matriarchy," in Hilary Callan (ed.) *The International Encyclopedia of Anthropology*, Hoboken, NJ: John Wiley, 2018.

Schneider, David M., "Introduction: The Distinctive Features of Matrilineal Descent Groups," in David M. Schneider and Kathleen Gough (eds.), *Matrilineal Kinship* (Berkeley and Los Angeles: University of California Press, 1961), 1–29.

Schröder-Butterfill, Elisabeth, and Ruly Marianti, "Understanding Vulnerabilities in Old Age," *Ageing and Society* 26:1 (2006), 3–8.

Schulte Nordholt, Henk, and Gerry van Klinken (eds.) *Renegotiating Boundaries: Local Politics in Post-Suharto Indonesia,* Leiden: Brill, 2007.

Selinaswati, *Women in Politics in Matrilineal Society: A Case Study of West Sumatra, Indonesia*, Ph.D. dissertation: Deakin University, 2014.

Siegetsleitner, Anne, "Matriarchy", in H. James Birx (ed.) *Encyclopedia of Anthropology* (Thousand Oaks, CA: SAGE Publications, 2006), 1554–5.

Simon, Gregory M., *Caged in on the Outside: Moral Subjectivity, Selfhood, and Islam in Minangkabau, Indonesia*, Honolulu: University of Hawaii Press, 2014.

Tanner, Nancy, "Matrifocality in Indonesia and Africa and Among Black Americans," in Michelle Z. Rosaldo and Louise Lamphere (eds.), *Woman, Culture and Society* (Stanford: University of Stanford Press, 1974), 129–56.

Turner, M., O. Podger, M. Sumardjono, and W.K. Tirthayasa (eds.), *Decentralisation in Indonesia: Redesigning the State*, Canberra: Asia Pacific Press, 2003.

Utomo, Ariane J., and Peter F. McDonald, "Internal migration, group size, and ethnic endogamy in Indonesia," *Geographical Research* (2020), 1–22.

van Bruinessen, Martin, "Introduction: Contemporary Developments in Indonesian Islam and the 'Conservative Turn' of the early twenty-first century," in Martin van Bruinessen (ed.), *Contemporary Development in Indonesian Islam: Explaining the "Conservative Turn"*, (Singapore: Institute of Southeast Asian Studies, 2013), 1–20.

van Dijk, Kees, Gregory Acciaioli, and Roger Tol (eds.), *Authority and Enterprise among the Peoples of South Sulawesi*, Leiden: KITLV Press, 2000.

van Reenen, Joke, *Central Pillars of the House: Sisters, Wives and Mothers in a rural community in Minangkabau, West Sumatra*, Leiden: Research School CNWS, Leiden University, 1996.

von Benda-Beckman, Franz, *Property in social continuity: Continuity and change in the maintenance of property relationships through time in Minangkabau, West Sumatra*, The Hague: Martinus Nijhoff, 1979.

von Benda-Beckmann, Franz, and Kebeet Von Benda-Beckmann, "Transformation and Change in Minangkabau," in Lynn L. Thomas and Franz Von Benda-Beckmann (eds.), *Change and Continuity in Minangkabau: Local, Regional, and Historical Perspectives on West Sumatra* (Athens: Ohio University Center for International Studies, 1985), 235–78.

von Benda-Beckmann, Franz, and Kebeet von Benda-Beckmann, "Ambivalent Identities: Decentralization and Minangkabau Political Communities," in H. Schulte-Nordholt and G. van Klinken (eds.) *Renegotiating Boundaries: Local Politics in Post-Suharto Indonesia* (Leiden: KITLV Press, 2007), 417–42.

von Benda-Beckmann, Franz , and Kebeet von Benda-Beckmann, *Political and Legal Transformations of an Indonesian Polity: The Nagari from Colonisation to Decentralisation*, New York: Cambridge University Press, 2013.

Whalley, Lucy A., *Virtuous Women, Productive Citizens: Negotiating Tradition, Islam and Modernity in Minangkabau, Indonesia*, Ph.D. dissertation: University of Illinois, 1993.

Adat Perpatih in Malaysia: Nature, History, Practice, and Contemporary Issues

Alexander Wain and Norliza Saleh

INTRODUCTION

Modern-day Malaysia is famed for its culturally, religiously, and ethnically diverse makeup. Although a Muslim majority nation, it is home to a broad variety of different religious and cultural groups drawn from across wider Asia and from much further afield. Far from a recent phenomenon, this diversity stretches back millennia, being a natural by-product of the commercial interaction characteristic of Malaysian history. The mercantile nature of Malaysia's earliest polities prompted extensive interaction with and, finally, migration from other parts of the world, including the broader Southeast Asian region. Ultimately, this allowed a unique matrilineal tradition known as *adat perpatih*

A. Wain (✉)
School of Divinity, University of St Andrews, St Andrews, UK
e-mail: adrw1@st-andrews.ac.uk

N. Saleh
International Institute of Advanced Islamic Studies (IAIS) Malaysia,
Kuala Lumpur, Malaysia

© The Author(s), under exclusive license to Springer Nature
Switzerland AG 2024
A. Panakkal, N. M. Arif (eds.), *Matrilineal, Matriarchal, and Matrifocal Islam*, Palgrave Series in Islamic Theology, Law, and History, https://doi.org/10.1007/978-3-031-51749-5_2

(or *lareh bodi caniago*) to develop on the Malay Peninsula, primarily in the region known today as Negeri Sembilan (The Nine States).

Matrilineal culture first arrived in Negeri Sembilan from Minangkabau, a highland region of West Sumatra in modern-day Indonesia. For centuries, Minangkabau had practised a form of matrilineality known as *adat alam Minangkabau* (traditions of the Minangkabau world). From at least the fifteenth century, this unique system began to disperse across wider Southeast Asia under the aegis of another Minangkabau tradition called *merantau* (lit. 'wandering'). This migratory practice saw many Minangkabau people leave their homeland in search of new frontiers; after travelling far and wide, a large proportion of them settled in what is now Negeri Sembilan, where succeeding centuries saw their complex matrilineal culture combine with pre-existing local customs and Islamic practices to form *adat perpatih*. This resultant and unique matrilineal system not only emphasised women's rights, but also equality before the law, respect for nature, and the moral necessity of correction and reform. This chapter describes the nature, history, practice, and contemporary condition of this tradition. In particular, we consider *adat perpatih*'s approach to community leadership, marriage, and property ownership (including inheritance). Each of these issues is discussed in ideal terms, as they would manifest were *adat perpatih* given full rein. While considering how *adat perpatih* converges and diverges with Islamic orthopraxis, we argue that behind an array of superficial differences lies a common desire to protect the status of women. Finally, the chapter considers *adat perpatih*'s decline in the wake of European colonialism.

The Nature of *Adat Perpatih*

To begin, let us consider what *adat perpatih* is, precisely. Academic literature typically defines the Malay word *adat* (from the Arabic *ādāt* or 'custom') in legalistic terms as denoting a prescriptive set of (often codified) laws governing social interaction.[1] Traditional manifestations of this concept, however, including *adat perpatih*, subsume far more than just law. As succinctly outlined by R. J. Wilkinson:

---

[1] For example, see M. B. Hooker, "A Note on the Malayan Legal Digests," *Journal of the Malaysian Branch of the Royal Asiatic Society* 4:1 (1968), 157–70.

Adat includes laws of nature, the conventions of society, the rules of etiquette and even the doctrines of common sense. *Adat* is right action in matters of everyday life as well as in obedience to the laws of the land.[2]

Rather than a strictly legal concept, therefore, *adat* denotes "right action" in a more general sense, incorporating the observance of perceived natural laws, commonly held cultural norms, and generally accepted ethical and moral standards. In this context, *adat perpatih* constitutes the central plank in a complex social system defined by familial descent, whether individual or collective, through the female line. From specific individuals to households (*rumpun*) to overarching matriclans (*suku*), this system expresses identity in terms of common female ancestry.[3] The majority of the ideals underlying this matrilineal system are encoded in *perbilangan* (proverbs), traditional oral statements transmitted as either prose or poetry. Although written down over the late nineteenth and early twentieth centuries, these proverbs are still memorised by ruling chiefs and *adat* officials (below) so that they can be passed from generation to generation as a guide in decision-making processes. They cover various aspects of life, including the appointment of leaders, the punitive justice system, and social conduct. All ruling chiefs or leaders must understand them and be skilled in their use.[4]

Another common perception within the literature is that *adat*, both generally and in terms of *adat perpatih* specifically, is oppositional to *sharīʿa*. The more *adat* a tradition contains, the less Islamic it is often thought to be.[5] Although consistently applied to *adat perpatih*,[6] this

---

[2] Richard James Wilkinson, "Rembau: Its History, Customs and Constitution," *Journal of the Straits Branch of the Royal Asiatic Society* 56 (1910), 13–14.

[3] Tsuyoshi Kato, "Change and Continuity in the Minangkabau Matrilineal System," *Indonesia* 25 (1978), 3.

[4] This chapter cites numerous *perbilangan*, each taken from Negeri Sembilan's *adat perpatih* tradition, with some additions from nearby Naning, Melaka. Readers should note that all cited *perbilangan* have an (often direct) equivalent in Minangkabau. See Michael B. Hooker, *Adat Laws in Modern Malaysia* (Oxford: Oxford University Press, 1972), 34.

[5] Hooker, "Note on Malayan Legal Digests," 169; Yock Fang Liaw, *Undang-Undang Melaka: The Laws of Melaka*, Bibliotheca Indonesica 13 (The Hague: Martinus Nijhoff, 1976), 31–2.

[6] For example, see Cecil William Chase Parr and W.H. Mackray, "Rembau, One of the Nine States: Its History, Constitution and Customs," *Journal of the Straits Branch of the Royal Asiatic Society* 56 (1910), 1–57.

46   A. WAIN AND N. SALEH

perspective is problematic; adherents of the tradition itself interpret it as complementary to Islam rather than contradictory, being an expression of the same natural order.[7] As clearly stated in one *perbilangan*:

Adat bersendi hukum.	*Adat* is based on religious law.
Hukum bersendi kitabullah.	Religious law on the Book of God.
Kuat adat, tak gaduh hukum.	If *adat* is strong, religious law is not troubled.
Kuat hukum, tak gaduh adat.	If religious law is strong, *adat* is not troubled.
Ibu hukum muafakat.	The mother of religious law is consensus.
Ibu adat muafakat.	The mother of *adat* is consensus.

This proverb clearly posits a dependency between *adat* and *sharīʿa*, rooting the former in the latter and making the legitimacy of both dependent on *kitabullah* (the Book of God, or the Qurʾān).[8] Islam and *adat* are therefore interrelated, with both constituting a law of values (what is proper, good, and right) leading to the existence of God.[9] Some Muslim jurists, including Wahbah al-Zuhayli, have argued that several Qurʾānic verses openly enjoining the observance of *adat* (termed *ʿurf*, 'that which is known') reinforce this sense of interdependence. Verse 7:199, for example, states: "Keep to forgiveness, enjoin *ʿurf*, and turn away from the ignorant". Al-Zuhayli perceives this and similar verses as textual authority for incorporating *adat* into *sharīʿa*; *adat* that does not contravene the principles of *sharīʿa* is considered valid and authoritative.[10]

Finally, as a complete system, *adat perpatih* can be seen as the embodiment of two core principles: *muafakat* (from Arabic *mūwāfaqa*, 'consensus') and *budi* ('virtue' or 'good character').[11] The importance of *muafakat* is illustrated by the tribal decision-making processes characteristic of *adat perpatih*, in which consultation (similar to the Islamic concept of *shūrā*) is key. Elaborated on more fully below, this idea of *muafakat* is manifested

---

[7] Taufik Abdullah, "Adat and Islam: An Examination of Conflict in Minangkabau," *Indonesia* 2 (1966), 3.

[8] This interdependence is also spelt out within an *adat perpatih* legal digest, codified in Sungai Ujong in 1904. The fourth *fasal* (section) of this digest states: "Truth arises out of three things: out of discussion, out of Allah's Book, and out of ancestral law." See Richard Olaf Winstedt and Patrick Edward de Josselin de Jong, "A Digest of Customary Law from Sungai Ujong," *Journal of the Malayan Branch of the Royal Asiatic Society* 27:3 (1954), 8.

[9] Hooker, *Adat Laws in Modern Malaysia*, 218–19.

[10] Wahbah al-Zuhayli, *Usul al-Fiqh al-Islami* (Damscus: Dar al-Fikr, 1998), 828.

[11] Wan Kamal Mujani, Wan Hamdi Wan Sulaiman, and Ermy Azziaty Rozali, "Sistem Federalisme Dalam Adat Perpatih di Negeri Sembilan," Researchgate, https://www.researchgate.net/publication/329338031_SISTEM_FEDERALISME_DALAM_ADAT_PERPATIH, 5 (accessed October 16, 2020).

in the proverb, "*bulat air dek pembetung, bulat kata dek muafakat*" (water is shaped by the bamboo pipe, decisions by *muafakat*). The concept of *budi*, on the other hand, similar to the Arabic *iḥsān*, establishes a foundation for positive values like righteousness, generosity, and respect for elders, family members, and leaders. This concept is mentioned in another proverb, "*kok tua dimuliakan, kok muda dikasihi*" (if the elderly are respected, the youngsters are loved).[12]

Having discussed something of the nature and form of *adat perpatih*, let us now consider the how and when of its development in Negeri Sembilan.

Negeri Sembilan's *Adat Perpatih* Tradition

As briefly mentioned, the origins of *adat perpatih* lie in the West Sumatran highland region of Minangkabau. According to Minangkabau's rich legacy of *tambo* (origin tales), initially committed to writing during the nineteenth century, the region was once governed by two semi-legendary maternal half-brothers, Datuk Ketemenggungan and Datuk Perpatih Nan Sebatang.[13] Although the *tambo* are vague about chronologies, other regional sources place these two brothers in the mid-fourteenth century: they are mentioned, for example, as Patih[14] Ketemenggungan and Patih Suatang in the late fourteenth- to early fifteenth-century *Hikayat Raja Pasai* (court chronicle of Samudera-Pasai, North Sumatra) as co-rulers of Periangan (an old name for Minangkabau)[15] and contemporaries of

---

[12] Nordin Selat, "Leadership in Adat Perpatih," *Federation Museums Journal* 17 (1972), 75–6.

[13] Their mother, Puti Indera Jelita, was the daughter of a local *penghulu* (district chieftain). Her first husband, and Datuk Ketemenggungan's father, was a non-Muslim Raja from India called Marajo who established himself at Pagaruyung, the Minangkabau royal capital, with the Indic title Sri Maharaja di-Raja (King of Kings). After his death, Puti Indera Jelita married Marajo's former mystical adviser, the South Indian (probably Hindu) holy man, Cateri Bilang Pandai. From this second union came Datuk Perpatih Nan Sebatang. See Ibrahim Dt. Sanggoeno Diradjo, *Tambo Alam Minangkabau: Tatanan Adat Warisan Nenek Moyang Orang Minang* (Bukit Tinggi: Kristal Multimedia, 2015), 12–14.

[14] Patih (Javanese, 'governor') is roughly equivalent to the Malay Datuk.

[15] The *tambo* describe how Marajo found Minangkabau under the control of two *penghulus* resident in the villages of Periangan and Padang Panjang. To honour these tribal leaders, Marajo named his kingdom Periangan Padang Panjang once he became Sri Maharaja di-Raja. The designation 'Minangkabau' appeared later. See Diradjo, *Tambo Alam Minangkabau*, 14.

Majapahit's famed prime minister, Gajah Mada (in office from 1329 to c.1364), with whom they came into conflict.[16] In Minangkabau, the *tambo* describe how these brothers reigned over an animistic population who revered "the womb of the mother" (*bundo kandung*).[17] Under Datuk Perpatih Nan Sebatang, who acted as head of all the local *penghulu* (district chieftains),[18] this matrilineal tradition crystalised into *adat alam Minangkabau*. Henceforth associated with tribal agricultural communities based in the hinterlands, *adat alam Minangkabau* sat in contrast to *adat temenggung*, an alternative and patriarchal body of praxis supposedly compiled by Datuk Ketemenggungan for use in the royal court.[19] Both traditions were considered complementary parts of the same system, however, representing the male and female united in a sacred marriage.[20]

At what point *adat alam Minangkabau* began to penetrate Negeri Sembilan and evolve into *adat perpatih* is difficult to determine. Malay tradition divides the history of Negeri Sembilan into three parts: first, the semi-legendary Sakai period, when three indigenous tribes—the Sakai, Semang, and Jakun—occupied four proto-states at Klang (in modern-day Selangor), Sungai Ujong, Jelebu, and Johol; second, the Minangkabau period, when increased settlement from Sumatra resulted in significant Minang intermarriage with the indigenous population (notably the Sakai), creating the Beduanda *suku* (clan) and nine Minangkabau *luak* (districts) in Rembau, Sungai Ujong, Jelebu, Klang, Ulu Pahang, Johol, Segamat, Jelai, and Naning (in modern-day Melaka); and third, the modern period, when four of the above nine Minangkabau *lauk* (Rembau, Sungai Ujong, Jelebu, and Johol) formed a constitutional monarchy under a Yamtuan

---

[16] See Russell Jones, *Hikayat Raja Pasai* (Kuala Lumpur: Yayasan Karyawan and Penerbit Fajar Bakti, 1999). Whether Patih Suatang is indeed Datuk Perpatih Nan Sebatang is uncertain but, given the context, plausible. The Old Javanese poem, *Nagarakertagama* (written 1365), lists Minangkabau among the conquests of Gajah Mada, see Damaika Saktiani, *Kakawin Nagarakertagama* (Jakarta: PT Buku Seru, 2016).

[17] There are hints of an earlier matrilineal tradition; the *tambo* mention two pre-*adat perpatih* forms of matrilineal law: the *undang-undang Nai Tigo* and *adat tarik baleh*. See Yatim, *Adat*, 214–15.

[18] Diradjo, *Tambo Alam Minangkabau*, 14.

[19] Rais Yatim, *Adat: The Legacy of Minangkabau* (Kuala Lumpur: Yayasan Warisanegara, 2015), 66.

[20] Abdullah, "Adat and Islam," 4.

(lord).[21] While precisely how *adat perpatih* links with these periods is obscure, several preliminary conclusions are possible. According to the *Sejarah Melayu* (the court chronicle of Melaka, written in 1612), two of the four Sakai proto-states—Sungai Ujong and Klang—were Melakan vassals.[22] Although the text does not mention Minangkabau settlement or matrilineal practices within either region, at modern-day Kampung Pengkalan Kempas, in what was then Klang, a Melakan gravesite survives. Belonging to an Melakan official called Ahmat Majanu and dated 1467, it is accompanied by a contemporary assemblage of megaliths. Although rare on the Malay Peninsula, comparable grave markers are common throughout Minangkabau, where they are called *batu tagak* and associated with Minangkabau's matrilineal culture.[23] They therefore tentatively indicate the latter's influence in Negeri Sembilan contemporary to the Melaka period. Indeed, the *Suma Oriental* of Tomé Pires (written in Melaka between 1512 and 1515) describes Minangkabau as Melaka's principal source of gold, and therefore as an important trading partner. Under Melaka's Sultan Muzaffar Shah (r.1445–59), Pires claims Melaka even absorbed two Minangkabau provinces, Kampar and Indragiri, and converted them to Islam.[24] The Portuguese conqueror of Melaka, Afonso d'Albuquerque, refers to Minangkabau migration to the city, although without giving a sense of scale.[25]

---

[21] Richard James Wilkinson, "Notes on the Negri Sembilan," in Richard James Wilkinson (ed.) *Papers on Malay Subjects* (Kuala Lumpur: Oxford University Press, 1971), 283; Martin Lister, "Malay Law in Negri Sembilan," *Journal of the Straits Branch of the Royal Asiatic Society* 22 (1890): 302; Jan Petrus de Josselin de Jong, *Minangkabau and Negri Sembilan: Socio Political Structure in Indonesia* (Leiden: Ijdo, 1951), 123, 151–2.

[22] Under Melaka's Sultan Muzaffar Shah (r.1445–59), the prominent noble Tun Perak was *penghulu* of Klang, while under Sultan Mansur Shah (r.1459–77) Sungai Ujong was governed by Tun Tukah, a relation of the Melakan Bendahara (chief minister). See Boon Keng Cheah, *Sejarah Melayu: MS Raffles No. 18 Edisi Rumi Baru*, MBRAS Reprint 17 (Kuala Lumpur: Malaysian Branch of the Royal Asiatic Society, 2010), 136–7, 219.

[23] Ivor H. N. Evans, "A Grave and Megaliths in Negri Sembilan with an Account of some Excavations," *Journal of the Federated Malay States Museums* 9:3 (1921), 155–73; Elizabeth Lambourn, "The Formation of the Batu Aceh Tradition in Fifteenth-Century Samudera-Pasai," *Indonesia and the Malay World* 32:93 (2004), 241.

[24] Tome Pires, *Suma Oriental: An Account of the East, from the Red Sea to China, Written in Malacca and India in 1512–1515*, vol. 2, ed. Armando Cortesao (New Delhi: Asian Educational Services, 2005), 244–5.

[25] Cited in Josselin de Jong, *Minangkabau and Negri Sembilan*, 123.

All this notwithstanding, oral traditions collected by the British in Rembau and Sungai Ujong over the late nineteenth century, while lacking a clear chronology, trace Minangkabau migration to events surrounding the lifetime of Bendahara Sekudai, an important ancestral figure within both the Rembau and Sungai Ujong *luak*s. Also known as Tun Jinal, Bendahara Sekudai appears in longer versions of the *Sejarah Melayu* as an early seventeenth-century Johor official;[26] he may be the aged Bendahara Sekudai whom that text describes as leading the Dutch-Johor assault against Portuguese Melaka in 1641.[27] It is therefore significant that the British encountered traditions tracing Minangkabau migration to a period immediately before his arrival in Negeri Sembilan, as Johor's governor of the region, in the early seventeenth century. His lifetime, it seems, marked the beginning of a transition from the earlier Sakai period to the later Minangkabau period. Indeed, the first certain reference to Minangkabau settlement in Negeri Sembilan does appear over this period; the 1613 account of Melaka written by Portuguese-Bugis explorer, Godinho de Eredia, references Minangkabau settlement at both Naning and Rembau, then vassals of Portugal and Johor, respectively.[28] This vassalage implies the existence of distinct political and geographic entities that, coupled with their Minangkabau identity, would be consistent with the formation of *luak*, although without necessitating them. Indeed, official seals firmly establishing the existence of Minangkabau *luak* in Negeri Sembilan, and therefore the Minangkabau period, do not emerge until the 1700s. Issued by Johor as their suzerain, the first appears in Naning (1705), followed by Rembau (1707), and then a succession of other *luak* until Jelebu (1760).[29]

[26] Jan Petrus de Josselin de Jong, "Who's Who in the Malay Annals," *Journal of the Malayan Branch of the Royal Asiatic Society* 34:2 (1961), 76.

[27] Wilkinson, "Notes on the Negri Sembilan," 288.

[28] Godinho de Eredia, *Description of Malaca, Meridional India, and Cathay*, trans. John Vivian Mills, MBRAS Reprint 14 (Kuala Lumpur: Malaysian Branch of the Royal Asiatic Society, 1997), 21–3.

[29] Wilkinson, "Notes on the Negri Sembilan," 290. See also Annabel Teh Gallop and Venetia Porter, *Lasting Impressions: Seals from the Islamic World* (Kuala Lumpur: Islamic Arts Museum Malaysia, 2012), 152.

Although *adat alam Minangkabau* presumably accompanied early Minang migrants to Negeri Sembilan, precisely when *adat perpatih* began to emerge and take hold across the state's *luak* is uncertain. Circumstances surrounding the appointment of Negeri Sembilan's first Yamtuan, however, suggests an early eighteenth-century date. In 1699, the Bendahara of Johor, Tun Abdul Jalil, supported by the Bugis of Riau, assassinated Johor's Sultan Mahmud Shah II and usurped the Johor throne. The resultant civil war extended over much of the early 1700s and saw Negeri Sembilan's Minangkabau *luak* side with a Sumatran pretender to the throne, Raja Kecil, who claimed posthumous descent from Sultan Mahmud. In consequence, Negeri Sembilan came into conflict with Tun (now Sultan) Abdul Jalil, who placed the state under Bugis occupation. In the ensuing chaos, the *penghulu*s of Sungai Ujong, Jelebu, Johol, and Rembau petitioned the Raja of Siak, in East Sumatra—a deputy of the by then defunct Sultanate of Minangkabau—for a ruler capable of restoring order and reuniting Negeri Sembilan, notably by enforcing *adat perpatih*. By the early 1700s, then, at least a notional conception of *adat perpatih* existed. Whether it was enforced, however, is uncertain: the initial three candidates despatched by the Raja of Siak to rule Negeri Sembilan—Raja Kasah, Raja Adil, and Raja Khatib—all failed to enforce *adat perpatih* and, for that reason, were rejected by the *luak*s. Only in 1773 did a fourth contender for the throne, Raja Melewar, succeed. Appointed by the *penghulu*s as the first Yamtuan Besar of Negeri Sembilan, Raja Melewar governed the state according to the norms of *adat perpatih* until 1795, cementing the tradition's centrality within the state.[30]

With this brief outline of both the nature and history of *adat perpatih* in mind, we now turn to three issues demonstrating its unique character: leadership, marriage, and property ownership.

LEADERSHIP IN *ADAT PERPATIH*

Adat perpatih leadership has its own uniqueness, being divisible into four separate institutions that each govern a different section of society, as described in the following *perbilangan*:

---

[30] Wilkinson, "Notes on the Negri Sembilan," 295–6.

Alam beraja.	The state has its Raja.
Luak berpenghulu.	The *luak* has its *penghulu.*
Suku berlembaga.	The *suku* has its *lembaga.*
Anak buah berbuapak.	The people have their *buapak.*
Orang semenda bertempat semenda.	The affine has affinal relatives.

Di atas Raja.	At the top is the Raja.
Di tengah penghulu.	In the middle the *penghulu.*
Di bawah lembaga.	Beneath [them] the *lembaga.*
Raja berdaulat dalam alamnya.	The Raja governs his state.
Penghulu berdaulat dalam luaknya.	The *penghulu* governs his *luak*
Lembaga bernobat dalam anak buahnya.	The *lembaga* is appointed over his people.

From the highest to the lowest, *adat perpatih* therefore incorporates the following authority figures: *yamtuan besar* (the Raja or lord), *penghulu* (or *undang*, district chieftain), *lembaga* (clan chieftain), and *buapak* (sub-clan chieftain).

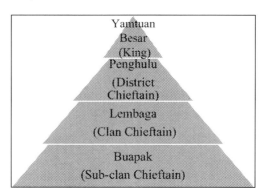

While the institution of *yamtuan besar* (henceforth Yamtuan) is patrilineal, as we shall see, the posts of *penghulu*, *lembaga*, and *buapak* are all transmitted matrilineally—although, ultimately, all three are also held by men. The above proverbs clearly describe how the Yamtuan holds the highest position within the *adat perpatih* power hierarchy, being the supreme ruler of the state. This individual's official title is Yang di-Pertuan Besar Negeri Sembilan, and several conditions determine eligibility for his office: candidates must be male, Muslim, and of the lineage of Raja

Lenggang (the third Yamtuan).[31] Traditionally, the Yamtuan has been a symbol of unity in Negeri Sembilan, albeit with no actual political authority beyond being the final arbiter in legal disputes. The only *luak*, or district, he has had any political power over is the royal town of Seri Menanti, his place of residence. His role is therefore merely ceremonial; real political power has customarily resided with the *penghulus*. Indeed, the Yamtuan is essentially an elected officer selected by unanimous vote from among the four most prominent *penghulus*—those of Sungai Ujong, Jelebu, Johol, and Rembau.[32] As a result, there have been several power struggles between the *penghulus* and the Negeri Sembilan royal family.

Aside from this elective political power, each *penghulu* (or *undang*) is also considered a leader of custom, often being referred to as its "mother".[33] Their role in society is outlined by the following proverbs:

Boleh menghitam dan memutihkan.	With authority to pronounce black and white.
Boleh memanjang dan memendekkan.	With authority to lengthen and shorten.
Boleh mengesah dan membatalkan.	With authority to confirm and annul.
Sah batal pada undang.	Confirmation and annulment are with the *undang*.
Keris penyalang pada undang.	So too the execution *kris*.

In short, *penghulu* are responsible for interpreting *perbilangan* and, therefore, for protecting and executing *adat*. The *penghulus* and *adat* are

---

[31] Hooker, *Adat Laws in Modern Malaysia*, 116–7. Initially, the Yamtuan was elected from among the descendants of the Minangkabau sultan. This tradition, however, was not long-lasting, being soon challenged by local princes. The last so-called prince of Pagaruyong was Raja Labu Lenggang, who died in 1824 and was succeeded by his son. See Khoo Kay Kim, "Adat dan Perkembangan Politik: Pembangunan Masyarakat Negeri Sembilan," in A. Samad Idris, Norhalim Hj. Ibrahim, Muhammad Tainu and Dharmala N. S. (eds.) *Negeri Sembilan: Gemuk Dipupuk, Segar Bersiram: Adat Merentas Zaman,* (Seremban: Jawatankuasa Penyelidikan Budaya Negeri Sembilan, 1994), 5. The following is a list of all the Yamtuan Besar of Negeri Sembilan since the state's unification in 1773. Pagaruyung dynasty: Raja Melewar (r.1773–95), Yamtuan Hitam (r.1795–1808), and Yamtuan Labu Lenggang (r.1808–24). Local princes: Yamtuan Radin ibnu Langgang (r.1830–61), Yamtuan Imam (r.1861–9), Yamtuan Puan Intan (or Pemangku Raja) (r.1869–72), Yamtuan Antah (r.1872–88), Tengku Muhammad (r.1888–1933), Tengku Abdul Rahman (r.1957–60), Tuanku Munawir (r.1960–7), Tungku Jaafar (r.1967–2008), and Tuanku Muhriz (r.2008–present).

[32] Rosiswandy bin Mohd. Salleh, *Sejarah Pengamalan Adat Perpatih di Negeri Sembilan* (Jelebu: Muzium Adat Jelebu, Negeri Sembilan, n.d.), 7; Khoo, "Adat dan Perkembangan Politik," 3.

[33] Mohammad Fadzeli Jaafar, "Lexical Patterns in Customary Sayings," *Indonesian Journal of Applied Linguistics* 8:1 (2018), 231.

54   A. WAIN AND N. SALEH

complementary.[34] The title *penghulu* connotes nobility and attracts respect. A position for life, it is usually conferred on someone of high status who will have authority over his people. *Penghulu*s are assisted in their activities by a council of advisors, called the *orang besar undang*. All decisions are based on consultation with this council, a process conducted through *muafakat* (above). Additionally, a *penghulu* must be surrounded by his *anak buah* (kinship group), who should be loyal and submissive; *anak buah* should always sit around the *penghulu* and serve him with particular politeness, as a sign of respect.[35] The relationship between a *penghulu* and his *anak buah* is one of mutual care involving obedience, respect, affection, and loyalty. As described in the following *perbilangan*, the *anak buah* should:

Kok malu membangkitkan,	Restore his [the *penghulu*'s] dignity when he is humiliated,
Haus memberi air,	give him drink when he is thirsty,
Kok litak memberi nasi,	give him rice when he is hungry,
Hilang mencari,	find him when he is lost,
Sakit mengubat,	seek a cure when he is ill,
Mati menanam.	bury him when he dies.

When a *penghulu* dies, his successor must be appointed before his burial, as the latter will conduct the funeral ceremony.

*Penghulu*s can be removed from office if found guilty of going against *adat*. Each *penghulu* is responsible for his own district or *luak*, of which there are currently fourteen in Negeri Sembilan: Seri Menanti, Tampin, Sungai Ujong, Jelebu, Johol, Rembau, Ulu Muar, Jempol, Terachi, Gudung Pasir, Inas, Gemencheh, Ayer Kuning, and Linggi. *Penghulu*s are also responsible for dividing up ancestral land between female members of their *luak* in accordance with the requirements of *adat* (discussed below). They protect all land within their territory from outside aggression; a *penghulu* must always be ready to help his people when they are in trouble. Moreover, no one may leave the *luak* without his permission.[36]

Below the *penghulu* is the *lembaga*, or clan head. The clan, or *suku*, is the largest descent group within *adat perpatih* society. There are currently twelve *suku* in Negeri Sembilan: Biduanda, Paya Kumbuh, Tiga Nenek, Batu Belang, Tiga Batu, Semelenggang, Selemak, Mungkal, Tanah Datar, Batu Hampar, Anak Melaka, and Anak Aceh. The election of *lembaga* is by

---

[34] Selat, "Leadership in Adat Perpatih," 80, 85.
[35] Selat, "Leadership in Adat Perpatih," 79–80.
[36] Selat, "Leadership in Adat Perpatih."

ADAT PERPATIH IN MALAYSIA: NATURE, HISTORY, PRACTICE...   55

fixed rotation. It is interesting to note that candidates must be married to a woman from the *suku* they are to represent; only by virtue of this connection are they eligible for the position, meaning it is dispensed matrilineally.[37] The responsibilities of each *lembaga* are limited to his own people, both socially and legally. In practice, he has limited authority; he can only settle trifling issues among *suku* members. More serious issues have to be resolved according to *adat* as administered by the *penghulu*.[38] Nevertheless, all *lembaga* within a *luak* have responsibility for appointing their *penghulu*, which they do through mutual consultation.

The smallest unit in *adat perpatih* society is the *perut*, which forms a sub-division of the *suku*. *Perut* have been described as "matri-unilocal" groups, being a conglomeration of *keluarga* (families) or *rumpun* (individual households) descended from a common female ancestor who all own, work, and reside on the same ancestral land. These units are led by a *buapak* who must be the brother or maternal uncle of a prominent female member of the *perut*. They are elected by all the female adult members of the lineage. As with the *lembaga*, therefore, the *buapak* inherits his position matrilineally. Their appointment, however, must be approved by the local *lembaga*, with whom they work closely for the good of their *perut*. The *buapak*'s responsibilities are limited to their *perut* alone. *Buapak* primarily administer customary land and act as mediators in inheritance disputes.[39] Although they have some responsibility for implementing *adat*, this role is largely confined to being present at lineage ceremonies.

Overall, the delegation of power within *adat perpatih* society moves from the smallest unit (the *perut*) to the highest authority (the Yamtuan). In short, those in power must be elected by the people they are to rule. The relationship between the rulers and the ruled is therefore very dynamic and exhibits clear democratic traits. For example, each *buapak* is elected unanimously by the ordinary members of their tribe, the *anak buah* (affines). The *lembaga* above him can only approve his appointment; he cannot suggest it or force it into being. Typically, all *adat perpatih* post holders, regardless of rank, will remain in office for life unless those

---

[37] Hooker, *Adat Laws in Modern Malaysia*, 22.

[38] Norhalim Hj. Ibrahim, "Some Observations on Adat and Adat Leadership in Rembau, Negeri Sembilan," *Southeast Asian Studies* 26:2 (1988), 157.

[39] Sueo Kuwahara, "A Study of a Matrilineal Village in Negeri Sembilan," *Senri Ethnological Studies* 48 (1998), 35.

beneath them deem them unfit for the position, in which case they can be deposed.

It is striking how this socio-political structure mirrors many salient features within early Islamic political culture, notably the emphasis on consultation and accountability. Consultation (*shūrā*) was regularly used during the lifetime of the Prophet Muhammad to elect officials and reach other important decisions. The Prophet reportedly said:

> If your leaders are the best among you, your wealthy the most generous among you, and your affairs are conducted after consultation among you, the Earth's surface will be better for you than its interior.[40]

Certainly, the Prophet Muhammad often consulted his Companions when making crucial decisions. For instance, during the Battle of Uhud, he followed majority opinion by meeting the attacking army at Medina.[41] After his death, a (varying) form of election based on *shūrā* was used to select his successors, a process that eventually became enshrined in classical Islamic political thought as the ideal means of choosing a *khalīfa*.[42] The distinguished Qur'ānic commentator, Ibn ʿAtiyya (d. 546/1151), even commented concerning *shūrā* that:

> Shūrā is one of the basics of Islamic law (*sharīʿa*), and a mandatory rule; and any [who are entrusted with public authority] who does not take the counsel of those who have knowledge and are conscious of God, should be dismissed from his [or her public] position, and there is no argument about that.[43]

Concerning accountability, each *adat* chief (*penghulu, lembaga,* and *buapak*) is responsible for the people within their jurisdiction, whose welfare they must protect—whether materially or morally. The various

---

[40] Abu Isa Muhammad ibn Isa ibn Surah al-Tirmidhi, *Sunan al-Tirmidhi*, ed. Abd al-Rahman Muhammad Uthman (Madinah: Al-Maktabah al-Salafiyyah, 1974), 3:261.

[41] Ibn Ishaq, *The Life of Muhammad (Sirat Rasul Allah)*, trans. Alfred Guillaume (Oxford: Oxford University Press, 2010), 370.

[42] Abu al-Hasan Ali al-Mawardi, *Al-Ahkam as-Sultaniyah: The Laws of Islamic Governance*, trans. Asadullah Yate (London: Ta-Ha Publishers, 1996), 13.

[43] Ibn. Atiyya, *Al-Muharrar al-Wajiz*, vol. 3 (Fez: Ministry of Awqafand Islamic Affairs, 1997), 280–1.

chieftains must never transgress the limits of their authority, and only settle disputes within their jurisdiction according to the principles of *adat*. There is no room for a tyrant in *adat perpatih*, as demonstrated by these *perbilangan*:

Kalau keruh air di hulu,	If the water is murky at the river source,
Sampai ke muara keruh juga.	it will be murky right down to the mouth.

Tumbuhnya ditanam.	He (the ruler) grows because he is planted.
Tingginya dianjung.	He is high because he is held aloft.
Besarnya diampu.	He is great because he is made great.

Raja Adil Raja disembah.	A just ruler is revered.
Raja zalim Raja disanggah.	An unjust ruler is deposed.

Kok gadang jangan melanda.	The great must not oppress.
Kok cerdik jangan menipu.	The clever must not swindle.

Similar ideals emerge within early Islamic political thought. Guarding the welfare of the general populace, for example, was a central theme within the inaugural speech of Abū Bakr, the Prophet's immediate successor:

> The weak among you is deemed strong by me, until I return to them that which is rightfully theirs, insha Allah. And the strong among you is deemed weak by me, until I take from them what is rightfully (someone else's), insha Allah.[44]

This strong commitment to social justice, likewise enshrined in the Qur'ān, notably in its call for Muslims to pay *zakat* (compulsory charity, see 2:177), mirrors the underlying concerns structuring *adat perpatih* leadership—and, arguably, its principles of landownership too (below). However, the ability of *anak buah* to depose their leaders should the latter abuse their power, notably by flouting *adat*, has no equivalent in Islam; no mechanism exists to allow Muslims to overthrow a *khalīfa* or other authority figure. Nevertheless, there is a similar intolerance in Islam towards the flouting of ethical norms. Returning to Abū Bakr's inaugural speech, he reputedly said:

---

[44] Ali Muhammad As-Sallabee, *The Biography of Abu Bakr As-Siddiq* (Riyadh: Darussalam, 2007), 246.

Obey me so long as I obey Allah and His Messenger. And if I disobey Allah and His Messenger, then I have no right to your obedience.[45]

At the very least, this allows Muslims to engage in civil disobedience should their leaders disobey Islam. Although more restrictive than the course of action available in *adat perpatih*, this quotation embodies the same principle of accountability.

In summary, the political values underlying *adat perpatih*, rooted in the concepts of accountability, checks and balances, and compromise, contribute to the maintenance of its political system and find numerous parallels (if not equivalencies) within the Islamic tradition. With this observation in mind, let us progress to the next part of our discussion: marriage.

MARRIAGE IN *ADAT PERPATIH*

At the core of *adat perpatih* marriage custom lies the principle of exogamy; to marry within the same *suku* is strictly forbidden. All members of the same clan are considered siblings, between whom marriage is unacceptable for the sake of the *suku*'s long-term health and prosperity.[46] Marriages are instead perceived as alliances between *suku*, formalised as oral contracts after due discussion and consideration.[47] This exogamous approach to marriage contrasts sharply with Islamic practice. While Muslim marriages are also contractual (and usually oral), the Qur'ān only prohibits wedlock within immediate family units:

---

[45] As-Sallabee, *The Biography of Abu Bakr As-Siddiq*, 253.

[46] Mat Noor Mat Zain, Che Maryam Ahmad, and Zuliza Mohd. Kusrin, "Perkahwinan Adat Rembau, Negeri Sembilan, dalam Penulisan C.W.C. Parr dan W.H. Mackray," *Jurnal Melayu* 9 (2012), 179. The exception is Rembau, where marriage within the same *suku* is permitted, provided the individuals concerned are from different *perut*. See Jonathan Cave, *Naning in Melaka: History, the Culture, Tribes and Clans, the War, Independence*, MBRAS Monograph no. 16 (Petaling Jaya: MBRAS, 1989), 412.

[47] In practice, this emphasis on tribal alliance means polygamy is rare (although not forbidden). This is because the bride's family dislikes both sharing a bridegroom and negotiating with multiple *suku* (that of the bridegroom and any existing wives). See Cave, *Naning in Melaka*, 418–19.

Forbidden for you to marry are your mothers and daughters, sisters, aunts on both sides, the daughters of your brothers and sisters, milk-mothers, milk-sisters, mothers-in-law, stepdaughters who are in your care—that is, born of wives with whom you have had sexual intercourse, but if you have not yet consummated the marriage, then there is no harm—or women belonging to your actual sons; it is also forbidden to have intercourse with two sisters together. (4:22–23)

In Islam, therefore, broad familial associations are not a bar against marriage, as in *adat perpatih*. While this clearly serves to differentiate the two traditions, arguably such variance masks a shared objective: to prevent marriage between close family members for the benefit of wider society. As demonstrated by the above verse, Islam defines membership of a family unit in terms of the shared possession of two life-giving substances, either blood or milk (where the latter refers to individuals suckled by the same woman). Two people with such ties cannot marry.[48] In *adat perpatih*, the same principle applies: although suckling is not referred to, individuals who share close blood-ties also may not marry, for the same reasons. The difference, however, lies in the perceived boundaries of that affinity; in *adat perpatih*, the limits are set much wider, across an entire clan.

Concerning betrothal, in *adat perpatih* (as in Islam) potential bridegrooms may decide whom they wish to marry, after which they inform their father and *buapak* of their choice. These elders then visit the family of the proposed bride, where they meet their counterparts and discuss the suitability of the match, usually in terms of the relative reputation and prestige of the two *suku*. As in broader Malay *adat* (based on Hindu practice), if the match is agreed upon, the bridegroom confirms betrothal by presenting the bride with a *tanda suka* (lit. 'sign of liking', usually a ring). Subsequently, on the wedding day, he provides *mas kahwin* (lit. 'marriage gold') and *wang hantaran* (lit. 'money sent'). The first, which may be deferred, is presented to the bride as her inalienable right, the second to the bride's family, often to help defray wedding costs. The contract of marriage, however, is established by the *tanda suka*; if the contract is subsequently breached before finalisation (that is, before the *nikah*, or Islamic

---

[48] Jacob Neusner, Tamara Sonn, and Jonathan E. Brockopp, *Judaism and Islam in Practice: A Sourcebook* (London: Routledge, 2000), 65–6.

marriage ceremony), twice the *wang hantaran* is payable. This is based on the proverb, "*menerima satu tangan, tolak dua tangan*" (receive with one hand, push away with two).[49] The *nikah* itself is conducted by a *khatib* (Muslim preacher) in accordance with Islamic norms: the consent of the bride is required, in addition to the presence of a *wali* (male guardian) and two witnesses.

A marriage solemnised without the above *adat* practices (that is, by *nikah* alone) remains valid but is considered improper; traditionally associated with elopement, such marriages only occur when opposition to them is so intractable that the couple must bypass *adat* altogether, usually because they are from the same *suku*. As J. Cave notes, such bypassing "was extremely rare, and occurred when the bride was lost to feelings of family respectability and social display".[50]

Overall, the centrality of betrothal within *adat perpatih* is noteworthy. Sufficient to establish the marriage contract, its primacy differs significantly from betrothal as envisioned in Islam. Although mentioned in the Qur'ān (2:235), betrothal is not a legal obligation under *sharī'a* and can be dispensed with, if necessary. Even when pursued, far from establishing a contract of marriage, betrothal has little legal effect beyond preventing other suitors from approaching the fiancée.[51] Both *adat perpatih* and Islam agree, however, that betrothal should be accompanied by a suitable gift, which the fiancée retains, even if the engagement is broken off.[52] They also agree on the need for a *wali* during the *nikah*, but disagree concerning that individual's identity. According to *adat perpatih*, the *wali* must be

---

[49] Cave, *Naning in Melaka*, 412–14.

[50] Cave, *Naning in Melaka*, 417. In the event of such unusual marriages, the *mas kahwin* becomes a fine payable by the *lembaga* of the bridegroom to the *lembaga* of the bride. This is contrary to Islamic practice. See Mat Zain, Ahmad, and Kusrin, "Perkahwinan Adat Rembau," 181.

[51] On the basis of the *hadith*, "Do not ask for a woman in marriage if another Muslim has already done so" (*Muwatta' Imam Malik*, Chapter 311, hadith #1062). Neusner, Sonn, and Brockopp, *Judaism and Islam in Practice*, 63–7.

[52] Neusner, Sonn, and Brockopp, *Judaism and Islam in Practice*, 64.

either the father of the bride, the maternal grandfather, or a maternal uncle. Paternal male relations, by contrast, are excluded; necessarily members of different *suku*, they are ineligible to act on their niece's behalf.[53] Such a restriction, however, is foreign to Islam.[54] Of the two further monetary payments mandated by *adat perpatih*, *mas kahwin* corresponds to the Islamic *mahr*, which is likewise deferrable and payable only to the bride (see Qur'ān 4:4). *Wang hantaran*, on the other hand, although widely observed among Malay Muslims, has no Islamic equivalent, being rooted in earlier Hindu practice.[55]

After marriage, the husband becomes *orang semanda* (from *senda*, 'to pledge'), signifying his new status as 'pledged' to his wife's *suku*.[56] Losing all active association with his mother's clan, in Negeri Sembilan the *orang semanda* enters the household of his wife in a process called *tempat semenda* (situating the one who is pledged).[57] Traditionally, in Minangkabau, the *orang semanda* would barely interact with his wife's *suku*, merely sleeping in her ancestral house at night before returning to his mother's *suku* to work their land during the day. This led to comparisons between the *orang semanda* and a bull buffalo, borrowed for the sake of impregnation.[58] In Negeri Sembilan, however, the *orang semanda* has always played a more active role in his wife's family. Most notably, the

---

[53] For example, if two brothers marry women from different *suku*, they cannot be *wali* to each other's daughters. This is because their responsibility is towards their wife's *suku*; the connection with their own (and so to each other) ends upon marriage (below). See Mat Zain, Ahmad, and Kusrin, "Perkahwinan Adat Rembau," 177.

[54] Neusner, Sonn, and Brockopp, *Judaism and Islam in Practice*, 86–7.

[55] Ahmad Badri Abdullah, Mohammad Hashim Kamali, and Mohamed Azam Mohamed Adil, *Malay Traditional Customs: Towards a Shariah Compliant Practice*, IAIS Malaysia Policy Issue Paper 12 (Kuala Lumpur: IAIS Malaysia, 2020).

[56] Kato, "Minangkabau Matrilineal System," 6.

[57] Lister, "Malay Law in Negri Sembilan," 316.

[58] Kato, "Minangkabau Matrilineal System," 7.

wife's *suku* is expected to provide him with a livelihood, when available.[59] For his part, the *orang semanda* should build (or at least provide) a house for his wife, often on her ancestral land, and meet her (and any children's) living costs.

While the degree of dominance the above arrangement accords the wife's *suku* is perhaps at odds with Islamic norms, which generally assume the husband's centrality within a marriage,[60] *adat perpatih* as practiced in Negeri Sembilan still upholds the expectation that husbands provide for their wives and children, as demanded by Islamic teachings. As stated in the Qur'ān: "Men are the protectors and maintainers of their wives, because God has given the one more (strength) than the other, and because they support them from their means" (4:34).

Concerning any offspring produced during a marriage, in Minangkabau children (both male and female) traditionally maintain only minimal contact with their paternal relations, including their father. Their mother and her *suku*, to which they belong, dominate their lives.[61] In Negeri Sembilan,

---

[59] In 1908, J. L. Humphreys witnessed the ritualised recital of an *adat perpatih* poem during a wedding in Kelemak, Alor Gajah, Naning. Delivered by the *penghulu* of the Mungkar *suku*, who was a relative of the bridegroom, it urged the bride's *suku* to guard the welfare of the *orang semanda*:

Tiap-tiap menerima orang semenda itu,	All who receive the *orang semanda*,
Ditentukan pula dengan benar dengan muafakat:	do so according to what has been agreed:
Kalua ada berkata ada,	if (there is land), let it be stated,
Kalau tidak berkata benar.	if there is not, say so truthfully.
Ke baruh sawah yang selepah lantak yang bertukul,	To the lowly (give) a paddy field with planted posts,
Ke darat kampung yang sesudut pinang yang sebatang,	to the high an orchard with betel-palms for a mark,
Tempat ke bukit mencari minum	to the hills for drink,
Tempat ke lurah mencari makan.	to the valleys for food.

Quoted in John Lisseter Humphreys, "A Naning Wedding Speech," *Journal of the Straits Branch of the Royal Asiatic Society* 72 (1916), 28.

[60] Neusner, Sonn, and Brockopp, *Judaism and Islam in Practice*, 86.

[61] Kato, "Minangkabau Matrilineal System," 6–8.

however, although children likewise identify with their mother's *suku*, even adopting a matronym to express that connection, the realities of parenthood and cohabitation entail a more shared experience, where both parents have authority (*perintah*) over their children. The father's Islamically sanctioned status as *wali*, taken more seriously in Negeri Sembilan than in Minangkabau, also ensures that he maintains a central role in his children's life-defining moments, like marriage. In the event of divorce[62] or premature death, however, responsibility for any children falls exclusively to the mother's *suku*; that of the father has no claim over them. If a man is predeceased by his wife, for example, his association with her *suku* ends; following a forty-four-day mourning period, he must vacate the family home and cease all contact with his children. In practice, however, such separation is considered too disruptive; children effectively lose both parents in a short space of time, damaging their welfare. More commonly, therefore, widowers marry a younger sister of their deceased wife, allowing them to remain within their children's *suku*. Alternatively, if any of his daughters are old enough to inherit their mother's property upon her death, the widower is often permitted to remain within the family home, although his formal association with the *suku* ceases.[63]

Arguably, little of the above resonates with Islamic praxis, in which children typically identify with their father and his family (including any tribal grouping), as demonstrated by the prevalence of *nasab* (Arabic patronyms). Nevertheless, in the event of either the premature death of the father or divorce, Muslim children are similarly entrusted to the care of their mother or her relatives, especially when still young. In the context of divorce, the Qur'ān states:

---

[62] Like the *nikah*, divorce in *adat perpatih* conforms to Islamic norms, being achieved by the husband's thrice repetition, whether at once or at intervals, of *ṭalāq* (Arabic for 'divorce') in front of two witnesses. As in wider Islamic practice, women adhering to *adat perpatih* must observe an *'iddah* (waiting) period of three months before remarrying (see Qur'ān 2:225–32).

[63] Cave, *Naning in Melaka*, 421–2.

The mothers shall suckle their [new-born] offspring for two whole years, if the father desires to complete the term. But he shall bear the cost of their food and clothing on equitable terms. (2:233)

Jurists have traditionally understood this Qur'ānic two-year custody period as a minimum. In reality, mothers are typically accorded custody of their sons until they reach puberty and of their daughters until they are old enough to marry. In consequence, although not (as in *adat perpatih*) compulsory, young Muslim children are likewise entrusted to the care of their mothers. Moreover, in the event of the mother's death, before paternal relations are considered as potential custodians, the maternal grandmother or a maternal aunt will be approached. Unlike in *adat perpatih*, however, financial responsibility for children always resides with their father and his family.[64]

Now that the *adat perpatih* conceptions of leadership and marriage have been considered, let us turn to the third issue defining that tradition: property ownership and inheritance.

PROPERTY OWNERSHIP AND INHERITANCE IN *ADAT PERPATIH*

Adat perpatih recognises two over-arching forms of property: *harta pusaka* (hereditary/ancestral) and *harta pencarian* (acquired). Along with matrilineal descent, *harta pusaka* constitutes a defining characteristic of *adat perpatih*. A communally held, individually managed resource, *harta pusaka* usually takes the form of agricultural or occupational land (but can also consist of houses, ponds, or *adat* titles) and is inalienable; it belongs to the *suku* in perpetuity, for the benefit of all. Within an agricultural setting, therefore, it constitutes a guarantee of future land ownership.[65] While men can benefit from *harta pusaka*, typically by working agricultural land, they are only able to do so via their association with female members of the *suku*; *harta pusaka* may only be 'owned' by women, who inherit

---

[64] Neusner, Sonn, and Brockopp, *Judaism and Islam in Practice*, 124–5.

[65] Azizah Kassim, "Women, Land and Gender Relations in Negeri Sembilan: Some Preliminary Findings," *Southeast Asian Studies* 26:2 (1988), 137.

ADAT PERPATIH IN MALAYSIA: NATURE, HISTORY, PRACTICE... 65

custody of it from their mothers, as their mothers did before them, in an upbroken line down to the very beginnings of the *suku*. *Harta pusaka* therefore carries a unique sense of sanctity linked to a far distant matrilineal past.[66] In line with its communally held nature, *harta pusaka* can neither be sold nor subjected to rent and/or taxes. It is generally only transferrable by inheritance from one woman to another, usually within the same *perut*.[67]

Harta pencarian, on the other hand, is earned personal property acquired through individual effort. As outlined below, male and female members of a *suku* are both entitled to possess *harta pencarian*. This type of property is transformed into *harta pusaka* after two generations of continuous (female) ownership within the same *rumpun*, initially becoming *harta pusaka warisan* (ancestral property belonging to a particular family) and then, after the fourth generation, *harta pusaka* proper.[68] While traditionally *harta pusaka* has constituted the economic foundation of *adat perpatih* society, from the mid-nineteenth century, *harta pencarian* has gained considerable significance in the wake of rapid population growth and increased use of cash cropping. These factors have combined to render *harta pusaka* inadequate as a means of supporting all members of a *suku* within an increasingly monetised economy.[69] The next section, on contemporary issues, elaborates on this point more fully.

In the context of marriage, the rules of property ownership and inheritance run as follows. Any property owned by a bridegroom prior to the *nikah* ceremony, whether earned or obtained as a gift (he cannot 'own' or

---

[66] Cave, *Naning in Melaka*, 408–9.

[67] The transfer of land between *perut* within the same *suku* is, however, possible. Although considered a gift (*pemberian*), such transfer is often accompanied by a nominal cash payment passed from the recipient to the donor. See Kassim, "Women, Land and Gender Relations in Negeri Sembilan," 137. It is exceptionally rare for *harta pusaka* to be acquired by someone from outside a *suku*. Such may only occur under very specific circumstances and with universal agreement from among the *suku*'s leadership. Valid circumstances include the need to (1) repair or rebuild an *adat* house; (2) finance the inauguration of a *lembaga*; (3) finance the marriage of a girl within the lineage; or (4) provide the funeral expenses of a lineage member. See Kato, "Minangkabau Matrilineal System," 3n.4; J. M. Gullick, "D.O.'s and Dato's: Dialogue on the 'Adat Perpatih'," *Journal of the Malaysian Branch of the Royal Asiatic Society* 73 (2000), 41.

[68] Cave, *Naning in Melaka*, 408.

[69] Kato, "Minangkabau Matrilineal System," 9.

inherit *harta pusaka*), is considered *harta pembawaan* (brought). A sub-division of *harta pencarian*, it is considered to be his alone—although if he fails to declare it as *harta pembawaan* from the outset, it will become the property of his wife. In the event of divorce or death, *harta pembawaan* reverts back to the bridegroom or his *suku*, respectively.[70] Property brought to the marriage by the bride, on the other hand, is *harta pendapatan* (possessed). This category may include both *harta pusaka* and *harta pencarian*. Likewise considered her property, it remains so in the event of divorce.[71] If she dies, it is inherited by her nearest female relatives (usually her sisters or daughters). By contrast, any property acquired during marriage by either party is *harta pencarian* and co-owned by both spouses. In the event of divorce, it is divided equally. If the husband predeceases his wife, his share may be bequeathed to his children or *suku* using the Islamic concept of *hībah* (gifting).[72] Otherwise, the entirety of it automatically becomes the property of his wife's *suku*. If she predeceases her husband, he may inherit her share.[73] These principles of marital ownership are rooted in the proverb:

Pembawa Kembali.	What the bridegroom brings returns.
Dapatan Tinggal.	What the bride brings stays.
Carian bahagi.	What is earned is shared.
Mati laki tinggal ke bini.	If the husband dies, it goes to his wife.
Mati bini tinggal ke laki.	If the wife dies, it goes to her husband.

In short, the above categories of property are alien to but not, it seems, incompatible with Islam. In sharīʿa, property (termed *al-māl*) is defined very broadly as any material item or usufruct a person may possess. The Shāfiʿī school, predominant across Southeast Asia, expands on this

---

[70] Lister, "Malay Law in Negri Sembilan," 316.

[71] Mat Zain, Ahmad, and Kusrin, "Perkahwinan Adat Rembau," 184. Should *harta pendapatan* include agricultural land that is subsequently improved by the husband, the latter is entitled to compensation upon divorce for any consequent increase in its value. A house built upon ancestral land is *harta pusaka*. If built on normal land, it is *harta pencarian*. See Cave, *Naning in Melaka*, 422–3.

[72] Kato, "Minangkabau Matrilineal System," 10; Cave, *Naning in Melaka*, 419–20.

[73] Abdullah, "Adat and Islam," 21. Beginning in 1920s Naning, divorced husbands could issue assurances (*tentukan*) stating that, upon their death, some or all of their *harta pencarian* could pass to the children of the defunct marriage. See Cave, *Naning in Melaka*, 426.

definition by arguing that property must be (1) possessable; (2) of clear benefit to its owner; (3) by virtue of that benefit, of definable value; and (4) exchangeable for that value.[74] Within this context, while notions of *harta pusaka*, *harta pencarian*, *harta pembawaan*, and *harta pendapatan* find no direct equivalent within Islam, the latter's definition of property is general enough to allow their absorption. Thus, all forms of *adat perpatih* property are possessable, of benefit to their owners, of inherent value, and transferable (albeit within limits). Arguably, therefore, each category is compatible with the essentials of Islamic law in this area. Rather, the only seemingly significant difference between *adat perpatih* and Islam emerges with inheritance.

The Qur'ān apportions fixed inheritance shares to specific family members. Giving women only one half of what men inherit (reflecting the latter's greater financial responsibilities, above), the Qur'ān states:

> God directs you [the man] as regards your children: to the male the portion of two females. If there are more than two women, they will have two-thirds of what you leave. But if she is only one, then she will have one-half. Each one of your parents will have one-sixth of what you leave, if you have children. If you have no children, and your heirs are your parents, your mother will have one-third; but if you have brothers, your mother will have one sixth, after any bequest you bequeath, or any debt. As for your father and your sons, you do not know which of them is more beneficial to you. Division of shares is from God, and God is all knowing, wise.
>
> You [the man] will have one-half of what your wives leave, if they have no children; but if they have children then you will have one-fourth of what they leave, after any bequest they bequeath, or any debt. They will have one-fourth of what you leave, if you have no children; but if you have children, then they will have one-eighth of what you leave, after any bequest you bequeath, or any debt. If a man, or a woman, has no heir, but he has a brother or a sister, each of them will have one-sixth. If there is more than two, they share in one-third, after any bequest he bequeaths, or any debt that takes precedent. (4:11–12)

While additional individual bequests are permitted, by which *adat perpatih* norms could be accommodated, such are limited to one-third the

---

[74] Muhammad Wohidul Islam, "Al-Mal: The Concept of Property in Islamic Legal Thought," *Arab Law Quarterly* 14:4 (1999), 361, 364.

value of an estate. While the degree of dissimilarity between the above and *adat perpatih* praxis is striking, as elsewhere it arguably masks a convergence of intention. Thus, save on one occasion, when it mentions the father, the Qur'ān only names mothers, wives, daughters, and sisters when allocating inheritance shares. In practice, this means those said individuals take priority when an estate is divided. Depending on the specific situation, women can therefore inherit the lion share of a man's property. For example, if a man dies and leaves two daughters (one-third each), a wife (one-eighth), and his mother (one-sixth), then more than nine-tenths of his estate will be divided between his female relatives before any male relation is considered. Like *adat perpatih*, therefore, Islamic inheritance norms seem designed to protect female property rights, even if that intention is not immediately apparent.[75]

CONTEMPORARY ISSUES

As stated at the outset, this chapter's presentation of *adat perpatih* is somewhat idealised, reflecting how that tradition would manifest were it given full rein. To better understand *adat perpatih* as a lived tradition, it behoves us to consider two leading factors underlying *adat perpatih*'s contemporary decline, both borne of British colonialism: the gradual undermining of *harta pusaka* by capitalist norms and the erosion of traditional power structures.

Since the mid-nineteenth century, *adat perpatih* property ownership norms have steadily declined across Negeri Sembilan. This process, which has only accelerated over the twentieth and early twenty-first centuries, was catalysed by the arrival of the British in 1874. Quickly establishing themselves at Sungai Ujong, the British rapidly extended their influence across Negri Sembilan until, on 8 August 1895, they were able to sign an agreement with the *penghulu*s of six *luak*, drawing each into a centralised administrative arrangement under the control of a British Resident at Seremban.[76] In the long run, this colonialisation of Negeri Sembilan

---

[75] Neusner, Sonn, and Brockopp, *Judaism and Islam in Practice*, 106–7.

[76] Gullick, "D.O.'s and Dato's," 39. The six *luak* that became part of British Negeri Sembilan were Rembau, Sungai Ujong, Jelebu, Ulu Pahang, Johol, and Jelai. Of the remaining three, Klang was incorporated into Selangor, Naning into Melaka, and Segamat into Johor. This apportionment of *luak* persists today.

served to severely destabilise *adat perpatih* society, both economically and politically.

Beginning with the economic ramifications of colonialism, soon after the British took control of Negeri Sembilan, they introduced an aggressive form of colonial capitalism, revolutionising the state's traditional agrarian economy. From the mid-1870s, both local and foreign (male) investors were urged to undertake widespread land clearance across Negeri Sembilan in order to establish largescale rubber plantations capable of meeting British demand. Expensive to plant and slow to yield produce, these plantations represented significant long-term cash investments for their owners. Problematically, therefore, many local male investors sought to utilise the *harta pusaka* (ancestral land) of their wives' *suku*, a course of action that presented significant risk: to establish a plantation, several lots of *harta pusaka* were often required, each with its own custodian whose permission would be required. If a custodian should subsequently change her mind or die, or if a male investor divorced his wife, that investor risked losing control of part or all of his plantation.[77] For many, this situation proved too prohibitive. The British, therefore, seeking to maintain and encourage further investment, instituted numerous land law reforms based on their own Common Law system. Beginning in the 1890s, it became possible for male occupiers of land to obtain official legal titles recognising their right of ownership while also giving them exclusive use of the land, the right to dispose of it as they saw fit (whether by sale or gift), and the right to mortgage it. These legal titles also imparted an obligation to pay an annual land tax to the British. All of this, however, ran contrary to *adat perpatih* norms, undermining its principles of communal, female-directed property ownership (above). Although increasing local hostility to these changes eventually forced the British to issue a Customary Tenure Enactment (1909) recognising the existence of "customary land", little effort was made to identify such land so that it could be correctly registered. In consequence, permanent individual (male) ownership continued to increase.[78] Under the British, therefore, although large sections of

---

[77] Azima Abdul Manaf, "Masalah dan Cabaran Tanah Adat Minang di Dunia Melayu Malaysia dan Indonesia," *Geografia: Malaysian Journal of Society and Space* 5:1 (2018), 81.

[78] Gullick, "D.O.'s and Dato's," 48; Azizah Kassim, "Women, Development and Change in Negeri Sembilan: A Micro-Level Perspective," *Southeast Asian Studies* 34:4 (1997), 717–8.

harta pusaka would survive, significant amounts were either re-apportioned or fell into disuse when it became apparent they were unsuitable for larg-escale cultivation.

The legacy of these developments survives into the present: rubber and (more recently) palm oil plantations continue to be established and maintained throughout Negeri Sembilan, often on what was (or still is) *harta pusaka*. Additionally, the post-independence growth of Malaysia's wage economy means most household incomes are now attained through fixed salaries, with the small-scale agricultural activities associated with *harta pusaka* becoming obsolete. All of this has further undermined this core element of *adat perpatih* society. Some *harta pusaka* has also been re-purposed by the authorities for building schools or for widening roads.[79]

The British intervention in Negeri Sembilan also disrupted the state's traditional power structures. Under the British, *adat* chiefs (the *penghulu*, *lembaga*, and *buapak*) rapidly lost their administrative powers, becoming mere figureheads with authority to preside over only religious and royal ceremonies. This decline was further compounded in 1897, when the then British Resident, Ernest Birch, created a new administrative position within each *suku*. Expressly designed to rival the *lembaga*, these new offi-cials were (somewhat confusingly) called *penghulu* and served as British agents, collecting taxes and enforcing a degree of order. Although not permitted to interfere in *adat*, these *penghulu* hastened the decline of the *lembaga* and *buapak* by positioning themselves as rival authority figures to whom the people could turn in times of need.[80] This served to further diminish the utility of traditional *adat* chieftains, damaging their relation-ship with the people. In the long-term, this proved of considerable conse-quence; as the repositories of the *perbilangan* upon which *adat perpatih* rested, the decline of the *adat* chieftains' societal relevance made it increas-ingly difficult to ensure the continuation of the tradition.[81]

Heading into the early twenty-first century, the severity of this situation has become increasingly apparent. Malaysia's post-independence govern-ments have largely replicated British policy towards the *adat* chiefs, fur-ther diminishing their social stature. In consequence, younger generations

---

[79] Kassim, "Women, Development and Change in Negeri Sembilan," 699.
[80] Gullick, "D.O.'s and Dato's," 38.
[81] Kuwahara, "A Study of a Matrilineal Village in Negeri Sembilan," 45.

born within *adat perpatih suku* have found themselves without compelling traditional authority figures, making it harder for them to maintain active ties with their cultural roots. Moreover, as ever greater numbers of Negeri Sembilan's youth migrate to Malaysia's urban centres, whether to pursue tertiary education or employment opportunities, greater barriers have emerged to the continuance of *adat perpatih*. Living, working, and marrying outside Negeri Sembilan, this new generation has ceased to follow *adat perpatih* norms, which have become little more than an historical curiosity. In consequence, although Negeri Sembilan's older generation still preserves knowledge of *perbilangan* and wider *adat perpatih* tradition, their responsibility to pass down that information is being undermined by a failure to get younger people actively involved in *adat*-related activities.[82] Ultimately, *adat perpatih*'s long-term survival will depend on the capability of its people to adapt to these societal changes in order to facilitate the continuance of their cultural heritage.

CONCLUSION

Although often discussed in legalistic terms, Malaysia's *adat perpatih* tradition constitutes a complex, matrilineally focused social system incorporating perceived natural laws, commonly held cultural norms, and generally accepted ethical and moral standards. With its origins in fourteenth-century Minangkabau (Indonesia), the tradition began its evolution in Negeri Sembilan during the fifteenth century, finally prevailing there over the late eighteenth. As well as elevating the status of women, this tradition embodies the principles of consensus (*muafakat*) and virtue (*budi*). This chapter examined three issues of defining importance to this tradition— leadership, marriage, and property and inheritance—including their relation to Islamic orthopraxis, before briefly considering its decline over the post-colonial period.

Regarding leadership structures, *adat perpatih* recognises four authority figures, each responsible for a different section of society: the *yamtuan besar* (head of state), *penghulu* (or *undang*, district chieftain), *lembaga* (clan chieftain), and *buapak* (sub-clan chieftain). Although all male,

---

[82] Bernama, "Is the Younger Generation Unaware of Adat Perpatih?" *Borneo Post*, October 162013,https://www.theborneopost.com/2013/10/16/is-the-younger-generation-unaware-of-adat-perpatih/ (accessed October 16, 2020).

several of these individuals inherit their positions matrilineally, via association with their female relatives. Moreover, within *adat perpatih* society those in power must be elected by the people they govern; without the consent of the people, they must relinquish their office. This parallels the principles of consultation and accountability inherent within early Islamic political thought.

Concerning marriage, *adat perpatih* upholds only exogamous marriage and demands that husbands move from their own *suku* (clan) to that of their wives, upon which they become dependent. Although this contradicts Islamic practice, many other details of *adat perpatih* marriage, including the *nikah*, *mas kahwin*, and financial responsibility of the husband towards his wife and children, are consistent therewith. Turning to property and inheritance norms, *adat perpatih* promulgates a number of property types that have no direct equivalents in Islam—most notably, ancestral property (*harta pusaka*) and acquired property (*harta pencarian*). Nevertheless, the Islamic concept of property (*al-māl*) is broad enough to absorb these categories, rendering the two traditions compatible. Regarding inheritance, *adat perpatih*'s specific rulings, favouring the passing of property from mothers to daughters, contrasts sharply with Islamic practices as outlined in the Qur'ān. Nevertheless, both traditions manifest the same desire to protect women's rights to inheritance. Any outward variations, therefore, arguably mask a shared intention.

Finally, the chapter ended with a consideration of two contemporary issues with the potential to impede *adat perpatih*'s survival in Negeri Sembilan. Both rooted in the British colonial period, the first pertained to the gradual undermining of *harta pusaka* by capitalist norms, while the second highlighted the erosion of traditional power structures. Both these factors have weakened key *adat perpatih* identity markers, making it difficult for the tradition to perpetuate itself. *Adat perpatih*'s long-term survival will depend on the ability of its adherents to adapt to these changing circumstances.

Bibliography

Abdullah, Ahmad Badri, Mohammad Hashim Kamali, and Mohamed Azam Mohamed Adil, *Malay Traditional Customs: Towards a Sharīʿa Compliant Practice*, IAIS Malaysia Policy Issue Paper 12, Kuala Lumpur: IAIS Malaysia, 2020.

Abdullah, Taufik, "Adat and Islam: An Examination of Conflict in Minangkabau," *Indonesia* 2 (1966), 1–24.

Bernama, Is the Younger Generation Unaware of Adat Perpatih? Borneo Post, 16 October 2013, https://www.theborneopost.com/2013/10/16/is-the-younger-generation-unaware-of-adat-perpatih/ (accessed October 16, 2020).

Cave, Jonathan, *Naning in Melaka: History, the Culture, Tribes and Clans, the War, Independence*, MBRAS Monograph no. 16, Petaling Jaya: MBRAS, 1989.

Cheah, Boon Keng, *Sejarah Melayu: MS Raffles No. 18 Edisi Rumi Baru*, MBRAS Reprint 17, Kuala Lumpur: Malaysian Branch of the Royal Asiatic Society, 2010.

de Eredia, Godinho, *Description of Malaca, Meridional India, and Cathay*, trans. J. V. Mills, MBRAS Reprint 14, Kuala Lumpur: Malaysian Branch of the Royal Asiatic Society, 1997.

Evans, Ivor H. N., "A Grave and Megaliths in Negri Sembilan with an Account of some Excavations," *Journal of the Federated Malay States Museums* 9:3 (1921), 155–73.

Gallop, Annabel Teh, and Venetia Porter, *Lasting Impressions: Seals from the Islamic World*, Kuala Lumpur: Islamic Arts Museum Malaysia, 2012.

Gullick, J. M., "D.O.'s and Dato's: Dialogue on the 'Adat Perpatih'," *Journal of the Malaysian Branch of the Royal Asiatic Society* 73 (2000), 31–52.

Hooker, M. B., "A Note on the Malayan Legal Digests," *Journal of the Malaysian Branch of the Royal Asiatic Society* 41:1 (1968), 157–70.

Hooker, Michael Barr, *Adat Laws in Modern Malaysia*, Oxford: Oxford University Press, 1972.

Humphrey, J. L., "A Naning Wedding Speech," *Journal of the Straits Branch of the Royal Asiatic Society* 72 (1916), 25–33.

Hussain, Khalid M., *Hikayat Iskandar Zulkarnain*, 2nd edition, Kuala Lumpur: Dewan Bahasa Pustaka, 1986.

Ibn Atiyya, *Al-Muharrar al-Wajiz*, vol. 3, Fez: Ministry of Awqaf and Islamic Affairs, 1997.

Ibn Ishaq, *The Life of Muhammad (Sirat Rasul Allah)*, trans. A. Guillaume, Oxford: Oxford University Press, 2010.

Ibrahim, Norhalim Hj, "Some Observations on Adat and Adat Leadership in Rembau, Negeri Sembilan," *Southeast Asian Studies* 26:2 (1988), 150–65.

Islam, Muhammad Wohidul, "Al-Mal: The Concept of Property in Islamic Legal Thought," *Arab Law Quarterly* 14:4 (1999), 361–8.

Jaafar, Mohammad Fadzeli, "Lexical Patterns in Customary Sayings," *Indonesian Journal of Applied Linguistics* 8:1 (2018), 226–34.

Jones, Russell, *Hikayat Raja Pasai*, Kuala Lumpur: Yayasan Karyawan and Penerbit Fajar Bakti, 1999.

de Josselin de Jong, P. E. "Who's Who in the Malay Annals," *Journal of the Malayan Branch of the Royal Asiatic Society* 34:2 (1961), 1–89.

de Josselin de Jong, P.E., *Minangkabau and Negri Sembilan: Socio Political Structure in Indonesia*, Leiden: Ijdo, 1951.

Kassim, Azizah, "Women, Development and Change in Negeri Sembilan: A Micro-Level Perspective," *Southeast Asian Studies* 34:4 (1997), 696–721.

Kassim, Azizah, "Women, Land and Gender Relations in Negeri Sembilan: Some Preliminary Findings," *Southeast Asian Studies* 26:2 (1988), 132–49.

Kato, Tsuyoshi, "Change and Continuity in the Minangkabau Matrilineal System," *Indonesia* 25 (1978), 1–18.

Kim, Khoo Kay, "Adat dan Perkembangan Politik: Pembangunan Masyarakat Negeri Sembilan," in A. Samad Idris, Norhalim Hj Ibrahim, Muhammad Tainu, and N. S. Dharmala (eds.) *Negeri Sembilan: Gemuk Dipupuk, Segar Bersiram: Adat Merentas Zaman* (Seremban: Jawatankuasa Penyelidikan Budaya Negeri Sembilan, 1994), 3–8.

Kuwahara, Sueo, "A Study of a Matrilineal Village in Negeri Sembilan, Malaysia," *Senri Ethnological Studies* 48 (1998), 27–52.

Lambourn, E., "The Formation of the Batu Aceh Tradition in Fifteenth-Century Samudera-Pasai," *Indonesia and the Malay World* 32:93 (2004), 211–48.

Liaw, Yock Fang, *Undang-Undang Melaka: The Laws of Melaka*, Bibliotheca Indonesica 13, The Hague: Martinus Nijhoff, 1976.

Lister, Martin, "Malay Law in Negri Sembilan," *Journal of the Straits Branch of the Royal Asiatic Society* 22 (1890), 299–319.

Manaf, Azima Abdul, "Masalah dan Cabaran Tanah Adat Minang di Dunia Melayu Malaysia dan Indonesia," *Geografia: Malaysian Journal of Society and Space* 5:1 (2018), 69–78.

al-Mawardi, Abu al-Hasan Ali, *Al-Ahkam as-Sultaniyah: The Laws of Islamic Governance*, trans. Asadullah Yate, London: Ta-Ha Publishers, 1996.

Mat Zain, Mat Noor, Che Maryam Ahmad, and Zuliza Mohd. Kusrin, "Perkahwinan Adat Rembau, Negeri Sembilan, dalam Penulisan C.W.C. Parr dan W.H. Mackray," *Jurnal Melayu* 9 (2012), 171–89.

Neusner, Jacob, Tamara Sonn, and Jonathan E. Brockopp, *Judaism and Islam in Practice: A Sourcebook*, London: Routledge, 2000.

Parr, C.W.C., and W.H. Mackray, "Rembau, One of the Nine States: Its History, Constitution and Customs," *Journal of the Straits Branch of the Royal Asiatic Society* 56 (1910), 1–57.

Pires, Tome, *Suma Oriental: An Account of the East, from the Red Sea to China, written in Malacca and India in 1512–1515*, ed. Armando Cortesao, New Delhi: Asian Educational Services, 2005.

Saktiani, Damaika, *Kakawin Nagarakertagama*, Jakarta: PT Buku Seru, 2016.

As-Sallabee, Ali Muhammad, *The Biography of Abu Bakr As-Siddiq*, Riyadh: Darussalam, 2007.

Salleh, Rosiswandy bin Mohd, *Sejarah Pengamalan Adat Perpatih di Negeri Sembilan*, Jelebu: Muzium Adat Jelebu, Negeri Sembilan, n.d.

Sanggoeno Diradjo, Ibrahim Dt., *Tambo Alam Minangkabau: Tatanan Adat Warisan Nenek Moyang Orang Minang*, Bukit Tinggi: Kristal Multimedia, 2015.

Selat, Nordin, "Leadership in Adat Perpatih," *Federation Museums Journal* 17 (1972), 73–98.

al-Tirmidhi, Abu Isa Muhammad ibn Isa ibn Surah, *Sunan al-Tirmidhi*, ed. Abd al-Rahman Muhammad Uthman, Medina: Al-Maktabah al-Salafiyyah, 1974.

Wilkinson, R. J., "Notes on the Negri Sembilan," in R.J. Wilkinson (ed.) *Papers on Malay Subjects* (Kuala Lumpur: Oxford University Press, 1971), 277–321.

Wilkinson, R. J., "Rembau: Its History, Customs and Constitution," *Journal of the Straits Branch of the Royal Asiatic Society* 56 (1910), 1–157.

Winstedt, J. O., and P. E. de Josselin de Jong, "A Digest of Customary Law from Sungai Ujong," *Journal of the Malayan Branch of the Royal Asiatic Society* 27:3 (1954), 5–71.

Yatim, Rais, *Adat: The Legacy of Minangkabau*, Kuala Lumpur: Yayasan Warisanegara, 2015.

al-Zuhayli, Wahbah, *Usul al-Fiqh al-Islami*, Damscus: Dar al-Fikr, 1998.

Cultural and Social Integrations in Matrilineal, Matriarchal, Matrifocal Muslim Communities of South India

Abbas Panakkal

INTRODUCTION

Evidence of early traces of matrilineal Islam in the Indian subcontinent can be found in the manuscript copy of *Futūhāt al-Jazāʾir* ("Triumphs of the Islands") believed to have been penned by Qāḍī Abū Bakr, son of Shaykh ʿUbayd Allāh bin Muḥammad bin Abū Bakr as-Ṣiddīq, who, according to the manuscript, reached Amini Island—one of the islands in modern Lakshadweep—in 41 A.H./662 C.E.[1] Shaykh ʿUbayd Allāh, also known

---

[1] His journey took place four years after the death of his father, Muḥammad ibn Abū Bakr (631–58), who was the adopted son of ʿAlī, the fourth Rāshidūn caliph. ʿAlī married Muḥammad ibn Abū Bakr's mother, Asmā, after the death of Abū Bakr and appointed his adopted son as his general in Egypt after the battle of Siffin.

A. Panakkal (✉)
School of History, University of St Andrews, St Andrews, UK
e-mail: ap399@st-andrews.ac.uk

© The Author(s), under exclusive license to Springer Nature
Switzerland AG 2024
A. Panakkal, N. M. Arif (eds.), *Matrilineal, Matriarchal, and Matrifocal Islam*, Palgrave Series in Islamic Theology, Law, and History, https://doi.org/10.1007/978-3-031-51749-5_3

as ʿUbayd Allāh Thangal and Mumb Maulā,[2] had set out on his voyage in response to guidance he received in a dream of the Prophet. His example of integrating regional cultural practices with Islamic principles demonstrates the long history of matrilineal traditions in Muslim communities of the Indian subcontinent. This pious and learned scholar, who lived before the four schools of Islamic law came into existence, created a firm foundation for a matrilineal Islamic society, forming the necessary legal grounds for an integrated Islam.

The Lakshadweep Islands lie in the Indian Ocean, just off the Malabar Coast of South-West India. By the time of Shaykh ʿUbayd Allāh's arrival, the islands already had a long history of human habitation. Megalithic findings on Androth Island confirm the presence of early human settlement by a maritime culture whose boats were designed to withstand the rough seas; N. Muthukoya compared the Lakshadweep style of boat-building and seafaring with those of Polynesian peoples and their cultures.[3] Matriliny has a long history in the region: its spread in Proto-Oceanic society was documented by Per Hage, who showed that Oceanic-speaking double-descent societies are matrilineal, while cognatic societies also show high levels of matricentricity compared to other world cultures; Polynesian society, for example, followed the same traditions.[4]

In Lakshadweep, indigenous traditions integrated with Islamic culture. However, earlier studies on the matrilineal traditions of the islands have led to serious misunderstandings. Leela Dube and A. R. Kutty both argued that, although human settlement on the island dates back to the second century B.C.E., Islam only arrived in the region in the fourteenth century, imported by immigrants from the Malabar coast, while the indigenous inhabitants of the islands are descendants of Hindu settlers from the coast of Kerala.[5] Dube states the situation as follows:

[2] "Thangal" is a term of respect, literally meaning "noble personality." This is normally used to denote a descendant of the Prophet Muḥammad, an alternative vernacular term for Sayyid/Sharīf. The name Mumb Maulā, which means "the first," is found in the manuscripts of *Futūhāt al-Jazāʾir*, *Mawlid*, and *Māla*.

[3] N. Muthukoya, *Lakshadweep Noottanudkaliloode* (Kottayam: Vidyarthi Mithram Book Depot, 1986), 32.

[4] Per Hage, "Was Proto-Oceanic Society Matrilineal?" *Journal of the Polynesian Society* 107:1 (1998), 365–79.

[5] Leela Dube, *Matriliny and Islam: Religion and Society in the Laccadives* (Delhi: National Publishing House, 1969), 12; A.R. Kutty, *Marriage and Kinship in an Island Society* (Delhi: National Publishing House, 1972), 9.

CULTURAL AND SOCIAL INTEGRATIONS IN MATRILINEAL, MATRIARCHAL... 79

There is no doubt that centuries ago a matrilineal kinship system with duolocal residence was brought to these islands by migrants from the coastal regions of Kerala. The circumstances in which the migrants came to settle, and whether all of them originally followed the same pattern of kinship and marriage, are not known. But it is clear that the islands provided a congenial setting for the flowering of this system. Subsistence activities and trade with the mainland made teamwork and coordination necessary and meant that some men were periodically absent. The people lived on a narrow strip of land within easy reach of one another. These factors seem to have facilitated the adoption of matriliny and duolocal residence by the various groups of settlers who were thrown together, as well as the continued existence of these patterns. The migrants' political and economic organization and their system of graded groups also seem to have been adapted from what prevailed in the region from which they came. The migrants depended on rice as a staple, which gave rise to regular trade with the mainland in which coconuts and their products were exchanged for rice and other necessaries.[6]

Yet this understanding of history can be taken as part of a blatant continuation of the colonial historiography that simplistically connected administrative areas through vernacular networks, relying on stories of Malabar Muslims who were linked to the islands. Persistent colonial efforts to draw parallels between cultures, languages, and ethnicities in order to create shared administrative zones were the underlying motivation for such narratives, visible in Whyte Ellis's dissertation on the various languages and Dravidian attributions to the administrative zonal vernaculars—a thesis that used to bolster the policy of the colonial Madras Presidency.[7] Writers from the islands themselves also tried to connect their history with that of the mainland, where the history of Islam was linked with the popular history of Cheraman Perumal.[8] Yet the islands have their own distinct history; we now turn to the arrival of Shaykh ʿUbayd Allāh, in the seventh century C.E.

---

[6] Dube, "Who Gains from Matriliny? Men, Women and Change on a Lakshadweep Island," *Sociological Bulletin* 42:1 (1993), 17.

[7] Whyte Ellis, "Dissertation on the Second on the Malayalma Language," 1815; Robert Caldwell, *A Comparative Grammar of the Dravidian or South Indian Family of Languages*, London: Trubner and Co., 1875.

[8] P.I. Pookoya, *Dweepolpathi—an up-to-date History of Laccadive, Minicoy and Amindivi Islands* (Calicut: Falcon Press, 1960), 46. Cheraman Perumal was the first king who accepted Islam, mentioned in the manuscript of *Qiṣṣat Shakarwatī Farmāḍ*.

80   A. PANAKKAL

THE MANUSCRIPT OF *FUTŪHĀT AL-JAZĀ'IR*

According to the manuscript of *Futūhāt al-Jazā'ir*, one day young ʿUbayd Allāh fell asleep in the Medina mosque and dreamed of the Prophet Muḥammad, who encouraged him to travel to spread the religion in far-off lands. ʿUbayd Allāh accepted the mission and started his voyage from Jeddah on the eleventh of Shawwāl in the year 41/662. After a gruelling fifty-day journey the ship was wrecked in a fierce rainstorm, and Shaykh ʿUbayd Allāh was saved by clinging on to a piece of the deck that carried him to Amini Island.[9] The manuscript tells that during Shaykh ʿUbayd Allāh's hardships, the Prophet appeared once again in a dream and reassured him, promising him ease in his future life. The manuscript also provides evidence of Shaykh ʿUbayd Allāh's preference for adhering to an integrated family tradition of matrilineal kinship in his own family:

> ʿUbayd Allāh said, "I kept calling them to believe in Allah again and again, but they did not heed my call, except a woman, who responded to my call and said to me, stretch out your hand and I will testify that there is no God but Allah alone and Muhammad is His Servant and Messenger. She became a Muslim and I lived with her in her house, and I named her Hamidah, the purified one. She was the only one who responded to my call from all the village. I married her, and she gave birth to fifteen children; ten boys and five girls.[10]

At the time of the Shaykh's arrival, it is believed that people on the islands were following a traditional Polynesian lifestyle with matrilineal customs. Shaykh ʿUbayd Allāh's family also followed matrilineal kinship and matrilocal practices, and in accordance his children were known by his wife's family name. His children's names are specified in the manuscript, which details the advent of Islam on various islands, the building of mosques, and how jurists (*qāḍīs*) were assigned. Shaykh ʿUbayd Allāh was able to convince the people of Amini, Kawaratti, and Agatti and spread the message of Islam throughout the Lakshadweep Islands, integrating it into their cultural traditions. During the last part of his life, he went to Androth Island, where he spent the rest of his days. The Shaykh died in Androth

---

[9] Qāḍī Abū Bakr bin ʿUbayd Allāh, *Futūhāt al-Jazāʾir* (Madin Manuscript Library, Malappuram), 1.

[10] *Futūhāt al-Jazāʾir*, 3.

CULTURAL AND SOCIAL INTEGRATIONS IN MATRILINEAL, MATRIARCHAL... 81

and was buried near the Juma mosque, now one of the principal attractions in Lakshadweep.[11]

Matrilineal traditions of the islands thus began before the four schools of law came into existence in the Islamic legal field. There is no doubt that Shaykh ʿUbayd Allāh, who was born and grew up in Arabia, was aware of the Islamic family traditions of Arab patriarchy, which gave prominence to male members of the family, yet he did not impose these cultural practices. Instead, he integrated the new religion with local customs, including matriliny, legalising their traditions of matrilineal property through *waqf* and integrating the prominent role of the female members of the family. The rank of *qāḍī* (judge) was also passed down through the sister's son throughout the islands, in accordance with matrilineal traditions. The Pattakkal family in Androth Island is a clear example: there is a popular story—narrated by Puradam Kunjikoya Thangal in *Safina Pattu*—that Muhammed, son of Aboobacker, claimed the position of *qāḍī* after his father's death. The people of the area chose Aboobacker's sister's son instead, however, abiding by the matrilineal tradition, and eventually Muhammad left the island.[12] Another manuscript, known as *Mawlid*, also mentions how Shaykh ʿUbayd Allāh established an endowment for the matrilineal traditional home, understood as measuring ninety-nine traditional yardsticks in one side. It was unambiguously signed and documented, detailing that the boundaries of the residence measure nine carpenter's handsticks from the foundation of the house in another direction.[13]

The indigenised legal tradition continued to be followed in the islands, and there were few questions or cultural clashes relating to this tradition even after the implementation of colonial law, which tried to rein in Muslim matrilineal traditions throughout British India. Local traditions have been maintained, in many cases differing somewhat from those of the mainland. There is, for example, a tradition of serving food in the evening

---

[11] During my research visit, I found that people often held ritualistic prayers at the shrine before commencing important activities.

[12] Muthukoya, *Lakshadweep Noottanudkaliloode*, 52. I was personally able to see a copy of the *Safina Pattu*, a text composed by M. K. Muhammed Koya Thangal which recounts the advent of Islam in the islands and the construction of mosques.

[13] Anonymous, *Mawlid of Mumb Maulā* (Manuscript not listed), 15. The copy of the manuscript I refer to in this study is kept in the personal collections of Aboobacker Saqafi of Agathi Island.

while reciting the *Mawlid*, which is believed to be adopted from the time of the death of Shaykh Ubayd Allāh.[14]

The history of the advent of Islam in the Lakshadweep Islands was narrated in various manuscripts and liturgical literatures on the life of Mumb Maulā or ʿUbayd Allāh Thangal. These were codified in two collections, *Mawlid* and *Māla*, written both in Arabic and in the vernacular, and used to be proudly recited in the islands as their own narratives, unlike the other traditional songs of Muhiyudheen Māla,[15] Manqūs Mawlid,[16] Muhiyudheen, and Ahmad ibn ʿAlī Ar-Rifāʿī Ratheebs[17] imported from the Malabar mainland and abroad. Confidence in the legal rectitude of matrilineal practices can be seen in the narratives of Islamic scholars of the islands, who quoted *Futūhāt al-Jazāʾir*, while the local people were reassured by the vernacular *Māla*, which emphasises the validity of the regional cultural traditions integrated by ʿUbayd Allāh.

The *Mawlid* narrates the history of Muslim ethnic groups on the islands and indicates that Shaykh ʿUbayd Allāh followed matrilocal tradition when he married a wife from the islands, preferring matrilineal kinship for his own descendants, and emphasises his courage and strong personality.[18] Though the author of the *Mawlid* is unknown, its contents suggest that it was composed with reference to the manuscript copy of *Futūhāt al-Jazāʾir*; it is composed in the traditional mixed mode narrative, which comprises prose as well as poetry, with rhythmic renditions to each stanza. The use of Arabic script for writing in the vernacular became very popular among Muslim communities, and there were traces of manuscript cultures moving between the islands and the Malabar mainland. Popular works by Malabar scholars, such as Muhiyudheen Māla and Manqūs Mawlid, were well accepted and orally circulated in the islands. Early barriers created by differences in language and culture were washed away by the popular integrated linguistic tradition, which was identified by the regional vernacular. This integrated language tradition helped to create better connections between the islands and the Malabar mainland, but have misled historians

---

[14] Muthukoya, *Lakshadweep Noottanudkaliloode*, 123.

[15] Muhiyudheen Māla is a popular vernacular poem on Sheikh Muhiyudheen Abdul Qādir Gīlānī, composed by the prominent scholar and poet, Khazi Muhammad of Kozhikode.

[16] Manqūs Mawlid is a famous eulogy popular from the sixteenth century, composed by Zayn al-Din Sr.

[17] Muhiyudheen Ratheeb and Rifaʿi Ratheeb are equally popular in the region. Rifaʿi Ratheeb is a more ritualistic performance by the followers of Sheikh Ahmed al -Rifaʿi.

[18] *Futūhāt al-Jazāʾir*, 10.

CULTURAL AND SOCIAL INTEGRATIONS IN MATRILINEAL, MATRIARCHAL... 83

who understood these literary connections to mean that the history of Islam and Muslim matrilineal traditions of the islands and mainland were interlinked.

THE *QISSAT SHAKARWATĪ FARMĀD* MANUSCRIPT AND MATRILINEAL PORT TOWNS

South Indian Muslims still enjoy two types of kinship organisation, both matrilineal and patrilineal. The Muslims from the Malabar coastline follow matrilineal kinship, which is deeply rooted in the port towns where integrated Islamic cultures developed over centuries. It is clear from this scenario that when people accepted Islam as their religion, they never insisted on changing their social systems if its structures were not in conflict with the basic beliefs of Islam. Matrilineal, matrilocal, and matriarchal systems were easily incorporated into religion, supported by scholars.

When Islam arrived in Malabar it became indigenised, with the cooperation of non-Muslim rulers. This story of integration and indigenisation was illustrated in *Qissat Shakarwatī Farmād*, a manuscript in the British Library that contains detailed descriptions of how mosques were established across the coastal region of Malabar and Ma'bar, alongside the appointment of judges (*qādī*s) and the port masters (*shāhbandar*s) who were pivotal figures in foreign trade.[19] Traditional sources from Malabar also describe the conversion of the king, Cheraman Perumal, to Islam, although the time frame is debated among early historians.

I was able to find three additional manuscript copies of *Qissat Shakarwatī Farmād*, two from the personal libraries of Ahmed Koya Shāliyāti (1885–1955) and Pangil Ahmed Kutty Musliyār (1888–1946) and one from the old mosque library in Madayi. All four of these manuscripts provide details of the exact locations and land endowments for the early mosques, including dates and days of their construction and the names of the Muslim judges and port masters delegated to different port towns of the region.[20] The *Qissat Shakarwatī Farmād* contains comprehensive sketches of the details of mosque construction, including their exact land endowments, described in terms of Islamic law as *waqf*.[21] The

[19] Anonymous, *Qissat Shakarwatī Farmad*, British Library MS, IO, Islamic 2807d.
[20] Abbas Panakkal, lecture given at the International Islamic University Malaysia (2018), 1167–89.
[21] *Qissat*, 99–102.

names of the judges, the foundation dates of mosques, and the chronological order of endowments are identical in all four manuscripts. This text was written on the Malabar mainland in 21 A.H., twenty years before Shaykh ʿUbayd Allāh's arrival in the Lakshadweep Islands. Even though matrilocal cultures or matrilineal traditions are not directly mentioned in the manuscripts, it is interesting to note that the Muslim communities of these prominent port towns specifically uphold the matrilineal traditions.

Matrilineal Muslim communities are mainly found along the shorelines of the early port towns of Malabar (Barkur to Kollam) and Ma'bar—the Coromandel coast mentioned in *Qiṣṣat*. A similar description of the establishment of mosques on various islands and allocations of *waqf* lands also features in *Futūḥāt al-Jazāʾir*. These manuscripts make it clear that the region was under the influence of matrilineal kinship before the advent of Islam, and that early Muslims incorporated the tradition and integrated it into their family life. The distinctive nature of *Futūḥāt al-Jazāʾir* makes it clear that this is not simply another story of the conversion of local rulers, a generalisation put forward by Yohanan Friedman, who cited the similarities between the *Qiṣṣat* and shoreline stories from other regions of the Indian Ocean yet provided no specific documented evidence.[22]

The names documented in the *Qiṣṣat* manuscript reveal that early *qāḍī*s and *shāhbandar*s originated from various countries: the name "al-Madanī" shows that one came from Medina, for example, while "al-Miṣrī" came from Egypt. These names demonstrate the multicultural and multi-ethnic roots of early Islamic tradition and law in Malabar. This account of Islamic tradition was also described in the early Brahmanical document *Keralolpatti*, which gives a mythical history of the provinces and stories of various Hindu tribes based on the Brahman settlements. The chronology of the mosques and the names of appointed legal experts given in *Qiṣṣat* are identical to those in *Keralolpatti*.[23]

The matrilineal system of inheritance became a special feature of Muslim communities living in Malabar and Ma'bar port towns, where women played an active, visible role in society. Malabar, where traders and settlers from various parts of the world lived together, was a paradigm of an integrated, multi-national Muslim community. Peaceful co-existence as well as

---

[22] Yohanan Friedmann, "Qiṣṣat Shakarwatī Farmāḍ: A Tradition concerning the Introduction of Islam to Malabar," *Israel Oriental Studies* 5 (1975), 233–58.

[23] Hermann Gundert, Keralolpatti—*Origin of Malabar* (Mangalore: Basel Mission press, 1868), 147.

undisturbed trade and commerce became part of the identity of these port towns, which were prominent in the international markets.[24] South Indian ports were comfortable trading centres and a second home for traders and travellers, who spent a certain period of time on the coast every year awaiting the seasonal changes in the monsoon winds necessary for long-range voyages.[25] Arabs, in particular, were based in various port towns, exploring commodities of value to expand their commercial enterprises.[26] A mosque inscription mentioning the year 5 A.H. in Madayi Juma Majid proves that Islam was already known in the region before the time of *Qiṣṣat Shakarwatī Farmāḍ* and *Futūhāt al-Jazāʾir*. The Malabar port towns became prominent in different centuries as focal points of interaction between local rulers and foreign traders.[27] Traders from the Arabian Peninsula depended particularly heavily on the monsoon winds, which meant that they remained in the ports for some time every year and thereby strengthened the integrated nature of matrilineal kinship in the region.[28]

All prominent port towns mentioned in *Qiṣṣat* adopted matrilineal Islam, with the support of Muslim jurists of diverse backgrounds. The Moroccan traveller Ibn Battuta (1304–1377), a follower of the Mālikī School, described the juristic character of Muslims at various port towns of the region and mentioned judges from various backgrounds: one from Mogadishu who was educated in Mecca and Medina, and others from Baghdad, Oman, and Qazwin in Persia.[29] He also met Faqeeh Husain, who wrote the *Qaidul Jami-e* (1342 C.E.), an early legal text from Malabar.[30] Such networks of Muslim scholars demonstrated the openness

---

[24] Tara Chand, *Influence of Islam on Indian Culture* (Allahabad: The Indian Press Limited, 1936), 36.

[25] F. Fernandez Armesto, *Pathfinders: A Global History of Exploration* (London: Oxford University Press, 2006), 36.

[26] G. Haurani, *Arab Seafaring in Indian Ocean in Ancient and Early Mediaeval Times* (Princeton, NJ: Princeton University Press, 1951), 83.

[27] Steven E. Sidebotham, *Berenike and the Ancient Maritime Spice Route* (Berkeley, CA: University of California Press, 2011), 191.

[28] Omani sailors still routinely spend three months of the year in Calicut, waiting for the weather to return. I interviewed some of these sailors and published this research in my article "Beypūṛinum Sūrinum Idayil," *Gulf Focus* 2:2 (2015), 28–34.

[29] Ibn Battuta, *The travels of Ibn Battuta in Asia and Africa*, vol. 4, ed. H. A. R. Gibb (Cambridge: Cambridge University Press, 1962), 66–103.

[30] The manuscript copy of *Qaidul Jami-e* kept in the Ma'din Manuscript Library gives the author's name as Hussain bin Ahmed al Mahfani, while the copy in the Juma al Majid Library of Dubai gives it as Abu Abdullah Hussain bin Ahmed al Mahfani, along with the extended title of the text *Mukhthasar fi Ahkam al-Nikah*. Prefixes such as Abu Abdullah confirm his Arab connections, and the place name Mahfan shows his country of origin.

and legal integration that resulted in support of matrilineal patterns in the early port towns of Malabar.

In the sixteenth century, scholars of the port town of Ponnani[31] also took initiatives to integrate regional practices by broadening the local community's understanding of Islam. This intellectual atmosphere set the framework for a systematised Shāfiʿī school of thought in Malabar and provided liberal support for matrilineal traditions in the religious milieu of Ponnani. After establishing the prominent Ponnani Muslim College in the sixteenth century, Zayn al-Din Sr. and his son Abd al-Aziz published texts on various subjects, in particular addressing the legal arguments about contradictory practices, but never condemning matrilineal traditions.[32] Zayn al-Dīn al-Malaybārī's *Fath al-Muʿīn* shows how regional culture was widely reflected in the interpretation of Islamic law. Legal reasoning based on the principles of the Qur'ān and Sunna allowed him to make room for ʿ*urf* (custom), and the text raised no questions about the matrilineal traditions flourishing in the region since they were considered compatible with religion. The highest customary position in Ponnani's Muslim community was also handed down through matrilineal traditions, as noted in British gazette records:

> In the South the *makkathayam* system is usually followed, but it is remarkable that succession to religious *sthanams* [positions], such as that of the Valiya Tangal of Ponnani, usually goes according to the *marumakkattayam* [matrilineal] system.[33]

Muslim jurist clans of the Ponnani Makhdum family abided by matrilineal kinship patterns to pass positions on to their descendants.

---

[31] Ponnani was called the "Mecca of Malabar" because it was a prominent centre of Muslim cultural and intellectual development. During the medieval period, Ponnani, under the ruler Zamorin, emerged as one of the most important port towns of the region.

[32] Abd al-Aziz's prolific writings demonstrate his scholarship. He followed his father in promoting enlightened integration and defending the integrity of Ponnani College. He also supported opposition to Portuguese imperialism and encouraged Muslims to protect the power of the Hindu king of Calicut. He died in 1585 and was buried in Ponnani.

[33] C. A. Innes, *Madras District Gazateers, Malabar and Anjengo.* (Madras: Government Press, 1908), 198.

Adoption of *Waqf al-Aulād* in Malabar

The traditions of *Futūhāt al-Jazā'ir* and *Qiṣṣat Shakarwatī Farmāḍ* are different in their characteristics, reflecting cultural differences between the Malabar mainland and the Lakshadweep Islands, especially the traditions of matrilineal family property possession through *waqf*. *Qiṣṣat Shakarwatī Farmāḍ* gives categorical statements on the provisions of *waqf*, which were retained on the mainland; legislation of matrilineal property rights through *waqf al-aulād* was not specific in Malabar before the British passed legislation to pare down matrilineal traditions, labelling them "un-Islamic." In the Lakshadweep Islands, colonial law and the propaganda surrounding it were not as powerful as in the mainland Malabar region, despite being under the same jurisdiction. When this colonial attack on local tradition engulfed Malabar's matrilineal Islam, the Arackal authorities therefore adopted the model of *waqf* followed on the islands, which were under their rule. This illustrates how difficult it was for the colonial government to uproot matrilineal culture—even with the successive legislations of the Malabar Partition Bill of 1910, the Succession Act of 1918, and the Mappila Marumakkathayam Act of 1939. The Arackal ruling family was against the Partition Bill, which allowed the partition of joint family houses that were passed down through the female line; in order to maintain the exalted matrilineage of their own family, *waqf-al-aulād* was adopted as the only way to retain these customs as part of Islamic law.[34] If matrilineal properties were dealt with according to the *waqf-al-aulād*, the British could hardly raise the concern that this practice was "un-Islamic."

Most people were unconcerned about whether their matrilineal practices had a place in the structure of Islam, while some ardent Sunnī scholars tried to use the jargon of *waqf-al-aulād* to amend the traditions. This can be taken as iconic evidence for the adaptation of legal jargon from Lakshadweep by the Malabar mainland as part of an effort to legitimise matrilineal systems even after the implementation of anti-matrilineal edicts. Two particular property types in Lakshadweep also demonstrate the written legal orientation of the island, which was little affected by the colonial attempt to 'Islamise' matrilineal customs. "Friday" property is matrilineal and communal, while "Monday" property describes personal

---

[34] Manaf Kottakkunnummal, "Indigenous Customs and Colonial Law: Contestations in Religion, Gender and Family among Matrilineal Mappila Muslims in Colonial Malabar, Kerala, c. 1910–1928," Sage Open, January 2014.

holdings; the distinction between these two distinct types of property has helped keep the matrilineal system intact for centuries. Monday property may be disposed of at its owner's personal discretion, whereas the divisions and transactions of Friday property were regulated by custom and tradition. Earlier researchers considered Monday property as structured and standardised by Islamic law, while Friday property was not. Leela Dube also identified the nature of the *waqf* system followed by Lakshadweep people to preserve matrilineal property: "Some held that *Taravad* property was a kind of wakf property created for the benefit of the women and children of the matrilineage."[35] This practice was adopted by Malabar matrilineal families to preserve the matrilineal *tharavads* of Malabar.[36] Under the British influence, however, the historiography of the matrilineal system in the islands was overlooked, considered as being an imitation of the mainland, thus neglecting these solid historic models.

Contrary to Dube and Kutty's argument that Malabar was the origin of the matrilineal kinship of Lakshadweep, it is therefore clear that often socio-cultural influence sometimes went in the other direction: Malabar, in fact, adopted centuries-old *waqf* formulas from the islands. Dube's argument on early migration from Kerala as the origin of the matrilineal system needs to be reoriented.[37]

Expressions of Matrilineal Culture (*Marumakkathayam*)

The word *marumakkathayam* literally means "inheritance by sisters' children," derived from *marumakkal*, meaning nephews and nieces. Different types of matrilineal customs in the region have been gathered into the concept of *marumakkathayam*, an umbrella term that includes a number of different matrilineal, matrilocal, and matriarchal practices. In this system the inheritance of the family is transferred through the female line, and family power—the *karanavar* position—is bestowed on the eldest

---

[35] Dube, "Who Gains from matriliny?" 26.

[36] A *tharavad* is the ancestral home consisting of the extended family.

[37] Similar misinformation was also put forward by André Wink, who stated that before converting to Islam, the Lakshadweep Islands had been Hinduised by settlers from the Malabar coast, and after becoming Muslims they maintained a caste hierarchy and the Malabari matrilineal kinship system. Wink also wrongly stated that the Minicoy islands retained a patrilineal system (Wink, André, *Al-Hind: The making of the Indo-Islamic world, vol. I. Early medieval India and the expansion of Islam, 7th–11th centuries*, Leiden: Brill, 1990).

CULTURAL AND SOCIAL INTEGRATIONS IN MATRILINEAL, MATRIARCHAL... 89

female member of the household; families respect female elders as *karanavathi*. In some families, three customs prevail: matrilineal, matrilocal, and matriarchal. Some other families follow a collaborative version of either matrilineal or matrilocal systems.

Etymologically, matriarchy means rule by mothers, and a deeper definition signifies domination by female members of society. Matriarchy was specifically visible in the queendom of Arackal, which maintained authoritarian matrilineal kinship with the explicit political dominance and ruling authority of the Beebi, the female head. In the Arackal royal house the eldest member in the maternal line, whether male or female, succeeded to the throne, and many women took the royal throne with the title of Beebi.[38] This Arackal Swarupam[39] is one example of Muslim matriarchy, and it is believed that it derived from an earlier tradition.[40] The Arackal royal house maintained friendly relations with the Ottoman empire, which accepted this Muslim matrilineal inheritance and the matriarchal leadership of the kingdom.[41] The Arackal Swarupam was the only Muslim ruling family that exclusively followed three forms of matricentric Islam together, using matrilineal, matrilocal, and matriarchal traditions as part of the system of the sovereign state. The Arackal effectively exercised power in the Lakshadweep and Kannur regions, where people followed matrilineal kinship. Notably, this was the only Swarupam—in which the eldest person in the family was selected as ruler—where women were fully eligible to become the head of their country and never excluded from the *muppumura*,[42] making them free to attain the highest position in the chain of command. The Arackal Beebis enjoyed their position as queen and head of the family; they were also in charge of the mosques and held the power to declare the date of auspicious Islamic days such as Ramadan, Eid, and other celebrations.[43]

---

[38] Ronald E. Miller, *Mappila Muslims of Kerala: A Study in Islamic Trends* (Bombay: Orient Longman, 1976), 57–58.

[39] The official name of political houses in pre-colonial Malabar.

[40] Binu John Mailaparambil, Lords of the Sea: The Ali Rajas of Cannanore and the Political Economy of Malabar (1663–1723), (Leiden: Brill, 2012), 46, K.K.N. Kurup, *The Ali Rajas of Cannanore* (Trivandrum: College Book House, 1975), 2.

[41] William Logan, A Collection of Treaties, Engagements and other Papers of Importance Relating to British Affairs in Malabar, (Calicut: Minarva Press, 1879), 22–23.

[42] The official order of seniority in a *swarupam* or *tharavad*.

[43] Interview with the head of the Arackal Kingdom.

90   A. PANAKKAL

Some families follow matrilineage and matrilocal systems, but are not matriarchies. The Kozhikode *qāḍī* family, for example, follows matrilineal family inheritance, but patriarchal inheritance for succession to the position of *qāḍī*. Faqrudheen Usman, who was *qāḍī* of Calicut from 1343 to 1370, was succeeded by his son, and this pattern was generally followed, although in some cases the former *qāḍī*'s brothers inherited his position. The family names of Muslim jurists from the same lineage always varied, however, as they followed matrilineal kinship traditions.

Some Muslim families descended from the Prophet's family have been settled in Calicut for centuries. They customarily follow matrilocal traditions at home and keep their matrilineal heritage in their designated places of burial, but not in their kinship. The Jifri house of Kozhikode models this practice, reserving the nearest burial space for a daughter and son-in-law in the holy shrine of Shaykh Jifri. The younger generation of the Thangal family, on the other hand, preferred matrilocal customs, but not matrilineal affinity.[44] I was able to examine their family trees, which are separately prepared so as to link the sides of both the father and the mother. The general public addresses them using the matrilineal family name, because they were all born and brought up adhering to matrilocal customs in their personal lives. There are also Thangal families that follow matrilineal kinship, for example Fazal Koyamma Thangal Koora, son of Sayyid ʿAbdurahmān al-Bukhāri, Ullal Thangal, and they are proud to be associated with their mother's family name.

LEGACY OF MATRILINEAL KINSHIP

The matrilineal nature of southern India was noted by early travellers. Ibn Battuta (1304–1369) explained the succession of political sovereignty in Malabar through mother-lines, observing that the rulers of that country left their royal position to their sister's son to the exclusion of their own children.[45] The rulers of Cochin, Travancore, and Calicut were matrilineal, the ruler's heir being the eldest son of his sisters. Abd-al-Razzāq Samarqandī (1413–1482), the Persian chronicler who was ambassador from Shah Rukh—the Timurid ruler of Persia—to Calicut in the early 1440s, discussed the matrilineal inheritance practised by the kingdom of Calicut as well as non-Muslim matrilineal traditions in the following words:

---

[44] Interview with Sayyid Salih Jifri of Calicut.
[45] Ibn Battuta, *The Travels of Ibn Battuta*, 76.

The sovereign of this city bears the title of Sameri.[46] When he dies it is his sister's son who succeeds him, and his inheritance does not belong to his son, or his brother, or any other of his relations. No one reaches the throne by means of the strong hand. The Infidels are divided into a great number of classes, such as the Brahmins, and others. Although they all agreed upon the fundamental principles of polytheism and idolatry, each sect has its peculiar customs. Amongst them there is a class of men, with whom it is the practice for one woman to have a great number of husbands, each of whom undertakes a special duty and fulfils it. The hours of the day and of the nights are divided between them and each of them for a certain period takes up his abode in the house, and while he remains there no other is allowed to enter. The Sameri belongs to this sect.[47]

The Namboothiri followed the Brahmin tradition that restricted marriages of brothers of the same family to women from the Brahmin community. The older brother of the family kept nuptial ties with girls from his own clan, and the other young men had no right to connubial life, practising hypergamy with Nair women.[48] Nair families also considered it a point of pride for their women to have Brahmin partners as a means of preserving their high status, and the younger sons of Brahmins were accepted as sexual mates in Kshatriya and Nair households. Niccolò de' Conti (c. 1395–1469), the Italian merchant and explorer, illustrated the customs that existed in Malabar:

> In this district alone, the women are allowed to take several husbands, so that some have ten and more. The husbands contribute amongst themselves to the maintenance of the wife, who lives apart from her husbands. When one visits, he leaves a mark at the door of the house, which being seen by another coming afterwards, he goes away without entering. The children are allotted to the husbands at the will of the wife. The inheritance of the father does not descend to the children.[49]

The children born out of these relations were not Brahmins, and neither the woman nor her child was conferred with the privileges of kinship, although the children were accepted into the mother's caste by virtue of

---

[46] Vernacular variant of the official title of Zamorin, the ruler of Calicut.

[47] Richard Henry Major, *India in the Fifteenth Century* (London: Hakluyt Society, 1857), 17.

[48] Nair, sometimes spelt Nayer, is a Hindu caste comprising a number of subdivisions.

[49] Major, *India in the Fifteenth Century*, 20.

matrilineage.[50] Among these polyandrous communities paternity was uncertain, and as a result the mother's line was used to guarantee the lineage; succession therefore passed through the mother. The children born out of these relationships were thus always considered Nairs, and this affiliation formed the foundations of the Nairs' matrilineal and matrilocal systems.[51]

There is a false perception that the Nairs were the sole progenitors of the matrilineal ethnicities of southern India, and that all Muslims adopted the *marumakkathayam* law of inheritance and the rule of non-division from them. This concept arose from colonial historiography, which created a distorted image of the history of integrated Muslim cultures and even depicted these Muslims as fanatics:

> The origin of this extraordinary custom which once established among the *Nairs* became fashionable and adopted by castes even by the fanatic Mappilas who are followers of the Prophet.[52]

In *Kinship Organization and Marriage Customs Among Moplahs on the South West Coast of India*, Victor S. D'Souza wrote that matrilineal Muslim traditions were originally formed through intermarriage between maritime Arab traders and local women, and that contemporary Muslim communities are heterogeneous and characterised by ethnic, regional, and social diversity.[53] Ronald E. Miller opined that among the native Hindu community, Nair women were sexually available outside of wedlock and as a result marriage was of little importance along the coastline; it was no great matter to find a partner from the region.[54] Kathleen Gough and C. F. Fuller linked the formation of Malabar matriliny to the medieval Nair militia, relying on the theory that the Nair forces of Malabar recruited a large number of local militia men who were often away from home, so

---

[50] Kathleen Gough, "Mappila North Kerala," in David M. Schneider and Kathleen Gough (eds.), *Matrilineal Kinship* (Berkeley: University of California Press, 1961), 320.

[51] K.M. Panikkar, "Some Aspects of Nayar Life," *Journal of the Royal Anthropological Institute* 48 (1918), 265.

[52] Walter Kelly Firminger, *Fifth Report from the Select committee on the Affairs of the Indian Company* Vol. VIII (Calcutta: R. Cambray, 1917), 300.

[53] Victor. S. D' Souza, "Kinship Organization and Marriage Customs Among Moplahs on the South West Coast of India," in Imtiaz Ahmad (ed.), *Family, Kinship and Marriage among Muslims in India* (New Delhi: Manohar Books, 1976), 141.

[54] Miller, *Mappila Muslims of Kerala*, 49.

these *tharavads*—ancestral homes consisting of extended families—by necessity became matrilineal.[55] André Wink, quoting D'Souza, wrote: "Mappillas, assimilating converted Hindus from early on, became ethnically quite diverse. They spoke Malayalam and dressed like the Nairs, from whom they often took over the matrilineal kinship organization as well."[56] S.M. Mohamed Koya recounted the theory that Muslims living in Kolathunad were obliged to conform to the general practices—including matrilineal ones—prevailing in the region, and also affirmed that this system was adopted from the Nair communities as a result of intermarriages and conversions. The kinship units closely resembled the matrilineal units of the Nairs of Malabar, with reforms and revisions.[57]

Matrilineal systems, as popularly believed, were adopted not just from the Nairs but from all ethnic matrilineal groups who accepted Islam. When Nair families embraced Islam, they integrated Muslim practices by restricting unlawful sexual bonds with many men, while their descendants preserved permissible matrilineal family customs. Earlier studies tried to establish the erroneous concept that the whole system was associated with the Nair practice of polyandry to ensure the family descendants came from the same bloodline. The general perception of the emergence and development of Muslim matrilineal structures needs to be redefined, given that a number of tribal groups abide by matrilineal traditions in South India. Adivasi groups, the aboriginal peoples of the region, and other lower castes also follow the matrilineal kinship system. The Kurichiyar, for example, are a matrilineal scheduled tribe living mainly in the Wayanad and Kannur districts of Kerala State. This tribal group also observes a joint family system. The Adiyans are a bilingual community who also follow a system of succession through the mother's lineage. This tribal group is divided into clans called "Mantu" or "Chemmam," and the clan head is known as "Chemmakkaran." A. Sreedhara Menon's *Kozhikode District Gazetteer* noted matrilineal customs and traditions practiced by Kshatriyas, Nairs, the Ambalavasis, the Pulayars, the Vellalans, and aboriginal people such as the Waynadan Chettis, the Kurichiyas, Karimpalans, the Kadar, the

---

[55] Kathleen Gough, "Changing Kinship Usages in the Setting Up of Political and Economic Change among Nayars of Malabar," *Journal of Royal institute of Great Britain and Ireland* 82, No 1 (1952), 76; C.J. Fuller, *The Nayars Today* (Cambridge: Cambridge University Press, 1976) 123–4.

[56] André Wink, *Al Hind: The Making of the Indo-Islamic World*, vol. I. *Early Medieval India, and the Expansion of Islam, 7th–11th Centuries* (Leiden: Brill, 1990), 75.

[57] S.M. Mohammed Koya, *Mappilas of Malabar* (Calicut: University of Calicut, 1983), 64.

94   A. PANAKKAL

Tachanad Muppans, and the Kunduvatiyand.[58] In north Malabar, the *marumakkathayam* system is also closely associated with the Tiyyans.[59] During my field work in Appapara, Thirunelli Wayanad district, I personally found that a number of Adivasi families had changed their matrilineal traditions to patriarchy. Tribal culture and tradition had also been replaced by Hindu tradition, and their marriage rituals were solemnised by Pujari of the Hindu temple, replacing the Moopan of the tribe. In earlier times, marriages followed local customs with traditional bands, dances, and special performances, but today these celebrations have been fully transformed into *tali kettu kalyanam*, the tradition of "tying the marriage knot." I also found that these tribes consider matrilineal and matrilocal systems to be shameful to their community, and they stated that this was an old system which they now seldom follow. This change also reflected legal concerns, since tribal peoples fall under the jurisdiction of Hindu Law.

India's 1891 census of Travancore in 1891 counted 530,000 families, of which 56% were classed as matrilineal and 44% were patrilineal.[60] This would be similar in Malabar and Cochin.[61] In the nineteenth century, half the population of different castes and communities adhered to matrilineal practices.[62] Tiyyas or Ezahvas[63] comprised 30–40% of the population. Yet some historians argue that the discrepancies based on higher and lower caste denominations result from the fact that low-caste groups practised matriliny that was not genuine, like that of the Nairs, but in imitation of them.[64]

---

[58] Menon A. Sreedhara (ed.), *Kozhikode District Gazetteer* (Trivandrum: Superintendent of Government Press, 1962), 228.

[59] Andreas Haberbeck, "Muslims Customs and The Courts (Application of Customary Laws to Mappillas of North Malabar, Khojas and Cutchi Memons)," *Journal of the Indian Law Institute* 24:1 (1982), 132–58.

[60] Census of India 1891, Travancore vol 1 (London: Her Majesty's Stationary office, 1893), 252.

[61] Robin Jeffrey, "Legacies of Matriliny: The Place of Women and the 'Kerala Model'," *Pacific Affairs* 77:4 (2004), 649.

[62] G. Arunima, *There Comes Papa: Colonialism and the transformation of matriliny in Kerala, Malabar, c.1850–1940*, New Delhi: Orient Longman, 2003; Joseph and Elzy Tharamngalam, "Capitalism and Patriarchy: The Transformation of Matrilineal System in Kerala," International congress on Kerala studies, Thiruvananthapuram, 1994.

[63] The Ezhava, the largest Hindu community—also known as Chovas or Chokons—are based in Central Travancore, and the Thiyyar or Tiyyas in the Malabar region. They used to work as agricultural labourers, small-scale cultivators, and toddy tappers.

[64] A. Aiyappan, "Fraternal Polyandry in Malabar," *Man in India* 15 (1935), 111–2; Filippo and Caroline Osella, Social Mobility in Kerala (London: Pluto, 2000), 85.

Robin Jeffrey, without considering the matrilineal nature of tribal groups, reached the conclusion that matriliny in Kerala did not date from prehistoric times. According to him, it developed around the eleventh century C.E., possibly as a result of a prolonged war between the Chera and Chola dynasties and their subordinates; but whatever the origins, matrilineal practices were firmly established—particularly among the Nair caste—by the time Europeans began arriving regularly on the Kerala coast in the 1500s.[65] Jeffrey mentions that Pattam A Thanu Pillai (1885–1970), twice Chief Minister of Kerala, and Mannath Padmanabhan (1878–1970), founder of the NSS (Nair Service Society), had Brahmin fathers. Daughters grew up to receive their men in their own family home, while their brothers visited women of appropriate status in their houses. The system linked the Nairs to Brahmin religious authorities, who were sometimes great landlords, and Kshatriyas, who visited women of Nair houses. It is therefore evident that the Nair community were, in many cases, polyandrous, and the absence of identifiable fathers became a burning issue for their families. G. Arunima referred to this as a clarion call for the end of matriliny.[66]

European missionaries and British government servants in India derided the "quaint and immoral" practice of matriliny.[67] Robin Jeffrey cites a letter from Oomen Mamen to the Secretary of the CMS, dated 21 September 1867: "The high caste females are grossly immoral as they don't know the sanctity of marriage."[68] In the "ideal type," women of the house were visited by males from other Nair families, or by Brahmins or Kshatriyas. In an example much relished by audiences today, a man who was no longer wanted would find his sleeping mat and personal effects left outside the door of the house where he was accustomed to visiting, signalling the relationship was over.[69] In 1896, in the course of attempts to modify the law of matriliny, P. Thanu Pillai had no qualms of conscience in levelling the reproach: "Your wives are concubines, and your sons are bastards."[70]

---

[65] Robin Jeffrey, *Politics, Women, and Well-being: How Kerala became 'a Model'* (London: Palgrave Macmillan, 1992), 24–5.

[66] Arunima, *There Comes Papa*, 2.

[67] T K Gopal Panikkar, *Malabar and Its Folk*, Madras, 1900; Augusta M. Blandford, The Land of the Conch Shell (London: CEZMS, 1901), 39.

[68] Jeffrey, *Politics, Women and Well-Being*, 654.

[69] Jeffrey, "Legacies of Matriliny," 469.

[70] P. Thanu Pillai, "Travancore Council, 20 June 1896," *Travancore Government Gazette* vol 34, no. 25, June 1896.

96   A. PANAKKAL

André Wink also reconfirmed this matricentric culture as taboo in these words:

> They have ensured themselves of a spouse in the harbours which they frequented, and this was of extra importance in Malabar on account of the strong taboos on commensality which developed here among the Hindus. The women with whom such marriages were contracted were often, if not always, of low fishermen and mariner castes. Their offspring multiplied in the harbour towns and belonged to the mother, in conformity to the matriarchal custom of Malabar, but was raised in Sunni Islam.[71]

Issues of polyandry and unidentified fathers were seldom discussed in Muslim matrilineal families. Focusing on these issues was therefore a misguided interpretation from scholars who had a monochromic view of the system, one that focused only on Nair societies and tried to view all others through the same lens. Concerns about caste-based concubines were taken as typical of the larger case of Hindu women generally. Meanwhile, even Hindu women from other societies and castes enjoyed the benefits of matriliny without the drawbacks of keeping many men and difficulties in identifying their own children's father. The matrilineal system was considered to be an acceptable custom among traditional Muslims and Hindu groups in which women were respected and kept legally identified single husbands in their homes. Kathleen Gough also mentioned that Muslim traders put an end to endogamy in the region.[72]

INTEGRATED FAMILY CUSTOMS AND CULTURES

The matrilineal system emerged and developed among South Indian Muslim communities as a result of the incorporation of the local ethos into Islamic culture. This flourished and was supported by later generations as part of their family traditions, and came to be seen as an active model for living in diversity. Women held positions of prominence in these matrilineal Muslim families; the highest female authority was the *karanavatthi*—the eldest and most powerful woman in the family—who wielded power in economic and social decisions, and even in ritual actions related to the *tharavad*. In coastal towns of Malabar, Muslims and other

---

[71] Wink, *Al Hind*, 72.
[72] Gough, "Mappila North Kerala," 418–9.

CULTURAL AND SOCIAL INTEGRATIONS IN MATRILINEAL, MATRIARCHAL... 97

communities lived in the same locality, even in adjacent houses, mingling and dining freely with each other. Women attended educational centres such as the *othu palli*, traditional schools where pupils learned the basics of religion as well as ritual practices, run by female teachers known as *mullachis*. The public had great respect for women scholars as well as female heads of families, and admired their leadership, scholarship, and contributions to society.

Cultural integration was also reflected in matrilineal houses, which adapted traditional architecture to suit the climate, using available building materials and the craftsmanship of traditional builders to create a comfortable living space for the matrilineal family group. There were three patterns of matrilineal houses among the Muslim as well as the Hindu communities of Malabar, depending on their financial status as lower class, middle class, or aristocracy. Muslims and non-Muslims built the same type of houses, choosing from one of these three designs according to their fiscal situation. Aristocratic houses followed unique old patterns, sticking strictly to the conventional *vastu* architecture. Built in the style of *nalukettu* and *ettukettu*, the traditional ancestral houses of Malabar consisted of a *padippura*, a gate house, and a long *varanda*, the legacies of traditional regional architecture. The long-established Muslim *tharavads* were replicas of conventional Hindu houses and were all built strictly following traditional *vastu* style, suiting the environment of the region, and with rooms called by the same names. Muslim houses reserved specific places for ritual purposes with built-in platforms on either side of the entrance in the open area between the *kolaya* and *naduvakam*—the central hall of the house—for performing traditional ritual arts such as rateeb, mawlid, and so on.

These large houses, normally with two storeys and a wooden staircase to the second floor, were designed to accommodate matrilocal customs and include an *arras*—a luxurious private bedroom or leisure area for visiting husbands. Residents of the house normally paid much respect to the *puthiyapla* (bridegroom) who remained and was considered as the respected guest of the family forever. The central courtyard area of the house normally had a square opening on the roof that allowed some natural wind inside the house, keeping it cool, which was naturally adapted to the special climatic seasons of Malabar; the architectural style thus represents the integration of the traditional Malabar house with the Muslim way of life.

In a matrilocal system, the husband is given a special room in the wife's house, with all facilities. He enjoys breakfast in this special room, his wife serving him or the mother-in-law taking care to make him happy. In the middle-class house, all these are arranged on a single floor, and they live according to the space, family status, and regional social situation. Middle-class houses are rectangular in shape, but a miniature of the same architectural structure with single-floor facilities. They also contain an *arras*, or bedroom, with available facilities. Lower classes of the community also followed prevailing local matrilineal practices. In the matrilineal system, the ceremony of *arayilakkal*[73] is an important event in the bride's house. On the wedding night, the bride is led to the bridal chamber, accompanied by *oppana* singers, while the bridegroom, with his close relatives and friends, is served a delicious dinner known as *thakkaram*. Some families find this an important and prestigious event, and the tradition lives on as a result of the desire to maintain a link down the generations through such ceremonies and feasts. During my field study in the South Pacific on the "cultural moorings of Malabar," I was able to meet people who were proudly hosting a *thakkaram* in their house for their daughter's new husband. Zulaikha Khthoon, for example, a mother from the Fijian Malabar community who now lives with her family in Melbourne, Australia, feels a strong pride in the Malabar tradition. She told me that she would hold a *thakkaram* for her eldest daughter in the same elegant fashion that her parents had for her.

There were numerous *puthiyaplas* (bridegrooms) in the various villages of the Kannur district. Muhammed Abdulrahman Nalu Purappadil Puthiyapurayil from Madayi, one of the oldest port towns, talked about the last buses carrying matrilocal husbands to various villages; they were known locally as the "*Puthiyapla* bus." In the modern context, it is sometimes argued that the matrilineal system in Malabar originates with the phenomenon of male migration for work; this is a groundless argument, however, as a great number of men from patrilineal societies also migrate for the same reason.[74]

There was a drastic change in the authoritarian structure of Nair families after the declining prominence of the *tharavad* in the early twentieth century. The administration of the *tharavad* was reduced in importance to the role of sexual procreation, and away from an active role in various ways

---

[73] During this ceremony, the bridegroom is officially taken to *maniyara* (bridal chamber) accompanied by significant people, with traditional arts performed by friends and relatives.

[74] Collected from interviews of various matrilineal networks.

of social reproduction.[75] There was also an attempt to curb the matrilineal nature of Muslim family structure as a result of the so-called Salafi "reforms," which curtailed women's rights and limited them to household activities and childcare.[76]

'REFORMATION' TO CURB MATRILINEAL ISLAM

The Wahhābī-Salafi "reformers" condemned traditional Malabar Muslims for integrating traditional customs into their religious practice, labelling them "folk worshippers" and considering them provincial and parochial. With the backing of the British, the Wahhābī-Salafi movement was highly critical of the integration and indigenisation of Islam in the region, calling traditional Islam "un-Islamic" and denouncing local Muslim customs as "aberrant" and "unethical." From the last quarter of the nineteenth century onwards, these "reformists" campaigned against local practices and admonished Malabar Muslims to revert to the "real Islam," becoming increasingly prominent by the early twentieth century.

Sanulla Makti Thangal (1847–1912) was considered to be the "forerunner of reformists" by followers of Salafi-Wahhābī movements.[77] Unlike other later "reformists," he was proud of his family's lineage, which could be traced back to the Prophet, although as a "reformist" he was more inclined to texts than to traditions.[78] Inspired by the desire to "decontaminate" Islam in the region, he published a journal *Nabinanayam* from Cochin,[79] and established a printing press—the Muḥammadiya Press—based in Aleppey. He used this printing press to issue numerous pamphlets condemning the *marumakkathayam* matrilineal traditions of the Malabar Muslims, which he considered to be relics of Hindu culture. As he saw it, Muslims were continuing to follow these traditions when even the Hindus had realised the discrimination inherent in the matrilineal system and considered it an injustice that a man could be required to leave the family

---

[75] Arunima, G. (2003). *There Comes Papa: Colonialism and the transformation of matriliny in Kerala, Malabar c. 1850–1940.* Hyderabad: Orient Longman, pp. 53, 56.

[76] The Salafi movement was described as *iṣlāḥī*, meaning reformist, even though it had an extremely negative impact on the freedom of women.

[77] K.K. Muhamad Abdul Kareem, *Makti Thangalude Sampoorna Krithikal*, (Tirur: Kerala Islamic Mission, 1981), 9–16.

[78] K.K. Muhamad Abdul Kareem, *Sayid Sanaulla Makti Tangal*, (Tirur: Kerala Islamic Mission, 1981), 19, Maktih Thangal, *Nabi Nanayam*, 2–3.

[79] *Nabinanayam* means "the Prophet's coin."

home by his wife or father-in-law. In his own words, based on a strongly patriarchal worldview: "Be ashamed of permitting wives to act as husbands. A man cannot allow this system, which goes against human nature itself."[80] Makti Thangal's biography even records him saying, in a sermon at Shaduli mosque in Koothumparamba, that "animals would not follow a matrilineal system, and the admirers of this practice would never be entitled to the benevolence of God and the Prophet."[81]

Makti Thangal opposed women's education, recommending that they should only be instructed in obligatory Islamic knowledge—*ʿilm al-farḍ*, or *farḍ al-ʿayn*—in an article written to counter the arguments of Moosakutty (d. 1930), who supported women's empowerment through both secular and religious education.[82] Later, he revised his views somewhat, accepting that women had the right to an education provided it did not go beyond the limits of *sharīʿa*, and even agreeing that boys and girls could study together at mixed schools.[83] This argument was a result of his alliance with the colonial powers, who also considered matrilineal traditions "un-Islamic," and he went on to admonish his supporters to accept colonial rule, claiming that "separatist demands were pointless, rebellious, and disloyal to the colonial Government."[84]

Salafi influence also reached Lakshadweep and started negating traditional practices of the islands. Kerala Nadvathul Mujahideen, a Salafi organisation founded in 1952, opened branches in Lakshadweep and brought out publications questioning the tradition of *Futūhāt al-Jazāʾir* and litanies such as the Māla and Mawlids. The Saudi-trained Fathahudheen SM Koya argued effusively against the traditional practices and litanies and branded them as "un-Islamic."[85] Koya made these contentions—roughly based on general descriptions available in English and Malayalam, without

---

[80] K.K. Muhamad Abdul Kareem, *Maktih Thangal, Parkaleetha Porkalam, Makthi Thangalude Sampoorna Krithikal* (Calicut: Vachamam Books, 2015), 224–5.

[81] Abdul Kareem, *Sayid Sanaulla Makti Tangal*, 48.

[82] In Makti Thangal's article, *Nareenarabhichari*, he argued that women were created solely for the pleasure of men; Moosakutty responded with counter-arguments in *Swadeshabhimani*, to which Makti Thangal replied with two further articles (Muhamed, *Maktih Thangal*, 924–5).

[83] This article was titled *Rajyabhakhthiyum Desabhimanavum* ("Loyalty and Patriotism").

[84] Muhamed, *Maktih Thangal*, 726.

[85] Fathahudheen SM Koya, *Lakshadweepum and Ubayd Allāhyum* (Kavarathi: Kerala Nadvathul Mujahideen, Kavaratti Branch, 2000).

seeing a copy of the *Futūhāt al-Jazāᵓir* manuscript[86]—in his first book, prepared using extremely shaky evidence, in which he commented on the prominent Muslim rulers of Arackal who controlled the islands.[87]

Colonial Laws Against "un-Islamic" Matrilineal Practices

British documents from the colonial period show an unequivocal attempt to realign the matrilineal, matriarchal, and matrilocal Muslim communities in the region. Gazette records show that the British aimed to destroy the matrilineal and matriarchal Muslim way of life, labelling it "un-Islamic" and curtailing female-centric family practices as well as property possession. There was no desire for change within the community itself: the unique nature of Muslim family life in the region demonstrated the merits of woman-centric structures, and the traditions were supported by male as well as female members. Women, as owners of the family land and property, enjoyed more prestigious positions, but men found satisfaction in their own roles and in the safety the system accorded their female relatives. Nevertheless, the colonial rulers sought to uproot the integrated woman-centric Muslim family on the basis of unintegrated Arab-centric Islamic texts and culture, resulting in the fragmentation of societal cohesion.

The British considered the matrilineal organisation of property rights and inheritance to be "corrupt" from the religious perspective. As Charles Alexander Innes (1874–1959), a settlement officer in Malabar and deputy secretary to the British Government, wrote in one report: "In North Malabar Mappilas as a rule follow the *marumakathayam* system of inheritance, though it is opposed to the precepts of the Koran."[88] They therefore took steps to change the traditional system by implementing Anglo-Muhammadan law, curtailing the freedom of Muslim women to own property. This legal framework was based on the misguided and patriarchal assumption that Arab culture was the essence of Islam, and ignored the fact that Islamic law allows customary rights and freedom to women. It was also a pretext for the extension of colonial powers, clear from the fact that similar legislation was applied to non-Muslim woman-centric

---

[86] Fathahudheen SM Koya, *Mahanmaraya Awliyakkalum Anthroth Dweepum* (Ernakulam: Thaha Book Centre, 1996), 10.

[87] Koya, *Mahanmaraya Awliyakkalum Anthroth Dweepum*, 50.

[88] Innes, *Madras District Gazeteers*, 198.

cultures: restrictions on matrilineal traditions were also imposed on other communities, such as the Ezhava, who saw their traditional practices reorganised by the colonial powers.[89]

Some of the first legislative steps taken by the British government were to codify customary laws through the Malabar Marriage Act of 1896 and the Malabar Will Act of 1898, both imposing legislation to shore up existing matrilineal practices.[90] The Malabar Marriage Act permitted the registration of *sambandham*[91] as a legal marriage in response to the recommendations of Malabar Marriage Commission of 1891, but this did not affect Muslim communities, who practised *marumakkathayam* and never observed *sambandham*, which was outside their religious framework. The Malabar Will Act declared the testamentary power of persons governed by the *marumakkathayam* law of inheritance and provided rules for the execution, corroboration, revocation, and revival of their wills, enabling those who followed matrilineal traditions to bequeath their property as they wished. These Acts, unlike later legislation, did not attempt to curb the power of the region's remarkable woman-centric social customs.

Based on Anglo-Muhammadan legislation, the Mappila Succession Act came into existence in 1918.[92] The first phase emerged as part of public litigation regarding intermarriage between matrilineal and patriarchal families, addressing regulations concerning their various customs in the division of ancestral properties.[93] The Tellicherry court expressed its discontent about the existing system as early as 1861: in some instances, when women from a matrilineal family background married a man from a patrilineal family, clashes arose between the two family systems.[94] As a result, the administration attempted to codify the laws by means of an

---

[89] Meera Velayudhan, "Reform, law and gendered identity: Marriage among Ezhavas of Kerala," *Economic and Political Weekly* 33:38, 1998; J. Devika, "The Aesthetic Woman: Re-forming Female Bodies and Minds in Early Twentieth-Century Keralam," *Modern Asian Studies* 39:2 (2005), 461–87.

[90] Jeffrey, "Matriliny, Women, Development—and a Typographic Error," 15–25.

[91] Sambandham was defined in Act IV of Malabar Marriage Act, 1896, as an alliance or cohabit or intend to cohabit as husband and wife between a man and a woman in accordance with the custom of their communities.

[92] Indian Law Reports 16 (Madras, 1892), 201.

[93] L. R. S. Lakshmi, *The Malabar Muslims: A different Perspective* (New Delhi: India Foundation Books, 2012), 50.

[94] H. M. A. Wigram, *A Commentary on Malabar Law and Custom* (Madras: Granes, Cookson and Co., 1882), 153; Lewis Moore, *Malabar Law and Custom* (Madras: Higginotham & Co., 1905), 324.

CULTURAL AND SOCIAL INTEGRATIONS IN MATRILINEAL, MATRIARCHAL... 103

"Islamification" that curtailed the rights that women enjoyed according to local custom.[95] In response, local Muslims petitioned the courts to protest the erosion of their way of life; a number of similar petitions written in the vernacular are found in the Tellicherry litigation records collected by Herman Gundert (1814–1893).

The Mappila Succession Act was the first of three pieces of legislation established between 1918 and 1939 to impose a more "Islamic" legal framework on Muslim families, and was followed by the Mappila Wills Act of 1928 and the Mappila Marumakkathayam Act of 1939. These laws accelerated the process of the Arabisation of Islam in the subcontinent, to the detriment of the integrated nature of Islam that had enriched co-existence in Malabar society for centuries. The Mappila Marumakkathayam Act of 1939 abolished women's customary rights over their property and family life, and legalised the partition of joint property of the family on formal request by a majority of family members. This was followed by the implementation of laws to regulate matrilineal kinship property rights in the non-Muslim communities of Malabar, who were considered to be the originators of the system.

Anglo-Muhammadan law affected various aspects of the lives of matri-lineal Muslims of the region. The Muslim Personal Law Act of 1937 became the definitive legislative framework for all Muslims throughout India,[96] with Section Two stating: "Notwithstanding any custom or usage to the contrary in matters involving inheritance, marriage, dissolution, financial maintenance, dower, gifts and other matters of personal status and finance, the deciding rule in cases where the parties are Muslim shall be the Muslim Personal Law Act, 1937."[97] Centuries-old matrilineal tradi-tions were thus set aside as a result of the combined power of the colonial ideology and the Arab-centric Salafi religious "reform" movement. These self-declared "reformists" were not prepared to accept the existing local Muslim matrilineal system; religious clergy influenced by Salafi thought claimed that matrilineal customs were "un-Islamic," and manipulated the Legislative Assembly to pass a bill—The Mappilla Marumakkathayam (Amendment) Act of 1963—specifying that property inheritance must pass through the male lineage. The Salafi-based reform movements were

---

[95] Joseph Skariya, *Thalasseri Rekhakal*, Kottayam: D.C. Books, 1998.

[96] Anver M. Emon, "Conceiving Islamic law in a Pluralist Society: History, Politics and Multicultural Jurisprudence" *Singapore Journal of Legal Studies* (2006), 342.

[97] The Muslim Personal Law Application Act, 1937, Act No. XXVI of 1937.

supported by further legislation, eroding the cultural benefits of woman-centric Islam and its integrated practices in the region. Far from constituting real "reform," these legislations legitimised a backward form of patriarchy that deprived women of their basic rights and brought drastic upheaval to the entire community, particularly in cases when properties had been owned exclusively by women.

The matrilineal system persisted despite the influence of this law, however; although under the Salafi influence some families restructured themselves to fit the new ethos of male supremacy. Other Malabar Muslim families, however, maintained their matrilineal practices without being swayed by the imported Arab-centric unilateral Islam. Though the law reined in matriarchal benefits, fiscal dominance, and property possession, matrifocal culture was maintained through keeping the ancestral home as the bedrock of family life and using the provision of *waqf* to ensure that it continued to be passed down the female line. Time has proved that it is not easy to discard centuries-old matrilineal traditions from the lives of Malabar Muslims through the imposition of new legislation; it is a way of being innate to the people of the region.

In my own research I collected the family trees of matrilineal joint families and reviewed documents related to property ownership, and found examples of those who prefer to maintain their ancestral prestige by bestowing ownership of the *tharavad* on female members of the family. The elder male family members ensure that their family properties are transferred to women, sacrificing their own legal ownership rights. One of the family trees from the Madayi area had been prepared by Abdu Rahiman Nalu Purappadil Puthiya Purayil, whose family name has been passed down through the female line: his mother Aleema, grandmother Nafeesa, and great-grandmother Mariyam all carry the name Nalu Purappadil Puthiya Purayil. This family tree reveals the matrilineage of Abdu Rahiman, who is proud of maintaining the woman-centric traditions of his culture, ensuring that his own son is also part of a matrilineage through taking his mother's name. He built a house for his wife on land that she owned in her name; it is this male pride in matrilineal tradition that preserves the family bond as durable and resilient. Family men like Abdu Rahiman believe that it is a duty and obligation to build their wives a house that will become part of property owned by her lineage. Another example came from the Saidammadakath family, who claim to be descendants of the Kunjalimarakkar. Their family name is derived from the term Shaheedanmarakath, which means "martyr's house." Examining the documents related to their family land, registered in 1976 and 1991, I found that they were all in the name of Biyythutty Umma, the female head of the family. Even though this did not come under the *waqf* system, male family members had made the decision that the house should belong to the eldest women of the family. Such documents show that women's ownership of property has continued, thanks to the generous support of male family members in keeping the female-centric family traditions alive.

It is clear that the British administrators made deliberate attempts to conceal their endeavours to curtail women's right through implementing law against the matrilineal system of inheritance and kinship. William Logan, an officer of the British government, exemplified the attitudes of the colonial rulers. In his history of the Malabar Coast, he works on the assumption that indigenous people were following *marumakkathayam* long before they embraced Islam, and that early Muslim settlers in north Malabar changed their existing inheritance laws in order to fit into the local community. He therefore argued that *marumakkathayam* traditions were a later adoption for the Muslims in the region, and the Anglo-Muhammadan Law represented a return to true Islamic tradition and practice. To prove his case, Logan cited the example of the Nambuthiris from Payyannur in North Malabar, where *marumakkathayam* prevailed. Hindu Brahmin immigrants from the north had been permitted to settle there on the condition that they adopted the *marumakkathayam* law.[98] This example was flawed, however, since Muslim settlers in Malabar and elsewhere along the coast had never been obliged to follow the traditions of *marumakkathayam*, but had naturally integrated it into their way of life. The matrilineal practices of Malabar Muslims were not incorporated at a later date, as Logan argued, but formed an intrinsic part of the culture. Logan's argument is now understood to have been a misguided attempt to conceal the British rulers' misogynistic attack on women's rights, which had previously been upheld under the *marumakkathayam* system.

Later researchers such as Kathleen Gough were also influenced by the prevailing colonial discourse. In her discussion of the Nair and Tiyyars, she suggested that the disintegration of matrilineal groups was a social trend among Muslim families in the region—yet the very fact that matrilineal, matrilocal, and matrifocal culture continues to thrive decades after

---

[98] William Logan, *A collection of Treaties, Engagements and other papers of importance relating to British Affairs in Malabar* (Calicut: Minerva Press, 1879), 272.

legislation was passed to suppress it is evidence that this analysis was flawed.[99] Some Muslim historians, too, have described the *marumakkathayam* as un-Islamic and argue that the matrilineal Arackal system is against *sharīʿa*, in many cases unaware that they were adopting a colonial perspective. S. M. Mohamed Koya also argued that the region was seeing a gradual shift from matriliny to patriliny, continuing over decades, although the reality of life in the region today makes it clear that matrilineal Muslim culture has in no way been eradicated, despite almost a century of legislation against it.[100]

Conclusion

Matrilineal Islamic practices were accepted and adopted by early Muslim scholars and the leaders of Malabar. In more recent times, however, Salafi, Wahhābī, and other political Islamist movements attacked the distinctive nature of matrilineal Islam and labelled its practices "un-Islamic." Rather than supporting woman-centric Islam in matrilineal Muslim communities, they excluded incorporated practices, classifying them as heretical. This attitude was mirrored by the British colonial powers, who sought to legislate against matrilineal culture.

The Muslims of Malabar succeeded in countering the assault on their traditions through adopting the practice of *waqf* in relation to Friday property custom that was in use on the Lakshadweep Islands. There was a strong call to force a change in lifestyles, food habits, dress codes, and even architecture to reflect Arab models, rather than accepting the integrated and centuries-old vernacular Islam. In this context it is important to note that even before the advent of Islam in the region there had been considerable interaction with Arab traders, who used to spend months there as part of the monsoon navigation. Cultural integration was promoted rather than an inflexible single tradition; this prevented any feeling of alienation and helped matrilineal culture to flourish in diversity. It is also important to emphasise that the matrilineal structures of Lakshadweep are deep-rooted, extending, for example, to customs around the succession of Muslim jurists.

---

[99] Gough, "Mappila North Kerala," 432.
[100] S.M. Mohamed Koya, "Matriliny and Malabar Muslims," *Proceedings of the Indian History Congress* 40 (1979), 419–31.

This study has provided a review of the legal and social integration of matrilineal culture in the Lakshadweep and the Malabar region, and differs from early studies which suggested that the matrilineal traditions of Lakshadweep were an adaptation of those from the mainland. In both these Muslim communities, the centrality of women was unambiguously visible in their amalgamation of matrilineal, matrifocal, and matriarchal traditions. Every aspect of life—including inheritance rights, property ownership, marriage, the raising of children, control over production, and policy-making—involved women at some level. Men seldom made decisions without consulting them, and legal terminology developed to shore up the traditional family structure. These matrilineal Indian Muslim societies made every effort to preserve their cultural heritage in the face of opposition from patriarchal and colonial legislation, and men from the communities were glad to sacrifice the privileges granted them by law in order to uphold their integrated family traditions.

BIBLIOGRAPHY

Abdul Kareem, K.K. Muhamad, *Sayid Sanaulla Makti Tangal*, Tirur: Kerala Islamic Mission, 1981a.

Abdul Kareem, K.K. Muhamad, *Makti Thangalude Sampoorna Krithikal*, Tirur: Kerala Islamic Mission, 1981b.

Abdul Kareem, K.K. Muhamad, *Maktih Thangal, Parkaleetha Porkalam, Makthi Thangalude Sampoorna Krithikal*, Calicut: Vachamam Books, 2015.

Aiyappan, A, "Fraternal Polyandry in Malabar," *Man in India* 14 (1935), 108–18.

Arunima, G., *There comes papa: Colonialism and the transformation of matriliny in Kerala, Malabar, c.1850–1940*, New Delhi: Orient Longman, 2003.

Blandford, Augusta M., *The Land of the Conch Shell*, London: CEZMS, 1901.

Caldwell, Robert, *A Comparative Grammar of the Dravidian or South Indian Family of Languages*, London: Trubner and co., 1875.

Census of India 1891, Travancore vol 1, London: Her Majesty's Stationary office, 1893.

Chand, Tara, *Influence of Islam on Indian Culture*, Allahabad: The Indian Press Limited, 1936.

Devika, J., "The Aesthetic Woman: Re-forming Female Bodies and Minds in Early Twentieth-Century Keralam," *Modern Asian Studies* 39:2 (2005), 461–87.

D'Souza, Victor S., "Status groups among the Moplahs on the West Coast of India," in Imtiaz Ahmad (ed.), *Caste and social stratification among Muslims in India*, Delhi: Manohar, 1978.

108   A. PANAKKAL

D'Souza, Victor S., "Kinship Organization and Marriage Customs among Moplahs on the South West Coast of India," in Imtiaz Ahmad (ed.), *Family, Kinship and Marriage among Muslims in India*, New Delhi: Manohar Books, 1976.

Dube, Leela, *Matriliny and Islam: Religion and society in the Laccadives*, Delhi: National Publishing House, 1969.

Dube, Leela, "Who Gains from matriliny? Men, Women and Change on a Lakshadweep Island," *Sociological Bulletin* 42:1 (1993), 15–36.

Ellis, Francis Whyte, *Dissertation the Second on the Malayalma Language*, 1815.

Emon, Anver M., "Conceiving Islamic law in a pluralist society: History, politics and multicultural jurisprudence," *Singapore Journal of Legal Studies* (2006), 331–55.

Fernandez, Armesto F., *Pathfinders: A Global History of Exploration*, London: Oxford University Press, 2006.

Firminger, Walter Kelly, *Fifth Report from the Select committee on the Affairs of the Indian Company*, Vol. 8, Calcutta: R. Cambray, 1917.

Friedmann, Yohanan, "Qiṣṣat Shakarwatī Farmāḍ: A Tradition concerning the Introduction of Islam to Malabar," *Israel Oriental Studies* 5 (1975), 233–58.

Fuller, C.J., *The Nayars Today*, Cambridge: Cambridge University Press, 1976

Ganesh, K. N. (ed.), *Culture and modernity: Historical explorations*, Calicut: Calicut University Press, 2004.

Gough, Kathleen, "Changing Kinship Usages in the Setting Up of Political and Economic Change among Nayars of Malabar," *Journal of Royal institute of Great Britain and Ireland* 82:1 (1952), 71–88.

Gough, Kathleen, "Mappila North Kerala," in David M. Schneider and Kathleen Gough (eds.), *Matrilineal Kinship* (Berkley and Los Angeles: University of California Press, 1962), 415–41.

Gundert, Hermann, *Keralolpatti—Origin of Malabar*, Mangalore: Basel Mission Press, 1868.

Haberbeck, Andreas, "Muslims Customs and The Courts (Application of Customary Laws to Mappillas of North Malabar, Khojas and Cutchi Memons)," *Journal of the Indian Law Institute* 24:1 (1982), 132–58.

Hage, Per, "Was Proto-Oceanic society matrilineal?" *Journal of the Polynesian Society* 107:1 (1998), 365–79.

Haurani, G., *Arab Seafaring in the Indian Ocean in Ancient and Early Mediaeval Times*, Princeton: Princeton University Press, 1951.

Ibn Battuta, *The travels of Ibn Battuta in Asia and Africa*, vol. 4, ed. H. A. R. Gibb, Cambridge: Cambridge University Press, 1962.

Innes, C. A., *Madras District Gazetteers, Malabar and Anjengo*, Madras: Government Press, 1908.

Jeffrey, Robin, 'Matriliny, women, development—and a typographic error', *Pacific Affairs* 63:3 (1990), 375.

Jeffrey, Robin, *Politics, Women and Well-Being: How Kerala Became "a Model"*, New Delhi: Oxford University Press, 2001.

Jeffrey, Robin, "Legacies of Matriliny: The Place of Women and the 'Kerala Model'", *Pacific Affairs* 77:4 (2004), 469.

Kottakkunnummal, Manaf, "Indigenous customs and colonial law: contestations in religion, gender and family among matrilineal Mappila Muslims in colonial Malabar, Kerala, c. 1910–1928," Sage Open, January 2014.

Koya, S.M. Mohammed, "Matriliny and Malabar Muslims," *Proceedings of the Indian History Congress* 40 (1979), 419–31.

Koya, S.M. Mohammed, *Mappilas of Malabar*, Calicut: University of Calicut, 1983.

Koya, S.M. Mohammed, "Survival of a social institution: Matriliny among the Mappilas", in K. N. Ganesh (ed.), *Culture and modernity: Historical explorations* (Calicut: Calicut University Press, 2004).

Koya, S.M. Fathahudheen, *Mahanmaraya Awliyakkalum Anthroth Dweepum*, Ernakulam: Thaha Book Centre, 1996.

Koya, S.M. Fathahudheen, *Lakshadweepum and Ubayd Allāhyum*, Kavarathi: Kerala Nadvathul Mujahideen, 2000.

Kurup, K.K.N., *The Ali Rajas of Cannanore*, Trivandrum: College Book House, 1975.

Kutty, A.R., *Marriage and kinship in an island society*, Delhi: National Publishing House, 1972.

Lakshmi, L. R. S., *The Malabar Muslims: A different Perspective*, New Delhi: India Foundation Books, 2012.

Logan, William, *A collection of Treaties, Engagements and other papers of importance relating to British Affairs in Malabar*, Calicut: Minerva Press, 1879.

Mailaparambil, Binu John, *Lords of the Sea: The Ali Rajas of Cannanore and the Political Economy of Malabar (1663–1723)*, Leiden: Brill, 2012.

Moore, Lewis, *Malabar law and custom*, Madras: Higginbotham and Co., 1905.

Major, Richard Henry, *India in the fifteenth century: being a collection of narratives of voyages to India, in the century preceding the Portuguese discovery of the Cape of Good Hope*, London: Hakluyt Society, 1857.

Miller, Ronald E., *Mappila Muslims of Kerala: A Study in Islamic Trends*, Bombay: Orient Longman, 1976.

Muthukoya, N., *Lakshadweep Noottanudkaliloode*, Kottayam: Vidyarthi Mithram Book Depot, 1986.

Osella, Filippo and Caroline, *Social Mobility in Kerala*, London: Pluto, 2000.

Panakkal, Abbas, "Beypūṛinum Sūrinum Idayil," *Gulf Focus* 2:2 (2015), 28–34.

Panikkar, T.K. Gopal, *Malabar and Its Folk*, Madras: 1900.

Panikkar, K.M., "Some Aspects of Nayar Life," *Journal of the Royal Anthropological Institute* 48 (1918), 254–93.

Pillai, P. Thanu, "Travencore Council, 20 June 1896," *Travancore Government Gazette* vol 34, no. 25, June 1896.

110   A. PANAKKAL

Pookoya, P.I., *Dweepolpathi: an up-to-date history of Laccadive, Minicoy and Amindivi Islands*, Calicut: Falcon Press, 1960.

Seethi, Saheb K.M., *The Muslims of Kerala and the Marumakkathayam Law*, Cochin: Kerala Muslim Directory, 1960.

Sidebotham, Steven E., *Berenike and the Ancient Maritime Spice Route*, Berkeley, CA: University of California Press, 2011.

Skariya, Joseph, *Thalasseri Rekhakal*, Kottayam: D. C. Books, 1998.

Sreedhara, Menon A. (ed.), *Kozhikode District Gazetteer*, Trivandrum: Superintendent of Government Press, 1962.

Tharamngalam, Joseph and Elzy, "Capitalism and Patriarchy: The Transformation of Matrilineal Systems in Kerala", International congress on Kerala studies, Thiruvananthapuram, 1994.

Velayudhan, Meera, "Reform, law and gendered identity: Marriage among Ezhavas of Kerala," *Economic and Political Weekly* 33:38, 1998.

Wigram, H. M. A., *A commentary on Malabar law and custom*, Madras: Granes, Cookson and Co., 1882.

Wink, André, *Al-Hind: The making of the Indo-Islamic world, vol. I. Early medieval India and the expansion of Islam, 7th-11th centuries*, Leiden: Brill, 1990.

MANUSCRIPTS

Anonymous, *Qiṣṣat Shakarwati Farmad*, British Library MS, IO, Islamic 2807d.

Anonymous, *Mawlid* of *Mumb Maulā* (Manuscript not listed).

Qāḍī Abū Bakr bin ʿUbayd Allāh, *Futūḥāt al-Jazāʾir*, Madin Manuscript Library, Malappuram.

Makhdum II, *Tuhfat al Mujahidin*, British Library, MS. IO Islamic 2807e.

PART II

Northeast Asia

Affective Matrivocality and Women's Voices: A History of Muslim Women Writers in China

Jing Wang

INTRODUCTION

While China has a long tradition of "Han Chinese patriarchy" defined by the patrilineal Confucian order,[1] scholars have become increasingly aware of the unique heritage of matriliny and matrifocality among ethnic minorities. Two of the most distinctive cases of gender egalitarianism can be

[1] Shanshan Du, "Gender Norms among Ethnic Minorities: Beyond '(Han) Chinese Patriarchy'", in *Handbook on Ethnic Minorities in China* (Cheltenham, UK: Edward Elgar Publishing, 2016), 240–62.

J. Wang (✉)
School of Journalism and Mass Communication, University of Wisconsin-Madison, Madison, WI, USA
e-mail: jingwang.media@proton.me

© The Author(s), under exclusive license to Springer Nature Switzerland AG 2024
A. Panakkal, N. M. Arif (eds.), *Matrilineal, Matriarchal, and Matrifocal Islam*, Palgrave Series in Islamic Theology, Law, and History, https://doi.org/10.1007/978-3-031-51749-5_4

found among the Lahu and Mosuo communities in Southwest China.[2] Both the Lahu and Mosuo communities highlight the role of mothers or the mother-uncle relationship, which form the foundation for the preservation of matrilineal lineage. Moreover, the compatibility of religion and matriliny has also been observed among ethnic minorities such as the Lahu, the Bai, and the Zhuang.[3] The Lahu, for instance, use the symbolism from Mahayana Buddhism to promote gender equality and the bond between husband and wife.[4] Hui Muslims in Central China also have a long tradition of women's mosques based on the idea of "gender cooperation" and complementarity.[5]

In this chapter, I mainly focus on Hui Muslim women through what I call "matrivocality" to further highlight the Hui Muslims' distinctive contribution to the study of Islam, matriliny, and matrifocality. Historical and ethnographic studies show how different matrilineal patterns of descent, property, and pre-Islamic religious practices have long co-existed with Islam and continue to evolve in the post-colonial period across the Indian

[2] Du, "Gender Norms among Ethnic Minorities"; Chuan-kang Shih, *Quest for Harmony: The Moso Traditions of Sexual Union and Family Life.* (Palo Alto, CA: Stanford University Press, 2010); Eileen Rose Walsh, 'From Nü Guo to Nü'er Guo: Negotiating Desire in the Land of the Mosuo', *Modern China* 31:4 (2005), 448–86.

[3] Shanshan Du, "Is Buddha a Couple? Gender-Unitary Perspectives from the Lahu of Southwest China", *Ethnology* 42:3 (2003), 253–71; Ruizhi Lian, "Surviving Conquest in Dali: Chiefs, Deities, and Ancestors", in David Faure and Ts'ui-p'ing Ho (eds.) *Chieftains into Ancestors: Imperial Expansion and Indigenous Society in Southwest China* (Vancouver: University of British Columbia Press, 2013), 86–110; James Wilkerson, "Negotiating Local Tradition with Taoism: Female Ritual Specialists in the Zhuang Religion", *Religion* 37:2 (2007), 150–63.

[4] Du, "Is Buddha a Couple?"

[5] Shui, Jingjun and Maria Jaschok, *The History of Women's Mosques in Chinese Islam (Zhongguo Qingzhen Nusi Shi 中国清真女寺史)* (Beijing: Sanlian Hafou Yanjing xueshucongshu, 2002); Maria Jaschok, "Religious Agency and Gender Complementarity: Women's Mosques and Women's Voices in Hui Muslim Communities in Central China", *Review of Religion and Chinese Society* 5:2 (2018), 183–207.

Ocean and Africa.[6] Thus, in her discussion of the matrilineal Muslim society in Comoros, Blanchy resonates with Saul's idea to conceptualise matriliny more as "a cluster of features" than a system.[7] This is also a critical point of departure for the discussion of Islam and matrivocality in China. By matrivocality, I refer to a historically changing "cluster of features" that define Chinese Muslim women's roles and voices in a predominantly patrilineal society under both the Islamic and Confucian patriarchal systems. On the one hand, the concept of matrivocality is firmly situated within the studies of matriliny and matrifocality in Muslim societies around the world more generally, and regarding ethnic minorities in China in particular. On the other hand, the combination of *matri-* and *-vocality* broadens the meanings of matriliny and matrifocality to incorporate women's own voices in a women-centric approach within predominantly patriarchal structures.

First, this chapter offers a historical review of Hui women's changing status in social and religious lives. In particular, the emergence of women's mosques (*nüsi* 女寺) and the role of women imams (*nü a'hong* 女阿訇) in Central China laid the foundation for Hui women to further participate in religious education. Thanks to the heritage of mosque-based education, many of these women were engaged in China's twentieth-century transformations through both religious and secular education. The second part of the chapter traces the active participation of Hui women in the public sphere from the early twentieth century until the present day, particularly through new modes of education, mass media, and literature. In conclusion, I argue that Hui Muslim women have been cultivating a moderate,

---

[6] Evelyn Blackwood, "Representing Women: The Politics of Minangkabau Adat Writings", *The Journal of Asian Studies* 60:1 (2001), 125–49; Sophie Blanchy, "A Matrilineal and Matrilocal Muslim Society in Flux: Negotiating Gender and Family Relations in the Comoros", *Africa: The Journal of the International African Institute* 89:1 (2019), 21–39; Liazzat Bonate, "Matriliny, Islam and Gender in Northern Mozambique", *Journal of Religion in Africa* 36:2 (2006), 139–66; Liazzat Bonate, "Islam and Matriliny along the Indian Ocean Rim: Revisiting the Old 'Paradox' by Comparing the Minangkabau, Kerala and Coastal Northern Mozambique", *Journal of Southeast Asian Studies* 48:3 (2017), 436–51; Jeffrey Hadler, *Muslims and Matriarchs: Cultural Resilience in Indonesia Through Jihad and Colonialism* (Ithaca, NY: Cornell University Press, 2008); Tsuyoshi Kato, *Matriliny and Migration: Evolving Minangkabau Traditions in Indonesia* (Ithaca, NY: Cornell University Press, 1982).

[7] Mahir Saul, "Matrilineal Inheritance and Post-Colonial Prosperity in Southern Bobo Country", *Man* 27:2 (1992), 341–62; Blanchy, "Project MUSE—A Matrilineal and Matrilocal Muslim Society in Flux".

116   J. WANG

non-factional image of Islam in China through cultural representations in the public sphere. The changing gender consciousness manifested through Huo Da, Ma Jinlian, and other Hui women writers' work reflects what I call the affective dimension of matrivocality within the heterogeneous Hui communities in China, thus challenging the stereotypical misconception of Muslim women as passive, submissive, and voiceless.

HISTORICAL REVIEW OF HUI MUSLIM WOMEN IN CHINA FROM THE SEVENTH TO THE TWENTIETH CENTURY

Wives, Mothers, and Daughters

Historically, *Hui* is a fluid ethno-religious category often referring to Chinese-speaking Muslims or Sino-Muslims.[8] In pre-1949 China, *Huijiao* was widely used to refer to Islam, while terms such as *Huihui* and *Huijiaotu* (followers of the Islamic religion) were often used to include Muslims of different ethnic identities. After 1949, *Huizu* or Hui nationality became the largest Muslim minority in the PRC's ethnic identification system, together with nine other Muslim minorities: Uyghur, Kazakh, Tartar, Dongxiang, Bao'an, Uzbek, Kyrgyz, Salar, and Tajik. Today, Hui Muslims live across China in "large dispersion, small settlements" (*da fensan xiao juju*) with the highest concentration in Northwest and Southwest China. According to the Sixth National Census of People's Republic of China (PRC), the total population of Huizu is 10,586,087, constituting about 0.79% of the total population.[9] The population of Hui women is 5,212,346, about 49.2% of the entire Huizu population by 2011. In this chapter I use the terms Hui, Hui Muslims, and Chinese Muslims interchangeably, rather than Huizu, to discuss the unique heritage of Hui women both before and after 1949.

In the history of Islam in China, marriage plays a key role in shaping the identities of Muslim men and women. A common saying among the Hui communities across China today often attributes the origin of Hui Muslims

[8] Dru Gladney, *Ethnic Identity in China: The Making of a Muslim Minority Nationality* (New York: Harcourt Brace College Publishers, 1998); Jonathan Neaman Lipman, *Familiar Strangers: A History of Muslims in Northwest China* (Seattle, WA: University of Washington Press, 1998).

[9] National Bureau of Statistics of China, "2010 Census of National Ethnic Groups Based on Age and Gender [Quanguo Ge Minzu Fen Nianling, Xingbie de Renkou]" (National Bureau of Statistics of China, 2011).

to the intermarriages between Hui grandfathers and Han grandmothers (*huihui baba* and *hanren nana*). If non-Muslim men married Chinese Muslim women, they were required to convert; when non-Muslim women married Muslim men, conversion was strongly encouraged, but not required.[10] Since Islam came to China via the Silk Roads in the seventh century, during the Tang Dynasty (618–907), male Muslim traders, merchants, artisans, ambassadors, scholars, and soldiers from Arabia, Persia, and Central Asia have been long regarded as the forefathers of Hui Muslims in China.[11] Yet few came with their wives. During the Yuan Dynasty (1271–1368) in particular, many Muslim men with Central Asian origins managed to climb in social and political status under the Mongol rule as officials, generals, scientists, and religious practitioners.[12] For instance, Sayyid Ajjal Shams al-Din Omar al-Bukhari (Sai Dianchi, 1211–1279), one of the most prominent Muslim officials in the Yuan Dynasty, was the first governor of Yunnan province in Southwest China today.[13] As Muslim men started to settle down, they married Chinese women from local communities.[14] In a sense, the family structure in Chinese Muslim households profoundly influenced the formation of Chinese Muslim identities.

Furthermore, China's broader socio-political contexts also shape women's role in Chinese Muslim communities. In one of the earlier works on gender and Islam in China, Barbara Pillsbury noted that "for centuries Muslim women in China have occupied *a doubly subordinate status* [author's italicisation],"[15] referring to Chinese Muslim women being considered as inferior by both Muslim men and Han society. In the classic Confucian hierarchy of the Han Chinese society, the idea of "men as superior, women as inferior" (*nanzun nübei*) dictated that the appropriate roles for women in general should be "virtuous mothers" and "good

---

[10] Personal correspondence with Dr. Jacqueline Armijo, December 2020.

[11] Shouyi Bai, *Huimin Qiyi (Hui Rebellion)* (Shanghai: Shanghai Shudian Chubanshe, 2000); Raphael Israeli, *Islam in China: Religion, Ethnicity, Culture, and Politics* (Oxford: Lexington Books, 2002).

[12] Yijiu Jin, *The History of Islam (Yisilan Jiao Shi)* (Jiangsu: Jiangsu renmin chubanshe, 2008).

[13] Jacqueline Armijo, *Sayyid'Ajall Shams al-Din: A Muslim from Central Asia, Serving the Mongols in China, and Bringing Civilization to Yunnan*, Ph.D. dissertation: Harvard University, 1997.

[14] Shui and Jaschok, *The History of Women's Mosques in Chinese Islam*, 91.

[15] Barbara L. K. Pillsbury, "Being Female in a Muslim Minority in China", in Lois Beck and Nikki Keddie (eds.) *Women in the Muslim World* (Harvard University Press, 1978), 652.

wives." Tani Barlow translated this classic notion of women in pre-modern China thus: "[B]efore [women] are married they are *nü*/female/daughters, when they get married they are *fù*/wives, and when they give birth to children, then they are *mu*/mothers."[16] Living amongst the dominant Han-majority society, Hui Muslims have also been heavily influenced by the Confucian conceptualisation of gender. The social and familial division of labour in the form of "men managing external affairs, women internal" (*nan zhuwai, nü zhunei*) is widely spread and accepted across Muslim communities.[17] Even today, this binary division of gender roles is still often regarded as a normative reference among some Muslim communities in Northwest China, where Muslim women receive relatively little formal education and do not have economic independence.[18]

Gender Complementarity: Han Kitab and Women as Cultural Preservers

In the late Ming and early Qing dynasties (approximately the sixteenth and seventeenth centuries), women's roles as mothers and wives were given a new layer of meaning: family educators and cultural preservers. The history of Hui Muslim women in China reflects what Shui and Jaschok defined as "gender complementarity."[19] Tracing this idea to the Han Kitab and Hui Confucians, such as Li Zhi and Wang Daiyu, Muslim women's religious agency is conceptualised in the tradition of "gender coopera-

[16] Tani E. Barlow, "Theorizing Women: Funu, Guojia, Jiating (Chinese Women, Chinese State, Chinese Family)", in Inderpal Grewal and Karen Caplan (eds.) *Scattered Hegemonies: Postmodernity and Transnational Feminist Practices* (Minneapolis, MN: University of Minnesota Press, 1997), 1173–96.

[17] Liping Hu, "From the Gender's Perspective: Contemporary Huizu Muslim Female Education Taking a Girls' School in Yunnan Zhaotong as Example (Shehui Xingbie Shijiao Xia de Dangdai Musilin Nuxue: Yi Yunnan Zhaotong Mou Huizu Nuxiao Wei Li 性别视角下的当代穆斯林女学——以云南昭通某回族女校为例)", *Journal of Hui Muslim Minority Studies (Huizu Yanjiu)* 2 (2013), 109–14; Guihua Luo, *Shaan-Gan-Qing Huizu Women Traditional Social and Cultural Transformations (Shaan-Gan-Qing Huizu Nuxing Shehui Wenhua Bianqian Yanjiu* 甘青宁回族女性传统社会文化变迁研究) (Beijing: Minzu Chubanshe, 2007).

[18] Guifen Ma, *Participant Social Research among Muslim Women in the Northwest (Xibei Musilin Funu Shehui Canyu Yanjiu: Jiyu Gansu Sheng Huizu and Dongxiangzu Funu de Ge'an Yanjiu* 西北穆斯林妇女社会参与研究——基于甘肃省回族、东乡族妇女的个案研究) (Beijing: Renmin chubanshe, 2017).

[19] Shui and Jaschok, *The History of Women's Mosques in Chinese Islam*; Jaschok, "Religious Agency and Gender Complementarity".

tion" (*xingbie hezuo* 性别合作).[20] Heavily influenced by the Daoist idea of "*yin-yang* mutual nourishing" (*yinyang hubu* 阴阳互补), Hui Muslim culture in Central China from the sixteenth century onward has incorporated the idea that men and women complement each other in family life, religious spaces, and social roles.

The emergence of women's mosques ultimately goes back "to a crisis for Islam in China that threatened the very survival of the faith and of Muslims as a tolerated minority identity."[21] Hui Confucians and religious clergy (predominantly male *ahongs* or imams) started to advocate for the religious education of Muslim women through scripture-hall education (*jingtang jiaoyu*). While Hui intellectuals and religious practitioners reinterpreted Islamic teachings through Confucianism, they also realised the importance of women in the transmission and preservation of Islamic tradition in China. Hui Confucians (*Huiru*)—also known as the authors of the Han Kitab (*Han ketabu*), a collection of Chinese Islamic texts—offered an Islamic interpretation of classic Confucianist and Daoist texts, including a reinterpretation of women's role in society.[22] Scholars such as Li Zhi (1527–1602) and Wang Daiyu (1570–1660) argued, based on the Islamic scriptures, that men and women are created equal. Whereas Confucian scholars believed that "women without education are virtuous" (*nüzi wucai bian shi de*), Li Zhi advocated for equality between men and women in terms of intelligence and virtue, insisting that "Grand Dao doesn't differentiate between men and women" (*da dao bu fen nan nü*).[23] Inspired by Li Zhi and the Daoist idea of *yin-yang* complementarity, Wang Daiyu placed the husband-wife relationship at the pinnacle of the ethical hierarchy—radically different from the classic Confucian order, which ascribed more value to the relationship between emperors and subjects, or fathers and sons.[24] Radical in nature, Wang's theorisation of gender still very much conformed to the neo-Confucian order in a sense that he also tried to legitimise the subordinate role of women within families. Despite the

---

[20] Jaschok, "Religious Agency and Gender Complementarity," 186.

[21] Jaschok, "Religious Agency and Gender Complementarity," 193.

[22] Zvi Ben-Dor Benite, *The Dao of Muhammad: A Cultural History of Muslims in Late Imperial China, The Dao of Muhammad* (Leiden: Brill, 2020); Shui and Jaschok, *The History of Women's Mosques in Chinese Islam.*

[23] Weilin Fu, "Li Zhi Biography (Li Zhi Zhuan 李贽传)" in *History of Ming: On Other Religions (Mingshu: Yijiao Zhuan 明书·异教传)*, vol. 160 (Beijing: Zhonghua Shuju, 1985).

[24] Han and Ma, "On Wang Daiyu's Confucian Construction about the Values of Muslim Women", 44.

limits set by the Han Kitab, we cannot overlook their revolutionary implication for the emergence of women's mosques. In fact, Hui men were among the first to promote women-based religious education in pre-modern China.[25]

The earliest forms of women-based mosque education emerged in and around Central China (*zhongyuan*), in the contemporary Chinese provinces of Henan, Shanxi, Hebei, Anhui, and part of Shandong. According to the pioneering research of Shui and Jaschok,[26] Muslim women's religious education from the sixteenth to seventeenth centuries manifested significant regional differences. In Northwest China (today's Ningxia, Qinghai, Gansu, and Shaanxi), women's education was mostly confined within families. In Southwest China (mostly in Yunnan), the wives of imams (*shiniang* 师娘) often took up the responsibility of providing basic religious education to Muslim women in the male-led mosques. In Central China, Wangjia Hutong Women's Mosque in Kaifeng, Henan, is documented as being China's earliest women's mosque, dating back to the Jiaqing period (1796–1820).[27] From the Jiaqing to the Guangxu era (1875–1908), Henan and Yunnan both saw female *ahongs* in charge of religious instruction, while this phenomenon was almost non-existent in Northwest China.[28]

In general, men were the leading figures in early women's mosque education. They advocated for the inclusion of women's religious education in men's mosques (*nansi*), compiled textbooks for them, and trained female students to become woman *ahong*. The texts for instruction and learning were written in the Persian-Arabic scripts (*xiao'er jing*). Women *ahong*, and the wives of male *ahong*, would then teach Muslim women the basic Islamic knowledge of faith and prayer. Apart from the male *ahongs* in mosques and madrasas, some female *ahongs* also learned from their fathers or other family members to excel in their religious studies. This trend, as Hui scholar Yang Wenjiong characterised it, marked the transition of a mono-track structure (*dangui jiegou*) of Islamic transmission to a duo-track structure (*shuanggui*), i.e., from "Jamaat (*zhemati*, meaning a

---

[25] Apart from religious education, whether Chinese Muslim women were also encouraged to take traditional Chinese classical education remains a question. If readers have any references, please reach out to the author at jing.wang@asc.upenn.edu.

[26] Shui and Jaschok, *The History of Women's Mosques in Chinese Islam*, 108–9.

[27] Jaschok, "Religious Agency and Gender Complementarity," 195.

[28] Shui and Jaschok, *The History of Women's Mosques in Chinese Islam (Zhongguo Qingzhen Nusi Shi)*, 121.

community or congregation) > mosque (scripture-hall education, men's study or *nanxue*) > men (fathers, sons) > family (wives, children) > Jamaat," to "Jamaat > mosque (scripture-hall education, men's study and women's study or *nüxue*) > family (all members) > Jamaat."[29]

Rise of Women's Studies and Modern Education in the Twentieth Century

From the late Qing dynasty into the first half of the twentieth century, this transition into a duo-track structure was furthered by a new wave of women's mosque construction and the rise of modern education. During famines, floods, and wars in the early twentieth century, the migration and dispersion of Hui Muslims from Central China helped facilitate the construction of women's mosques in Northwest China where they settled. For instance, the only independent women's mosque in Xi'an today was established by Hui Muslim women from Henan.[30] After the May Fourth Movement (1919) and the New Culture Movement (1910s–1920s), the role of women in the survival of the Chinese nation was accentuated by many writers, intellectuals, social activists, and politicians.[31] Educating women was regarded as an essential part of modernisation, a phenomenon not dissimilar to the transformation of women's status during the Kemalist reforms in Turkey.[32] During this period of socio-political transformation, Hui Muslims were active participants rather than passive observers. For instance, the first Muslim girls' modern middle school, Crescent Girl Middle School (*xinyue nüzi zhongxue* 新月女子中学), was established in Beijing in 1935.[33] There was only one class of forty female students when

---

[29] Wenjiong Yang, "Women's Madrassa: Development of Mosque Education and Displacement of the Role of Cultural Transmission: Taking Lanzhou, Xi'an and Linxia as Examples" (Nuxue: Jingtang Jiaoyu de Tuozhan Yu Wenhua Chuancheng Juese Zhongxin de Weiyi: Yi Lanzhou, Xi'an, Linxia Diaocha Wei Ge'an 女学:经堂教育的拓展与文化传承角色中心的位移——以兰州、西安、临夏调查为个案), *Journal of Hui Muslim Minority Studies (Huizu Yanjiu)*, no. 1 (2002), 25–31.

[30] Qiang Ma, *Inside and Outside Hui Quarter: Studies of Xi'an Muslims during the Process of Urban Modernization [Huifang Neiwai: Chengshi Xiandaihua Jincheng Zhong de Xi'an Yisilanjiao Yanjiu]* (Beijing: China Social Sciences Press, 2011).

[31] Barlow, "Theorizing Women", 182; Yinhe Li, *Feminism (Nuxing Zhuyi 女性主义)* (Shanghai Wenhua Chubanshe, 2018), 40–2.

[32] Nilüfer Göle, *Islam and Secularity: The Future of Europe's Public Sphere* (Durham, NC: Duke University Press, 2015): 104.

[33] Ma, *Participant Social Research among Muslim Women in the Northwest*, 91.

the school was first established. Ma Ruye (马汝邺),[34] the wife of Muslim general Ma Fushou, donated the initial funding for the school and also took on the role of Chairwoman of the school board. Students were taught the standard curriculum, in addition to Arabic and the basics of Islamic religious education. The school was closed in 1937 after the Sino-Japanese War broke out. Institutionally, the establishment of the Crescent Girl Middle School marked the beginning of a Muslim women-oriented education beyond the spheres of the family and women's mosques.

Since the establishment of the People's Republic of China, the Chinese Communist Party (CCP) aimed to transform Chinese women into socialist female workers equal to their male counterparts in the construction of a new nation.[35] Accordingly, women's legal rights (such as the passing of marriage laws in 1950) and their access to education were institutionalised through laws and social institutions. In 1950, for example, the National Hui College (*guoli huimin xueyuan* 国立回民学院) in Beijing opened its first women-only class, training young Hui Muslim women as intellectuals, educators, and translators. The first cohort of women excelled in their studies and their class was named the Zoya Class (卓娅班) after Zoya Kosmodemyanskaya, one of the most revered heroines of the Soviet Union. Yet, from the late 1950s to late 1970s, political turmoil, especially during the Cultural Revolution (1966–1976), had a devastating effect on almost all formal education and religious activities in China, including women's mosques and schools. While many Hui women started to work in work units (*danwei*) in the social and political domains, they lost the access to mosque-based education and were not allowed to publicly display their religious identity through the wearing of headscarves (*gaitou*).[36] Despite all these hardships, some Hui women and men still endeavoured to prevent some mosques from being torn down, or made efforts to preserve their faith privately.[37] In the early 1980s, religious activities started

---

[34] Ma Ruye was born in Chengdu in the late Qing era, but her exact birthday was not well documented. Her father Ma Xuwu, a Qing official, was commissioned to go to England and Japan to inspect their educational systems. Her father hired a Japanese teacher for Ma Ruye to learn Math, music, and other subjects. Ma Ruye taught in primary schools for over a decade in Northeast China. She returned to Chengdu in her old age and died there in the 1930s.

[35] Barlow, "Theorizing Women", 184.

[36] Maris Gillette, *Between Mecca and Beijing: Modernization and Consumption among Urban Chinese Muslims* (Palo Alto, CA: Stanford University Press, 2000).

[37] Fieldwork interviews between 2015 and 2016 in Shaanxi Province.

AFFECTIVE MATRIVOCALITY AND WOMEN'S VOICES: A HISTORY...   123

to resume after the issuance of the No. 19 file addressing the religious issue in 1982.[38] The No.19 file acknowledges the importance of religion to the "material and spiritual civilisations of socialism." It states that the Party's basic religious policy is to "respect and protect religious freedom." Since then, Hui Muslim women have been playing an ever more important role in the revival of Islam in post-Mao China.

The revival of Islamic education is one of the key areas to which Hui Muslim women have been making significant contributions. At the local level, market-oriented reforms since the late 1970s have indirectly reduced the amount of educational resources previously allocated by the state. In the poor Hui communities of China's northwestern and southwestern regions, boys still tend to get more opportunities for formal education than girls. A famous example was that of Ma Yan (马燕), a Hui girl born in Xiji county, Ningxia Province. She almost had to quit school due to poverty and the prioritisation of boys over girls within her family, until French journalist Pierre Haski discovered her diary and published it in French in 2002. The publication of *The Diary of Ma Yan*[39] not only gave her the chance to go back to school but also exposed the serious problems faced by many other Hui girls. Faced with this challenge, Hui women have taken the initiative to start different forms of education suitable for people in various local communities. Hui women established pre-school programmes for young children, after-school and summer programmes for school-age children, daytime and evening classes for the elderly and working adults, and Islamic schools for those who aspire to become female *ahongs* and Arabic teachers or translators.[40] Based on her five-year fieldwork in Southwest China, Armijo also observed how Hui women played a proactive role in pursuing Islamic education both at home and abroad, establishing girls' schools, promoting Islam among other Muslims, and serving as imams in women's mosques.[41]

[38] Central Committee of CCP, "Basic Views and Policies on Religious Issues under Socialism in PRC (Guanyu Woguo Shehui Zhuyi Shiqi Zongjiao Wenti de Jiben Guandian He Jiben Zhengce 关于我国社会主义时期宗教问题的基本观点和基本政策)" (Beijing, 1982).

[39] Yan Ma and Pierre Haski, *The Diary of Ma Yan (Ma Yan Riji 马燕日记)* (Tianjin: Tianjin jiaoyu chubanshe, 2006).

[40] Jacqueline Armijo, "A Unique Heritage of Leadership: Muslim Women in China", *Georgetown Journal of International Affairs* 10:1 (2009), 37–45.

[41] Jacqueline Armijo, "Muslim Education in China: Chinese Madrasas and Linkages to Islamic Schools Abroad", in Farish Noor, Yoginder Sikang, and Martin van Bruinessen (eds.) *The Madrasa in Asia: Political Activism and Transnational Linkages* (Amsterdam: Amsterdam University Press, 2008), 169–89.

Sino-Arabic women's schools (*zhong'a nüxiao*中阿女校, abbreviated as SAWS) are a prominent example of the Hui people's efforts to integrate religious and secular education for Muslim women in China. Ma Qiang, a Hui scholar from Northwest China, defined SAWS as the officially recognised, institutionalised cultural associations dedicated to teaching Chinese, Arabic, and Islamic culture.[42] Besides the formal institutions of SAWS, there are also spaces for women to study similar topics in women's madrasas, whether in mosques or private homes. Influential Sino-Arabic women's schools include Linxia SAWS (临夏中阿女校), Zhangjiachuan SAWS (张家川中阿女校), Yinchuan Minle Arabic School Women's Section (银川民乐阿校女生部), Changzhi SAWS (长治中阿女校), Dali Muzhuan Women's Section (大理穆专女生部), and others.[43] In Zhaotong county of Yunnan province, for example, Shouwang SAWS (守望中阿女校)—originally established by a well-respected male *ahong* in 1982—has accepted over 2000 students, of whom about 300 women had formally graduated by 2012.[44] Some women continued, after graduation, to pursue further religious studies, to teach Arabic in local communities, or to become translators in coastal cities like Yiwu.

These formal SAWS, informal women's study opportunities, and women's mosques provide a collective, physical space for the cultivation of Muslim subjectivities and ethics for Hui women, thus becoming a critical source of Muslim women's empowerment. Anthropologist Saba Mahmood raised an important critique of the liberal-secular notion of feminism through her study of the women's mosque movement in Cairo, Egypt.[45] She pointed out that the agency of urban Egyptian Muslim women did not manifest itself in a binary form of either submission or resistance. Rather, the broader Islamic revival or Islamic Awakening (al-Ṣaḥwa al-Islāmiyya), partly channelled through the development of the women's mosque movement, allowed Muslim women to exercise their agency through Islamic ethics. "Agential capacity," as Mahmood put it, "is entailed not only in those acts that resist norms but also in the multiple

---

[42] Qiang Ma, "Urbanization and Development of Women's Masjid and Women's School in China (Dushihua Jincheng Zhong de Qingzhen Nusi He Nuxue 都市化进程中的清真女寺和女学)", *Journal of Hui Muslim Minority Studies (Huizu Yanjiu)*, no. 2 (2011), 110–16.

[43] Ma, "Urbanization and Development of Women's Masjid and Women's School in China", 111.

[44] Hu, "From the Gender's Perspective", 111.

[45] Saba Mahmood, *Politics of Piety: The Islamic Revival and the Feminist Subject* (Princeton, NJ: Princeton University Press, 2011).

ways in which one inhabits norms."[46] Although Hui Muslim women live in a socio-political context different from that of the Egyptian women, it is not inappropriate to notice a similar trend of women's empowerment in a Muslim-majority country like Egypt and in a Muslim-minority country like China amidst the global movements of Islamic revival.

Ethnographic materials attest to the validity of such a comparison on the ground. As Hu noticed, many female participants in Shouwang SAWS emphasised a renewed sense of their self-identification as dutiful Muslim mothers, wives, and daughters in everyday life.[47] This observation was also confirmed in my multiple field trips in Northwest China between 2015 and 2020. During my encounters with Hui Muslim women, many would affirm their equal rights as human beings created by God but also emphasise their differentiated gender role as women. For example, Fatima, a Muslim woman in her early forties who has been teaching Arabic in women's mosques and private homes in Gansu, is an active member of the religious and social spheres in her local community. She needs to take care of family chores, educate her two children, and teach Qur'ānic recitation classes, while enduring the loneliness of the often long-term separation from her husband who is doing business in Pakistan. Despite all these difficulties, she appreciates her husband's deep commitment to the family and emphasises the importance of learning for all her family members: "Learning is the divine duty for every Muslim man and woman (*qiuxue shi meige musilin nannü de zhuming*)." Fatima commented on her daughter's life choices: "My daughter's fluent in four languages—Chinese, English, Arabic, and Urdu. As long as she wants to continue her studies, her father and I will support her. But we also want her to find a good husband and to be a good mother in the future." Fatima's unapologetic stance is a testimony to Muslim women's agency in everyday life, thanks to their continuous efforts of religio-ethnical cultivation as pious Muslim women. With the promotion of equality between men and women (*nannü pingdeng*) in the twentieth century, the previous idea of mutual nourishing was challenged yet adapted to have a renewed sense of gender complementarity: "Muslim women see a paradigmatic gender relationship in terms of complementarity, as *hezuo*, a conception that frames women's unique history in Islam in central China, and they view their negotiation of gender and strategic political alliances as the most effective way forward in a rap-

---

[46] Mahmood, *Politics of Piety*, 14–5.
[47] Hu, "From the Gender's Perspective," 111–2.

126   J. WANG

idly modernising society."[48] Fatima's case is also part of this growing sense of agency shared by Muslim women outside central China today.

FROM GENDER COMPLEMENTARITY TO AFFECTIVE MATRIVOCALITY IN CONTEMPORARY CHINA

Hui Women's Voices in Public Spheres in the First Half of the Twentieth Century

While it is of great importance to keep tracing, documenting, and understanding Hui Muslim women's mosques and religious agency, we also need to pay more attention to the growing presence of their voices in China's public sphere. Nurtured by the tradition of women's mosques, Hui Muslim women have also been cultivating a unique heritage of cultural representations through literature and mass media. Anthropologists of Islam have noted how literary, visual, and other modes of women's self-representations give rise to, sustain, and transform Muslim women's agency in both private and public spaces. For instance, anthropologist Lila Abu-Lughod showed how the Awlad Ali Bedouin women in Northern Egypt used the poetic form of *ghinnāwas* (little songs) to share everyday sentiments of love, joy, sorrow, pain, and other sentiments.[49] As Abu-Lughod pointed out, the link between poetry as a form of literary expression and matters of everyday life is so strong that *ghinnāwa*s can be defined as a "discourse of love."[50] This discourse is shared by "individuals whose ordinary actions and statements conform to the modesty code, who take pains to present themselves as moral and worthy of respect."[51] The poetic expressions and performances, in a sense, become a collective self-expression by, among, and for women. These affective dimensions of matrivocality expressed through literary forms are also manifested through Hui women writers' works.

While rural Bedouin women's poetic expressions were mostly shared in private spaces such as kitchens and living rooms, urban Turkish women in the first half of the twentieth century found themselves at the epicentre of

---

[48] Jaschok, "Religious Agency and Gender Complementarity," 186.

[49] Lila Abu-Lughod, *Veiled Sentiments: Honor and Poetry in a Bedouin Society* (Berkeley & Los Angeles: University of California Press, 1986).

[50] Abu-Lughod, *Veiled Sentiments*, 232.

[51] Abu-Lughod, *Veiled Sentiments*, 232.

Turkish modernism. The state's efforts to transform Muslim women into public citizens led to a series of policies, such as the removal of the veil, the change of marriage law, and the rights of voting and holding public office—all targeting women, their bodies and minds, as the site of modern transformation.[52] With the implementation of compulsory coeducation, women's literacy rates were significantly improved. Literature became a contesting ground for constructing the image of modern Muslim women and their daily struggles between the Western notion of modernity and Islamic ethics of modesty. Göle used Turkish author Yakup Kadri Karaosmanoğlu (1889–1974) and his novel *Ankara* (1934) as an example to illustrate how the female antagonist, Selma, embodied such struggles in her everyday life.[53] Undeniably, most representations of women were still written or portrayed by men in the late Ottoman Empire and early Turkish republic. Yet, from the late nineteenth century onwards in Turkey, female novelists also started to carve out a space—albeit very limited—for their own voices. Fatma Aliye Topuz (1862–1936),[54] for instance, is often credited as the first female novelist in Turkish literature.[55] Her sister, Emine Semiye, was also a writer and social activist, advocating for women's rights in public spaces. Other prominent female writers included Azmiye Hami Güven (1904–1954) and Halide Edib Adivar (1884–1964). The emergence of women both as an object (topic) and as a subject (agency) in modern Turkey bears some striking resemblances to the experiences of Hui Muslim women in modern China.

From the late nineteenth to twentieth century, Hui Muslim women began taking more initiatives to cultivate their own voices through literature and mass media. Hui social activist women Liu Qingyang (刘清扬 1894–1977) and Guo Longzhen (郭隆真 1894–1931) established influential women-oriented modern newspapers such as *Women's Daily (funü ribao* 妇女日报) and *Women's Friends (funü zhiyou* 妇女之友), which were not confined to Hui female readers.[56] In the *Hui Women Magazine (yisi-*

---

[52] Nilüfer Göle, *The Forbidden Modern: Civilization and Veiling* (Ann Arbor, MI: University of Michigan Press, 1996); Göle, *Islam and Secularity*, 110.

[53] Göle, *Islam and Secularity*, 111–2.

[54] Before Fatma Aliye, Zafer Hanim also published a novel in 1877. However, very little is known about her life and death.

[55] İlknur Bahadır, "Fatma Aliye's Discourse of Women in the Context of the Islamic Modernization and Tradition" (Master's dissertation: Istanbul Şehir University, 2018).

[56] Li Liu and Jing Zhou, "Analysis of the Journal Publications by Hui Muslim Women in the Republic Era (Minguo Shiqi Huizu Nuxing Zuozhe de Baokan Shuxie Pingxi 民国时期回族女性作者的报刊书写与评析)", *Journal of Hui Muslim Minority Studies (Huizu Yanjiu)*, no. 3 (2018), 84–8.

lan funü zazhi 伊斯兰妇女杂志), Hui female writers such as He Ru (何如) argued that the subjugation of women was part of "feudal ethics" (*fengjian lijiao*) in China and that Islam respected women's rights and saw their duties as equal to those of men.[57] Ma Xiuzhen (马秀珍), a Hui female intellectual, wrote:

> After the furious waves of the May Fourth Movement, haven't we seen all the efforts by women to overthrow oppression? However, among all these passionate women, did we see any Muslim women? Alas! It's disheartening to realise that no Muslim women participated in the waves [of May Fourth Movement]. As for those who consciously stand up to break the shackles, I have found none. ... Why have we Muslim women been staying silent while other women could stand up to break their shackles? ... The reason why we are willing to be confined by feudal ethics is really because we haven't gained self-enlightenment and consciousness yet! ... Now, we [as Muslim women] need to have a deep understanding of our own status. We also need to have a deep understanding of the true meaning of liberty and of the principle of equality. ... Our purpose is not only to liberate Muslim women from oppression [of feudal ethics] but also to fight for other women under oppression. Our purpose is to make sure that all women around the world will enjoy real freedom and equality, walking the path of enlightenment, happiness, and peace.[58]

In Ma's essay, she echoed He Ru that the root cause of oppression of Muslim women was "feudal ethics" in Chinese history rather than the true Islamic teachings. She reflected upon the silence of Muslim women and their lack of effort to break free. It was of paramount importance to raise "self-enlightenment and consciousness" so that Muslim women could "have a deep understanding of their (our) own status." Furthermore, Ma also emphasised that it was not enough to just "liberate Muslim women from oppression [of feudal ethics]" but also to "fight for other women under oppression." This realisation of women's universal plight beyond religious and national boundaries was representative of Ma, He, and other Hui women intellectuals in the first half of the twentieth century.[59] In

---

[57] Ru He, "Islam and Women (Yisilanjiao Yu Funu 伊斯兰教与妇女)", *Hui Women Magazine (Yisilan Funu Zazhi)*, 1936.

[58] Xiuzhen Ma, "Awakening of Muslim Women (Yisilan Funu de Juewu 伊斯兰妇女的觉悟)," *Hui Women Magazine (Yisilan Funu Zazhi* 伊斯兰妇女杂志), 1936.

[59] Liu and Zhou, "Analysis of the Journal Publications by Hui Muslim Women in the Republic Era."

AFFECTIVE MATRIVOCALITY AND WOMEN'S VOICES: A HISTORY... 129

other words, they situated Muslim women's issues within the broader context of modernity, both within China and beyond. Islamic teachings became part of their ethical and intellectual legacy from which they could draw inspiration to legitimise their fights for freedom and equality.

To a certain extent, this development marks a radical shift of Muslim women's social spaces from primarily within the family and women's mosques to larger Chinese society during a period of dramatic socio-political transformations. Typically, sporadic records of women in the historical accounts of Muslims in China do not include the voices of women themselves.[60] The most well-known Muslim women in imperial China were perhaps Empress Ma (马皇后 1352–1382), a Hui woman married to Emperor Zhu Yuanzhang (1328–1398), and Xiang Fei (香妃), a legendary Uyghur Muslim woman in the reign of Emperor Qianlong (1711–1799).[61] Yet none of these Muslim women left their own narratives. Only very few Hui Muslim women managed to publish literary or religious texts, either during their lifetime or posthumously. For instance, within Hui Muslim communities, the story of Cai Gutai (蔡姑太)—who lived during the Qing Dynasty—is well known among the Qadiri Sufi order.[62] Cai Gutai has been credited as the scribe for a miniature handwritten copy of the Qur'ān.[63] Ma Jinliang, the current shaykh living in the mosque complex where Cai Gutai's shrine (*gongbei*, its pronunciation likely derived from "gonbad" in Persian) is located, explained that their particular saintly lineage tends to attract more female Muslims, not just locally but also from across the region today.[64] Ding Yunhui (丁蕴辉), a female teacher born in 1894 in Shandong Province, is now credited as the first (and perhaps the only) female translator of Islamic classics in ancient China. Ding translated Ou'mudai (欧母戴), a scripture-hall textbook originally written in Persian, into classical Chinese.[65] As for poetry or other

[60] Shui and Jaschok, *The History of Women's Mosques in Chinese Islam*, 91–3.

[61] James A. Millward, "A Uyghur Muslim in Qianlong's Court: The Meanings of the Fragrant Concubine", *The Journal of Asian Studies* 53:2 (1994): 427–58; Pillsbury, "Being Female in a Muslim Minority in China," 654.

[62] A Sufi order is called *menhuan* in Chinese (*ṭarīqa* in Arabic). The Qadiriyya is one of the major Sufi orders in China, besides the Khufiyya, Jahriyya, and Kubrawiyya. Most followers of Sufi orders live in Northwest and Southwest China. Unlike the other three sects, the shaykhs in the Qadiri order are celibate.

[63] Shui and Jaschok, *The History of Women's Mosques in Chinese Islam*, 119.

[64] Interview in Qinghai, August 2020.

[65] Zhou, *Qingzhen Dadian* (清真大典), 531–61.

non-religious texts, even fewer female Hui writers are recorded. Li Shunxian (李舜弦, living around the nineteenth century) is often credited as the first recorded female Muslim poet in ancient China.[66] Still, it is still too early to say that Hui Muslim women rarely left any works or publicly voiced their concerns simply because few records have survived.

It is also important to note that the voices of Muslim women in public spheres in the Republic era (1912–1949) were limited in terms of its quantity and scale. Most Muslim social activists, intellectuals, editors, and writers were still men. From 1930 to 1945, about thirty female Muslim writers published twenty-five articles in nine magazines, most of whom lived in big cities like Shanghai, Beijing, and Chongqing.[67] One important factor that contributed to the emergence of Hui women writers was the strong support from Hui Muslim men during that time. For instance, upon the establishment of the aforementioned Crescent Girl Middle School, Ma Songting (1895–1992) sent his eldest daughter, Ma Guojing (马国靖), as one of the first enrolled female students. Ma Songting *ahong*, born in a traditional Hui family in Beijing, was himself a key figure in the development of modern Islamic education in China. He co-established Chengda Normal School (成达师范学校) in 1925 and the *Light of Moon* (*Yuehua* 月华) magazine in 1929. Together with other editors and teachers, prominent male Hui educators such as Ma Songting, Zhao Zhenwu (1895–1938), and Tang Kesan (1882–1950) helped educate a generation of talented female Hui writers and educators.[68] In terms of topics, this generation of educated Hui women not only wrote about the education of women but also made forays into other areas, such as the relationship between youth and politics, sociological investigations, Islamic studies, and patriotism.[69] In this sense, both Muslim men and women start to see "a paradigmatic gender relationship in terms of complementarity" through

---

[66] My interlocutor Shalan and I only found three recorded names (Li Shunxian and Ma Xianglan 马湘兰) in the entire volume of *Ancient Period* (before late nineteenth century) in *General History of Huizu Literature in China*, ed. Yingsheng Zhang (2014).

[67] Liu and Zhou, "Analysis of the Journal Publications by Hui Muslim Women in the Republic Era (Minguo Shiqi Huizu Nuxing Zuozhe de Baokan Shuxie Pingxi 民国时期回族女性作者的报刊书写评析)," 85.

[68] Bozhong Ma, "On the Hui Women Writers in Yuehua Magazine (Tantan Yuehua de Huizu Nuxing Zuozhe 谈谈《月华》的回族女性作者)," *Chinese Muslims (Zhongguo Musilin)*, 2005.

[69] Ma, "On the Hui Women Writers in Yuehua Magazine".

AFFECTIVE MATRIVOCALITY AND WOMEN'S VOICES: A HISTORY...   131

the "negotiation of gender and strategic political alliances as the most effective way forward in a rapidly modernising society."[70]

From Gender Complementarity to Affective Matrivocality Since the 1950s

All these concerted efforts in the first half of the twentieth century further prompted the growing voices of Hui Muslim women, not just in the *ummah* (or "jamaat" as Yang characterised it in the duo-track model of China's Islamic studies) but also in China's wider public sphere. They laid the foundation for the re-emergence of Hui Muslim women's distinctive voices in post-1949 China, especially after the Cultural Revolution. Based on my fieldwork in Northwest China in the summer of 2020 and continuing collaborative archival research with Hui interlocutors, there are over ninety identifiable Hui women writers born between the 1940s and 1980s who have formal publications in different presses, magazines, newspapers, academic journals, and digital platforms. I argue that these women writers, together with many anonymous women writers online, do not only work under the paradigm of gender complementarity to have their voices heard in public space but also create a space of affective matrivocality that expresses their emotional and ethical struggles in everyday life. Female protagonists in the works of various Hui women writers open up ambivalent spaces for fostering gender consciousness within and beyond the Muslim communities in mainland China. Hui women writers such as Huo Da and Ma Jinlian, despite their different literary styles, reflect a shift away from the male-centric self-representation of the history of Islam in China to more multivocal cultural representations of the lived experiences of diverse Hui Muslim communities through women's voices.

Huo Da (霍达 1945–), born into a Hui family that used to specialise in jade and jewellery, is one of the most influential Hui woman writers in post-Mao China. Trained in the subject of Chinese history during her youth, Huo Da began her career as a professional writer after 1976. During the early years of her career she wrote many screenplays for films and TV dramas, with a focus on historical subjects. From the mid-1980s, she began to write both fiction and non-fiction with a wide range of topics

---

[70] Jaschok, "Religious Agency and Gender Complementarity," 186.

related to modern Chinese history.[71] For instance, her novella *The World of Mortals* ("Hongchen" 红尘)[72] tells the story of a Beijing woman and her traumatic experiences during the Cultural Revolution. Her novel *Amend the Breach in Heaven* ("Bu Tianlie" 补天裂)[73] focuses on late nineteenth-century Hong Kong, especially around the Chinese reactions towards the signing of the Convention Between Great Britain and China Respecting an Extension of Hong Kong Territory (also known as The Second Convention of Peking, 1898). Both novels, together with her other works, tend to draw inspiration from the traumatic memories of ordinary people in modern Chinese history. Yet Huo Da's most classic work deals not just with traumas in modern Chinese history but, more specifically, with the history of a Hui family through tragic love stories.

Entitled *The Jade King: History of a Chinese Muslim Family* ("Musilin de zangli" 穆斯林的葬礼),[74] the book traces the rise and fall of a jade business, originally owned by Liang Yiqing, over three generations. Liang is portrayed as a typical Hui Muslim—a blend of Chinese and Islamic cultures, dedicated, pious, persistent, and conservative. Liang adopts Han Ziqi, a Han Chinese orphan, and passes all his craftsmanship on to him. Han Ziqi converts to Islam and tries to modernise the traditional model of Hui business. After accumulating a great deal of wealth through the jade business, he loses it all during political upheavals. Han Xinyue, Han's daughter and the third generation in the family, is a talented Hui woman who manages to attend Peking University and study English. Han Xinyue falls in love with Chu Yanchao, a Han Chinese teacher who deeply admires Xinyue's romantic idealism and intellectual talent. The story ends in tragedy, with Han Xinyue's untimely death from heart disease. The novel won the Mao Dun Literature Prize—the highest literature prize in mainland China—in 1991. It has since been translated into various languages such as English, Arabic, and Urdu. Thanks to the descriptions of Hui history and Islamic practices in the novel, the book is often considered as one of the most influential novels written by a Hui writer.

---

[71] Hui Zhao, "Biographical Introduction of Contemporary Hui Women Writers (Dangdai Huizu Nuzuojia Sanlun 当代回族女作家散论)", *Ningxia Daxue Xuebao* 17:3 (1995), 20–5.

[72] Da Huo, *The World of Mortals (Hongchen* 红尘) (Beijing: Beijing Shiyue wenyi chubanshe, 2005).

[73] Da Huo, *Amend the Breach in Heaven (Bu Tianlie* 补天裂) (Beijing: Beijing chubanshe, 1997).

[74] Da Huo, *The Jade King: History of a Chinese Muslim Family (Musilin de Zangli* 穆斯林的葬礼) (Beijing: Beijing Shiyue wenyi chubanshe, 1988).

AFFECTIVE MATRIVOCALITY AND WOMEN'S VOICES: A HISTORY...   133

For our purpose here, this chapter mainly focuses on the portrayal of women and their agency in the works of Hui writers. Huo's novel, together with other work by Hui women writers, opens up an affective space to show the ethical struggles of women themselves outside a male-centric framework. In *The Jade King*, Huo Da's depiction of the female protagonists in the novel reflects the complexity of Hui women's struggles from around the 1920s to 1980s. Two of the key female protagonists, Liang Junbi and Liang Bingyu, are Liang Yiqing's daughters. They grow up with Han Ziqi and both fall in love with him. Yet they make very different choices. Junbi, the elder sister, marries Han Ziqi. Her husband, though talented in craftsmanship and business, is timid and indecisive in everyday life. Unlike Ziqi, Junbi is a traditional Hui housewife, pious, materialistic, often opinionated, and dedicated to her family and family business even while her husband goes away for over a decade. Bingyu, the younger sister and an independent-minded woman, is romantic, idealistic, courageous, and independent. She manages to attend Peking University, one of China's the most universities, at a time when most young women of her age hardly had a high school degree. At college, Bingyu supports anti-Japanese protests by fellow students and is outspoken in her criticism of inequality. During the Sino-Japanese War, Han goes to England in a desperate attempt to save his business. After a failed relationship at Peking University, Bingyu also decides to study in England. Unfortunately, the war soon engulfs Europe, and Han Ziqi and Liang Bingyu are trapped abroad for ten years during which they develop a deep love and appreciation for each other. After the war, they go back to China with their daughter, Han Xinyue, and realise that Junbi and her son are still alive. Han Ziqi refuses to leave Beijing again, but is indecisive in making a choice between the two relationships. The two sisters are left to make their own choices. Although still deeply in love with Han Ziqi, Bingyu chooses to return to England rather than share the same "husband" with her sister or even be married off to another man to cover up the family "scandal." "I am an independent human, not belonging to you or to Liang Junbi." Faced with Han's indecisiveness and her sister's rage, Bingyu says, "You want to be treated as a human being in this family and society, so do I."[75] She leaves, while Junbi decides to raise Xinyue. In 1979, sixteen years after Xinyue's death, Bingyu goes back to look for her daughter in Beijing only to realise

---

[75] Da Huo, *The Jade King*, 543. Author's translation.

the irrecoverable loss of her daughter when she visits the Muslim public cemetery.

In a sense, the female protagonists in Huo's novel subtly challenge the typical image of Hui Muslim women often depicted by Hui male writers of Huo Da's time. Particularly, Zhang Chengzhi (1948–), a prominent and prolific Hui Muslim writer, offers an opportune reference point for comparison. Both Huo and Zhang were born in Hui families in Beijing before 1949. Both published their most influential works around the same time: *The Jade King* was published in 1988, followed by Zhang Chengzhi's *The History of Soul* ("Xinlingshi").[76] Both books have been regarded as the most important contemporary literary works written by Hui Muslim writers in mainland China. Both authors regarded their works as a recapitulation of Hui history, but from different perspectives. As Huo Da comments, *The Jade King* is not just a "summary of the first half of her life experiences and writing practices" but also a "recapitulation of Chinese Hui Muslim history."[77] Zhang Chengzhi, in the Preface to *The History of Soul*, claims that he intends to become "a pen of Jahriyya" ("zheherenye de bi").[78] The specific Hui communities that Huo and Zhang choose to write about, however, are very different. Huo focuses on the history of Hui Muslims in twentieth-century Beijing, whereas Zhang highlights the history of the Jahriyya Sufi order in Northwest China from the Qing Dynasty until just before the early twentieth century. While Huo's literary style is commonly shared by many Hui and Han Chinese writers, Zhang blends different genres of historical, religious, and literary texts to write an "apocryphal counter-history" previously unknown to Han readers, and even to most Muslim readers in China.[79]

In Zhang's portrayal of different female figures, it is common to see both Muslim and non-Muslim women depicted as more or less passive figures who do not take initiative to make their own life choices. For instance, in *The History of Soul*, Zhang praises the bravery of Lady Xifu in salvaging the sacred relic passed down the Jahriyya Sufi order in China in

---

[76] Chengzhi Zhang, *The History of Soul (Xinlingshi* 心灵史*)* (Huacheng chubanshe, 1991).

[77] Yiqing Ding, *History of Huizu Literature (Huizu Wenxue Shi* 回族文学史*)* (Beijing: Minzu Chubanshe, 2015), 331.

[78] Anthony Garnaut, "Pen of the Jahriyya: A Commentary on The History of the Soul by Zhang Chengzhi", *Inner Asia* 8:1 (2006), 29–50; Zhang, *The History of Soul*.

[79] Jian Xu, "Radical Ethnicity and Apocryphal History: Reading the Sublime Object of Humanism in Zhang Chengzhi's Late Fictions", *Positions: East Asia Cultures Critique* 10:3 (2002), 525–46.

the late Qing Dynasty. For Zhang, "Lady Xifu is the kind of woman who devotes her life to heroes; she only seeks to share the same destiny as those heroes … their [women's] lives, despite their own intentions, are particularly dazzling since they are born in great times and give themselves to great men."[80] In his other works with female protagonists, Zhang also tends to portray women as strong yet silent mothers or beautiful daughters in need of salvation. As Hui female literary commentator Li Xiuping puts it, women are "voiceless" (*shiyu*) and lacklustre next to male figures in Zhang's works—women's images are often "blurry, pale, and weak."[81] In contrast, in *The Jade King* Huo Da shows how Hui women could be cunning, materialistic, pious, generous, cruel, revolutionary, romantic, naive, and most importantly that they have their own voices and a distinctive gender consciousness as Muslim women in China.

Seen from the perspective of affective matrivocality, another distinctive feature in the works of Hui women writers is the focus on the everyday Islam, thus offering a non-sectarian perspective in understanding the diverse Hui communities in both rural and urban settings. Veena Das proposes critically engaging with the ordinary, mundane aspects of everyday life in order to understand more complex socio-political contexts through her study of interfaith conflicts in India.[82] Kathleen Stewart highlights the power of the embodied affects—though often fragmented or seemingly trivial in everyday life—in illuminating cultural politics and shaping public sentiments.[83] Building upon the anthropological works on affectivity and the everyday, Charles Hirschkind further argues that the idea of the everyday helps break the fascination with a "set of immutable texts" and open up "a domain of ambiguity, contingency, skepticism, and pragmatic concern" in the anthropology of Islam and the Middle East studies.[84]

---

[80] Zhang, *The History of Soul*, author's translation.

[81] Xiuping Li, "The Construction and Deconstruction of Male Myth: On the Gender Consciousness in Zhang Chengzhi's Writings (Nanxing Shenhua de Goujian He Xiaojie: Zhang Chengzhi Bi Xia de Xingbie Yishi 男性神话的构建和消解——张承志笔下的性别意识)", in *Qingjie Zhi Qi: Lun Zhang Chengzhi de Xinling Zhi Lu* (清洁之旗——论张承志的心灵之旅) (Beijing: Zhishi chanquan chubanshe, 2013), 76–96.

[82] Veena Das, *Life and Words: Violence and the Descent into the Ordinary* (Berkeley, CA: University of California Press, 2006).

[83] Kathleen Stewart, *Ordinary Affects* (Durham, NC: Duke University Press, 2007).

[84] Charles Hirschkind, "Charles Hirschkind's Commentary on Everyday Islam Curated Collection", *Curated Collections, Cultural Anthropology Online*, 2014.

The literary texts produced by Hui women writers in China, though still texts, try to show how affective and ethical struggles unfold in everyday life, particularly among ordinary Muslim women. By showing "the experiences of ambiguity, confusion, and contradiction"[85] in literary forms, Hui women writers reveal the intersectional challenges they face as women, Muslims, mothers, daughters, wives, an ethnic minority, peasants, and migrant workers, amongst a myriad of identities.

The works of Ma Jinlian (马金莲 1982–) are representative of the depiction of everyday Islam among Hui women writers in China. Born into a Hui family in Xiji, Ningxia Hui Autonomous Region (NHAR), Ma Jinlian is known for her portrayal of everyday life in the region. Her own life experiences—ranging from being a farmer, teacher, and local official—attune her to the everyday lives and sentiments of rural Hui villagers. Most of her literary works take place in a fictional village called Fan Valley Village (shanziwan 扇子湾), a typical Hui village in the Yellow Earth Plateau stricken by poverty. Hunger, the lack of water resources, and rapid social transformations in modern China set the stage for her stories. Ningxia is home to different Islamic sects: both Sunni Islam and Sufism are widely practised in the region. Zhang Chengzhi's *The History of Soul* also takes place in Ningxia, but his work focuses on the region's role as the centre of the Jahriyya Sufi order with its history of rebellion, oppression, and revival. While religious practices do permeate everyday life, religion does not come to the foreground as the main subject matter in Ma Jinlian's novels. Rather, she foregrounds everyday struggles in the form of farming, digging wells, making money, raising children, and maintaining *jamaat* in rural Hui communities through poignant descriptions of marriages, funerals, and various religious works (*ermaili*, from the Arabic *amal*).

Ma often uses first-person narrative from the perspectives of women and young girls. In the story *The Little Wife* ("Sui xifu" 碎媳妇),[86] the female protagonist Xuehua experiences a series of humiliations that begin on her wedding day. For Xuehua, the biggest tragedy is the feeling of abandonment she experiences after giving birth to her children. In another story, *Embroidering Mandarin Ducks* ("Xiu yuanyang" 绣鸳鸯),[87] the

---

[85] Charles Hirschkind, "Charles Hirschkind's Commentary on Everyday Islam Curated Collection".

[86] Jinlian Ma, *Little Wife (Sui Xifu 碎媳妇)* (Ningxia renmin chubanshe, 2012).

[87] Jinlian Ma, *Embroidering Mandarin Ducks (Xiu Yuanyang 绣鸳鸯)* (Zhongguo yanshi chubanshe, 2017).

younger sister in the family tells the tragic love story between her elder sister and a vagabond salesman. Her grandparents, a couple of kind-hearted Muslims, rescue a vagabond salesman who has almost lost his life in a snow blizzard. During his long convalescence, the elder sister who is taking care of him falls in love with him. However, he eventually departs, leaving the elder sister pregnant out of wedlock. She chooses to give birth to her baby, who is tacitly adopted by her own mother, who had always wanted to have a son. In the story *Goldflower Sister* ("Jinhua dajie" 金花大姐),[88] the narrator traces the divergence of life paths between her and her elder sister Jinhua, or Goldflower. Though named after a golden flower, Jinhua does not enjoy the prosperous life her name suggests. As the first-born daughter in a poor family, Jinhua quits school early on and stays at home to help her mother with family chores. She also tries her best to support her talented younger sister to get a basic education. As the two sisters grow up, they also grow apart. Jinhua chooses to marry a kind-hearted *ahong* and follows her husband to Xinjiang. However, due to the financial constraints of a rapidly changing society, her husband gives up his religious post. Jinhua tries all kinds of menial jobs as a migrant worker, only to find her job prospects constrained by her illiteracy. The couple works hard to ensure their three children get an education so that they might have a better chance to change their own destiny. The younger sister, on the other hand, moves to the city, finds a stable job, and settles there with her family. As time goes by, the two sisters begin to reconnect, yet still find it hard to bridge the socio-economic gap within the family. What binds them together is their shared fond memories of the past and their strong sisterly bond.

If Huo Da's 1988 novel still reminds readers of a grand historical narrative revolving around the conflict between religious and secular values, the struggles of ordinary Hui women and their everyday sentiments in Ma Jinlian's literary world have taken centre stage. As Ma Jinlian writes in the epilogue to her novella *Long River* ("Changhe" 长河),[89] "[I]n the long river of time, our individual lives are motes of dust. Through my writing, I want to excavate the bright lustre given off by these specks before they return to dust." The voices of women are expressed through their ordinary affects—sorrow, confusion, happiness, longing for love, anger, the sense of loss, and so on—to reflect the multifaceted experiences of Hui

---

[88] Jinlian Ma, *Embroidering Mandarin Ducks*.
[89] Jinlian Ma, *Long River (Changhe* 长河*)* (Zuojia chubanshe, 2014).

women and men in contemporary China. This focus on everyday Islam has been widely shared by many contemporary Hui women writers through the use of different literary forms, including novels and novellas, poems, essays, travelogues, Ramadan diaries, blog posts, and articles in social media platforms.

In the first twenty years of the twenty-first century, digital media—the internet and social media platforms—have played an increasingly important role in making the voices of Hui women writers heard in public spheres.[90] According to my interview with Shalan in 2020, a Muslim woman and bookseller who used to manage the literature section on 2Muslims.com (one of the largest Muslim websites in China before its permanent closure in 2016), there has been a significant growth of Hui women writers in cyberspace since the early 2000s. Another Hui woman writer, Yikalina from Northwest China, also commented that she had started writing fiction while learning Arabic and teaching Qur'ānic recitation in women's mosques in Yunnan: "There are many [women] like me, actually. I just like writing but I am not that talented [as a writer]." When I asked about her writing experiences in the summer of 2020, Yikalina replied, "There are many realistic constraints in life that prevent me from writing, such as taking care of my son or teaching my students. But I still try to write diaries during Ramadan. It's the best time for reflection and writing." Yikalina's experience is not a unique case. In Ma, Romli, and Rahman's study of the Ramadan Diary project among Muslim women on 2Muslim.com before its closure, they found three major themes shared by thirty-three women from over thirty cities or regions in China: their everyday efforts to deepen their understanding of Islam, maintain their Muslim identity, and improve their social relations with Muslims and non-Muslims alike. As Ma, Romli, and Rahman observed, "They freely express their happiness and sorrow, and chronicle their lives with family, colleagues, and community."[91] In other words, the practice of writing by Hui women has extended beyond literature to encompass more diffuse forms of literary expression both online and offline. This trend, in turn, further promotes the visibility and audibility of Hui Muslim women in contemporary China.

---

[90] Ting Ma, Romlah binti Romli, and Nik Adzrieman Abdul Rahman, "Chinese Muslim Women in the Virtual Community: Identity, Expression and Empowerment", *New Media and Mass Communication Online* 65 (2017).

[91] Ma, Romli, and Rahman, "Chinese Muslim Women in the Virtual Community".

Conclusion

To conclude, Hui Muslim women's voices constitute their own unique lineage and continue to influence both Muslims and non-Muslims in China and beyond. In modern China, Hui Muslim women have been cultivating a moderate, non-factional image of Islam in China through literature and mass media. The voices of Hui women writers discussed in this chapter mostly complement rather than challenge various religious interpretations predominantly mediated through Hui Muslim men. Hui women writers' work problematises the framework of gender complementarity and Islamic ethics widely accepted among both Hui men and women. Women writers tend to depict the multifaceted aspects of their female protagonists. It is common to find women—especially mothers—depicted as the pillars who nurture family and preserve Islamic culture and practices. The gender consciousness manifested through Huo Da, Ma Jinlian, and other Hui women writers' works reflects the affective dimension of matrivocality within the heterogeneous Hui communities in China, thus challenging the stereotypical misconception of Muslim women as passive, submissive, and voiceless among both Muslim and non-Muslim readers.

Furthermore, more questions still remain regarding the women-centric Muslim communities in China. While this chapter mainly focuses on the voices of Hui Muslim women, what about women from China's other nine Muslim minorities: the Uyghur, Kazakh, Kyrgyz, Uzbek, Tartar, Salar, Tajik, Dongxiang, and Bao'an? How should we take into account the growing voices of women who convert to Islam as a result of education, marriage, migration, or for other reasons? What about the influence of the matrilineal and matrifocal groups upon local Muslim communities through their interactions both in pre-1949 and in post-1949 China? And how are we to understand the Hanafi school's influence on women-centric Islam in China, given that the majority of Chinese Muslims follow the Hanafi school? Shui and Jaschok, in their groundbreaking work on women's mosques, briefly mention that almost all their research subjects follow the Hanafi school of law (mainly Gedimu and Ikhwani).[92] They also note that there have been internal disagreements regarding the legitimacy of women's mosques at various levels, especially regarding how to interpret the phenomenon of *bidʿa* (innovation in religious affairs) in the socialist

---

[92] Shui and Jaschok, *The History of Women's Mosques in Chinese Islam.*

context.[93] However, more detailed ethnographic work is still needed to understand how the Hanafi school actually facilitates and/or hinders China's women-centric Islam in specific situations. Moreover, it will be interesting to see how Sufism plays a role in shaping matrivocality among Chinese Muslim women. The Qadiriyya, one of the Sufi orders in China, has female saints and mausoleums dedicated to them, as in the case of Cai Gutai. Since the Qadiri tariqa is heavily influenced by the Hanbali rather than the Hanafi school, it is worth asking how certain women-centric Qadiriyya followers practice Islam under the influence of both Islamic and Chinese traditions. This is not in any sense an exhaustive list of questions regarding women-centric Muslim communities in China. More historical and ethnographic studies are still urgently needed to give a more comprehensive image of Islam in China, particularly regarding the lives and voices of Muslim women.

Acknowledgement I would like to sincerely thank my friends and interlocutors—Shalan, Abdullah Wu, Ma Bin, Feng Ahong, Fatima Wu, Dawud, Yikalina, Fatima Ma, Ma Daxiang, and Ye Ge—who generously shared their time, enthusiasm, and resources with me throughout the process of this research. I want to thank Chai Shaojin for encouraging me to write this chapter for this book in the first place. I also want to thank Abbas Panakkal for working with me throughout the pandemic. I am grateful to Jacqueline Armijo for her constructive feedback and advice.

BIBLIOGRAPHY

Abu-Lughod, Lila, *Veiled Sentiments: Honor and Poetry in a Bedouin Society*, Berkeley and Los Angeles: University of California Press, 1986.

Armijo, Jacqueline, "A Unique Heritage of Leadership: Muslim Women in China," *Georgetown Journal of International Affairs* 10:1 (2009), 37–45.

Armijo, Jacqueline, "Muslim Education in China: Chinese Madrasas and Linkages to Islamic Schools Abroad," in Farish Noor, Yoginder Sikang, and Martin van Bruinessen (eds.), *The Madrasa in Asia: Political Activism and Transnational Linkages* (Amsterdam: Amsterdam University Press, 2008), 169–89.

Armijo, Jacqueline, *Sayyid'Ajall Shams al-Din: A Muslim from Central Asia, Serving the Mongols in China, and Bringing Civilization to Yunnan*, Ph.D. dissertation: Harvard University, 1997.

Bahadır, İlknur, *Fatma Aliye's Discourse of Women in the Context of the Islamic Modernization and Tradition*, Masters dissertation: Istanbul Şehir University, 2018.

---

[93] Shui and Jaschok, *The History of Women's Mosques in Chinese Islam*.

Bai, Shouyi, *Huimin Qiyi (Hui Rebellion)*, Shanghai: Shanghai Shudian Chubanshe, 2000.

Barlow, Tani E. "Theorizing Women: Funu, Guojia, Jiating (Chinese Women, Chinese State, Chinese Family)," in Inderpal Grewal and Karen Caplan (eds.), *Scattered Hegemonies: Postmodernity and Transnational Feminist Practices* (Minneapolis, MN: University of Minnesota Press, 1997) 1173–96.

Benite, Zvi Ben-Dor, *The Dao of Muhammad: A Cultural History of Muslims in Late Imperial China*, Leiden: Brill, 2020.

Blackwood, Evelyn, "Representing Women: The Politics of Minangkabau Adat Writings," *The Journal of Asian Studies* 60:1 (2001), 125–49.

Blanchy, Sophie, "A Matrilineal and Matrilocal Muslim Society in Flux: Negotiating Gender and Family Relations in the Comoros," *Africa: The Journal of the International African Institute* 89:1 (2019), 21–39.

Bonate, Liazzat, "Islam and Matriliny along the Indian Ocean Rim: Revisiting the Old "Paradox" by Comparing the Minangkabau, Kerala and Coastal Northern Mozambique," *Journal of Southeast Asian Studies* 48:3 (2017), 436–51.

Bonate, Liazzat, 'Matriliny, Islam and Gender in Northern Mozambique,' *Journal of Religion in Africa* 36:2 (2006), 139–66.

Central Committee of CCP, "Basic Views and Policies on Religious Issues under Socialism in PRC (Guanyu Woguo Shehui Zhuyi Shiqi Zongjiao Wenti de Jiben Guandian He Jiben Zhengce 关于我国社会主义时期宗教问题的基本观点和基本政策)," Beijing, 1982.

Das, Veena, *Life and Words: Violence and the Descent into the Ordinary*, Berkeley, CA: University of California Press, 2006.

Ding, Yiqing, *History of Huizu Literature (Huizu Wenxue Shi 回族文学史)*, Beijing: Minzu Chubanshe, 2015.

Du, Shanshan, "Gender Norms among Ethnic Minorities: Beyond "(Han) Chinese Patriarchy,"" in *Handbook on Ethnic Minorities in China* (Cheltenham, UK: Edward Elgar Publishing, 2016), 240–62.

Du, Shanshan, "Is Buddha a Couple? Gender-Unitary Perspectives from the Lahu of Southwest China," *Ethnology* 42:3 (2003), 253–71.

Fu, Weilin, "Li Zhi Biography (Li Zhi Zhuan 李贽传)," in *History of Ming: On Other Religions (Mingshu: Yijiao Zhuan 明书·异教传)*, Vol. 160, Beijing: Zhonghua Shuju, 1985.

Garnaut, Anthony, "Pen of the Jahriyya: A Commentary on The History of the Soul by Zhang Chengzhi," *Inner Asia* 8:1 (2006), 29–50.

Gillette, Maris, *Between Mecca and Beijing: Modernization and Consumption among Urban Chinese Muslims*, Palo Alto, CA: Stanford University Press, 2000.

Gladney, Dru, *Ethnic Identity in China: The Making of a Muslim Minority Nationality*, New York: Harcourt Brace College Publishers, 1998.

Göle, Nilüfer, *Islam and Secularity: The Future of Europe's Public Sphere*, Durham, NC: Duke University Press, 2015.

142 J. WANG

Göle, Nilüfer, *The Forbidden Modern: Civilization and Veiling*, Ann Arbor, MI: University of Michigan Press, 1996.

Hadler, Jeffrey, *Muslims and Matriarchs: Cultural Resilience in Indonesia Through Jihad and Colonialism*, Ithaca, NY: Cornell University Press, 2008.

Han, Zhongyi, and Yuanyuan Ma, "On Wang Daiyu's Confucian Construction about the Values of Muslim Women (Shitan Wang Daiyu Dui Musilin Funu Guan de Ruhua Goujian 试探王岱輿对穆斯林妇女观的儒化构建)," *Qinghai Minzu Studies* 23:2 (2012), 43–6.

He, Ru, "Islam and Women (Yisilanjiao Yu Funu 伊斯兰教与妇女)," *Hui Women Magazine (Yisilan Funu Zazhi伊斯兰妇女杂志)*, 1936.

Hirschkind, Charles, "Charles Hirschkind's Commentary on Everyday Islam Curated Collection," *Curated Collections, Cultural Anthropology Online*, 2014.

Hu, Liping, "From the Gender's Perspective: Contemporary Huizu Muslim Female Education Taking a Girls' School in Yunnan Zhaotong as Example (Shehui Xingbie Shijiao Xia de Dangdai Musilin Nuxue: Yi Yunnan Zhaotong Mou Huizu Nuxiao Wei Li 性别视角下的当代穆斯林女学——以云南昭通某回族女校为例)," *Journal of Hui Muslim Minority Studies (Huizu Yanjiu)*, 2 (2013), 109–14.

Huo, Da, *The Jade King: History of a Chinese Muslim Family (Musilin de Zangli 穆斯林的葬礼)*, Beijing: Beijing Shiyue Wenyi Chubanshe, 1988.

Huo, Da, *Amend the Breach in Heaven (Bu Tianlie 补天裂)*, Beijing: Beijing Chubanshe, 1997.

Huo, Da, *The World of Mortals (Hongchen 红尘)*, Beijing: Beijing Shiyue Wenyi Chubanshe, 2005.

Israeli, Raphael, *Islam in China: Religion, Ethnicity, Culture, and Politics* (Oxford: Lexington Books, 2002).

Jaschok, Maria, "Religious Agency and Gender Complementarity: Women's Mosques and Women's Voices in Hui Muslim Communities in Central China," *Review of Religion and Chinese Society* 5:2 (2018), 183–207.

Jin, Yijiu, *The History of Islam (Yisilan Jiao Shi)*, Jiangsu: Jiangsu Renmin Chubanshe, 2008.

Kato, Tsuyoshi, *Matriliny and Migration: Evolving Minangkabau Traditions in Indonesia*, Ithaca, NY: Cornell University Press, 1982.

Li, Xiuping, "The Construction and Deconstruction of Male Myth: On the Gender Consciousness in Zhang Chengzhi's Writings (Nanxing Shenhua de Goujian He Xiaojie: Zhang Chengzhi Bi Xia de Xingbie Yishi 男性神话的构建和消解——张承志笔下的性别意识)," in *Qingjie Zhi Qi: Lun Zhang Chengzhi de Xinling Zhi Lu (清洁之旗——论张承志的心灵之旅)* (Beijing: Zhishi Chanquan Chubanshe, 2013), 76–96.

Li, Yinhe, *Feminism (Nuxing Zhuyi 女性主义)*, Shanghai: Shanghai Wenhua Chubanshe, 2018.

Lian, Ruizhi, "Surviving Conquest in Dali: Chiefs, Deities, and Ancestors," in David Faure and Ts'ui-p'ing Ho (eds.) *Chieftains into Ancestors: Imperial Expansion and Indigenous Society in Southwest China* (Vancouver: University of British Columbia Press, 2013), 86–110.

Lipman, Jonathan Neaman, *Familiar Strangers: A History of Muslims in Northwest China*, Seattle, WA: University of Washington Press, 1998.

Liu, Li, and Jing Zhou, "Analysis of the Journal Publications by Hui Muslim Women in the Republic Era (Minguo Shiqi Huizu Nuxing Zuozhe de Baokan Shuxie Pingxi 民国时期回族女性作者的报刊书写评析)," *Journal of Hui Muslim Minority Studies (Huizu Yanjiu)* 3 (2018), 84–8.

Luo, Guihua, *Shaan-Gan-Qing Huizu Women Traditional Social and Cultural Transformations (Shaan-Gan-Qing Huizu Nuxing Shehui Wenhua Bianqian Yanjiu 甘青宁回族女性传统社会文化变迁研究)*, Beijing: Minzu Chubanshe, 2007.

Ma, Bozhong, "On the Hui Women Writers in Yuehua Magazine (Tantan Yuehua de Huizu Nuxing Zuozhe 谈谈《月华》的回族女性作者)," *Chinese Muslims (Zhongguo Musilin)*, 2005.

Ma, Guifen, *Participant Social Research among Muslim Women in the Northwest (Xibei Musilin Funu Shehui Canyu Yanjiu: Jiyu Gansu Sheng Huizu and Dongxiangzu Funu de Ge'an Yanjiu)* 西北穆斯林妇女社会参与研究——基于甘肃省回族、东乡族妇女的个案研究, Beijing: Renmin Chubanshe, 2017a.

Ma, Jinlian, *Little Wife (Sui Xifu 碎媳妇)*, Yinchuan, Ningxia: Ningxia Renmin Chubanshe, 2012.

Ma, Jinlian, *Long River (Changhe 长河)*, Beijing: Zuojia Chubanshe, 2014.

Ma, Jinlian, *Embroidering Mandarin Ducks (Xiu Yuanyang 绣鸳鸯)*, Beijing: Zhongguo Yanshi Chubanshe, 2017b.

Ma, Qiang, *Inside and Outside Hui Quarter: Studies of Xi'an Muslims during the Process of Urban Modernization [Huifang Neiwai: Chengshi Xiandaihua Jincheng Zhong de Xi'an Yisilanjiao Yanjiu]*, Beijing: China Social Sciences Press, 2011a.

Ma, Qiang, "Urbanization and Development of Women's Masjid and Women's School in China (Dushihua Jincheng Zhong de Qingzhen Nusi He Nuxue 都市化进程中的清真女寺和女学)," *Journal of Hui Muslim Minority Studies (Huizu Yanjiu)* 2 (2011b), 110–16.

Ma, Ting, Romlah binti Romli, and Nik Adzrieman Abdul Rahman, "Chinese Muslim Women in the Virtual Community: Identity, Expression and Empowerment," *New Media and Mass Communication Online* 65 (2017).

Ma, Xiuzhen, "Awakening of Muslim Women (Yisilan Funu de Juewu 伊斯兰妇女的觉悟)," *Hui Women Magazine (Yisilan Funu Zazhi伊斯兰妇女杂志)*, 1936.

Ma, Yan, and Pierre Haski, *The Diary of Ma Yan (Ma Yan Riji 马燕日记)*, Tianjin: Tianjin Jiaoyu Chubanshe, 2006.

Mahmood, Saba, *Politics of Piety: The Islamic Revival and the Feminist Subject*, Princeton, NJ: Princeton University Press, 2011.

Millward, James A., "A Uyghur Muslim in Qianlong's Court: The Meanings of the Fragrant Concubine," *The Journal of Asian Studies* 53:2 (1994), 427–58.

National Bureau of Statistics of China, "2010 Census of National Ethnic Groups Based on Age and Gender [Quanguo Ge Minzu Fen Nianling, Xingbie de Renkou]," National Bureau of Statistics of China, 2011.

Pillsbury, Barbara L K., "Being Female in a Muslim Minority in China," in Lois Beck and Nikki Keddie (eds.) *Women in the Muslim World*, Cambridge, MA: Harvard University Press, 1978), 651–76.

Saul, Mahir, "Matrilineal Inheritance and Post-Colonial Prosperity in Southern Bobo Country," *Man* 27:2 (1992), 341–62.

Shih, Chuan-kang, *Quest for Harmony: The Moso Traditions of Sexual Union and Family Life*, Palo Alto, CA: Stanford University Press, 2010.

Shui, Jingjun, and Maria Jaschok, *The History of Women's Mosques in Chinese Islam (Zhongguo Qingzhen Nusi Shi)*, Beijing: Sanlian Hafou Yanjing Xueshucongshu, 2002.

Stewart, Kathleen, *Ordinary Affects*, Durham, NC: Duke University Press, 2007.

Walsh, Eileen Rose, "From Nü Guo to Nü'er Guo: Negotiating Desire in the Land of the Mosuo," *Modern China* 31:4 (2005), 448–86.

Wilkerson, James, "Negotiating Local Tradition with Taoism: Female Ritual Specialists in the Zhuang Religion," *Religion* 37:2 (2007), 150–63.

Xu, Jian, "Radical Ethnicity and Apocryphal History: Reading the Sublime Object of Humanism in Zhang Chengzhi's Late Fictions," *Positions: East Asia Cultures Critique* 10:3 (2002), 525–46.

Yang, Wenjiong, "Women's Madrassa: Development of Mosque Education and Displacement of the Role of Cultural Transmission: Taking Lanzhou, Xi'an and Linxia as Examples (Nuxue: Jingtang Jiaoyu de Tuozhan Yu Wenhua Chuancheng Juese Zhongxin de Weiyi: Yi Lanzhou, Xi'an, Linxia Diaocha Wei Ge'an 女学:经堂教育的拓展与文化传承角色中心的位移——以兰州、西安、临夏调查为个案)," *Journal of Hui Muslim Minority Studies (Huizu Yanjiu)* 1 (2002), 25–31.

Zhang, Chengzhi, *The History of Soul (Xinlingshi 心灵史)*, Guangzhou, Guangdong: Huacheng Chubanshe, 1991.

Zhao, Hui, "Biographical Introduction of Contemporary Hui Women Writers (Dangdai Huizu Nuzuojia Sanlun 当代回族女作家散论)," *Ningxia Daxue Xuebao* 17:3 (1995), 20–5.

Zhou, Xiefan (ed.), *Qingzhen Dadian (清真大典)*, vol. 15, Hefei, Anhui : Huangshan Chushe, 2005.

Matriarchal Family Structure in Korea's Jeju Island and its Implications for the Muslim Community in Korea

Hee Soo Lee

INTRODUCTION

Throughout its long, rich history, women—particularly mothers—have played a major role in Korean society. Women have always been the mainstay of the family economy; in addition, of course, at one time a queen ruled the ancient kingdom of Silla (57 B.C.E–935 C.E.) and the political authority of women was absolute. During the Goryeo period (918–1392), the status and rights of women were little different from those of men in the family sphere, including economic power, inheritance, ancestral rites, and so on. Matrilocal marriage prevailed, and it was quite common for a man to live in his wife's house; a mother enjoyed the same rights as her son, inheriting property in her own right and managing it as she chose. Sons and daughters alternated in taking responsibility for ancestral rites.

H. S. Lee (✉)
Hanyang University, Seoul, South Korea
e-mail: hslee@hanyang.ac.kr

© The Author(s), under exclusive license to Springer Nature
Switzerland AG 2024
A. Panakkal, N. M. Arif (eds.), *Matrilineal, Matriarchal, and Matrifocal Islam*, Palgrave Series in Islamic Theology, Law, and History, https://doi.org/10.1007/978-3-031-51749-5_5

145

Then came the establishment of paternal and patriarchal traditions in Korea today, likely the result of Confucian ideology and the Confucian-based educational system. During the five hundred years of the Joseon Dynasty (1392–1910), Confucianism was the national ideology, and all social systems and family relations were transformed into patrilineal and patriarchal structures. Women were completely excluded from inheritance, ancestor worship, and community decision-making. It became taboo for adult men and women to see each other or mix freely, and the social custom that "a boy and a girl should not sit together after the age of seven" (男女七歳不同席) was born.

Jeju Island, however, is an exceptional case of a semi-matriarchal society in Korea. On this island, located at the southwestern end of the Korean peninsula, almost all tasks—such as community collaboration, responsibility for family finances, inheritance, child-rearing, and education—are women-centred. Most women have the right to make decisions and implement them as the head of the household; most men do subsidiary work, including helping take care of the children and shopping. Although there is only a small Muslim population on the island, newly converted Muslim women continue to hold these roles within the female-centred local culture. Muslim women in Jeju are faced with the challenge of harmonising the local matriarchal and matrifocal traditions with Islamic tenets through reinterpreting the principles of the Qur'ān and *hadīth*.

The unique experience for Muslim women in Jeju seems likely to influence the rest of the Korean peninsula, where Muslim women are expected to gradually create a new more woman-centred model of Muslim society that conflicts as little as possible with the teachings of Islam. Korean Muslim women, who have the highest educational level in Asia, are therefore set to become global leaders in woman-centred social reforms. This chapter focuses on the case of a matriarchal society in Jeju Island, which operates beyond the scope of traditional Korean Confucian stereotypes, and hypothesises how this phenomenon will affect the Muslim community in Korea and help them move forward in the best possible direction.

1. The Status of Women in Korean History

As in other labour-intensive agrarian-sedentary societies in Southeast Asian countries, the role of Korean women in society, labour, and even the conduct of war has played an important part in both the maintenance of families and the national economy throughout the country's history.

Korea's founding myth begins with a tiger god and a bear goddess; the powerful and patient bear goddess is a mythical ancestor of the Korean people. In the mythology of ancient Korea, the role of women is closely linked to fertility and creating new life through sacrifice, concepts that are embodied in this protective deity.[1]

Throughout history, Korean women have contributed vastly to national development and played strong roles in political leadership. Until the end of the fifteenth century, at least, women's social status, economic power, and right to speak were always upheld.[2] When we look at the history of ancient Korea, we find numerous cases of the impact of individual female political leaders on the social role of women. The Silla kingdom produced two queens—Sendeok (r. 632–647) and Jindeok (r. 647–654)—in addition to numerous other female leaders. In the military academy and elite educational system, women also played a key role as *hwarang*, or military commanders. According to the *Sam Guk Sa Gi* (SGSG, "The History of the Three Kingdoms"), female *hwarang* named Nammu and Junjeong led groups of three hundred soldiers during the reign of King Jinheung around 576.[3]

Women's status, active social participation, and self-determination were further strengthened during the Goryeo Dynasty (918–1392). During this period, women mingled freely with men in the public sphere. They participated in national festivals such as Palgwanhoe (a festival in honour of the indigenous gods) and Yeondeunghoe (the Buddhist lantern festival), when young people had the opportunity to meet each other socially and form relationships. It seems clear that monogamy was the norm among ordinary people, although polygamy was prevalent among the nobility and incestuous marriages took place within the royal family. Divorce and remarriage were also much more widely accepted during this period. When a man died, his widow could become the head of the family, and there are documented examples of women exercising their right to property and inheritance. During the Goryeo period, women enjoyed equal inheritance rights which later disappeared until recent legislation in

---

[1] Jang Sik Chang, "Women's duty and its meaning in mythology" 신화를 통해 본 여성의 임무와 그 의미(), *Folklore Studies(민속학연구)* 3, 179.

[2] Kang Min-soon, "Social Status of Koryo Women in 'Koryo History'(고려사에 나타난 고려여성의 사회적 지위)" (Master's dissertation: Jeju National University, 2000), 3–4.

[3] Ki-dong Yi, "Hwarangdo", *Encyclopedia of Korean Culture(한국민족문화대백과사전)*, 1995.

the 1990s.[4] During the Goryeo and early Joseon periods in the fifteenth century, it was customary for married couples to live in the wife's parents' household. This arrangement suggests that the status of women was higher than it was during the later period of the Joseon Dynasty (1392–1910).

However, the establishment of the Joseon dynasty ushered in an era of change, as Korean society adopted a strict hierarchical division and patriarchal family structure that justified unequal social treatment and gender roles following a rigid Confucian ideology and Confucian-based education system. According to Confucian customs, a married woman would leave her parents' household to join that of her husband. During the Joseon period, widows were generally not permitted to remarry, and meeting other men was regarded as adultery. Further, the children of a widow who did not keep her chastity were barred from entering high-level government positions. As the core value of Korean society, Confucianism promoted women's obedience to men throughout their lives: "to the father when young; to the husband when married; and to the son in old age."[5]

For a long time, women's roles were limited to the home as housewives and mothers; they were obliged to take care of their husbands' family, including his parents.[6] When they went out, they wore a long robe called *the jang-ot* that covered them completely, including the hair and face. In the patriarchal and patrilineal Joseon society, the most important function of a wife and daughter-in-law was to produce sons, and she was held responsible if children were girls. Women did not have freedom of expression, nor the right to participate in community decision-making as men did; instead, they were expected to support their husbands' decisions.[7] From a Confucian point of view, a virtuous woman should embrace self-sacrifice and obey social and cultural norms such as serving her parents,

---

[4] Kang Min-soon, "Social Status of Koryo Women", 3–4.

[5] Marian Lief Palley, "Women's status in South Korea: Tradition and change," *Asian Survey* 30:12 (1990), 1136–53; see also Soon-Deok Moon, "Trend and Prospect of Research of Women's Life and Cultural History in Jeju", *The Korean Literature and Arts* 25 (2018), 233.

[6] Pil-wha Chang and Eun-Shil Kim, *Women's Experiences and Feminist Practices in South Korea*, Seoul: Ewha Woman's University Press, 2005.

[7] KOIS (Korea Overseas Information Services), "Women's Role in Contemporary Korea" *Asia Society* 2016, https://asiasociety.org/education/womens-role-contemporary-korea, accessed 14 December 2021.

becoming an obedient and dutiful wife and a wise and caring mother. The failure to bear a son and early widowhood were both considered as cardinal sins against a husband's family ancestors.[8]

With the arrival of Christian missionaries in Korea in the late nineteenth and early twentieth centuries, women experienced a remarkable rise in status. These missionaries established numerous modern schools including medical schools, universities, and even women's universities. As a result, Korean women had the opportunity to access high-level modern education for the first time. The first generation of these educated women became active in encouraging others to follow suit.[9] During the period of Japanese occupation from 1910 to 1945, many Korean women played significant roles in the independence movement,[10] and after independence, the Constitution granted them equal rights and opportunities.[11] While opportunities for higher education greatly improved, however, in other respects, this declaration of equality remained largely theoretical, and little changed in terms of women's participation in the political arena or access to paid work.[12]

In Korea today, the impact of modernity has greatly changed the prevailing understanding of gender roles, and women and men generally enjoy a similar status in terms of education, legal rights, and social activities.[13] Almost 99% of Korean women have completed secondary education, and over 50% are employed; furthermore, more than a quarter of married women are in full-time employment.[14] Legislation has also come to reflect women's rights: the abortion law was conditionally passed in 2019, following the abolition of the "head-of-the-family" system in 2005,

[8] Suk-Ki Hong, "Hae-Nyo, the diving women of Korea", in Herman Rahn and Tetsuro Yokoyama (eds.) *Physiology of Breath-Hold Diving and the Ama of Japan* (Washington DC: National Academy of Sciences/National Research Council, 2014), 99–112.

[9] KOIS, "Women's role in contemporary Korea."

[10] C. Sarah Soh, *The Comfort Women: Sexual Violence and Postcolonial Memory in Korea and Japan*, Chicago: University of Chicago Press, 2008.

[11] Article 11 of the 1948 National Constitution states that "all citizens shall be equal before the law, and there shall be no discrimination in political, economic, social or cultural life on account of sex, religion or social status."

[12] Palley, "Women's status in South Korea."

[13] Laurel Kendall, *Under Construction: The Gendering of Modernity, Class, and Consumption in the Republic of Korea*, Honolulu: University of Hawaii Press, 2002.

[14] Archie Resos, "The Empowerment of Women in South Korea," *Journal of International Affairs* (2014), online edition: https://jia.sipa.columbia.edu/online-articles/empowerment-women-south-korea, accessed 14 December 2021.

which had previously formed the core of the Korean family system.[15] In 2013, marital rape was criminalised, and the law also acknowledged that women could be perpetrators of rape. Male politicians still outnumber women in the political sphere, yet increasing numbers of women are becoming politically active. Since the election of South Korea's first female president, Park Geun-Hye, in 2013, the public sphere—particularly the economy—has become more open to women.

Nevertheless, prejudice against women in society remains widespread, and rigid gender stereotypes consistently encourage them to remain at home as housewives and accept a subordinate status to men, both in the domestic and in the public spheres.[16] This too appears to be changing, however, and it seems likely that most Korean women today enjoy more financial independence and play a greater role in household decision-making than previous generations. A clear example of a more woman-focused Korean society can be found in the case of Jeju Island.

2. The Matriarchal Tradition of Jeju Island

Jeju Island, located in the southwestern end of the Korean peninsula, is an exceptional case of a semi-matriarchal society. Throughout the history of the island from pre-modern times, almost all tasks have been woman-centred—including community collaboration and responsibility for family finances, child-rearing and education—with most women having the right to make decisions and implement them as the head of the household. The concept of "woman-centredness" was the spirit and essence of Jeju.[17] Ever since the traditional agricultural era, Jeju women have been the pillars of the domestic economy, actively participating in farming and work at sea. Female divers, known as *haenyeo*, became the first female marines to take part in the Korean War, in addition to being role models for female

---

[15] Woong Kyu Sung, "Abortion in South Korea: The Law and the Reality," *International Journal of Law, Policy and the Family*, 26:3 (2012), 278–305.

[16] Chang and Kim, *Women's Experiences and Feminist Practices in South Korea;* Fang Lee Cooke, "Women's participation in employment in Asia: a comparative analysis of China, India, Japan and South Korea," *The International Journal of Human Resource Management* 21:12 (2010), 2249–70.

[17] Ok-Kyung Pak, "The Women's Side of Jeju Identity: Women Centredness," *World Environment and Island Studies* 5:4 (2015), 327.

participation in the economy.[18] The gender norms on Jeju Island reverse those of both mainland Korea and most Western societies. The gulf between the *haenyeo*s of Jeju and the stereotype of the Korean woman—with her submissive, domestic, and dependent role—have been described as two conflicting streams of socio-cultural narrative.[19]

The matriarchal tradition of Jeju society, represented by *haenyeo* culture, manifests itself in a number of ways. The oral traditions and intangible heritage of Jeju—found in folk songs, working songs, seasonal rituals, and rite of passage customs—include numerous characterisations of Jeju womanhood, emphasising the virtues of toughness, diligence, independence, and patience.[20] Jeju's creation myth begins with the giant goddess Seolmundae Halmang (grandmother), who created the island and became the patron of the women divers. The folktale suggests that the centrality of women and mothers is at the very heart of Jeju culture; other goddesses in Jeju mythology are generally "superwomen" with powerful abilities. Many unique goddesses appear in Jeju myths, embodying the extraordinary power of women, such as Seolmundae, goddess of creation; Yeongdeung, goddess of wind; Jacheongbi, goddess of agriculture; and Gamunjangagi, goddess of fate.[21]

Traditionally, Jeju women were all-weather workers who were in charge of the home economy as a result of their hard work in the sea and the fields; even new mothers would be back at work within two days of giving birth. This tradition of strength contributed to legends of female heroes. Kim Man-Deok (1739–1812) exemplifies this heroic female figure, saving the poor of the island in 1794 by donating her entire fortune to relieve severe famine and starvation. A great businesswoman, her dedication to Jeju society, which had fallen into terrible poverty, is still praised to this day. Of course, legends and folktales are a product of the human imagination—yet these imaginative fictions reflect the beliefs, values, and aspirations of contemporary people. Women's position in Jeju mythology is absolute, reflecting beliefs at the heart of the culture about the role of

---

[18] Soon-Deok Moon, "The Practice and Question of the Culture of Jeju Women," *Jeju Studies*, 32 (2009), 89.

[19] Hong, "Hae-Nyo, the diving women of Korea," 64.

[20] Moon, "Trend and Prospect of Research of Women's Life and Cultural History in Jeju", 235; Moon, "The Practice and Question of the Culture of Jeju Women," 5.

[21] Mi-Jeong Ahn, *Jamnyeo in Korea, History and Culture of Haenyeeo (Women Diver)* (Seoul: Yeokrak, 2019), 23–4.

women. It seems highly likely that a women-centred, female-led society existed on Jeju Island long before modern ideas about gender equality.[22]

In addition to the mythological tradition of female power, the formation of a matriarchal society in Jeju was more specifically based on the influence and socio-economic position of *haenyeo*. The climate and geographical conditions of the island, covered in stony ground and blown by the winds, did not allow for a comfortable existence. In an environment of material scarcity, the participation of women in the labour force was essential. Perhaps as a natural result of women's economic activities, their status and authority were high; such a society requires both women and men for its survival. It is important to note that, although Jeju identity is often presented as woman-centred, with women's position seen as pivotal, everything in the village was done in cooperation with men.[23] Yet the food and resources harvested from the sea gradually gained importance, as farming alone was insufficient to provide for the community and the taxation demanded by the government rose ever higher. Harvesting seaweed and abalone was the responsibility of women, and as this area became more important, a woman-centred economy—in which women's contribution outstripped that of men—came into being.[24]

The development of Jeju's woman-centred tradition and the culture of women divers, or *haenyeo*, are therefore inseparable. Women divers were economically self-sufficient. They were often the main breadwinners of the family, while men took care of children and the shopping—in sharp contrast to the Confucian norms of mainland Korea. Women are the "social adults" who support their families and dominate the socio-economic sphere of village life, according to Heung-Kuk Cho; they are competent, dedicated social actors who are full of self-respect, and mutual assistance among women is the basic form of village collaboration.[25] *Haenyeo* culture is an egalitarian and women-centred form of social organisation, modelled on the concept of a symbiosis between nature and society—highly

---

[22] Jang Il-hong, "Jeju Women's Myth and Eroticism," *Jeju Sound*, 7 March 2018, http://www.jejusori.net/news/articleView.html?idxno=201195, accessed 25 January 2022.

[23] Pak, "The Women's Side of Jeju Identity: Women Centredness," 332.

[24] Moon, "The Practice and Question of the Culture of Jeju Women," 1010.

[25] Heung-Kuk Cho, *The History and Culture of Southeast Asia,* Seoul: Sonamu, 2019, 267.

surprising when considered in the context of mainland Korea's staunch patriarchy based on Confucian ideas.[26]

Originally, diving was an exclusively male profession in Korea, with the exception of women who worked alongside their husbands.[27] Change came after 1629, during the Joseon period, when Jeju women were confined to the island and banned from moving to the mainland for the next two hundred and fifty years. While men of the island were taken to the mainland to work on public projects, women became responsible for the economy of Jeju. When women first began to venture into the water, it was a shock to the male-centred Confucian worldview.[28] By the eighteenth century, however, so many men had lost their lives as a result of deep-sea fishing accidents or as casualties of war that female divers outnumbered men, and diving became the work of women.[29]

As sea-diving firmly established itself as a female-dominated industry, many *haenyeo* subsequently replaced their husbands as the main breadwinners of the family. From the late nineteenth century, their economic activities extended to the southern coast of the Korean Peninsula and was not limited to Jeju Island alone. As sea-diving became the sole source of income for the people of Jeju, the economic power of *haenyeo* meant that they eventually became recognised as the heads of their households, and responsible for domestic affairs. As a result, a semi-matriarchal society steadily developed, reversing the traditional roles and making the island an outlier from Korea's patriarchal mainland society.[30]

---

[26] According to the research of Dr. Ok-Kyung Pak, who made a comparative study on the "female dominance" in Jeju, Korea, and the Minangkabau of West Sumatra, Indonesia, neither women nor men are actually dominant. In Minangkabau, power is shared equally but genealogies are based on matrilineality; some Jeju people call the island a "matrilineal" society, but no formal analysis has been done. Pak, "The Women's Side of Jeju Identity: Women Centredness," 327–8.

[27] Suk-Ki Hong, "Hae-Nyo, the diving women of Korea", in Herman Rahn and Tetsuro Yokoyama (eds.) *Physiology of Breath-Hold Diving and the Ama of Japan* (Washington DC: National Academy of Sciences/National Research Council, 2014), 99–112.

[28] Ahn, *Jamnyeo in Korea*, 58.

[29] Joo-Young Lee and Hyo Hyun Lee, "Korean Women Divers 'Haenyeo': Bathing Suits and Acclimatization to Cold," *Journal of the Human-Environment System* 17:1 (2014), 1–11.

[30] Sang-Hun Choe, "Hardy Divers in Korea Strait, 'Sea Women' Are Dwindling" *New York Times,* March 29 2014, https://www.nytimes.com/2014/03/30/world/asia/hardy-divers-in-korea-strait-sea-women-are-dwindling.html, accessed 14 December 2021; Gwi-Sook Gwon, "Changing Labor Processes of Women's Work: The Haenyeo of Jeju Island", *Korean Studies* 29 (2005), 114–36.

Unique expressions of this semi-matriarchal culture included the custom of men paying a dowry to the family of the bride, meaning that families celebrated the birth of girls more than that of boys. At funerals, the women of the village would carry their departed relatives themselves, whereas in a Confucian-centred society, funerals are an important ritual for men alone.[31] Traditions surrounding ancestral rites in Korea are also thoroughly patriarchal; their subjects are men, and the participants and organisers are men. In Jeju, however, not only do women organise ancestral rites but ordinary women are honoured and celebrated in them. Such rituals are rare compared to other parts of Korea, yet even today the legendary female benefactor Man-Deok Kim (mentioned above) as well as women such as Soon-Ae Hong and other female leaders who saved the community in the face of hunger and crisis are celebrated in memorial rituals from village to village. In some aspects of Confucian ancestor worship, the exclusion of women is difficult to negotiate, yet the culture of Jeju still allows for a higher level of female participation in these rituals than is common in the rest of the country.

The preeminent position of the *haenyeo* in Jeju has clearly served to solidify women's roles, responsibilities, and social influence in the community. These strong women have contributed to the development of a uniquely matriarchal society in modern Korea, one that is strongly connected to the land, the sea, and spirituality. Nowadays, however, the tradition of female divers' dominance in their home economy has diminished due to dramatic changes of the way of life in Korea, particularly among younger generations. In present-day Jeju, the population of *haenyeo* is rapidly disappearing. In 1969—almost 50 years ago—there were 20,832 divers, but by 2019, only 3820 divers remained, with 90% of them over 50 years old.[32] As the population of divers decreases, so too does the influence of their culture and value system. The people of Jeju are therefore faced with the challenge of how to maintain and revive the spirit of *haenyeo* culture. The tradition is an essential part of life in Jeju, where women's economic autonomy is equal to men's, and where social organisation is

---

[31] Soon-Deok Moon, "The Historical and Cultural Meaning of Jeju Women Commemorated through the memorial rituals: Focusing on Kim Manduk, Mrs. Koh, Mrs. Park, and Hong Yoonae", *Tamra Culture* 63 (2020), 88–9.

[32] KOSIS (Korean Statistical Information Service), available online: https://kosis.kr/statHtml/statHtml.do?orgId=218&tblId=DT_21802_E001053_1&vw_cd=&list_id=00000106&scrId=&seqNo=&lang_mode=ko&obj_var_id=&itm_id=&conn_path=R1&path=

founded on egalitarian principles.[33] Moreover, this social model is close to global standards for gender equality and suggests hope for the development of the standards of wider Korean society—and particularly Muslim communities—in the future. The tradition of *haenyeo* deserves to be celebrated as one of Jeju's most valuable treasures; accordingly, in 2016, it was recognised by UNESCO as the island's Intangible Cultural Heritage.

3. The Emergence and Development of the Korean Muslim Community

1. Historical Background

Contrary to popular belief, Islamic history in Korea and Korea's relationship with the Muslim world predate the Korean War by more than a millennium. Striking artifacts from the fourth and fifth centuries point to an ancient history of commercial and political relations between Korea and the peoples of the Arabian Peninsula and Persia, which continued after the arrival of Islam. Written references are few and far between, but there is sufficient documentation to demonstrate the existence of significant commercial ties. Although the exact date of the arrival of the first Muslims in Korea has not yet been determined, it is believed that they came to Korea via China during the period of the Unified Silla Kingdom (676–935). Archaeological excavations, folklore, and oral tradition all show evidence of cultural exchange between ancient Korea and Western Asia, including the Byzantine Empire; the Persian epic *Kūshnāma*, for example, includes a love story between a Sassanian prince and a Silla princess.[34] Goods traded between two regions included Roman and Persian-type glassware, Persian carpets, and items made of Persian silver. These concrete pieces of evidence show that trade and cultural exchange with Western Asia has been part of Korean history for at least 1200 years.

Muslim manuals of navigation show that Muslim navigators were quite at home in the south-eastern China Sea, where the first Muslim colonies were established as early as the eighth century. According to such Muslim narrations as *Akhbār al-Ṣīn wa'l-Hind* ("Accounts of China and India") in the mid-ninth century, collected by Sulaimān al-Tājir and completed by Abū Zaid al-Sirafi, there were more than 100,000 Muslims on the

---

[33] Pak, "The Women's Side of Jeju Identity: Women-Centredness," 330.
[34] Hee Soo Lee, *Kushnameh*, Seoul: Cheong A Publication, 2014.

156 H. S. LEE

south-east coast of China.[35] Direct encounters between Koreans and Muslims in Korea are borne out by references to Silla found in the writings of Muslim historians and geographers—such as Ibn Khurdādhbih, Sulaimān al-Tājir, and Masʿūdī—between the ninth and fifteenth centuries.[36] Ibn Khurdādhbih was the first Arab to mention Muslims residing in Silla Korea, and Masʿūdī wrote about Iraqis who lived there. Shams al-Dīn al-Dimashqī, Aḥmad al-Nuwāyrī, and al-Maqrīzī mentioned the emigration of members of the ʿAlid family to Silla, seeking asylum from Umayyad persecution. Alas, there are no writings referring to the return of Muslims from Korea.

The first Korean historical text documenting relations with Muslims is *Goryeosa*, the official chronicle of the Goryeo dynasty (918–1392). According to the chronicle, a Tashi (Arab) group of a hundred members, headed by a certain al-Rāzī, came to Korea for trade in 1024, followed by several Muslim trade groups headed by Ḥasan, al-Rāzī, and Abū Nahab. During their stay in Korea they were treated as important guests by the king and returned loaded with gifts. When the Mongols invaded Korea in 1270, many Muslims serving in the Mongol administration came with them. During the period of Mongol influence (1270–1368), many Muslims settled permanently and assimilated into Korean society, thanks to the preferential treatment and profitable economic advantages offered to them.

Muslims in Korea formed their own communities in the Goryeo capital, Gae-seong, where they could maintain their culture, traditions, and Islamic feasts and practices. They built mosques called *yegung* and elected their own religious leaders. From time to time, the heads of the Muslim community had the exceptional honour of attending court ceremonies, where they recited the Qur'ān and prayed for the king's longevity and the prosperity of the country. Under the assimilation policy of the Joseon dynasty (1392–1910), however, Muslims in Korea—many of whom had secured high social and economic positions—suddenly abandoned their distinctive attire, customs, and rituals, including Islamic practices such as prayer and fasting. Influenced by the Neo-Confucianism of the Chinese Ming dynasty, a Joseon royal decree in 1427 prohibited what it declared

---

[35] Sulaymān al-Tājir, *Akhbār al-Ṣīn wa-l-Hind*, ed. and trans. J. Savagat, Paris: Societe D'edition Les Belles Lettres, 1948.

[36] Ibn Khurdādhbih, *Kitāb al-masālik wa-l-mamālik*, ed. M. J. de Goeje, Leiden: Brill, 1889.

to be "alien" Muslim culture and tradition. After that, there are no historical documents on cultural contacts between Korea and the Muslim world from the mid-fifteenth century until the early twentieth century.

In spite of the setbacks for Muslim society in Korea resulting from the forced assimilation policy of the Joseon Dynasty, Muslims made important contributions to astronomy, calendar science, and medicine, as well as the development of musical and scientific instruments in Korea. According to *Joseon Wangjo Silok* (the official chronicles of the Joseon dynasty), the Korean lunar calendar, which was widely used throughout the period, could be completed based on Islamic astronomy and calendar science. Islamic science may also have contributed to the invention of various scientific instruments in Korea in the mid-fifteenth century, such as the celestial globe, water clock, sundial, astronomic clock, and rainfall gauge.

Islamic activities in Korea resumed with the arrival of Russian Turks in the 1920s, fleeing the Bolshevik revolution. Around two hundred Muslim Russian Turks settled permanently in Korea and established their own national and religious federation *(Millî ve dinî cemiyet)*. They benefited from trade between Manchuria, Korea, and Japan and obtained high social status under the protection of the Japanese governor-general of Korea (1910–1945). However, after Korean independence in 1945 and the outbreak of the Korean War in 1950, they were pressured to emigrate to Turkey, Europe, and the USA.

A modern Muslim community in Korea emerged after 1955, founded by Turkish Muslim soldiers who had participated in the Korean War (1950–1953) and used their military mission to spread their faith in Korea. The construction of the Seoul Central Mosque in 1976 marked the rapid growth of Islam in Korea, and the number of Muslims increased to 10,000 in 1979. The Korean Muslim community contributed to Korean society by maintaining friendly relations with the government and creating bridges to the Muslim world. Today, there are around 200,000 Muslims in South Korea, including 50,000 Korean converts, and more than 25 mosques and 250 *muṣallā*s (prayer halls) in the major cities. There are no reliable records regarding Muslims in North Korea.

2. Socio-economic Conditions of Korean Muslims
The economic status of Korean Muslims in general runs parallel to wider economic development in Korea. Many of them are likely to be in a position to help their fellow believers and donate to the Muslim community. Their social position is less advantageous, however, due to certain

fundamental difficulties that make it challenging to balance religious obligations with everyday life—particularly for converts. From the mid-1970s, the number of Korean Muslim converts suddenly increased, mainly among labourers who wanted to advance in the Middle East construction market, students who moved to Arab countries while studying the language and culture, and those involved in business with oil-producing countries in the Middle East. However, since the 1980s this number has decreased significantly, becoming limited to those who choose the religion for spiritual reasons alone rather than for economic advantage or to increase their social status.

Converts to Islam often struggle to follow the schedule of daily prayers, however, since it is often impossible in the context of the workplace, and many may only be able to participate in the Friday prayer.[37] Few can fulfil the obligation to fast during the month of Ramadan, although most try to fast for at least a few days—and even this may be difficult if they are seen as "heretics" by the rest of their families. If Ramadan falls during the holiday season, fasting becomes easier, and many Muslim students join the *itikāf* camp, staying together at the mosque. The payment of *zakat* is uncommon in Korea, partly because there is no system to collect it and partly because there is little understanding that this is a religious duty. Similarly, very few are able to perform *hajj*. While several hundred pilgrims from Korea made the pilgrimage every year during the 1970s, since the 1980s the number has decreased substantially. Finally, even basic guidelines on permitted and prohibited food may be hard to follow, although most Muslims make an effort to avoid pork. Since the establishment of the *halāl* butcher shop in the Seoul Islamic Centre and the opening of many *halāl* grocery shops in cities with a stronger Muslim population, however, this is gradually becoming easier.[38]

There are few Muslim marriages in Korea. Most Korean Muslim bridegrooms choose non-Muslim Korean partners, on the condition that the bride will convert to Islam at some time in the future. In the case of Muslim women, however, it is very difficult to find a non-Muslim Korean partner who is prepared to consider conversion. Korean Muslim women with strong faith therefore tend to marry foreign Muslims. Recently, it has become increasingly common for foreign Muslim labourers—mostly from

---

[37] Hee Soo Lee, *Korea and the Muslim World: A Historical Account* (Istanbul: IRCICA, 2020), 293.

[38] Lee, *Korea and the Muslim World*, 293.

Pakistan and Bangladesh—to marry Korean women. Korean Muslim weddings are usually celebrated twice: once in the mosque, in the Islamic tradition, and then in the wedding ceremonial hall in the Korean style, similar to Western weddings. Many Korean Muslims conduct funeral ceremonies according to Korean traditions, which differ somewhat from those of Islam. There are no Muslim cemeteries, which poses another difficulty for the Muslim community.[39]

The question of how to remain faithful to Islamic teachings depends, of course, on an individual Muslim's personal intention and commitment. Yet to help each individual achieve this, the Muslim community also needs to make every effort to provide a positive environment for Islam to thrive within Korean society. In Korea, full freedom of religion is guaranteed by the constitution, and the government values the presence of Muslims and their contribution to national interests. In 1976, for example, the site of the Seoul Central Mosque and Islamic Centre was donated to the Korean Muslim Federation by Park Jung-Hee, then president of Korea.

Today, it is essential for the country to build stronger relations with Muslim nations, including those in the Arab World, due to high levels of dependence in terms of energy and the economy. Moreover, Korea's close cultural and commercial relations with the Muslim world countries have a much longer history, stretching back over a thousand years to the time of the Unified Silla Kingdom (676–935).[40] Nevertheless, many Koreans still have a negative perception of Islam. Misconceptions about certain aspects of Islam—such as polygamy, attitudes toward violence and terrorism, human rights, and the role of women—are widespread and have even found their way into some Korean school textbooks. Like most new converts in non-Muslim majority countries, Korean Muslims are faced with numerous difficulties in implementing their religious obligations. The lack of qualified Muslim leaders and Islamic literature, as well as insufficient financial backing, contribute to these difficulties. Moreover, the hostility that many Koreans feel towards Muslims, based on misunderstandings about the religion, has become a great psychological burden for Korean Muslims in their everyday lives.

---

[39] Lee, *Korea and the Muslim World*, 294.

[40] Hee Soo Lee, "1500 Years of Contact between Korea and the Middle East," *Middle East Institute Journal* (online), June 7, 2014, /https://www.mei.edu/publications/1500-years-contact-between-korea-and-middle-east, accessed 25 January 2022.

160 H. S. LEE

It seems likely that the Muslim women of Jeju, who are familiar with the island's matriarchal traditions, will be a leading force in bringing positive change to Korea's Muslim community. In wider society, women have long taken a leading role in the country's domestic economy, in both large and small cities, and, since the 1990s, women's human rights have gradually improved and there has been greater focus on a more female-centred approach to society. Gender equality in all fields is guaranteed by law, and today the civil service, the judiciary, and the medical sector are increasingly dominated by women. Korean Muslim society has reflected these wider social changes with regard to women's rights. We now turn to the case of Muslim women in Jeju, and consider how they may influence Islam in Korea more generally, providing an example of equitable gender roles beyond the scope of traditional Korean Confucian stereotypes.

4. Korean Muslim Women in Jeju and Matriarchal Traditions

In Korea, as in many other regions in Asia, inequality between women and men, and between girls and boys, has long been accepted as natural. Yet in a number of regions in Southeast Asia, there are examples of women playing an active role in social and economic life. A Chinese map, produced in 1526, went so far as to describe Southeast Asia as a barbaric region that "values women and despises men." In agricultural societies, where women's labour plays a vital part, their social participation and right to property followed naturally.[41]

The Minangkabau of West Sumatra, Indonesia, currently comprise the largest matrilineal society in the world; they are also Muslim. According to some anthropologists, their traditional social and political organisation seemingly reflects a state of "pure matriliny." Within this system, Minangkabau women occupy a distinctive place. The Minangkabau social structure is guided by *adat*, a behavioural code and worldview that sets the rules on matriliny in terms of village organisation, group membership, residence, and the inheritance of property. Among the Minangkabau, property such as land and traditional houses are inherited through the female line.[42]

---

[41] Cho, *The history and culture of Southeast Asia*, 218.
[42] Abdul Mahdi, Yonariza Mahdi, and Hanung Ismono, "Gender Inequality and the Oppression of Women within Minangkabau Matrilineal Society," *Asian Women* 32:3 (2016), 23–49.

It can therefore be seen that matrilocal and woman-centred traditions are not unique to Jeju society, but also found in other Southeast Asian Muslim communities. The prominence of women in Jeju's economy and society can provide a model for women's roles in Korea in the twenty-first century. Further, the matriarchal culture of Jeju could have a positive influence on wider Korean Muslim society. Accordingly, it is important to investigate whether Jeju's woman-centred traditions are shared by Muslim women living on the island.

The number of Korean Muslim women in Jeju is small. However, through intensive analysis of the lives of Muslim women from Jeju and in-depth interviews with them, my research aimed to reach a new understanding of the potential roles and development directions for other Muslim women in Korea. Fatima, a Muslim woman from the island, provides a clear example. She has been married to her husband, a Yemeni, for five years, and they have two children. Fatima runs a local *halāl* restaurant and is fully responsible for the family finances, in addition to raising and educating her children. She also attends and speaks at village meetings. While her situation as a Muslim woman with a foreign husband was initially regarded as alien, she has now been accepted by the local community as a strong Jeju woman in her own right, rather than simply seen as a Muslim, or as the wife of a foreigner. Much, of course, depends on a woman's individual personality; while some prefer to take a subordinate role to their husbands, in accordance with Islamic tradition, others maintain the Jeju ideal of strong independent womanhood. Yet Jeju's unique society inevitably has some impact on the Muslim women who live there, with positive implications for the potential of a more woman-centred development trajectory within Muslim minority communities in Southeast Asia.[43]

The role of Muslim women in Korea reflects the traditional role of Korean women more generally: to care for their husbands' family and to produce sons. Muslim women in Korea have thus been relegated to the domestic sphere of child-rearing and housekeeping, becoming what has been described as "inside people."[44] In contrast, Muslim women of Jeju have found a different role and strong voice through the challenge of engaging in paid work. Through their own resourcefulness, working in

---

[43] Interview with Mrs. Maryam Lee on October 11th, 2020.
[44] Cumings, Bruce, *Korea's Place in the Sun: A Modern History*, (New York: W. W. Norton and Company, 1998), 47.

groups and developing their physical strength, Jeju Muslim women gained financial independence and autonomy equivalent to that of men, and in some cases greater.

Most of the Muslim women I met during the course of my research in Jeju had converted to Islam as a result of marriage to foreign Muslim men. It is unclear whether Jeju Muslim women who live outside the island can continue to adhere to the Jeju concept of womanhood, given how much their ideals and thinking differ from those of other Korean Muslim women. Jeju Muslim women rarely wear traditional modest Muslim dress, for example. Wearing hijab in Jeju increases attention and can even be a threat to women due to Islamophobia within the community. While the original purpose of hijab was to protect women, in Jeju it can have the opposite effect: it increases the level of risk for them, and amplifies unnecessary interest. Some Muslim women on the island argue that it is better not to wear hijab, since in Korea it can be seen as symbolising the passivity of Muslim women who are confined to the home. Ayana Moon, a model who always wears a hijab in Indonesia as part of the Muslim *sunna*, feels uncomfortable wearing the same clothes in Korea, feeling it to be a symbol of female subjugation and represents economic dependency.[45]

In addition, Jeju Muslim women are almost always the breadwinners of the family, as well as having the final say in the upbringing and education of their children. Since the majority have foreign husbands, they are considered as heads of their household at community gatherings, and in the context of social and political decision-making. All Jeju women are actively aware of their legal rights, and Muslims are no exception; Korean law specifies the same inheritance rights for women and men, and Jeju Muslim women therefore claim an equal share. They also take part in religious duties and festivals on an equal footing to men, without any gender segregation. Such practices are also seen as acceptable by Muslim men on the island: Haji Bashir Kim, the founding director of the Jeju Islamic Centre, also expressed his strong belief that Jeju women's matriarchal traditions and leading role in the economic sphere would have a positive impact on Muslim women in other parts of Korea.[46]

---

[45] Zoom Interviews with Ayana Moon in September and October 2020.

[46] Interview with Haji Bashir Kim, the Founding Director of Jeju Islamic Center and Vice President of RISEAP, on 10 October 2020. Bashir Kim studied *shari'a* law at Qatar University in the 1980s.

Living on Jeju, Muslim women are strongly influenced by the independence of other Jeju women. They are so few in number that it is difficult to base any hypothesis on their experiences, yet it seems clear that these women will not choose a passive and subservient role. The long matriarchal traditions of the island differ significantly from both Korean and Islamic traditions; as such, the spirit of Jeju holds the potential for combining with Islamic teachings to open up new possibilities for contemporary Islam in Korea.

5. The Prospect and Challenge of Muslim Women in Korean Society

The example of Korean Muslim women in Jeju Island gives hope that women can play a more progressive and positive role in Muslim societies through the reinterpretation of Qur'ān and *hadīth* without having to abandon established personal practices or the traditions of family life. It suggests that it is possible to establish a new kind of relationship between Muslim couples that can benefit both individuals and wider society in the future.

The Korean Muslim community is small and has yet to open itself to the reinterpretation of religious texts and ideas of gender equality within Islam. No strong female leader of the Muslim community has yet emerged to challenge traditional thinking. Yet a new generation of Muslim women, such as Ayana Moon—a Korean Muslim woman who wears hijab, and enjoys huge popularity in Indonesia as a model—are gradually coming to prominence. Moon has the potential to become a future leader of the Korean Muslim community as a result of her fame in both Korea and Indonesia, and also through her active community service as a Muslim woman, as well as her work for the UN on global sustainability. In interviews that formed part of this research, she discussed desirable ways for Korean Muslim women to live, saying that,

> Islam's cultural tradition does not hinder women's political, economic, or social advancement. Moreover, it seems important for Muslim women themselves to recognise that women's social contributions and activities are in harmony with Islamic values.[47]

---

[47] Interview with Ayana Moon, September 2020.

It is important that women themselves should be aware of issues of religion and gender roles; one of the most serious obstacles to change is Korean Muslim women's unquestioning acceptance of their husbands' beliefs and practices as Islamic, when in many cases they are rooted in indigenous culture or misunderstanding of their faith. Their task is to recognise their own rights, as it is the task of Muslim men to respect women's participation in society and the economy. Through educating both women and men, the community can embrace a new form of Islamic culture based on the ideal of gender equality in its contemporary form, part of a Korean society that is already rapidly becoming more woman-centred. Islamic principles and the teachings of the Qur'ān are based on gender equality. We no longer live in a nomadic society where men were, by necessity, responsible for production; today's global society demands that both men and women share in economic life as well as in raising the family. As a result, we need a new understanding of the holy texts that is compatible with this new era, without violating Islamic tenets of faith regarding the roles of men and women. This will transform the current stereotype of Muslim women as passive and oppressed.

According to national inheritance laws, when a married man dies, the proportion of inheritance is one for each child, and one and a half for his widow. All children inherit the same amount, regardless of gender. The legal system of naming also changed recently, when the paternal family system was abolished in 2005, so children are no longer obliged to take their father's last name. While an overwhelming majority do adopt their father's surname, in accordance with tradition, an increasing number choose to use the surnames of both their parents. If, for example, the father's surname is Lee and mother's is Park, their daughter may decide to adopt the surname Lee Park. Traditionally, in Korea, women retain their own family name after marriage, and it is rare to find a woman who changes her name to that of her husband unless his family are Muslim; for these women, in particular, it is important to raise awareness of their rights as both women and Muslims.

In wider Korean society, the culture is rapidly moving towards gender equality, and the Muslim community is no exception. As the influence of Jeju's matriarchal culture spreads, understanding of women's rights among Korean Muslims is likely to increase. Female converts to Islam in Jeju remain faithful to their matriarchal traditions as well as to the teachings of their religion, creating the possibility of a more woman-centred Muslim community. Muslim women are thus expected to create a new model of a society in which women enjoy equal power in the family as wage earners, co-parents, and decision-makers, sharing domestic tasks equally with their husbands and having a voice in all areas of everyday life, from the family budget to their sexual lives. They already have equal rights to inheritance, political freedom, and the right to participate in social activities, since Korean society is now increasingly women-centred. Korean women enjoy some of the best opportunities in the world for higher education, suggesting that Korean Muslim women will become global leaders in the reinterpretation of Islamic texts and resulting social reform.

The role of women is an essential aspect of all Muslim societies, but all the more so when Muslims are a minority group. In this regard, the potential of Jeju's culture to influence the development of the wider Korean Muslim community through its women is a precious opportunity for positive, innovative change.

BIBLIOGRAPHY

Ahn, Mi-Jeong, *Jamnyeo in Korea: the History and Culture of Haenyeo Women Divers*, Seoul: Yeokrak, 2019.

Chang, Pil-wha, and Eun-Shil Kim, *Women's Experiences and Feminist Practices in South Korea*, Seoul: Ewha Woman's University Press, 2005.

Cho, Heung-kuk, *The History and Culture of Southeast Asia*, Seoul: Sonamu, 2019.

Choe, Sang-Hun, "Hardy Divers in Korea Strait, 'Sea Women' Are Dwindling" *New York Times*, March 29 2014, https://www.nytimes.com/2014/03/30/world/asia/hardy-divers-in-korea-strait-sea-women-are-dwindling.html, accessed 14 December 2021.

Cooke, Fang Lee, "Women's participation in employment in Asia: a comparative analysis of China, India, Japan and South Korea," *The International Journal of Human Resource Management* 21:12 (2010), 2249–70.

Cumings, Bruce, *Korea's Place in the Sun: A Modern History*, New York: W. W. Norton and Company, 1998.

Gwon, Gwi-Sook, "Changing Labor Processes of Women's Work: The Haenyeo of Jeju Island", *Korean Studies* 29 (2005), 114–36.

Hong, Suk-Ki, "Hae-Nyo, the diving women of Korea", in Herman Rahn and Tetsuro Yokoyama (eds.) *Physiology of Breath-Hold Diving and the Ama of Japan* (Washington DC: National Academy of Sciences/National Research Council, 2014), 99–112.

Ibn Khurdādhbih, *Kitāb al-masālik wa-l-mamālik*, ed. M. J. de Goeje, Leiden: Brill, 1889.

Il-hong, Jang, "Jeju Women's Myth and Eroticism," *Jeju Sound*, 7 March 2018, http://www.jejusori.net/news/articleView.html?idxno=201195, accessed 25 January 2022.

Kang, Min-soon, *The Social Status of Koryo Women in 'Koryo History'*(고려사에 나타난 고려여성의 사회적 지위), Masters dissertation: Jeju National University, 2000.

Kendall, Laurel, *Under Construction: The Gendering of Modernity, Class, and Consumption in the Republic of Korea,* Honolulu: University of Hawaii Press, 2002.

KOIS (Korea Overseas Information Services), "Women's Role in Contemporary Korea" *Asia Society* 2016, https://asiasociety.org/education/womens-role-contemporary-korea, accessed 14 December 2021.

Lee, Joo-Young and Hyo Hyun Lee, "Korean Women Divers 'Haenyeo': Bathing Suits and Acclimatization to Cold," *Journal of the Human-Environment System* 17:1 (2014), 1–11.

Lee, Hee Soo, *Kushnameh*, Seoul: Cheong A Publication, 2014a.

Lee, Hee Soo, "1,500 Years of Contact between Korea and the Middle East," *Middle East Institute Journal* (online), June 7, 2014b, /https://www.mei.edu/publications/1500-years-contact-between-korea-and-middle-east, accessed 25 January 2022.

Lee, Hee Soo, *Korea and the Muslim World: A Historical Account*, Istanbul: IRCICA, 2020.

Moon, Soon-Deok, "Trend and Prospect of Research of Women's Life and Cultural History in Jeju", *Korean Literature and Arts* 25 (2018), 221–51.

Moon, Soon-Deok, "The Historical and Cultural Meaning of Jeju Women Commemorated through the memorial rituals: Focusing on Kim Manduk, Mrs Koh, Mrs Park, and Hong Yoonae", *Tamra Culture* 63 (2020), 59–88.

Moon, Soon-Deok, "The Practice and Question of the Culture of Jeju Women," *Jeju Studies*, 32 (2009), 87–112.

Mahdi, Abdul, Yonariza Mahdi, and Hanung Ismono, "Gender Inequality and the Oppression of Women within Minangkabau Matrilineal Society," *Asian Women* 32:3 (2016), 23–49.

Pak, Ok-kyung, "The Women's Side of Jeju Identity- Women Centredness," *World Environment and Island Studies* 5:4 (2015), 325–38.

Palley, Marian Lief, "Women's status in South Korea: Tradition and change," *Asian Survey* 30:12 (1990), 1136–53.

Resos, Archie, "The Empowerment of Women in South Korea," *Journal of International Affairs*(2014), online edition: https://jia.sipa.columbia.edu/online-articles/empowerment-women-south-korea, accessed 14 December 2021.

Sik Chang, Jang, "Women's duty and its meaning in mythology", 신화를 통해 본 여성의 임무와 그 의미, *Folklore Studies (민속학연구)* 3, 179.

Soh, C. Sarah, *The Comfort Women: Sexual Violence and Postcolonial Memory in Korea and Japan*, Chicago: University of Chicago Press, 2008.

Sulaymān al-Tājir, *Akhbār al-Ṣīn wa-l-Hind,* ed. and trans. J. Savagat, Paris: Societe D'edition Les Belles Lettres, 1948.

Sung, Woong Kyu, "Abortion in South Korea: The Law and the Reality," *International Journal of Law, Policy and the Family,* 26:3 (2012), 278–305.

INTERVIEWS

Ms. Ayana Moon (via Zoom), September–October 2020.
Haji Bashir Kim, Director of the Jeju Islamic Center, 5–13 October 2020.
Ms. Mariyam Lee Kenan, Jeju, 11 October 2020.

The Maternal Initiative Role in the Japanese Muslim Community: Japanese Muslim Wives as Mediators Between Muslim Immigrants and Japanese Society

Yuki Shiozaki

INTRODUCTION

Muslim immigrants formed communities in European countries in the latter half of the twentieth century, while also settling in Northeast Asian countries and areas such as Japan, South Korea, Taiwan, and Hong Kong—where rapid economic growth in the region created a demand for immigrants to join the workforce—from the 1980s onwards. During the following decades of settlement in Northeast Asia, these Muslim settlers experienced drastic changes in their culture, customs, values, and even family systems. In the same way, Muslim settlers in Europe were unable to maintain all the cultural practices they had left behind in Indonesia, Pakistan, Bangladesh, and other countries. However, total assimilation

---

Y. Shiozaki (✉)
School of International Relations / Graduate School of International Relations, University of Shizuoka, Shizuoka, Japan

© The Author(s), under exclusive license to Springer Nature Switzerland AG 2024
A. Panakkal, N. M. Arif (eds.), *Matrilineal, Matriarchal, and Matrifocal Islam*, Palgrave Series in Islamic Theology, Law, and History, https://doi.org/10.1007/978-3-031-51749-5_6

169

into the local culture was unacceptable for many Muslim immigrants; sustaining their cultural identities and Islamic practices was a matter of great importance to them. As a result, new Muslim lifestyles developed, adapted to the host societies of Europe and Northeast Asia yet retaining aspects of their original cultures.

This chapter explores one aspect of the cultural changes in the family system that took place in the Muslim community in Japan from the 1980s onwards, a period when Muslims migrated to Japan mainly as manual labourers in the construction and manufacturing sectors. Even though most returned to their home countries after some years, a minority chose to remain in Japan. In the 2010s, Japan's Muslim population reached 100,000.[1] The majority are manual labourers, technical trainees, and international students—not permanent residents.

This study focuses on female Japanese Muslims who married foreign Muslim immigrants. Many Muslim married couples, where one partner is Japanese and the other foreign, leave Japan to live in Muslim countries overseas. This study discusses couples who have become permanent residents in Japan. Even though these permanent residents are a minority among the Muslims currently living in Japan, they are the core actors in the construction of the Japanese Muslim community. Couples in which one partner is Japanese and the other foreign are in a particularly strong position to mediate between Muslims and wider Japanese society. Japanese Muslim women, in their role as wives and mothers, are the key to shaping the new Muslim community and adapting it to Japanese social and cultural norms; these women take the initiating role both at home and in the local community.

The Transition of the Family System in Modern Japan

The transformation of the family system in modern Japan is one of the main background factors affecting the formation of new Muslim families. The Japanese family system became a topic of great controversy in the Japanese academy during the late nineteenth century, as it was considered crucial to the modernisation project. As in many Muslim countries, the implementation of a Western civil code was a central element of

---

[1] Hirofumi Tanada, "Sekai to Nihon no Musurimu Jinko 2018nen [Estimate of Muslim Population in the World and Japan, 2018]," *Waseda Journal of Human Sciences* 11:2 (2019), 253.

modernisation during the Meiji Restoration period from 1868. Before then, under the feudal social system, especially in the eighteenth and nineteenth centuries, the influence of Confucianism and its patrilineal family system was highest among the samurai class, which was largely composed of warriors and bureaucrats.[2] These samurai initiated the Meiji Restoration, leading to a new civil code that outlined a unilateral patrilineal family system for Japan.[3] In 1898 the new civil code, modelled after the German patrilineal civil code, was put into effect.[4]

The implementation of the new civil code was controversial and caused shockwaves in Japanese society. Firstly, the family system of the samurai class was not ideal for other classes, which held less strongly to Confucianism norms.[5] Secondly, there were regional variations in the family system and in traditions around courtship and mate-choice in Japan.[6] There were also regional variations in systems of household membership and property inheritance. Even though the Meiji regime unified the family system throughout the Japanese nation, practices concerning family have remained diverse in modern Japanese society.

Since the introduction of social science into modern Japan, the family system has become a major focus for anthropology, archaeology, ethnology, and history, and the diversity within it has been established through field research. In addition to regional diversity, there is variation in the influence of Confucian ideals. It is inadequate to describe the Japanese family system as either patrilineal or matrilineal; some aspects of the system are unilateral, while others are bilateral or ambilineal. In Japanese society, parent-child relationships with inheritance rights are often socially approved for both father-child and mother-child relationships. Inheritance rights may accrue to even non-kinship relatives. It depends on era and region. Muratake argued that in the analysis of the family system, the "family" should not be understood as simply a kinship group, and concepts of family and household should be differentiated.[7] The concept of the household can be defined as a "domestic group with common locality

---

[2] William Goode, *World Revolution and Family Patterns* (New York: The Free Press of Glencoe, 1953), 323.

[3] Goode, *World Revolution and Family Patterns*, 327.

[4] Goode, *World Revolution and Family Patterns*, 326.

[5] Goode, *World Revolution and Family Patterns*, 323.

[6] Goode, *World Revolution and Family Patterns*, 329.

[7] Seichi Muratake, *Kazoku no Shakai-Jinruigaku* [Social Anthropology of the Family], (Tokyo: Kobundo, 1973), x.

172   Y. SHIOZAKI

and spatiality".[8] Japanese family descent-lines are mostly straight-line patrilineal, and partly bilateral.[9] However, ancestor-based pedigree is not necessarily required for the succession of family-line or homestead-line. In the Japanese family system, the continuity of the homestead-line is considered a higher priority than the descent-line.

One of the common characteristics of the Japanese household system is inheritance by an adopted son.[10] The adopted son—usually a paternal or maternal relative—marries a daughter of the household, and thus becomes admitted as a householder. In rare cases, even an unrelated adopted son inherits the homestead-line.[11] Another characteristic of the Japanese household system is the long-established duolocal residence pattern. According to this pattern, a married man did not reside with his wife but visited her residence frequently while continuing to live with his matriclan. The duolocal residence pattern in Japan declined after the tenth century, when the family residence pattern became more neolocal. However, in rural areas in Japan—especially on remote islands—the duolocal residence pattern continued into the twentieth century, mainly in the early period of married life.[12] This pattern was also widely seen in Southeast Asia and is still partially practised today in some areas.[13]

The characteristics of the Japanese family system, including the bilateral family-line and a higher priority given to the homestead-line than descent-line, are similar to those of many other societies in Southeast Asia, where family systems include aspects of both "family as kinship group" and "family as household". In the kinship group, the patrilineal descent-line is mainly dominant. However, when it comes to inheritance of the homestead-line, bilateral or ambilineal succession is not uncommon, and some examples of matrilineal succession remain—such as the well-documented matrilineal inheritance of ancestral land in Minangkabau, Indonesia, and in Negeri Sembilan, Malaysia.

In the Southeast Asian Muslim societies of the archipelago, the bilateral and matrilineal family system was often controversial from the viewpoint

---

[8] Muratake, *Social Anthropology of the Family*, x.

[9] Muratake, *Social Anthropology of the Family*, xxiv–xxv.

[10] Goode, *World Revolution and Family Patterns*, 325.

[11] Muratake, *Social Anthropology of the Family*, xv–xvi.

[12] Muratake, *Social Anthropology of the Family*, 108–9.

[13] Muratake, *Social Anthropology of the Family*, 32–3; Tsuyoshi Kato, *Matriliny and Migration: Evolving Minangkabau Traditions in Indonesia* (Ithaca: Cornell University Press, 1982), 214.

THE MATERNAL INITIATIVE ROLE IN THE JAPANESE MUSLIM...   173

of jurisprudence. Since the fifteenth century, through the centuries of the Islamisation process, Southeast Asian Muslims faced the problem of contradictions between Islamic jurisprudence and local customary law or *adat*. For example, in the seventeenth century, the Sultanate of Aceh in Sumatra Island was ruled by four Sultanas or female monarchs. Later that century, however, a male monarch replaced them after the Sultanate received a *fatwa* from Mecca stating that a female ruler was not permissible.[14] After that, there were no more female rulers in the Sultanate of Aceh. In Japan, too, there are examples of female rulers or Empresses until the eighteenth century. This ended when the Meiji Restoration abolished the right of a female princess to succeed to the Imperial Throne.

In Minangkabau, the local family system, especially the *adat* of matrilineal inheritance, was a controversial issue. One of the most prominent Islamic scholars from Minangkabau, Ahmad Khatib al-Minankabawi, asserted the predominance of the *sharīʿa* over *adat* and demanded renouncement of the *adat*-based family system in his work *al-Manhaj al-mashrūʿ* ("The ordained method") published in 1893.[15] Yet despite the fierce attacks by Ahmad Khatib and other Islamic scholars of the Shāfiʿī school, matrilineal *adat* was legislated under Dutch colonial rule and survived into the twentieth century.

The bilateral and matrilineal family systems in Southeast Asia and Japan were gradually replaced by the patrilineal and unilateral system over time, even though traditional family systems partially remain, especially in rural areas. The transition to a patrilineal system was caused by the influence of Confucianism, Islamisation, and the implementation of the European model of the civil code.

From the late twentieth century onwards, another drastic shift—the nuclearisation of the family—has occurred in both Southeast Asia and Japan. The nuclear family, consisting of two parents and their children, increased as a result of industrialisation and urbanisation. As a result of the rapid industrialisation, the population, especially the younger generation, became concentrated in urban areas. New urban residents formed nuclear families and separated from the relatives and their traditional family system in the rural areas; in Japan, the majority of the households were nuclear

---

[14] Azymardi Azra, *Jaringan Ulama Timur Tengah dan Kepulauan Nusantara Abad XVII dan XVIII* (Bandung: Mizan, 1995), 196.

[15] Michael Laffan, *Islamic Nationhood and Colonial Indonesia: The Umma below the Winds* (New York: Routledge, 2003), 109–10.

families by the 1920s. For these urban nuclear families, the succession of descent-line and homestead-line became less of a priority. For them, the husband-wife relationship took on a greater significance than the relationship between the husband and his parents, and between other kinship groups in the local areas.[16]

The transition of the modern Japanese family system is the premise of this study on new Muslim families in Japan. Most Muslims with permanent resident status in Japan started to form families in urban areas in the late twentieth century. The focus of this study is one form of nuclear family—Muslim families consisting of a Japanese wife and foreign husband, along with their children. Although forming a Muslim family with a foreigner is extremely unusual in the traditional Japanese family system, this type of nuclear family faces fewer objections when they reside in an urban area. Like most other Japanese nuclear families, they live in urban areas, mainly around Tokyo, separating them from the influence of the traditional family system and kinship groups found in rural areas. Most of the foreign Muslim husbands—especially Indonesians, who are the largest Muslim group in Japan—are already familiar with the nuclear family, which is also prevalent in urban areas of their own countries.

Nevertheless, the characteristics of the traditional Japanese family system and its influence on the formation of the new Muslim family should be also considered, particularly the traditional prioritisation of the homestead-line and the possibility for an adopted son to inherit the homestead-line. The case study that formed part of this research provides an example of Muslim children who inherited their Japanese mother's family name, and adopting the family name is the key point in Japanese homestead-line succession. When it is inherited by an adopted son, for example, his children take the family name of the homestead. The adoption of the Japanese mother's family name in the new Muslim family, therefore, resembles the Japanese tradition of inheritance by an adopted son.

The traditions of the foreign husband's society of origin, including the bilateral family system in Southeast Asia, may also be relevant. In this case study, the foreign husbands were not necessarily negative about their children's adoption of the maternal family name. The amalgam of the traditional Japanese family system with the family system of the Muslim

---

[16] Goode, *World Revolution and Family Patterns*, 348.

THE MATERNAL INITIATIVE ROLE IN THE JAPANESE MUSLIM... 175

society—as well as the additional influence of contemporary transitions—affects the formation of the new Muslim family in Japan.

DEMOGRAPHY AND PRECEDING STUDIES ON THE MUSLIM FAMILIES IN JAPAN

Muslims in Japan are studied in the fields of sociology and anthropology, generally in the context of immigrant issues; most research focuses on the labour market, the education of international students, security, and social inclusion. The social lives and families of Muslim immigrants, however, have been very little studied.[17] The aim of this study was to conduct pioneering research on Japanese Muslim women and their key roles in the family and the community. Even though the majority of Muslims living in Japan are short-term residents such as manual labourers, trainees, and international students, these key actors are permanent residents.

Muslim society in Japan has only around a hundred years of history. The community of permanent Muslim residents in Japan started becoming visible only in the late nineteenth century. Before that time, the Tokugawa Shogun rule from the seventeenth to nineteenth centuries prohibited the entry of foreigners into Japan, and there were thus no records of any permanent Muslim residents during this period. After the Meiji Restoration in 1868, modernisation projects began and the entry of foreigners was permitted. In the early twentieth century, most Muslims in Japan were traders, especially the Indian Muslims of Kobe and Yokohama. Both of these cities were opened as trading ports at the end of the Tokugawa regime. After the Russian Revolution in 1918, Tatar Muslims from Central Asia escaped to Japan, fleeing the oppression of the Soviet Union. Yet still, in the 1930s, the Muslim population remained very small.

In 1990 there were only three mosques in the whole of Japan. By the end of 2008, there were 50 mosques and more that were in the process of being built. Most of these mosques are concentrated in the three biggest

---

[17] The two most important publications in this area to date—both focusing on Pakistani men and their Japanese wives—were conducted by Tomoko Fukuda and Masako Kudo: Tomoko Fukuda, *Toranshunashonaruna Pakisutanjin Imin no Shakaiteki Sekai* [Social Worlds of Transnational Pakistani Immigrants: From Immigrant Labors to Immigrant Entrepreneurs], Tokyo: Fukumura Shuppan, 2012. Masako Kudo, *Ekkyo no Jinruigaku: Zainichi Pakisutanjin Musurimu Imin no Tsumatachi* [An Anthropology of Border-Crossing in Japan: Japanese Wives of Pakistani Muslim Migrants], Tokyo: Tokyo Daigaku Shuppankai, 2008.

metropolitan areas of Tokyo, Osaka, and Nagoya. The Japanese government has been promoting tourism and student exchange, while the influx of immigrant workers—with the exception of technical trainees—is strictly restricted. Aside from students, however, most Muslim migrants come to Japan as workers, arriving on social visit visas and going on to work as physical labourers. Many Indonesians enter the country with visas for technical trainees and are treated as a very cheap physical labour force in manufacturing, agriculture, and other areas.

There has been rapid development of the Muslim society in Japan over the past 20 years, yet the presence of Muslims in Japan is still very limited. It is very rare to find Muslims in rural areas, and even in urban settings, foreigners form their own community and native Japanese people rarely interact with them. As a result, foreign Muslims are segregated from the Japanese. According to research conducted in Gifu city in 2012, 5% of respondents had no contact at all with any Muslims, although 8700 of the city's population of 420,000 were foreign Muslims.[18]

Although the Muslim population has been increasing, Islam and Muslims are still not fully embedded in Japanese society. As most Muslims in Japan are temporary residents with visas, difficulties in attaining or retaining visas and work permits, and associated social problems such as marriage and divorce, are rampant within the community. Marriage between a foreign Muslim man and a Japanese woman is closely related to the need to obtain a spouse visa. Their divorce is often triggered by a foreign Muslim man obtaining permanent residency. Discrimination against Muslims is limited in Japan, yet this is only because most Japanese do not recognise the existence of Muslims in their country.

Tanada estimated that the total Muslim population in Japan in June 2018 was around 200,000, consisting of 157,000 foreigners and 43,000 Japanese nationals.[19] Tanada also estimated that, of 157,000 foreign Muslims in Japan, only 31,097 had permanent resident status.[20] These estimates were taken from statistics of foreign resident nationals released by the Japanese Immigration Bureau; because the census and other

[18] Hirofumi Okai and Kiju Ishikawa, *Determination of Local Residents' Perceptions and Attitude Toward Islam and Muslims: A Case Study in Gifu City, Japan* (Tokyo: Institute for Multi-ethnic and Multi-generational Societies Waseda University, 2012), 6–12.

[19] Tanada, "Estimate of Muslim Population in the World and Japan, 2018," 260.

[20] Tanada, "Estimate of Muslim Population in the World and Japan, 2018," 259.

Japanese public statistical surveys do not ask the religious belief of respondents, there are no accurate statistics on religious demography in Japan.

There is, however, solid data on foreigners' nationalities and residence status from the Immigration Services Agency of the Japanese government. According to the Statistical Survey of Foreign Residents, the main five Muslim-majority countries of origin for resident foreigners are Indonesia, Pakistan, Bangladesh, Malaysia, and Turkey (Table 1). These immigrants are not necessarily Muslims; there is likely to be a large portion of Christians and Buddhists among the Malaysian nationals, for example. There were 19,102 holders of permanent residence status among foreign nationals from these five main Muslim-majority countries.

Those Muslim families whose members hold Japanese nationality or have permanent residence status are most fully and continuously engaged in the development of Japan's Muslim community, while other foreign Muslims is also important. Tanada estimated that around 2000 Japanese converts made their decision without marrying a foreign Muslim.[21] The other 41,000 Japanese Muslims are therefore the spouses of foreign Muslims, he argues, or Japanese nationals who were born into Muslim families. According to the census conducted by the Japanese government in October 2015, 2508 Japanese men married Indonesian women, while 1634 Japanese women married Indonesian men.[22] A large majority of Muslim families are understood to consist of foreign Muslims and Japanese nationals.

Table 1 Foreign residents in Japan from Muslim-majority countries at the end of December 2019

Nationality	Total	Permanent residence status	"Spouse of Japanese national" status	"Child of Japanese national" status
Indonesia	66,860	6662	1921	205
Pakistan	17,766	5015	718	4
Bangladesh	16,632	3500	401	0
Malaysia	10,862	2880	531	15
Turkey	5419	1045	794	2

Source: Immigration Services Agency of Japan, "Zairyu Gaikokujin Tokei Tokeihyo [Statistical Survey of Foreign Residents]", July 31, 2020

[21] Tanada, "Estimate of Muslim Population in the World and Japan, 2018," 260.
[22] Statistics Bureau of Japan, "Heisei 27nen Kokusei Chosa [Census 2015]."

The population of the Muslims in Japan, excluding short-term residents who stay no more than a few years, is assumed to be around 80,000.[23] Within this community, the role of Japanese Muslim women as wives, mothers, and local community members is extremely significant.

CASE STUDIES ON WOMEN'S ROLE IN THE MUSLIM FAMILIES IN JAPAN

In Muslim families in Japan, the position of the Japanese woman is essential; her place of birth, family of origin, and level of education are all vital to her family, since the skills and connections necessary for survival in Japan depend on having enjoyed a Japanese education and upbringing.

In the families discussed in this study, where the husband is foreign, the wife is the only one with this background. In order to navigate administrative procedure, entrepreneurship, local community activities, and the education system, her skills are indispensable. This study focuses on three aspects of the role of Japanese Muslim wives: the family name, livelihood, and local community activities, including school activities. The two preceding studies on Muslim families consisting of Pakistani husbands and Japanese wives by Fukuda and Kudo also address these three areas.[24] There have been virtually no studies on Muslim families in which the husband is of another nationality, despite the fact that foreign Muslims in Japan come from a wide range of countries.

This study considers four cases of Japanese Muslim women married to Indonesians and Arabs. The Indonesian community in Japan is the largest of any Muslim-majority country and therefore particularly significant for the development of Japanese Muslim society. The majority of people from Muslim countries who hold permanent resident status or are married to Japanese partners are Indonesian (Table 1). Yet this study is the first to consider the role of the Japanese wives of Indonesian Muslim men. The four informants are all Japanese Muslim women, two of whom are married to Indonesians and two to Arabs. As such, it is a small study and much

---

[23] 41,000 Japanese converts are married to foreign Muslims, 31,000 foreign Muslims have permanent resident status, and 8000 foreign Muslims have the status of "spouse of Japanese national". Tanada estimated that there are 8244 foreign Muslims with this status. (Tanada, "Estimate of Muslim Population in the World and Japan, 2018," 259.)

[24] Fukuda, *Social Worlds of Transnational Pakistani* Immigrants; Kudo, *An Anthropology of Border-Crossing in Japan.*

larger-scale research is needed in order to reach a clearer understanding of this under-investigated topic. This is simply the first step towards further research on the role of Japanese Muslim women.

Interviews with the four respondents focused on the family name, livelihood, and local community activities, including school activities. In this section, I analyse their responses, summarised in Table 2.

1. Family Name Inheritance

In the Japanese family registration system, all Japanese nationals must register their family names. In many of Muslim families of a foreign husband and Japanese wife, the foreign husband does not have Japanese nationality, or their home country's registration system may not require family name. The only option for the children of such families is therefore to adopt their mother's Japanese family name.

In Japanese society, the family name is very significant. It is usually the first form of identification in the relationships between Japanese, and relatives on the paternal side share a family name. The limited number of family names—around 300,000—means that a name is also proof of affiliation to traditional establishment families. In Japanese daily life, especially in the local community, having a well-known family name in the area is an indicator of belonging to that community. It is therefore advantageous for children of Muslim families with foreign fathers to take their mother's family name, since it confers belonging to both the maternal family and the local community. In addition, in many cases it is the only way for these children to obtain Japanese nationality.

Three of the four families who were part of this study had registered their children as Japanese nationals under the mother's family name. Only Mrs. C's family used the husband's Arab family name; this was possible because he had been naturalised as a Japanese citizen, and his original name was registered as his Japanese family name. Both the children and Mrs. C were also registered under this name. The other three husbands in the families that took part in this study were not naturalised Japanese citizens.

For children, the registration of their family names can be a lifelong momentous decision, as the family name becomes their main identification in Japanese society. It is therefore highly significant that the majority of children with foreign Muslim fathers take their mother's family name.

Table 2 Responses from four respondents from Muslim families in Japan on the family name, livelihood, and local community activities, including school activities

Informant	Family name	Livelihood	Local community activities, including school activities
Mrs. A, a Japanese Muslim married to a Muslim from Indonesia, with three children	The children are registered as Japanese nationals with the mother's family name	Both the husband and the wife are earners. The main earner is the husband, who graduated from a graduate school in Japan and works at an overseas subsidiary of a Japanese company. He remits money home to the family in Japan In Japan, Mrs. A is registered as the householder	While her husband works overseas as an expatriate, Mrs. A participates in all the activities of the PTA, clubs, and other events at school
Mrs. B, a Japanese Muslim married to an Indonesian Muslim. They have one child	The child is registered as a Japanese national, with the mother's family name	Both the husband and the wife are earners. The main earner is the husband. Both work in Japan, at different working places The husband is the registered householder	The husband can communicate in Japanese and is active in the residents' association, where he is a member of the management committee
Mrs. C, a Japanese Muslim married to a Muslim from an Arab country, with four children	The husband was naturalised as a Japanese citizen. He, Mrs. C, and the children are registered as Japanese naturals with the husband's Arab family name	Both Mrs. C and her husband are earners	The husband does not participate in the PTA and other school activities, as he speaks limited Japanese. Mrs. C plays a role in school activities. Her husband participates in residents' association activities, such as disaster prevention drills

(*continued*)

Table 2 (continued)

Informant	Family name	Livelihood	Local community activities, including school activities
Mrs. D, a Japanese Muslim married to a Muslim from an Arab country	The children are registered as Japanese nationals with the mother's family name	Only the husband is the earner. He is also registered as the householder	The wife undertakes the duties of the PTA, as in most other families. The husband occasionally supports her

Sources: Interviews conducted in September 2020

2. Livelihood

Proficiency in Japanese, including reading and writing Chinese character, is required a minimum skill in most work application processes in Japan. Many foreign Muslims lack basic language skills in Japanese, making it hard for them to be the breadwinners of their families. Fukuda pointed out the strong tendency among Pakistani Muslims—especially those married to Japanese women—to aspire to becoming self-employed businessmen.[25] In the 1990s, many Pakistanis came to Japan on short-term visas. Those who married Japanese citizens were granted special permission to stay in the country and could legally start a self-owned or family-operated business. Fukuda also noted the high unemployment rate of around 61–70% among Pakistani residents in Japan in the 1980s and 90 s, as a result of the lack of skills required for the Japanese job market.[26] Becoming self-employed is thus the only way out of unemployment for most of them. In 2000, 27% of Pakistanis holding jobs were entrepreneurs, second only to Koreans among foreign nationals in Japan. Moreover, 51.7% of these Pakistani entrepreneurs were owners of firms under private management.[27] The most popular business is used car trading, which has been at the core of the Pakistani Muslim community in Japan since the mid-1990s.[28] They buy up used cars in Japan and export them to Pakistan, UAE, South

[25] Fukuda, *Social Worlds of Transnational Pakistani Immigrants*, 79.
[26] Fukuda, *Social Worlds of Transnational Pakistani Immigrants*, 175.
[27] Fukuda, *Social Worlds of Transnational Pakistani Immigrants*, 176–7.
[28] Fukuda, *Social Worlds of Transnational Pakistani Immigrants*, 182–4.

182 Y. SHIOZAKI

America, Russia, and African countries.[29] Residential communities were formed around used car auction sites, especially north of the Tokyo area, where mosques built by Pakistanis are also located.

Kudo also described the predominance of the used car trading business among Pakistanis, Bangladeshis, and Sri Lankan Muslims.[30] In the 1980s and 90 s, many Pakistanis and Bangladeshis entered Japan on short-stay visas and worked as manual labourers in the construction and manufacturing industries. Even though most of them returned or were deported to their mother countries, those married to Japanese remained in Japan. In the 1990s, they moved from manual labour to being self-employed, especially in used car trading.[31]

The role of Japanese wives is indispensable in the process of starting a business. The registration of a corporation, bank loan, operating permission, acquisition of real property, accounting, and all other procedures require proficiency in Japanese and a Japanese national to stand as guarantor. One of the key roles of a Japanese wife is to be her husband's guarantor.[32] Virtually all Pakistani businesses could not be sustained without Japanese wives as associate partners or family employees.

In Muslim society in Japan, Japanese wives therefore play a crucial role in the Pakistani family business; this is also the case in families where the husband is from Bangladesh or Sri Lanka. Muslims from other countries—including Indonesians—are rarely involved in the used car trading business, however. It is a clear choice for Pakistani nationals, since their government tariff system permitted expatriates to import limited numbers of foreign cars, but other countries do not allow this.[33]

None of the four families in this study worked in the used car business. Mrs. C managed her own business, while the wage-earners of the other three families were all in paid employment. Foreign Muslim residents who have graduated from Japanese universities tend to find work at Japanese companies, since they are proficient in Japanese. Indonesia and Bangladesh are the two top Muslim-majority nationalities in Japanese higher education institutes in terms of international student numbers.

[29] Fukuda, *Social Worlds of Transnational Pakistani Immigrants,* 217–9.
[30] Kudo, *An Anthropology of Border-Crossing in Japan,* 91.
[31] Kudo, *An Anthropology of Border-Crossing in Japan,* 89–91.
[32] Fukuda, *Social Worlds of Transnational Pakistani Immigrants,* 198–200.
[33] Fukuda, *Social Worlds of Transnational Pakistani Immigrants,* 211.

The husbands of Mrs. A and Mrs. B both graduated from Japanese higher education and found employment in Japanese companies; among Indonesian Muslims with permanent residency, this is a typical life trajectory. Even for them, however, the role of their Japanese wives is crucial. Many Muslims who graduate from Japanese universities are employed overseas, working for subsidiary companies elsewhere in Asia like Mrs. A's husband. Many are away from their families for years. In such cases, the wife takes on a key role as both mother and household manager.

3. Local Community Activities, Including School Activities

In Japanese schools, parents must participate in activities of the Parent-Teacher Association, or PTA. The quality of Japanese school is maintained by daily contributions of parents in aspects of school management such as security along school route, cleaning activities, and organising clubs. The PTA are also involved in the management of various school events including sports festivals, cultural festivals, open lectures, and so on. The PTA's regular meetings, documents, and other communications are in Japanese. In most Muslim families with foreign husbands and Japanese wives, PTA duty falls to the wife—mainly due to the necessity of speaking fluent Japanese. However, PTA duties are generally undertaken by mothers in the majority of Japanese families, so this is not unusual.

In the local community, especially in rural areas in Japan, all residents are required to be members of residents' associations. The residents' association takes charge of local community governance, organising activities such as rubbish collection, recycling, security patrols, disaster prevention, health promotion, and so on. The residents' association is usually a counterpart of local government and acts as a liaison point for the community. These associations also organise local festivals held at the local Shinto shrine or Buddhist temple.

To avoid becoming isolated from the local community, it is crucial to be a member of the residents' association and to participate in its activities. Foreigners, including permanent resident Muslims, are required to participate even more actively than other residents if they wish to enjoy community life fully. Yet since the medium of regular meetings, circular notices, and other communication is Japanese, the participants from Muslim families are usually Japanese wives. Foreign husbands who were educated in Japanese higher education institutions are also able to undertake these duties, however. Mrs. B's Indonesian husband is proficient in Japanese, and even appointed as a management committee member. Mrs. C's Arab husband is able to participate in programs such as disaster prevention drills with the help of his wife.

JAPANESE MUSLIM WIVES AS MEDIATORS

Kudo described the critical role of Japanese wives in Muslim families as that of "mediator" for their husbands and children in business life, social life, and school life.[34] In civil life and interactions with the neighbours and business interactions, Japanese Muslim wives have a serious responsibility to mediate between family members and the outside world. All mediation and negotiation with public offices, trade partners, neighbours, and school teachers are undertaken by Japanese wives in Muslim families.

The role of Japanese Muslim wives as mediators is not limited to interactions with non-Muslim Japanese and their families. They are also required to mediate between Islamic values and Japanese values, especially for their children. Children are educated in Japan, and their mother tongue is Japanese. They are surrounded by Japanese culture, Japanese friends, and Japanese media. Like other Japanese children, they do not have any opportunities to form an understanding of Islam aside from TV news programs on overseas conflicts. Even if the fathers are more knowledgeable about Islam, their knowledge was learned in Urdu, Bengali, Indonesian, or other foreign languages. They are not capable of explaining Islamic knowledge to their children in Japanese. Yet despite the difficulties involved, those who are knowledgeable of both Islam and Japanese culture are able to do this, meaning that Japanese Muslim mothers have the potential to guide their children to a deeper understanding of Islam. In many areas, they form learning groups of mothers and children.

The increase of the Muslim population in Japan after the 1980s was mainly due to marriages between foreign Muslims and native Japanese women. However, their children—the second-generation Muslims—are not necessarily contributing to the development of the Muslim community in Japan because most were assimilated into Japanese society. The assimilation of Muslim children is the main obstacle for sustainable Muslim community development in Japanese society.

In Europe, there is also pressure from governments and society to assimilate. Muslim immigrants are required to accept the secular lifestyles

---

[34] Kudo, *An Anthropology of Border-Crossing in Japan*, 176–84.

of the other Europeans, and there are often negative public opinions of some Muslim customs such as wearing the headscarf and sacrificing animals for Eid-al-Adha. However, in European countries, there is a principle of religious freedom, so Islamic belief itself is not negated. Religious practices are considered a basic human right in Europe. In Japan, too, religious freedom is assured as a basic right in Article 20 of the Constitution. However, society is not necessarily generous towards non-Japanese cultural expression, including unfamiliar foreign religious practices, and residents in Japan are required to accept a high level of homogeneity of language and customs. Individuals and groups outside this homogenous culture are usually alienated or ignored in Japanese society. It is very hard for Muslims to be accepted as a part of Japanese society, and Muslims are allowed to stay only as foreigners and temporary residents.

In Europe, there is a tendency to return to Islam among second- or third-generation Muslims. Muslim youths are often more concerned with Islam than their parents. These Muslim youths study Islam with enthusiasm and become the core of the new generation of European Muslims. In Japan, where the history of the Muslim community is shorter than in Europe, there are fewer second- or third-generation Muslims, and it is unlikely that they will gravitate towards an Islamic identity. Most second- or third-generation Muslims have already been assimilated into Japanese society and largely lost their Muslim identity, behaving just like other Japanese youth.

One of the main reasons for such sweeping assimilation is the public education system in Japan. Muslim children are required to behave like other children in elementary school and junior high school, wearing the same uniforms, speaking the same language, and eating the same food. If they behave differently from other children, they are likely to be alienated or neglected by their peers. In Japan, Muslim permanent residents have no possibility of choosing an Islamic school for their children, and it is unavoidable that most of them attend Japanese public schools. If Muslim children accept the same lifestyle as other native Japanese children, there is little difficulty for them to become accepted members of Japanese society and become friends with native Japanese. They usually abandon their Muslim identity during this process of assimilation, however.

From elementary school to university, the Japanese educational syllabus is mainly imported from the West. However, Western knowledge has limited influence on Japanese society. The Japanese value system and worldview are implanted in Japanese children through daily life and pop-culture, especially cartoons and games. The way of imbibing value systems within Japanese society is sophisticated and unifies people in the country. It exerts a powerful force over Japanese and non-Japanese children alike in assimilating and integrating them into Japanese society. In media and cyberspace, pop-culture is a dominant factor in spreading the Japanese value system. It is thus very difficult for Muslim children in Japan to absorb Islamic knowledge at the same time, and they are assimilated into Japanese society through the school system and media. Immersed in Japanese values, Muslim children in Japan have a very limited opportunity to learn about their religion, since their everyday environment is saturated with Japanese values. They attend Japanese schools, watch Japanese cartoons, and play Japanese games with Japanese friends. It becomes natural for them to think and behave in the Japanese style, and feel as if Islam is unnatural.

It is only Japanese wives—the mothers of second-generation Muslims in Japan—who can guide their children in Islamic values and knowledge. First, they must seek an appropriate vocabulary to explain Islam in Japanese, as Islam was not part of Japanese culture until the twentieth century. There is very limited literature on Islamic knowledge in Japanese, aside from Orientalist studies. The first generation of Muslims, or foreign immigrants, are not capable of explaining Islam in Japanese, nor are they interested in doing so. Muslim society in Japan is divided by ethnicities, and there is no umbrella association. Institutions such as mosques are thus divided into communities such as the Indonesians, Pakistanis, Iranians, Turks, and so on. They have their own mosques and conduct sermons in their own languages.

The segregation within the Muslim community is one of the main reasons for the lack of institutionalisation of Islamic values. If the community is divided by ethnicities and organisations, it becomes impossible to institutionalise Islamic values and Muslim activities. For example, when Muslims in Japan discuss plans to establish a school, there is a difference of opinion on the educational medium. Pakistanis prefer Urdu, Arabs prefer Arabic, and Indonesians prefer Indonesian. However, children need to be taught why Islam is indispensable for them in their mother tongue: Japanese.

The rapid increase of the Muslim population started in the 1980s, and there were still very few mosques and limited educational activities in the 90 s. At that time, Muslim immigrants did not recognise Japan as their home and were only concerned about their birth countries. Today there are tens of mosques, and regular activities are organised by Muslim groups. They have gradually come to recognise that Japan is their country of permanent residence, especially for their children's generation.

For this second generation, Japan is their motherland. It is necessary to harmonise their lives as Japanese citizens and Muslims, and they cannot learn this at school, or from Japanese media, cartoons, or games. Only their Japanese mothers are able to guide the process of harmonisation. Mothers often have to negotiate with school teachers. In many cases, the foreign fathers simply reject unfamiliar rules of their children's schools such as unified school meals, school uniforms, wearing shorts for physical exercise, sexual education, and so on. The mothers therefore go to their children's schools and negotiate with teachers, explaining religious requirements and negotiating to find compromise solutions in Japanese. The mothers also discuss their children's futures with teachers, understanding the Japanese education system, entrance examinations, and career paths in greater depth than their foreign husbands.

It is extremely difficult to negotiate with teachers, neighbours, public officers, business customers, and other figures in Japanese public life. Negotiation requires an explanation of religious requirements. Muslims are recent arrivals in Japanese history, and many basic concepts are not shared, meaning that inventive ideas are necessary in order to make Islam more widely understood. Mothers usually have to undertake these onerous duties of negotiation and mediation on behalf of their husbands and children.

CONCLUSION

Muslim society in Japan has been transforming rapidly since the 1980s. From the 1980s to 2010s, the first generation of immigrants from Pakistan, Bangladesh, and, later, Indonesia, formed the majority of the Muslims in Japan. Today, the Muslim community is in transition to the second generation. Japanese Muslim wives—the mothers of this second generation—have always been key actors in the development of the community.

To become a sustainable Muslim community, Japanese Muslims require an environment conducive to absorbing Islamic values; a simple transplantation of the learning systems of the Middle East or South Asia—even Indonesia—is inappropriate. It is necessary to establish a sense of coherence between Islamic learning and social life in Japan. If the second generation grow up with an understanding of Islam in this environment, the relationship between Muslims and Japanese society will be very different. Muslims will become part of Japanese civil society, and no longer require mediators.

At present, the Japanese Muslim wife is obliged to take on the burden of responsibility as mediator, negotiator, and translator. They are mediators between their families and Japanese society. At the same time, they must translate Islamic learning into Japanese, and place it in the Japanese context. In the case of many Muslim families in Japan, only the mothers can explain Islam to neighbours, school teachers, and their own children, for whom they are usually the main source of Islamic knowledge.

To avoid isolation from the local community, Japanese Muslim women's role as mediators is indispensable. Without it, the second and third generations would simply become cut off from mainstream Japanese society or assimilated into it. Despite the heavy burden responsibility for women, Muslim society in Japan must continue to rely on their maternal initiative role.

Acknowledgements This chapter is partially supported by Dr. Hiroko Kushimoto, Associate Professor at Sophia University, who conducted interviews with informants and collected data.

BIBLIOGRAPHY

Azymardi Azra, *Jaringan Ulama Timur Tengah dan Kepulauan Nusantara Abad XVII dan XVIII*, Bandung: Mizan, 1995.

Fukuda, Tomoko, *Toranshunashonaruna Pakisutanjin Imin no Shakaiteki Sekai* [Social Worlds of Transnational Pakistani Immigrants: From Immigrant Labors to Immigrant Entrepreneurs], Tokyo: Fukumura Shuppan, 2012.

Goode, William, *World Revolution and Family Patterns*, New York: The Free Press of Glencoe, 1953.

Immigration Services Agency of Japan, "Zairyu Gaikokujin Tokei Tokeihyo [Statistical Survey of Foreign Residents]," July 31, 2020.

Kato, Tsuyoshi, *Matriliny and Migration: Evolving Minangkabau Traditions in Indonesia*, Ithaca: Cornell University Press, 1982.

Kudo, Masako, *Ekkyo no Jinruigaku: Zainichi Pakisutanjin Musurimu Imin no Tsumatachi* [An Anthropology of Border-Crossing in Japan: Japanese Wives of Pakistani Muslim Migrants], Tokyo: Tokyo Daigaku Shuppankai, 2008.

Laffan, Michael, *Islamic Nationhood and Colonial Indonesia: The Umma below the Winds*, New York: Routledge, 2003.

Muratake, Seichi, *Kazoku no Shakai-JInruigaku* [Social Anthropology of the Family], Tokyo: Kobundo, 1973.

Okai, Hirofumi and Kiju Ishikawa, *Determination of Local Residents' Perceptions and Attitude toward Islam and Muslims: A Case Study in Gifu City, Japan*, Tokyo: Waseda University, 2012.

Statistics Bureau of Japan, "Heisei 27nen Kokusei Chosa [Census 2015]," October 26, 2016.

Tanada, Hirofumi, "Sekai to Nihon no Musurimu Jinko 2018nen [Estimate of Muslim Population in the World and Japan, 2018]," *Waseda Journal of Human Sciences* 11:2 (2019), 254–62.

PART III

Africa

Muslim Family Under Portuguese Rule: *Sharīʿa* and Matrilineal Custom in Colonial Coastal Northern Mozambique (ca. 1900–1974)

Liazzat J. K. Bonate

INTRODUCTION

Muslims are estimated to form between 18 and 22 per cent of the population of contemporary Mozambique, and the northern coastal region has a deep historical presence of Islam. The ways in which Muslims have regulated family life there, however, remain little understood. This chapter attempts to shed some light on this issue by exploring Portuguese colonial approaches and perceptions of the family relations and personal status of coastal Muslims, gathered from historical, ethnographic, and legal records. The study focuses on how the colonial regime understood and depicted the family lives of the local Muslim population, including Islamic

---

L. J. K. Bonate (✉)
Chr. Michelsen Institute, Bergen, Norway

© The Author(s), under exclusive license to Springer Nature Switzerland AG 2024
A. Panakkal, N. M. Arif (eds.), *Matrilineal, Matriarchal, and Matrifocal Islam*, Palgrave Series in Islamic Theology, Law, and History, https://doi.org/10.1007/978-3-031-51749-5_7

193

marriage, gender relations within the Muslim family and household, property rights, divorce, inheritance, and the custody of children.

Although the Portuguese first arrived in coastal northern Mozambique at the end of the fifteenth century, in 1482, their actual influence and control over these societies did not occur until after the 'effective occupation' of the region following the 1884–1885 Berlin conference. From 1895 to 1913, the Portuguese undertook military conquests which met with fierce African resistance, spearheaded, in northern Mozambique, by Muslim rulers from the coast. The colonial regime was gradually imposed from 1897 onwards and lasted until 1974, yet the Portuguese colonial conceptualisation of Islamic law and matriliny has barely been addressed by the scholarship. This study examines Portuguese colonial approaches to *sharīʿa*, *fiqh*, and Islamic law, as well as customary norms, and compares them to those of the British, French, and Dutch. In the process, the following questions are addressed: did the Portuguese colonial regime adopt policies, legal reforms, and governance modes similar to the British, Dutch, and French with regard to the Muslim family? How did the Portuguese conceive of Islamic law and articulate the simultaneous existence of Islam and matriliny? How did the Portuguese understand the meaning of African customs, in particular matriliny and its coexistence with Islamic norms? How did the colonial rule depict the Muslim family and the ways it was regulated? What concrete legal steps did the Portuguese take to deal with the Muslim family, and what were the consequences of these actions?

Islam expanded into northern Mozambique through Indian Ocean networks and the Swahili coast from approximately the eighth century.[1] Despite centuries of Islamisation, the coastal northern Muslim Mozambicans remained matrilineal. Rather than favouring the agnatic side of the family as the Qurʾān prescribes, kinship relations, property rights, inheritance and succession, rights over children, and marital residence privileged the maternal line. The sense of belonging to matrilineal kin was bolstered by initiation rites for both boys and girls upon reaching puberty, which transformed them into full-fledged members of a kin group and the community at large. The survival of matriliny can be explained by the fact that Mozambique differed from other areas of coastal East Africa

---

[1] Malyn Newitt, *A History of Mozambique* (London: Hurst and Co., 1995), 3–13; Liazzat J. K. Bonate, "Islam in Northern Mozambique: A Historical Overview," *History Compass* 8:7 (2010), 574.

MUSLIM FAMILY UNDER PORTUGUESE RULE: *SHARI'A...* 195

in one essential respect: unlike the Swahili communities of the Tanzanian and Kenyan coasts, where the Ḥaḍramī *sharīfs*[2] began arriving in the fifteenth century and the Omanis established the Sultanate of Zanzibar in the eighteenth century, the number of Arab migrants to Mozambique was insignificant. The increase of Ḥaḍramī *sharīfs* with claims to Islamic knowledge and authority on the Tanzanian and Kenyan coasts, as Kelly M. Askew points out, had a deep impact on local conceptions of Islam; these came to incorporate many principles of Islamic 'orthodoxy', leading to the replacement of traditional matrilineal systems with the Arab patrilineal ideology in addition to weakening women's legal and social status.[3] Sophie Blanchy observes similar tendencies among the Arab *sharīfs* in matrilineal Muslim Comoros.[4] In northern Mozambique, the absence of an Arab competition over Islamic authority meant that indigenous traditions of matrilineal descent and inheritance continued to prevail among Muslim communities.[5] Furthermore, Portuguese colonialism also contributed to the maintenance of matriliny by incorporating it into legal and administrative systems, despite staunch opposition from the Catholic Church.[6]

Pauline E. Peters argues that it is more "useful to consider matriliny as a set of characteristics rather than a totality or 'system.'"[7] Mozambican matriliny also has its own peculiarities. On the one hand, while postmarriage residence patterns were matrilocal or uxorilocal in rural areas, a husband rarely moved into his wife or mother-in-law's home; this is different from the case of the Comoros, where matrilocal residence meant

[2] *Sharīfs* are descendants of the Prophet Muhammad.

[3] Kelly M. Askew, "Female circles and male lines: Gender dynamics along the Swahili coast," *Africa Today* 46 (1999), 67–102.

[4] Sophie Blanchy, "Beyond 'Great Marriage': Collective Involvement, Personal Achievement and Social Change in Ngazidja (Comoros)," *Journal of Eastern African Studies* 7:4 (2013), 570–1.

[5] Eduardo do Couto Lupi, *Angoche. Breve memória sobre uma das Capitanias-Móres do Distrito de Moçambique* (Lisbon: Typografia do Annuario Commercial, 1907), 144–6, 154–7; Pedro Massano de Amorim, *Relatório sobre a ocupação de Angoche: Operações de campanha e mais serviço realizados, Anno 1910* (Lourenço Marques: Imprensa Nacional, 1911), 120.

[6] Liazzat J. K. Bonate, "Matriliny, Islam and Gender in Northern Mozambique," *Journal of Religion in Africa* 36:2 (2006), 139–66; Liazzat J. K. Bonate, *Traditions and Transitions: Islam and Chiefship in Northern Mozambique, ca. 1850–1974*, Ph.D. dissertation: University of Cape Town, 2007.

[7] Pauline E. Peters, "Introduction: Revisiting the Puzzle of Matriliny in South-Central Africa," *Critique of Anthropology* 17:2 (1997), 137.

moving into the wife's family compound.[8] The Mozambican husband moved to live in the area of his wife's matrilineage, where he had to build his own hut or house. This changed during the colonial period when many people, especially men, ended up working far from their original homelands—on construction sites, on plantations, in the urban economy, in the mines, or at sea. When they moved, they acquired housing, sometimes granted by the plantation owners or urban administrators, and upon marriage men brought their wives to live with them. If the new residence belonged to a husband, the property was expected to be inherited by his own matrilineal kin rather than his wife and children upon his death. Both men and women retained rights to the land and property of their matrilinear kin group in their original homeland, which continued to be subject to the rules of matriliny.

On the other hand, in stark contrast to the case of the matrilineal Muslim Comoros, women in northern Mozambican Muslim societies could access political, spiritual, and decision-making power.[9] The purported 'first-comer' status to a territory played a crucial role in the political legitimisation of the ruling clans entitled to distribute land or to grant others access to it. In local origin myths, the supposed first-comers were perceived as a link between the world of the ancestral spirits left behind and the spirits of the new homeland. The spirits of the new land either had to be appeased, if the land had been standing vacant, or expelled along with its previous owners. Relations with the spirit world—and the associated well-being and fertility of the land and its inhabitants—were safeguarded by the women who founded the community and their female descendants such as the *pia-mwene*, or female chief (in Makua); the *nunu* or *mwana*, meaning lady or mistress in Swahili; and the putative or real elder uterine sisters of the male chiefs (*mwene, mwenye, munu, mwiyini*, or *mfalume*). Oral traditions underscore that each male chief was accompanied by a female counterpart, and sometimes a woman led a group on her own. A female ruler represented the spirit of the Great Ancestor Mother and presided over important political decisions.[10] Only she could bestow 'spiritual essence' (in Makua, *nihimu*) to a lineage or clan. The blessing of

---

[8] Sophie Blanchy, "A matrilineal and matrilocal Muslim society in flux: negotiating gender and family relations in the Comoros," *Africa: Journal of the International African Institute* 89:1 (2019), 24.

[9] Blanchy, "A matrilineal and matrilocal Muslim society in flux," 24.

[10] N. J. Hafkin, *Trade, Society, and Politics in Northern Mozambique, c. 1753–1913* (Ph.D. dissertation: Boston University, 1973), 80, 205.

the ancestors through her *epepa* (in Makua, 'sacred flour') ensured plenty of food and female fertility and provided guidance on important decisions and protection against evil. For this reason, women also could become rulers on their own right. In the nineteenth century, when the region was involved in the international slave trade, female leaders competed for control of the slave trade economy on a par with men. Some Muslim queens were as militarised as men and aggressively pursued wars and slave raiding. Queen Maziza, for example, did not hesitate to murder Bwana Heri, her superior, when he tried to accommodate Portuguese interests and obstruct the slave trade.[11] Fatima binti Zakariya, the *nunu* of Seremaje region of Mogincual and her mother Manaty, the previous *nunu*, both were known to be brutal slave raiders, who also strongly resisted Portuguese conquests.[12] The Namarral Queen Naguema not only led the resistance against the Portuguese but also withstood a direct military confrontation with Mouzinho de Albuquerque, the legendary Portuguese commander of the 'effective occupation' campaigns.[13]

After the establishment of the Portuguese New State (*Estado Novo*, 1926–1974), the colonial legislation did not preclude women from becoming rulers. Article 117 of the 1933 Overseas Administrative Reform Law (*Lei de Reforma Ultramarina*) permitted them to occupy the position of chiefs as long as local tradition allowed it and the "attributes of female chiefs were similar to those of male chiefs" (*Decreto-Lei* No 23: 229, 1933). Portuguese officer José Alberto de Melo Branquinho's 1960s survey shows that some *pia-mwene* were quite powerful, even though they themselves were not actual chiefs.[14]

---

[11] Hafkin, *Trade, Society, and Politics in Northern Mozambique*, 267–72.

[12] Liazzat J. K. Bonate, "Muslim Female Political Leadership in Pre-Colonial Northern Mozambique: The Letters by *Nunu* Fatima Binti Zakaria of Mogincual," in Viera Pawlikova-Vilhanova (ed.), *Ad Fontes: Reflections on sources of Africa's pasts, their preservation, publication, and/or digitisation* (Bratislava: Slovak Academic Press, 2019), 81–105.

[13] Joaquim Mouzinho de Albuquerque, *A Campanha contra os Namarrais* (Lisbon: Imprensa Nacional, 1897), 11–12, 50, 60; Bonate, "Muslim Female Political Leadership."

[14] José Alberto de Melo Branquinho, "Relatório da Prospecção ao Distrito de Moçambique (Um estudo de estruturas hierárquicas tradicionais e religiosas, e da sua situação político-social), Nampula, 22 April 1969" Arquivo Histórico de Moçambique, Maputo, Secção Especial No 20, Cotas S.E., 2 III P 6, Portugal (Lourenço Marques, 1969), 275, 278–82.

198 L. J. K. BONATE

SHARĪ͑A AND ORIENTALISM

Most of the colonial and some post-colonial literature on northern Mozambican Muslims reflects an Orientalist stance on Islam.[15] This means that Islam has been viewed not as a living faith but as one of the "transcendent, compelling Oriental facts," a single, unitary, continually reasserted, and all-defining object identified with a 'classical' body of principles, including *sharī͑a* (the divine path), found in the writings of the 'orthodox' *͑ulamā* (Islamic scholars).[16] European Orientalist scholarship—in addition to the British, Dutch, and French colonial administrators and their local Muslim associates—expanded the usage of the term 'Islamic law' by transforming the Islamic principles of *sharī͑a* and *fiqh* (Islamic jurisprudence) into law in the Western sense from the eighteenth to the twentieth centuries.[17] 'Islamic law' became a central and strategic field of enquiry in the colonial context, argues Wael B. Hallaq, because without it the colonialist enterprise could not have been realised.[18] The first such instance took place in 1774 when David Anderson translated the *Fatawa-i-Alamgiri*—a set of seventeenth-century religious decrees and extracts from Ḥanafī *fiqh* treatises—and in 1783 when Charles Hamilton translated *al-Hidāya* by Burhān al-Dīn Abu'l-Ḥasan al-Marghīnānī (1135–1197), considered one of the most influential compendia of Ḥanafī

---

[15] Eduardo C. Medeiros, *História de Cabo Delgado e do Niassa (c. 1836–1929)* (Maputo: Central Impressora, 1997), 61 and passim; Pélissier, R., *História de Moçambique: Formação e Oposição, 1854–1928*, translated from French into Portuguese by Manuel Ruas (Lisbon: Editorial Estampa Lda., 2000), vol. 1: 319–20.

[16] Edward Said, *Orientalism: Western Conceptions of the Orient* (London: Penguin Books, 1995), 259–61, 278–9, 281–3, 300–1.

[17] Brinkley Messick, *The Calligraphic State: Textual Domination and History in a Muslim Society*, Berkeley, CA: University of California Press, 1992; Shamil Jeppie, Ebrahim Moosa, and Richard Roberts, "Introduction: Muslim Family Law in Sub-Saharan Africa: Colonial Legacies and Post-Colonial Challenges," in Shamil Jeppie, Ebrahim Moosa, and Richard Roberts (eds.) *Muslim Family Law in Sub-Saharan Africa: Colonial Legacies and Post-Colonial Challenges* (Amsterdam: Amsterdam University Press, 2010), 13–60; L. Buskens and B. Dupret, "The Invention of Islamic Law: A History of Western Studies of Islamic Normativity and Their Spread to the Orient," in F. Pouillon and J. C. Vatin (eds.), *After Orientalism: Critical Perspectives on Western Agency and Eastern Reappropriation* (Leiden: Brill, 2015), 31–47.

[18] Wael B. Hallaq, "The Quest for Origins or Doctrine? Islamic Legal Studies as Colonialist Discourse," *UCLA Journal of Islamic and Near Eastern Laws* 1 (2003), 1–31.

jurisprudence.[19] These two sources paved the way for what became the Anglo-Muhammadan Law Code under Warren Hastings (1732–1818), who embarked upon establishing a hierarchy of courts charged with the task of implementing Hindu and Islamic laws in India.[20] The British wanted to establish a legal framework quickly and reduce the complexities of local practices; they therefore focused on written texts rather than fluid unwritten customs, believing that these textual sources contained clear-cut rules and could ensure the loyalty of the population, who were presumed to be deeply religious.[21] They assumed that these *fiqh* manuals represented a codification of the *sharīʿa*, established centuries earlier.[22] This method of creating and applying 'Islamic law' through specific *fiqh* manuals, translated into European languages for the benefit of the colonial administrators and judiciary, continued to be practised in other regions throughout the nineteenth and twentieth centuries. Thus, for the Indian Ocean rim areas, where the Shāfiʿī *madhhab* (legal school) predominated, Nawawī's *Minhaj al-Ṭālibīn* became the classical *fiqh* manual.[23] In Algeria and West Africa, where most Muslims were identified as followers of the Mālikī *madhhab*, the French colonial regime used *al-Muwaṭṭa* by Mālik ibn Anas (711–795) and *al-Mukhtaṣṣar* by Khalīl ibn Ishāq al-Jundī (d. c.1365).[24]

This approach was cemented further by legally inclined Orientalists such as Ignaz Goldziher, Joseph Schacht, Noel J. Coulson, and J. Norman

---

[19] Elisa Giunchi, "The Reinvention of 'Sharīʿa' under the British Raj: In Search of Authenticity and Certainty," *The Journal of Asian Studies* 68:4 (2010), 1124–7.

[20] Scott A. Kugle, "Framed, Blamed and Renamed: The Recasting of Islamic Jurisprudence in Colonial South Asia," *Modern Asian Studies* 35:2 (2001), 262–4, 272–4; William R. Roff, "Customary Law, Islamic Law and Colonial Authority: Three Contrasting Case Studies and their Aftermath," *Islamic Studies* 49:4 (2010), 459.

[21] Giunchi, "The Reinvention of 'Sharīʿa,'" 1124.

[22] Kugle, "Framed, Blamed and Renamed," 297; Buskens and Dupret, "The invention of Islamic law," 77.

[23] Messick, *The Calligraphic State*, 22, 66; Zubaida, Sami, *Law and Power in the Islamic World* (London: I.B. Tauris, 2005), 32.

[24] G. H. Bousquet, "Islamic Law and Customary Law in French North Africa," *Journal of Comparative Legislation and International Law* 32:3 (1950), 59–61; David Robinson, "Ethnography and Customary Law in Senegal," *Cahiers d'études africaines*, 32:126 (1992), 234; Barbara M. Cooper, *Marriage in Maradi: Gender and Culture in a Hausa Society, 1900–1989*, (Oxford: James Currey, 1997), 73–8; Buskens and Dupret, "The Invention of Islamic Law," 77.

200   L. J. K. BONATE

D. Anderson.[25] They defined *sharīʿa* as 'divine law' and a paradigm of the Islamic way of life, with *fiqh* representing the 'science' of *sharīʿa*—the methods of its interpretation by human beings, applied to the Qurʾān and the *ḥadīth*.[26] The codification of the *sharīʿa* in this framework was linked to the idea that the 'doors' of *ijtihād* (independent reasoning, used to interpret the divine texts) were allegedly closed in the tenth century. At this time, the *ʿulamāʾ* granted recognition to only four legal schools (*madhāhib*; singular, *madhhab*), namely Shāfiʿī, Ḥanafī, Hanbalī, and Malikī. From that time on, original critical thinking regarding source texts was prohibited and scholars were required to limit themselves to *taqlīd* (imitation), copying the methods and following the rules of the founders of the *madhāhib*. This idea, however, has been debunked by recent scholarship, which shows that independent and creative interpretation of fundamental Islamic sources has never ceased.[27]

Portugal remained largely unaffected by these modes of European colonial thought and administration. The nineteenth-century Portuguese legislation, including codification of the so-called *usos e costumes* (usages and customs) in the 1854 Code of Usages and Customs of the Non-Christian Inhabitants of Daman and Diu (*Código de Usos e Costumes de Habitantes Não-Cristãos de Damão e Diu*) and the Civil Code (*Código Civil Português*) both subsumed Muslim legal practices under the rubric of custom. In contrast to other European colonial regimes, the Portuguese collected data for the 1854 Code of Indian territories from local interlocutors and through the observation of legal practices in courts, without any consideration or study of *fiqh* manuals or other Islamic sources. Article 8 of the 1896 Civil Code stated that Portugal did not oppose "the usages

[25] Ignaz Goldziher, *Introduction to Islamic Theology and Law*, Princeton, NJ: Princeton University Press, 1981; Joseph Schacht, *An Introduction to Islamic Law*, Oxford: Clarendon, 1966; Noel J. Coulson, *A History of Islamic Law*, Edinburgh: Edinburgh University Press, 1964; J. Norman D. Anderson, *Islamic Law in the Modern World*, New York: New York University Press, 1959.

[26] Schacht, *An Introduction to Islamic Law*, 1.

[27] Bernard Weiss, "Interpretation in Islamic Law: The Theory of Ijtihad," *American Journal of Comparative Law* 26:2 (1978), 199–212; Wael B. Hallaq, "On the Origins of the Controversy about the Existence of Mujtahids and the Gate of Ijtihad," *Studia Islamica* 63 (1986), 129–41; Frank E. Vogel, "The Closing of the Door of Ijtihad and the Application of Law," *The American Journal of Islamic Social Sciences* 10:3 (1993), 396–401; George Makdisi, "Freedom in Islamic Jurisprudence: Ijtihad, Taqlid, and Academic Freedom," *Les Belles Lettres* (1985), 79–87.

and customs that were not in conflict with morals and public order," both of the "natives" and of the "oriental" immigrants such as "Banyans [Hindu Vaniya], Bhatia, Parsees, and Moors [i.e., Muslims]." Furthermore, following the provision of the new Civil Code, the Decree of November 18, 1869, directed lawmakers and colonial administrators to undertake the codification of customs of various regions, such as Macau, East Timor, and Africa. In 1885, Joaquim d'Almeida da Cunha published a small compendium of "usages and customs" of Mozambique which included a section of five pages on the *monhés*—the coastal Muslims of northern Mozambique, presumed to be of Arab-African mixed heritage—of the sultanate of Angoche, which was still largely independent of the Portuguese.[28] Da Cunha dedicated three pages to family issues, while the remaining two dealt with the history and culture of Angoche. Although highlighting the long history of Islam in that region and the pervasiveness of the Muslim faith there, da Cunha did not mention any Islamic sources or *fiqh* terminology.

During the period of the 'effective occupation' (1895–1913), the Portuguese military conquerors were ordered to collect detailed ethnographic accounts of local societies, intended to be used for building modern colonial administrative and justice systems resembling those of other European powers.[29] Reports written by officers such as Francisco António da Silva Neves (1901), Eduardo do Couto Lupi (1907), and Pedro Massano de Amorim (1911), among others, contained various kinds of ethnographic data, including research on Muslim families. However, as these researchers were not yet affected by European Orientalism, they did not assume a 'knowledge of Islam' or take translations of the *fiqh* manuals into account; instead, they recorded Islamic concepts as they were told about them by local people. Only Lupi mentions the word *sharīʿa* and, while pointing out the widespread use of the term in the region, does not equate it with 'Islamic law' but rather with an 'ethnic' legal system which he calls "the Makua code."[30] A handful of *fiqh* terms, such as *mahr* (dower, *mahari* in local vernacular) and *ṭalāq* (repudiation, *talaqa* in local vernacular), are scattered throughout the reports on northern Mozambican

---

[28] Joaquim d'Almeida da Cunha, *Provincia de Moçambique. Estudo Acerca Usos e Costumes dos Banianes, Bathias, Parses, Mouros, Gentios e Indígenas. Para cumprimento do que dispôs o artigo no 8, 1 do decreto de 18 de Novembro de 1869* (Mozambique: Imprensa Nacional, 1885), 43–8.

[29] Lupi, *Angoche*, 80.

[30] Lupi, *Angoche*, 80–1.

202   L. J. K. BONATE

Muslim societies that are overwhelmingly described as matrilineal and matrilocal.[31] These *fiqh* concepts, however, were not explained with reference to any Islamic sources or texts.

The influence of the Orientalist approach to Islam became palpable in Portuguese colonial thought only in the early twentieth century, when African Muslims were often described as illiterate, 'syncretic,' heterodox followers of 'Black Islam' (*islão negro*), allegedly mixing the 'true' orthodoxy with local culture or practices, and therefore unlikely to be abiding by the *sharī'a*.[32] The idea of *islão negro* emerged under the influence of the French term *islam noir*.[33] However, unlike other Orientalists, the Portuguese did not define what precisely Islamic 'orthodoxy' meant, except for equating it geographically with 'Arabia.'

In 1941, the Government-General of Mozambique commissioned a jurist, José Gonçalves Cota, to collect "all the ethnographic elements indispensable for the elaboration of the project of the civil and penal codes of the indigenous populations."[34] The results were "destined for those [colonial] functionaries, who by their office, have assumed the heavy responsibility of the social reform of the natives and also have to occupy themselves with the administration of justice."[35] Gonçalves Cota's findings were quite similar to those of the military officers of the conquest period, although his reports were detailed and elaborated into the projects of the civil and penal codes. His Civil Code project was divided into four sub-chapters: "1) patriarchal people; 2) non-Islamised matriarchal people;

---

[31] F. A. da Silva Neves, *Informações á cerca da Capitania-Mór de Angoche* (Lourenço Marques: Imprensa Nacional, 1901), 13; de Amorim, *Relatório sobre a ocupação de Angoche*, 102–4, 120–1; Lupi, *Angoche*, 154–7.

[32] Amorim, *Relatório sobre a ocupação de Angoche*, 98; António José de Mello Machado, *Entre os Macuas de Angoche: Historiando Moçambique* (Lisbon: Prelo, 1970), 249–53; Fernando Amaro Monteiro, *O Islão, o Poder, e a Guerra: Moçambique 1964–74* (Porto: Ed. Universidade Portucalense, 1993), 120–4, 195–208.

[33] Christopher Harrison, *France and Islam in West Africa, 1860–1960* (Cambridge: Cambridge University Press, 1988), 2–4, 99–103, 116–7, 127–36 and *passim*; David Robinson, "France as a Muslim Power in West Africa," *Africa Today* 46:3–4 (1999), 122; Louis Brenner, *Controlling Knowledge: Religion, Power and Schooling in a West African Muslim Society* (Bloomington and Indianapolis: Indiana University Press, 2001), 154–5, 164.

[34] José Gonçalves Cota, *Mitologia e Direito Consuetudinário dos Indígenas de Moçambique* (Lourenço Marques: Imprensa Nacional de Moçambique, 1944), 5.

[35] Gonçalves Cota, *Mitologia e Direito Consuetudinário dos Indígenas de Moçambique*, 7.

MUSLIM FAMILY UNDER PORTUGUESE RULE: *SHARĪ'A...*   203

3) Islamised people; 4) people in transition from matriarchy to patriarchy."[36] Like his predecessors, he noted the prevailing matriliny in northern Mozambique, including among the Muslim population.[37] His works contained some *fiqh* terms, such as *nikāh* (marriage contract, *nikahi* in the local vernacular), *mahr*, and *ṭalāq*, yet without reference to any classical or modern Islamic legal texts. Gonçalves Cota's projects were not enforced for various reasons, but mostly because of the vehement opposition from several colonial officials and the Catholic Church, who viewed his projects as impediments to the 'civilising mission' in Africa. A particular bone of contention was Gonçalves Cota's suggestion to legalise polygamous marriages and regulate them through appropriate legal provisions.[38] He also endorsed the rules of matrilineal descent, inheritance, and guardianship of children, all of which the Catholic Church found strongly objectionable.[39]

Various ethnographic studies were undertaken by the Portuguese until the mid-1960s, but they remained in essence similar to those of earlier periods. Changes came in the last decade of colonial rule, when Portugal, despite widespread international condemnation of its resistance to decolonisation and the ongoing war in African territories, tried to prolong its grip over the colonies and created a special branch of the Secret Service called the Services for Centralisation and Coordination of Information (SCCI, or SCCIM for Mozambique). This special branch was directed to study the ideology of independence and to prevent Africans from becoming susceptible to it. Between 1965 and 1973, the SCCIM collected data on Islam in general and Muslim leaders in particular, with the objective of obtaining detailed information on Islamic networks and the means of communication between various Muslim regions and the so-called poles of religious authorities.[40] These reports outlined the prevalence of matri-

---

[36] José Gonçalves Cota, *Projecto Definitivo do Código Penal dos Indígenas da Colónia de Moçambique* (Lourenço Marques: Imprensa Nacional de Moçambique, 1946.

[37] Gonçalves Cota, *Mitologia e Direito Consuetudinário dos Indígenas de Moçambique*, 240–1.

[38] Gonçalves Cota, *Projecto Definitivo do Código Penal dos Indígenas da Colónia de Moçambique*, 145–6.

[39] Gonçalves Cota, *Projecto Definitivo do Código Penal dos Indígenas da Colónia de Moçambique*, 146–8, 155–6.

[40] Monteiro, *O Islão, o Poder, e a Guerra*, 280–1, 305–7; Liazzat J. K. Bonate, "Governance of Islam in Colonial Mozambique," in V. Bader, A. Moors and M. Maussen (eds.), *Colonial and Post-Colonial Governance of Islam* (Amsterdam: Amsterdam University Press, 2011), 29–48.

liny in the northern Mozambican coastal Muslim regions and featured some *fiqh* terms, such as *ṭalāq*, *mahr*, and *nikāh*; the words *madhhab* and Shāfiʿī also appeared, though once again their meanings were not clarified.[41] The same goes for ethnographic works of the 1970s, such as those authored by António José de Mello Machado.[42] My own recent research confirms that African Muslims of northern Mozambique were in fact Shāfiʿī, not only because they consistently referred to themselves as followers of the Shāfiʿī *madhhab* but also because they used Shāfiʿī *fiqh* manuals—such as the mid-nineteenth-century *Safīnat an-Najāh* by Sālim ibn ʿAbdallāh ibn Samir al-Ḥaḍramī and Nawawī's *Minhaj al-Ṭālibīn*—in their day-to-day lives.[43] This is unsurprising, given that Islam spread to the Mozambican coast from the eighth century onwards through the Indian Ocean and Swahili networks, and the Shāfiʿī legal school historically predominated along the Indian Ocean rim as well as in East Africa.[44] However, in contrast with the Comoros, Mozambican Muslims did not have access to institutionalised forms of the Islamic normative order, as the Portuguese colonial rule neither articulated Islamic law nor endorsed the *qāḍī* courts as the French did.[45]

[41] Branquinho, "Relatório da Prospecção ao Distrito de Moçambique," 423; Fernando Amaro Monteiro, "As comunidades islâmicas em Moçambique: mecanismos de comunicação" *Africana* 4 (1989), 73–5.

[42] Mello Machado, *Entre os Macuas de Angoche*, 274.

[43] Bonate, *Traditions and Transitions*; Liazzat J. K. Bonate, "Muslim Family and Gender in Northern Mozambique: *Sharīʿa*, Custom and the State Laws in Pemba City," *Islamic Africa* 11:2 (2020), 184–207.

[44] J. Spencer Trimingham, *Islam in East Africa* (Oxford: Clarendon Press, 1964), 69; J. Norman D. Anderson, *Islamic Law in Africa* (London: Frank Cass and Co. Ltd, 1970), 1–170; Christelow, Allan, "Islamic Law in Africa" in N. Levtzion and R. L. Pouwels (eds.) *The History of Islam in Africa* (Athens, OH: Ohio University Press, 2000), 377; Anne K. Bang, *Sufis and Scholars of the Sea: Family Networks in East Africa, 1860–1925* (London and New York: Routledge Curzon, 2003), 162; Bonate, Liazzat J. K., "Islam and Matriliny along the Indian Ocean Rim: Revisiting the Old 'Paradox' by Comparing the Minangkabau, Kerala and the Coastal Northern Mozambique," *Journal of Southeast Asian Studies* 48:3 (2017), 436–51.

[45] Blanchy, "A matrilineal and matrilocal Muslim society in flux"; Iain Walker, "What Came First, the Nation or the State? Political Process in the Comoro Islands," *Africa: Journal of the International African Institute* 77:4 (2007), 582–605; G. M. Shepherd, "Two Marriage Forms in the Comoro Islands: An Investigation," *Africa: Journal of the International African Institute*, 47:4 (1977), 344–59.

Custom and Colonial Legal Pluralism

Under the Dutch and British colonial rules, normative orders stemming from matrilineal kinship relations became associated with the notion of custom, combining the Islamic concept of *adat* with European ideas of an ancient, ahistorical, and unchanging set of rules pertaining to common law.[46] But while Islamic law could be categorised by the process of sifting through the Qur'ān, *ḥadīth*, and written *fiqh* texts, custom was an unwritten, normatively fluid and adaptive praxis. Creating 'customary law' required local collaboration in collecting ethnographic data and establishing what could be legitimately incorporated into the new colonial regulations and judicial institutions.[47] As Richard Roberts and Kristin Mann put it, "the difficulty in administering native law was to find what was customary."[48] Similar to 'Islamic law,' "customary law was ... forged in struggles over property, labour, power and authority within an interactive colonial legal system, African and European, Christian and Muslim, traditional and modern."[49]

In Muslim societies, European Orientalist scholars and their local collaborators played a central role in defining custom in opposition to the legal realm of *sharīʿa*, assumed to be a completely separate field that could not accommodate local customs.[50] This led the British and French colonial regimes not to accept customary practices in Muslim regions until the early twentieth century.[51] The French applied Islamic law in Algeria in the nineteenth century without regard for custom, while the British, who thought that matriliny had no place in Islam, barred matrilineal Mappila

[46] Martin Chanock, *Law, Custom and Social Order: The Colonial Experience in Malawi and Zambia* (Cambridge: Cambridge University Press, 1985), 3.

[47] Chanock, *Law, Custom and Social Order*, 8.

[48] Richard Roberts and Kristin Mann, "Law in Colonial Africa," in K. Mann and R. Roberts (eds.) *Law in Colonial Africa* (Portsmouth, NH: Heinemann and London: James Currey, 1991), 21.

[49] Thomas Spear, "Neo-Traditionalism and the Limits of Invention in British Colonial Africa," *The Journal of African History* 44:1 (2003), 15.

[50] Coulson, *A History of Islamic Law*, 143–6; J. Norman D. Anderson, "The Future of Islamic Law in British Commonwealth Territories in Africa," *Law and Contemporary Problems*, 27:4 (1962), 621–3; Bousquet, "Islamic Law and Customary Law in French North Africa," 65.

[51] Bousquet, "Islamic Law and Customary Law in French North Africa," 63; Roff, "Customary Law, Islamic Law, and Colonial Authority," 457–9; Allan Christelow, "The Muslim Judge and Municipal Politics in Colonial Algeria and Senegal," *Comparative Studies in Society and History*, 24:1 (1982), 10–11.

Muslims from accessing the Muhammadan Code and *qādi* courts. The Mappila Muslims fell under the 1896 Malabar Marriage Act and 1898 Malabar Will Act that enforced prevailing matriliny without any regard for their Islamic faith.[52] By contrast, in the Dutch East Indies the colonial government ended up privileging local customs over *sharīʿa* in the nineteenth century, mainly thanks to Christiaan Snouck Hurgronje (1857–1936), who realised that customary practice rather than *fiqh* was a lived reality in Indonesia.[53] Under his influence, Cornelius van Vollenhoven (1874–1933) elevated *adat* as a source of law in the local pluralistic legal environment and systematised and codified it as 'customary law' (*adatrecht*).[54] In 1927, the Dutch colonial government officially established the primacy of *adat* over Islamic law as a formal legal policy in the East Indian colonies.

With the conquest of vast territories in Africa at the beginning of the twentieth century, the European colonial powers embarked upon controlling populations in whose normative orders customary practices played a major role. As David Robinson maintains, "the concern for establishing custom emerged from administrators preoccupied with centralisation, control and a strong paternalistic and interventionist approach to their African subjects."[55] Under the system of Indirect Rule, which claimed to preserve indigenous rules and laws, the British began to organise 'native courts' and developed methods of applying or overseeing the 'native customary laws.'[56] In the case of matrilineal Muslims, the British again barred the Mappila Muslims from the application of the Anglo-Muhammadan or

---

[52] Kunjulekshmi Saradamoni, *Matriliny transformed: Family, law and ideology in twentieth century Travancore* (London: Sage Publications, 1999), 86–110; G. Arunima, *There comes Papa: Colonialism and the transformation of matriliny in Kerala, Malabar, c. 1850–1940* (New Delhi: Orient Longman Private Limited, 2003), 15–25; Manaf Kottakkunnummal, "Contestations in religion, gender, and family among matrilineal Mappila Muslims in colonial Malabar, Kerala, c. 1910–1928," *SAGE Open*, 4:1 (January 2014).

[53] Euis Nurlaelawati, *The Kompilasi Hukum Islam and Legal Practice in the Indonesian Religious Courts* (Amsterdam: Amsterdam University Press, 2010), 47–8; R. M. Keener, "Indonesian Movement for the Creation of a 'National Madhhab,'" *Islamic Law and Society* 9:1 (2002), 103; Roff, "Customary Law, Islamic Law, and Colonial Authority," 456.

[54] Keener, "Indonesian Movement for the Creation of a 'National Madhhab,'" 104; Roff, "Customary Law, Islamic Law, and Colonial Authority," 455.

[55] Robinson, "France as a Muslim Power in West Africa," 237.

[56] A. N. Allott, "What Is to Be Done with African Customary Law? The Experience of Problems and Reforms in Anglophone Africa from 1950," *Journal of African Law* 28:1/2 (1984), 58.

Islamic laws, unless they renounced matriliny in favour of Islamic patriliny and patriarchy.[57] Among the Muslim Minangkabau of Negeri Sembilan in Malaya, the British shaped matrilineal *adat* around the rules of matrilineal kinship, inheritance, and women's prerogatives in property ownership.[58] The Minangkabau *adat* and the Mappila *marumakkatayam* thus became defined as 'customary laws' incorporating matriliny in opposition to Islamic law in which matriliny purportedly had no place. More recent scholarship on the history of Muslim societies, however, has acknowledged that custom and *sharīʿa* could generally coexist; the assumption that custom could only be recognised as a source of law if it did not contradict the *sharīʿa* has been shown to be flawed.[59]

The French adoption of the policies of association in the 1920s and early 1930s also led to the recognition of the customary rules, first in the Algerian Grand Kabylie and, gradually, in the rest of the colonised territories. Thus, by the early twentieth century, the Dutch, French, and British colonial regimes had elaborated a concrete legal pluralism whereby *sharīʿa*, customary law, and European legal systems operated side by side. While largely disempowering local traditional and Islamic authorities and institutions, colonial officials were engaged in appointing and selecting judges, creating customary and *qāḍi* courts, and compiling regulations that largely

[57] Aleena Sebastian, "Matrilineal practices among Koyas of Kozhikode," *Journal of South Asian Studies* 1:1 (2013), 73–9; Kottakkunnummal, "Contestations in religion, gender, and family."

[58] M. B. Hooker, "The early *adat* constitution of Negri Sembilan (1773–1824)," *Journal of the Malaysian Branch of the Royal Asiatic Society*, 44:1 (1971), 107; Michael G. Peletz, *A share of the harvest: Kinship, property, and social history among the Malays of Rembau* (Berkeley: University of California Press, 1988), 99, 104–27.

[59] Bousquet, "Islamic Law and Customary Law in French North Africa," 65; Noel J. Coulson, "Muslim Custom and Case-Law," *Die Welt des Islams*, 6:1–2 (1959), 17, 19; Anderson, "The Future of Islamic Law," 621–3; Knut S. Vikør, *Between God and the Sultan: A History of Islamic Law* (London: Hurst and Company, 2005), 166–7; Nahda Shehada, "Flexibility versus Rigidity in the Practice of Islamic Family law," *PoLAR: Political and Legal Anthropological Review* 31:1 (2009), 30; Robert W. Hefner, "Modern Muslims and the Challenge of Plurality," *Society* 51:2 (2014), 131–9.

208   L. J. K. BONATE

covered family relationships, since other areas—such as criminal and commercial law—were brought under the direct control of European rule.[60]

As the Portuguese did not engage with the notion of Islamic law, they did not address the question of the compatibility of Islam and custom. Muslim norms and laws were incorporated into the legal concept of *usos e costumes*, or custom. Before endorsing the 1869 Civil Code, Portugal codified Hindu customary practices in a separate piece of legislation, and the 1854 Code of Usages and Customs of the Non-Christian Inhabitants of Daman and Diu included the practices of Indian Muslims.[61] In Mozambique, also in the early 1850s, African customs were codified in Quelimane (*Regulamento para o Capitão-Mór da Villa de Quilimane e seu termo*, Portaria 393/A, June 4, 1853) and Inhambane (O *Codigo Cafreal do Districto de Inhambane*, September 29, 1852, and the 1889 *Código dos Milandos Inhambenses-Litígios e Pleitos*), although neither was completed or endorsed.[62] From 1861 until the early twentieth century, the *capitães-móres*, acting as administrators on behalf of the Portuguese Crown, who could be either Portuguese or local African political elites, served as judges settling legal disputes and presiding over non-European courts.[63]

After the conquest, Portugal adopted a new administrative and legal system called *Indigenato*, which was based on the Code d'Indigénat that France applied to Algeria in the nineteenth century.[64] In Mozambique, it began with forced labour, direct taxation, and the arbitrary punishment

---

[60] A. N, Allott, "The Judicial Ascertainment of Customary Law in British Africa," *The Modern Law Review* 20:3 (1957), 244–63; Christelow, "The Muslim Judge and Municipal Politics"; Abd-el Kader Boye, Kathleen Hill, Stephen Isaacs and Deborah Gordis, "Marriage law and practice in the Sahel," *Studies in Family Planning*, 22:6 (1991), 343–9; Brett L. Shadle, "'Changing Traditions to Meet Current Altering Conditions': Customary Law, African Courts and the Rejection of Codification in Kenya, 1930–60," *The Journal of African History* 40:3 (1999), 411–31; Katherine E. Hoffman, "Berber Law by French Means: Customary Courts in the Moroccan Hinterlands, 1930–1956," *Comparative Studies in Society and History* 52:4 (2010), 851–80.

[61] Cristina Nogueira Silva, "A dimensão imperial do espaço jurídico português. Formas de imaginar a pluralidade nos espaços ultramarinos, séculos XIX e XX," *Rechtsgeschichte—Legal History* 23 (2015), 187–205.

[62] Rui Mateus Pereira, "A 'Missão etognóstica de Moçambique'. A codificação dos 'usos e costumes indígenas' no direito colonial português. Notas de Investigação," *Cadernos de Estudos Africanos*, 2001.

[63] E. S. Martinez, "Uma Justica Especial para os Indigenas: Aplicacao da Justica em Mocambique (1894–1930)" (Ph.D. dissertation: University of Lisbon, 2001), 81.

[64] Gregory Mann, "What was the Indigénat? The 'Empire of Law' in French West Africa," *Journal of African History* 50 (2009), 331–51.

MUSLIM FAMILY UNDER PORTUGUESE RULE: *SHARI'A...* 209

laws of 1899, 1904, and 1907.[65] It reached its apogee during the Estado Novo (The New State, 1926–1974) which introduced the Native Labour Code in 1928, and the 1926 *Estatuto Político, Civil e Criminal dos Indígenas* (Political, Civil and Criminal Statutes of the Natives), a civil rights code that was later amended in 1929. The *Estatuto Político* reinstated the 1869 Civil Code's principle on 'usages and customs' with regard to the family, which was in effect maintained throughout the colonial period. The Estado Novo formalised the Indigenato Regime (*Regime do Indigenato*) with the legal reforms of the 1930s, such as the 1930 *Acto Colonial* and the *Carta Orgánica do Império Colonial Português*, as well as the 1933 *Reforma Administrativa Ultramarina* (Overseas Administrative Reform), all clearly differentiating between African and European legal rights and civil statuses. The Portuguese colonial legal system of the twentieth century, like that of other Europeans in Africa, was thus dualistic in nature, classifying the mostly rural African population as 'traditional,' 'indigenous,' or 'native' *subjects*, while Europeans were *citizens* of the metropolitan state.[66] However, the Portuguese regime, like that of the French, was also assimilationist. Africans could apply for the status of *assimilado*, corresponding to the French *évolué*, acquire an identity card, and follow the Civil Code provisions according to the 1917 *Portaria do Assimilado* (Decree on Assimilated Persons), strengthened further by the 1921 Native Assistance Code, *Indigenato* legislation and the 1933 Overseas Administrative Reform.[67]

The overwhelming majority of Africans lived within the jurisdiction of local 'traditional customs and usages' administered by the appointed chiefs, the *régulos/regedores* (small-scale king, or territorial chief), who were assisted by the elders or those considered knowledgeable of local customs and traditions and interpreters. Africans could have recourse to European legal curators (*curadores*), judges, administrators of the areas,

---

[65] Roberts and Mann, "Law in Colonial Africa," 17–18; Malyn Newitt, *Portugal in Africa: The Last Hundred Years* (London: Hurst and Co., 1981), 104–6.

[66] Mahmood Mamdani, *Citizen and Subject: Contemporary Africa and the Legacy of Late Colonialism*, London: James Currey, 1996; Boaventura de Sousa Santos, "The Heterogeneous State and Legal Plurality," in B. de S. Santos, J. C. Trindade and P. Meneses (eds.), *Law and Justice in a Multicultural Society. The case of Mozambique* (Dakar: CODESRIA, 2006), 3–29; Maria Paula Meneses, "O 'indígena' africano e o colono 'europeu': a construção da diferença por processos legais," *Cadernos-CES* (2010), 68–93.

[67] Narana Coissoro, "African Customary Law in the Former Portuguese Territories, 1954–1974," *Journal of African Law* 28:1/2 (1984), 72–9.

210 L. J. K. BONATE

and police commissaries.[68] The chiefs' courts were expected to deal with the cases of corporal injuries, arson, private incarceration, rape, all family and 'social' matters and disputes, and forced labour and taxation. Wherever possible, the written court records were kept and archived. In 1933, special courts for the natives were formalised as the Tribunais Privativos de Indígenas. Africans could appeal to the Portuguese legal curator or administrator and to the Directorate for Native Affairs (Direcção doe Serviços e Negócios Indígenas). Although the *Indigenato* regime was legally abolished in 1954 and Portuguese citizenship was extended to all, independent of creed and race, by the 1961 Overseas Administrative Reform, in practice most rural African areas remained within the *Indigenato* regime until the end of colonialism in 1974.

THE MUSLIM FAMILY BETWEEN *SHARĪ'A* AND MATRILINEAL CUSTOM

Portuguese colonial ethnographic and legal writings from the conquest period (1895–1913) until the end of colonialism (1974) present some general information about the regulation of African Muslim family life, showing that Muslim society in coastal northern Mozambique remained matrilineal and matrilocal at the end of the nineteenth century. The Portuguese officers responsible for these reports stated that inheritance and succession did not follow the paternal line but instead went to a woman's senior nephew or brothers, as in other matrilineal societies in the region; in the eyes of the Portuguese, the matrilineal system meant that husband and wife had equal rights in both marriage and property.[69] Children stayed with their mother after a divorce and generally belonged to her matrilineal kin under the guardianship of a maternal uncle or, sometimes, grandfather.[70] The marital residence was matrilocal, and men went to live on their mothers-in-laws' land where they built a hut or a house.[71] Adultery cases were settled with payment of a monetary indemnity to the

---

[68] Martinez, "Uma Justiça Especial para os Indígenas," 125–6, 130, 134, 139, 155.

[69] Da Cunha, *Provincia de Moçambique*, 47; da Neves, *Informações á cerca da Capitania-Mór de Angoche*, 11, 13; Lupi, *Angoche*, 154–7, 80; de Amorim, *Relatório sobre a ocupação de Angoche*, 102–4, 120–1; A. Camizão, *Governo do Distrito de Moçambique. Indicações Gerais sobre a Capitania—mór do Mossuril. Appendice ao Relatório de 1 de Janeiro de 1901* (Lourenço Marques: Imprensa Nacional, 1901), 4.

[70] Lupi, *Angoche*, 142.

[71] Lupi, *Angoche*, 84; de Amorim, *Relatório sobre a ocupação de Angoche*, 134–6.

MUSLIM FAMILY UNDER PORTUGUESE RULE: *SHARĪ'A...* 211

husband by the offending male party, a portion of which went to the chief of the region if disputes were settled in his or her court.[72] Many other norms governing local family life, however, conformed with the provisions of *fiqh*, including settlements of disputes within and between families by a council with the participation of a *mwalimu* (Qur'ānic teacher or Muslim community leader) or other religious dignitary.[73] Family disputes were taken to the chief's court only when the case was particularly difficult. In accordance with classical Islamic jurisprudence, young people were considered eligible for marriage on reaching puberty, yet boys were taken to the bush for initiation ceremonies, including circumcision, and girls to a female-only house, following local customs. Both ceremonies took place under the auspices of *nehanga* (master of initiation rites), with drums called *umzoma* for the boys and *nimuari* for the girls. Before puberty a girl was called *mwalati* or *numar*, and afterwards *mwali* or *mwari*.[74]

Muslims of northern Mozambique married and divorced as often as they do today, and a woman's first wedding—associated with her virginity—is known as *harusi*, from the Arabic *'arūs*, or bride; generally, girls married for the first time around the age of fifteen or sixteen.[75] The preliminaries and wedding ceremony corresponded to general Islamic principles, and when a boy wished to marry, his father would write a letter to the girl's father—in the local language, but using Arabic script (*ajami*)—asking for her hand.[76] Literacy in the Arabic script in local languages is a *longue-durée* historical tradition of the region, and both marriage intent and divorces were usually written down.[77] When the marriage was agreed, the groom was invited to a special dinner at the house of his future in-laws, which he then continued to visit until the wedding day, sending regular gifts of food and clothes. The bride's family would write down all the

[72] Camizão, *Governo do Distrito de Moçambique*, 7; de Amorim, *Relatório sobre a ocupação de Angoche*, 110–4; Lupi, *Angoche*, 143, 153.

[73] Amorim, *Relatório sobre a ocupação de Angoche*, 101.

[74] Amorim, *Relatório sobre a ocupação de Angoche*, 136.

[75] Da Cunha, *Provincia de Moçambique*, 47; da Neves, *Informações á cerca da Capitania-Mór de Angoche*, 11; de Amorim, *Relatório sobre a ocupação de Angoche*, 125, 136.

[76] Jamal J. Nasir, *Islamic Law of Personal Status* (London: Graham & Trotman, 1990), 42–5; Neves, *Informações á cerca da Capitania-Mór de Angoche*, 11; Liazzat J. K. Bonate, "Islam and Literacy in Northern Mozambique: Historical Records on the Secular Uses of the Arabic Script," *Islamic Africa* 7 (2016), 60–80.

[77] Bonate, "Islam and Literacy in Northern Mozambique"; Bonate, "Muslim Family and Gender in Northern Mozambique".

expenditures incurred by the groom's family in Arabic script in local language; if the wedding did not go ahead, they were expected to reimburse them. Weddings often took place on Fridays after the *juma* prayers, sometimes in a mosque, and were solemnised by a *mwalimu* or imam, following the Islamic requirement that a marriage must be made public before witnesses.[78] The *mahr*, agreed by the parties beforehand, was paid upon the wedding ceremony; Neves notes that the average *mahr* in Angoche was forty reis (the old Portuguese currency) at the end of the nineteenth century.[79] On the wedding night, a nominal 'godmother' of the bride remained in the bedroom to attest her virginity, proof of which was displayed the following day. Annulment of marriage after consummation was permissible if the bride was found not to be a virgin or if any physical defects were discovered.[80]

Polygamy was accepted, with a man permitted to marry up to four wives, with the eldest wife enjoying special privileges, while a political ruler could also have an unlimited number of concubines.[81] The co-wives lived in separate dwellings, and a husband was expected to provide for his wives and children by building their hut or house, and by delivering food, clothes, and other necessities.[82] Divorce was allowed and could be initiated by either the wife or the husband, in which case it was known as *talaqa*.[83] If the wife had children, she could continue to reside in her usual dwelling after the divorce until she remarried or went back to her own matrilineal kin group, taking the children with her.[84]

Even after the consolidation of colonial rule in Mozambique (1926–1974), rural areas generally continued to be governed by the chiefs and their associated authority, which upheld matriliny and local Islamic practices derived from the Shāfiʿī *madhhab*. Changes in governance only occurred when people moved away from their original homelands.

---

[78] Nasir, *Islamic Law of Personal Status*, 54–5.

[79] Neves, *Informações á cerca da Capitania-Mór de Angoche*, 11.

[80] Amorim, *Relatório sobre a ocupação de Angoche*, 126.

[81] Da Cunha, *Provincia de Moçambique*, 46; Lupi, *Angoche*, 85, 154; Camizão, *Governo do Distrito de Moçambique*, 4–5.

[82] Lupi, *Angoche*, 144; Amorim, *Relatório sobre a ocupação de Angoche*, 128.

[83] Da Cunha, *Provincia de Moçambique*, 47; Lupi, *Angoche*, 153; Amorim, *Relatório sobre a ocupação de Angoche*, 113, 128–9.

[84] Lupi, *Angoche*, 153; Amorim, *Relatório sobre a ocupação de Angoche*, 128; Da Cunha, *Provincia de Moçambique*, 47.

Gonçalves Cota's 1940s findings were quite similar to those of the conquest period, and he reported: "Muslims of the colony are almost entirely matrilineal, and inheritance and succession follow the maternal line: 1) senior nephew, son of the senior sister of the deceased; 2) elder brother; 3) male ascendants of the deceased; 4) female ascendants of the deceased; 5) senior nephew, son of the elder brother or his representatives." He adds that "in the matrilineal family, the tutelage of orphaned children goes to: 1) senior maternal uncle; 2) mother; 3) maternal grandmother; 4) senior maternal aunt."[85]

As in previous centuries, boys and girls went through initiation rites on reaching puberty, after which they were considered of age to marry. In contrast to earlier periods, however, it became common for parents to marry their daughters off as early as possible, probably due to increasing poverty resulting from the harsh colonial economic and labour policies. The wedding was celebrated by a *mwalimu*, *shaykh*, or imam in a mosque or sometimes on the land where the couple's future home was built. Only the future fathers-in-law took part in the ceremony, while the bride remained at home until the wedding day. At the end of the religious ceremony, the father or uncle of the groom presented the *mahr* to the father or uncle of the bride, estimated to be between one hundred and five hundred escudos.[86]

Gonçalves Cota's description of the conjugal rights and obligations among Muslims suggests that they followed classical *fiqh* provisions: the wife owed obedience to her husband, while the husband was obliged to maintain his family by providing shelter, food, and clothing and by giving his wife both jewellery and tools to work in the field, since she was "responsible for cereals and agriculture." The husband was the owner of the family property, while the wife had her own property; she also had access to the clan land on her family side. Like earlier authors, Gonçalves Cota recognised that divorce could be initiated by either the husband or the wife, which is also within the parameters of *fiqh*.[87]

De Mello Machado's 1970 study of Angoche reaffirmed the views of previous authors, although he conflated matriliny with matriarchy and

---

[85] Gonçalves Cota, *Mitologia e Direito Consuetudinário*, 240–1, 230.

[86] Gonçalves Cota, *Projecto Definitivo do Código Penal*, 47; Gonçalves Cota, *Mitologia e Direito Consuetudinário*, 217.

[87] Gonçalves Cota, *Projecto Definitivo do Código Penal*, 51–2; Nasir, *Islamic Law of Personal Status*, 126–31.

matrilocal residence.[88] He argued that women in these societies enjoyed economic and social privileges due to matriliny and stressed the fact that "matriarchal tradition is powerfully and deeply rooted, so women enjoy great liberty" and the "concept of property is profoundly linked to the matrilineal structure."[89]

CONCLUSION

Portuguese colonialism differed from that of other European regimes in that it did not engage with the concept of Islamic law; rather, Islamic norms and regulations were considered part of custom. The Portuguese set about codifying customary practices much earlier than the British and French colonies and catalogued the Hindu, Muslim, and Christian customs in their Indian colonies of Diu, Daman, and Goa in the mid-nineteenth century. They also codified the African customs in the Inhambane and Quelimane regions of central and southern Mozambique during the same period but with few practical consequences. The Civil Code endorsed the customs of local populations and opened avenues for further codification, although resistance from the Catholic Church proved an insurmountable obstacle.

Unlike other European colonial powers, the Portuguese did not take *fiqh* texts or other Islamic sources into account when codifying Muslim practices, but instead relied on the observation of local societies. More nuanced knowledge about Muslim societies of the northern Mozambican coast only emerged in the Portuguese records at the end of the nineteenth century, particularly during and after the conquests in 1895–1913. They showed that, while remaining matrilineal and matrilocal, Muslims were also following classical *fiqh* provisions. Yet it was not until the late 1960s that Portuguese officials and scholars highlighted that these *fiqh* provisions were derived from the Shāfiʿī *madhhab*; and even then, they made no attempt to explain the origin or implications of this.

Africans, along with other colonised peoples, became *inígenas* or 'natives' under the Indigenato regime (1926–1954/1961), which meant that they were required to abide by customary law, although in theory they had an option of acquiring the status of *assimilado* and following the Metropolitan legal system. The vast majority of Africans lived in rural areas

[88] Mello Machado, *Entre os Macuas de Angoche*, 181.
[89] Mello Machado, *Entre os Macuas de Angoche*, 191, 221.

MUSLIM FAMILY UNDER PORTUGUESE RULE: *SHARĪA...* 215

and continued to be ruled by local chiefs, who became part of the colonial administration in the twentieth century and oversaw local legal matters. The incorporation of African traditions and customs into the colonial administrative and legal systems meant that matriliny went unchallenged, especially in rural areas, which allowed women to become chiefs and control the land and other assets derived from the matrilineal side of their families. The family relations and personal status of coastal African Muslims thus continued to be regulated by a combination of matrilineal norms and the rules of the Shāfiʿī *madhhab*.

Acknowledgements This research was made possible by a grant from the Seoul National University Research Fund and fieldwork funding from Oxfam-America and the Centre of African Studies of the Eduardo Mondlane University. I am thankful to Anne K. Bang at the University of Bergen and Hassan Mwakimako at the Zentrum Modrener Orient (ZMO) in Berlin for the opportunity to present some preliminary results of this research. I am deeply grateful to Isabel Casimiro at the Centre of African Studies of the Eduardo Mondlane University in Mozambique for her unfailing support.

BIBLIOGRAPHY

Albuquerque, Joaquim Mouzinho de *A Campanha contra os Namarrais*, Lisbon: Imprensa Nacional, 1897.

Allott, A. N., "The Judicial Ascertainment of Customary Law in British Africa," *The Modern Law Review* 20:3 (1957), 244–63.

Allott, A. N., "What Is to Be Done with African Customary Law? The Experience of Problems and Reforms in Anglophone Africa from 1950," *Journal of African Law* 28:1/2 (1984), 56–71

Amorim, Pedro Massano de, Relatório *sobre a ocupação de Angoche: Operações de campanha e mais serviço realizados, Anno 1910*, Lourenço Marques: Imprensa Nacional, 1911.

Anderson, J. Norman D. *Islamic Law in the Modern World*, New York: New York University Press, 1959.

Anderson, J. Norman D. "The Future of Islamic Law in British Commonwealth Territories in Africa," *Law and Contemporary Problems*, 27:4 (1962), 617–31.

Anderson, J. Norman D., *Islamic Law in Africa*, London: Frank Cass and Co. Ltd, 1970.

Arunima, G., *There comes Papa: Colonialism and the transformation of matriliny in Kerala, Malabar, c. 1850–1940*, New Delhi: Orient Longman Private Limited, 2003.

216   L. J. K. BONATE

Askew, Kelly M., "Female circles and male lines: Gender dynamics along the Swahili coast," *Africa Today* 46 (1999), 67–102.

Bang, Anne K., *Sufis and Scholars of the Sea: Family Networks in East Africa, 1860–1925*, London and New York: Routledge Curzon, 2003.

Blanchy, Sophie, "Beyond 'Great Marriage': Collective Involvement, Personal Achievement and Social Change in Ngazidja (Comoros)," *Journal of Eastern African Studies* 7:4 (2013), 569–87.

Blanchy, Sophie, "A matrilineal and matrilocal Muslim society in flux: negotiating gender and family relations in the Comoros," *Africa: Journal of the International African Institute* 89:1 (2019), 21–39.

Bonate, Liazzat J. K., "Matriliny, Islam and Gender in Northern Mozambique," *Journal of Religion in Africa* 36:2 (2006), 139–66.

Bonate, Liazzat J. K., *Traditions and Transitions: Islam and Chiefship in Northern Mozambique, ca. 1850–1974*, Ph.D. dissertation: University of Cape Town, 2007.

Bonate, Liazzat J. K., "Islam in Northern Mozambique: A Historical Overview," *History Compass* 8:7 (2010), 573–93.

Bonate, Liazzat J. K., "Governance of Islam in Colonial Mozambique," in V. Bader, A. Moorsand, M. Maussen (eds.), *Colonial and Post-Colonial Governance of Islam* (Amsterdam: Amsterdam University Press, 2011), 29–48.

Bonate, Liazzat J. K., "Islam and Literacy in Northern Mozambique: Historical Records on the Secular Uses of the Arabic Script," *Islamic Africa* 7 (2016), 60–80.

Bonate, Liazzat J. K., "Islam and Matriliny along the Indian Ocean Rim: Revisiting the Old 'Paradox' by Comparing the Minangkabau, Kerala and the Coastal Northern Mozambique," *Journal of Southeast Asian Studies* 48:3 (2017), 436–51.

Bonate, Liazzat J. K., "Muslim Female Political Leadership in Pre-Colonial Northern Mozambique: The Letters by *Nunu* Fatima Binti Zakaria of Mogincual," in Viera Pawlikova-Vilhanova (ed.), *Ad Fontes: Reflections on sources of Africa's pasts, their preservation, publication, and/or digitisation* (Bratislava: Slovak Academic Press, 2019), 81–105.

Bonate, Liazzat J. K., "Muslim Family and Gender in Northern Mozambique: *Sharīʿa*, Custom and the State Laws in Pemba City," *Islamic Africa* 11:2 (2020), 184–207.

Bousquet, G. H., "Islamic Law and Customary Law in French North Africa," *Journal of Comparative Legislation and International Law* 32:3 (1950), 57–65.

Boye, Abd-el Kader, Kathleen Hill, Stephen Isaacs and Deborah Gordis, "Marriage law and practice in the Sahel," *Studies in Family Planning*, 22:6 (1991), 343–9.

Branquinho, José Alberto de Melo, "Relatório da Prospecção ao Distrito de Moçambique (Um estudo de estruturas hierárquicas tradicionais e religiosas, e da sua situação político-social), Nampula, 22 April 1969" Arquivo Histórico de

Moçambique, Maputo, Secção Especial No 20, Cotas S.E., 2 III P 6, Portugal, Lourenço Marques, 30 December 1969.

Brenner, Louis, *Controlling Knowledge: Religion, Power and Schooling in a West African Muslim Society*, Bloomington and Indianapolis: Indiana University Press, 2001.

Buskens, L. and B. Dupret, "The Invention of Islamic Law: A History of Western Studies of Islamic Normativity and Their Spread to the Orient," in F. Pouillon and J. C. Vatin (eds.), *After Orientalism: Critical Perspectives on Western Agency and Eastern Reappropriation* (Leiden: Brill, 2015), 31–47.

Camizão, A., *Governo do Distrito de Moçambique. Indicações Gerais sobre a Capitania—mór do Mossuril. Appendice ao Relatório de 1 de Janeiro de 1901*, Lourenço Marques: Imprensa Nacional, 1901.

Chanock, Martin, *Law, Custom and Social Order: The Colonial Experience in Malawi and Zambia*, Cambridge: Cambridge University Press, 1985.

Christelow, Allan, "The Muslim Judge and Municipal Politics in Colonial Algeria and Senegal," *Comparative Studies in Society and History*, 24:1 (1982), 3–24.

Christelow, Allan, "Islamic Law in Africa" in N. Levtzion and R. L. Pouwels (eds.) *The History of Islam in Africa* (Athens, OH: Ohio University Press, 2000), 373–96.

Coissoro, Narana, "African Customary Law in the Former Portuguese Territories, 1954–1974", *Journal of African Law* 28:1/2 (1984), 72–9.

Cooper, Barbara M., *Marriage in Maradi: Gender and Culture in a Hausa Society, 1900–1989*, Oxford: James Currey, 1997.

Coulson, Noel J., "Muslim Custom and Case-Law," *Die Welt des Islams*, 6:1–2 (1959), 13–24.

Coulson, Noel J., *A History of Islamic Law*, Edinburgh: Edinburgh University Press, 1964.

Da Cunha, Joaquim d'Almeida, Provincia de Moçambique. Estudo Acerca Usos e Costumes dos Banianes, Bathias, Parses, Mouros, Gentios e Indígenas. Para cumprimento do que dispôs o artigo no 8, 1 do decreto de 18 de Novembro de 1869, Mozambique: Imprensa Nacional, 1885.

Giunchi, Elisa, "The Reinvention of 'Sharīʿa' under the British Raj: In Search of Authenticity and Certainty," *The Journal of Asian Studies* 68:4 (2010), 1119–42.

Goldziher, Ignaz, *Introduction to Islamic Theology and Law*, Princeton, NJ: Princeton University Press, 1981.

Gonçalves Cota, José, *Mitologia e Direito Consuetudinário dos Indígenas de Moçambique*, Lourenço Marques: Imprensa Nacional de Moçambique, 1944.

Gonçalves Cota, José, *Projecto Definitivo do Código Penal dos Indígenas da Colónia de Moçambique*, Lourenço Marques: Imprensa Nacional de Moçambique, 1946.

Hafkin, N. J., *Trade, Society, and Politics in Northern Mozambique, c. 1753–1913*, Ph.D. dissertation: Boston University, 1973.

Hallaq, Wael B., "On the Origins of the Controversy about the Existence of Mujtahids and the Gate of Ijtihad," *Studia Islamica* 63 (1986), 129–41.

Hallaq, Wael B., "The Quest for Origins or Doctrine? Islamic Legal Studies as Colonialist Discourse," *UCLA Journal of Islamic and Near Eastern Laws* 1 (2003), 1–31.

Harrison, Christopher, *France and Islam in West Africa, 1860–1960*, Cambridge: Cambridge University Press, 1988.

Hefner, Robert W., "Modern Muslims and the Challenge of Plurality," *Society* 51:2 (2014), 131–9.

Hoffman, Katherine E., "Berber Law by French Means: Customary Courts in the Moroccan Hinterlands, 1930–1956," *Comparative Studies in Society and History* 52:4 (2010), 851–80.

Hooker, M. B., "The early *adat* constitution of Negri Sembilan (1773–1824)," *Journal of the Malaysian Branch of the Royal Asiatic Society*, 44:1 (1971), 104–16.

Jeppie, Shamil, Ebrahim Moosa, and Richard Roberts, "Introduction: Muslim Family Law in Sub-Saharan Africa: Colonial Legacies and Post-Colonial Challenges," in Shamil Jeppie, Ebrahim Moosa, and Richard Roberts (eds.) *Muslim Family Law in Sub-Saharan Africa: Colonial Legacies and Post-Colonial Challenges* (Amsterdam: Amsterdam University Press, 2010), 13–60.

Keener, R. M., "Indonesian Movement for the Creation of a 'National Madhhab,'" *Islamic Law and Society* 9:1 (2002), 83–115.

Kottakkunnummal, Manaf, "Contestations in religion, gender, and family among matrilineal Mappila Muslims in colonial Malabar, Kerala, c. 1910–1928," *SAGE Open*, 4:1 (January 2014).

Kugle, Scott A., "Framed, Blamed and Renamed: The Recasting of Islamic Jurisprudence in Colonial South Asia," *Modern Asian Studies* 35:2 (2001), 257–313.

Lupi, Eduardo do Couto, *Angoche. Breve memória sobre uma das Capitanias-Móres do Distrito de Moçambique*, Lisbon: Typografia do Annuario Commercial, 1907.

Makdisi, George, "Freedom in Islamic Jurisprudence: Ijtihad, Taqlid, and Academic Freedom," *Les Belles Lettres* (1985), 79–87.

Mamdani, Mahmood, *Citizen and Subject: Contemporary Africa and the Legacy of Late Colonialism*, London: James Currey, 1996.

Mann, Gregory, "What was the Indigénat? The 'Empire of Law' in French West Africa," *Journal of African History* 50 (2009), 331–51.

Martinez, E. S., "Uma Justica Especial para os Indigenas: Aplicacao da Justica em Mocambique (1894–1930)," Ph.D. dissertation: University of Lisbon, 2001.

Medeiros, Eduardo C., *História de Cabo Delgado e do Niassa (c. 1836–1929)*, Maputo: Central Impressora, 1997.

Mello Machado, António José, *Entre os Macuas de Angoche: Historiando Moçambique*, Lisbon: Prelo, 1970.

Meneses, Maria Paula, "O 'indígena' africano e o colono 'europeu': a construção da diferença por processos legais", *Cadernos-CES* (2010), 68–93.

Messick, Brinkley, *The Calligraphic State: Textual Domination and History in a Muslim Society*, Berkeley, CA: University of California Press, 1992.

Monteiro, Fernando Amaro, "As comunidades islâmicas em Moçambique: mecanismos de comunicação" *Africana* 4 (1989), 65–89.

Monteiro, Fernando Amaro, *O Islão, o Poder, e a Guerra: Moçambique 1964–74*, Porto: Ed. Universidade Portucalense, 1993.

Nasir, Jamal J., *Islamic Law of Personal Status*, London: Graham & Trotman, 1990.

Neves, F. A. da Silva, *Informações á cerca da Capitania-Mór de Angoche*, Lourenço Marques: Imprensa Nacional, 1901.

Newitt, Malyn, *Portugal in Africa: The Last Hundred Years*, London: Hurst and Co., 1981.

Newitt, Malyn, *A History of Mozambique*, London: Hurst and Co., 1995.

Nurlaelawati, Euis, *The Kompilasi Hukum Islam and Legal Practice in the Indonesian Religious Courts*, Amsterdam: Amsterdam University Press, 2010.

Peletz, Michael G., *A share of the harvest: Kinship, property, and social history among the Malays of Rembau*, Berkeley: University of California Press, 1988.

Pélissier, R., *História de Moçambique: Formação e Oposição, 1854–1928* (translated from French into Portuguese by Manuel Ruas), Lisbon: Editorial Estampa Lda., 2000.

Pereira, Rui Mateus, "A 'Missão etognósica de Moçambique'. A codificação dos 'usos e costumes indígenas' no direito colonial português. Notas de Investigação," *Cadernos de Estudos Africanos*, 2001.

Peters, Pauline E., "Introduction: Revisiting the Puzzle of Matriliny in South-Central Africa," *Critique of Anthropology* 17:2 (1997), 125–46.

Roberts, Richard, and Kelly Mann, "Law in Colonial Africa," in K. Mann and R. Roberts (eds.) *Law in Colonial Africa* (Portsmouth, NH: Heinemann and London: James Currey, 1991), 3–58.

Robinson, David, "Ethnography and Customary Law in Senegal," *Cahiers d'études africaines*, 32:126 (1992), 221–37.

Robinson, David, "France as a Muslim Power in West Africa," *Africa Today* 46:3–4 (1999), 105–27.

Roff, William R., "Customary Law, Islamic Law and Colonial Authority: Three Contrasting Case Studies and their Aftermath," *Islamic Studies* 49:4 (2010), 455–62.

Said, Edward, *Orientalism: Western Conceptions of the Orient*, London: Penguin Books, 1995.

Santos, Boaventura de Sousa, "From Customary Law to Popular Justice," *Journal of African Law* 28:1/2 (1984), 90–8.

220   L. J. K. BONATE

Santos, Boaventura de Sousa, "The Heterogeneous State and Legal Plurality," in B. de S. Santos, J. C. Trindade and P. Meneses (eds.), *Law and Justice in a Multicultural Society. The case of Mozambique* (Dakar: CODESRIA, 2006), 3–29.

Saradamoni, Kunjulekshmi, *Matriliny transformed: Family, law and ideology in twentieth century Travancore*, London: Sage Publications, 1999.

Sebastian, Aleena, "Matrilineal practices among Koyas of Kozhikode," *Journal of South Asian Studies* 1:1 (2013), 66–82.

Shepherd, G. M., "Two Marriage Forms in the Comoro Islands: An Investigation," *Africa: Journal of the International African Institute*, 47:4 (1977), 344–59.

Schacht, Joseph, *An Introduction to Islamic Law*, Oxford: Clarendon, 1966.

Shadle, Brett L., "'Changing Traditions to Meet Current Altering Conditions': Customary Law, African Courts and the Rejection of Codification in Kenya, 1930–60," *The Journal of African History* 40:3 (1999), 411–31.

Shehada, Nahda, "Flexibility versus Rigidity in the Practice of Islamic Family law," *PoLAR: Political and Legal Anthropological Review* 31:1 (2009), 28–46.

Silva, Cristina Nogueira, "A dimensão imperial do espaço jurídico português. Formas de imaginar a pluralidade nos espaços ultramarinos, séculos XIX e XX," *Rechtsgeschichte—Legal History* 23 (2015), 187–205.

Spear, Thomas, "Neo-Traditionalism and the Limits of Invention in British Colonial Africa," *The Journal of African History* 44:1 (2003), 3–27.

Trimingham, J. Spencer, *Islam in East Africa*, Oxford: Clarendon Press, 1964.

Vikør, Knut S., *Between God and the Sultan: A History of Islamic Law*, London: Hurst and Company, 2005.

Vogel, Frank E., "The Closing of the Door of Ijtihad and the Application of Law," *The American Journal of Islamic Social Sciences* 10:3 (1993), 396–401.

Walker, Iain, "What Came First, the Nation or the State? Political Process in the Comoro Islands," *Africa: Journal of the International African Institute* 77:4 (2007), 582–605.

Weiss, Bernard, "Interpretation in Islamic Law: The Theory of Ijtihad," *American Journal of Comparative Law* 26:2 (1978), 199–212.

Zubaida, Sami, *Law and Power in the Islamic World*, London: I.B. Tauris, 2005.

Asante Nkramo and Fantse Nkramo: Unravelling the Paradox of Islam and Matriliny in Ghana

Mustapha Abdul Hamid

INTRODUCTION

This chapter examines the practice of inheritance among two Muslim Akan groups in Ghana: the Asante and Fantse. Islam is often understood to prescribe a patrilineal descent system, where descent is traced through the father rather than the mother, and the legitimacy of a child is mostly based on the establishment of legal paternity.[1] Islamic laws of inheritance as detailed in the Qur'an and interpreted and developed by the ulama

---

[1] Mohamad Som Sujimon, "Implications and Consequences of Illegitimate Child (walad al-zina) in Islamic Law: A Classical View," *Jurnal Syariah* 7:1, 1999.

M. Abdul Hamid (✉)
Department of Religion and Human Values, University of Cape Coast,
Cape Coast, Ghana
e-mail: mabdul-hamid@ucc.edu.gh

© The Author(s), under exclusive license to Springer Nature Switzerland AG 2024
A. Panakkal, N. M. Arif (eds.), *Matrilineal, Matriarchal, and Matrifocal Islam*, Palgrave Series in Islamic Theology, Law, and History, https://doi.org/10.1007/978-3-031-51749-5_8

222   M. ABDUL HAMID

essentially follow patrilineal lines and ensure provision for the male heirs of the deceased, although the Qur'an also makes special provision for female relatives, who were completely neglected by the customs and traditions of the Arabs before the advent of Islam.

Yet, the most distinctive feature of the Akan ethnic group, of which the Asante and Fantse are a part, is matriliny. Indeed, matriliny—the unilineal descent of an ethnic group through the mother's bloodline—has been the single most important determinant of the survival of the Akan. The Akan saying, *wo nni wu'a, na w'ebusua asa*, meaning, "a mother's death is the termination of the bloodline," is perhaps the most powerful expression of the centrality of matriliny to Akan culture. So, how are Asante and Fantse Muslims able to maintain their identity as both Akans and Muslims? More importantly, how are they able to guarantee the Islamic system of inheritance for their descendants while ensuring that their Akan lineages do not die? This question is the crux of this chapter. Leela Dube makes an even clearer case for why a study of matrilineal Muslim societies is an important academic venture:

> Perhaps nowhere would a social system appear so incompatible with the ideology of Islam, and demand so much adjustment and accommodation as in a matrilineal society. Born and shaped in a patrilineal setting, and subsequently spread to similarly organised communities in the period of its development and crystallisation, Islam invariably assumed patriliny as the natural form of social organisation, emphasising a code of conduct and laying down a system of law in keeping with it. Whatever has been said in the Islamic holy books and legal texts about the family, particularly the duties and obligations of parents, children, and spouses; about the implications of marriage, particularly rules enjoining the husband to properly maintain the household, wife and children; about not driving away a wife from her household (except for adultery); about the maintenance and living arrangement of the children in the event of divorce; about the guardianship of the children in the event of the remarriage of the mother; about the laws of inheritance and guardianship of property for minor children, clearly indicates a patrilineal set-up.[2]

---

[2] Leela Dube, *Matriliny and Islam: Religion and Society in the Laccadives* (Delhi: National Publishing House, 1969), 5–6.

This chapter unravels how the Asante and Fantse Muslims of Ghana navigate this apparent contradiction between their matrilineal culture and the patrilineal interpretations of Islam.

Asante and Fantse Muslims are called Asante Nkramo and Fantse Nkramo. Nkramo being the Akan word for Muslims (singular, Kramo). Kramo derives from the Akan word, *kram*, which means to chant or recite. Nkramo therefore refers to people who chant or recite—an obvious reference to the recital of the Qur'an both during prayer and in Islamic schools. Comfort Asante, a linguist, says that Muslims are called Nkramo because of the *adhan* (the Muslim call to prayer), which the Akan people interpret as a sort of chant.[3]

Islam is a religion, while the Asante and Fantse belong to the broad Akan ethnic group in Ghana. They are part of the larger Akan group, which constitutes about 45.7% of Ghana's population (2021 Population Census).[4] Any discussion of religion and ethnicity will therefore seem on the face of it to be contradictory. While the assertion that religion and ethnicity are divergent concepts in general, in certain senses, they are not. Appleby argues that,

> Literally millions of people structure their daily routines around the spiritual practices enjoined by a religious tradition, and they do so quite publicly. Dress, eating habits, gender relations, negotiations of time, space and social calendar—all unfold beneath a sacred canopy.[5]

This chapter is a classical study of how a people—the Asante and Fantse Muslims—subsume their social fabric under the sacred canopy of Islam. This study is important because of the apparent contradiction that the labels Asante Nkramo and Fantse Nkramo present. There are about eight major ethnic groups in Ghana, according to the most recent census, and all of these groups include Muslims. Indeed, Islam is dominant amongst many of the ethnic groups in the northern parts of Ghana: nearly 95% of Dagombas profess Islam as their religion, for example. Yet Dagomba Muslims are not referred to as Dagomba Nkramo, and as a distinct marker, Nkramo is only used when reference is made to Muslims who are Asante or Fantse.

[3] Personal communication, 20 October 2020.
[4] Ghana Statistical Service, 2021 Population and Housing Census, 2021.
[5] R. Scott Appleby, *The Ambivalence of the Sacred* (Lanham, MA: Rowman & Littlefield Publishers, 2000), 3.

There are two main reasons why only Asante and Fantse Muslims are also described as Nkramo. Islam in Ghana is generally understood to be a religion of the people of the north, while Christianity is perceived as the religion of the people of the south. Christianity was introduced into Ghana (then the Gold Coast) by Portuguese Christian missionaries in 1482, when they first landed at Elmina, a town that borders the Atlantic Ocean in the southern-most tip of Ghana.[6] From the southern tip, Christianity slowly inched its way up-country, but it has remained the dominant religion of the south. Islam, on the other hand, was introduced into Ghana from the late fourteenth to early fifteenth centuries by itinerant Muslim traders from the Sahel region of West Africa, who came to the then Gold Coast to trade in gold and cola nuts.[7] They came through the northern-tip of the country, then made their way to the forest zones of Ghana. Since that time, Islam has remained dominant in the north. As a result of these historical circumstances, Christianity has been characterised as the religion of the south, while Islam has become the religion of the north. It is therefore a matter for academic and social curiosity when southern people, in this case the Asante and Fantse, profess Islam, a religion that is generally seen as alien to their geographical setting. Beyond history and geography, culture is also an important factor in why Asantes and Fantses who profess Islam are called Asante Nkramo and Fantse Nkramo. For the Akans, their culture is what defines them, and their culture is everything: law, culture, morality and ethics are inseparable. The Akan word for culture is *mbra*, which also means law. More appropriately, culture is referred to as *oman mbra* or *ammamre*, although both expressions are better translated as the 'law of the land.' People are thus defined by the culture and law of their land.

It is important to state that both matriliny and patriliny are unilineal systems of inheritance. Unilineal systems of inheritance trace an individual's descent through either the mother or the father, but never both. Descent guarantees the succession of future generations and therefore their very survival. It is to underline this fact that the Akan assert that when your mother dies, your lineage ends, which is to say that it is through mothers that the Akan ensure the sustainability of lineages. It therefore seems clear that matriliny is a non-negotiable aspect of Akan culture.

---

[6] Lamin Saneh, *West African Islam*, Maryknoll, NY: Orbis Books, 1983.

[7] Peter B. Clarke, *West Africa and Islam* (London: Edward Arnold, 1982), 58.

Using inculturation theory as a basis, this chapter will investigate how the Asante and Fantse navigate the matriliny of their ethnicity and the patriliny of their religion. The chapter adopts a case study methodology, triangulating data from about twenty key informants and two focus group discussions, and I conclude that Asante and Fantse Muslims have found an ingenious way of "observing Allah's law, while also acknowledging that Allah created us into tribes and nations."[8] First, however, I shall introduce the Asante and Fantse ethnic groups.

THE ASANTE AND FANTSE ETHNIC GROUPS

The origin of the Asante people is disputed. The Asantes themselves believe that they came forth from the ground a very long time ago, somewhere in the rainforest zone of the middle parts of Ghana.[9] What is generally agreed, however, is that the Asante are a part of the eight clans that form the Akan ethnic group of Ghana. They all speak varying forms of the Akan language, which have been named as Twi (spoken by the Asante), Fantse (spoken by the Fantse) and Akwapim Twi (spoken by the Akwapim). The eight clans of the Akan are the Oyoko, Nsona, Anona, Twidan, Aburadze, Ntwaa, Kwona and Adwenadze.[10] Specifically, the Asante kingdom is said to have been established from the Oyoko clan of the Akan group.[11] The Akan people are believed to have been part of the ancient kingdom of Ghana, which covered the land that today forms Mali and Mauritania. Indeed, it was the connection that Danquah established between the Akan of today and their progenitors in ancient Ghana, that led to the Gold Coast being renamed Ghana.[12]

Various factors are said to have caused these Akan clans to begin a series of migratory journeys from the Sahelian region they originally inhabited to the forest zones of present-day Ghana. Edgerton attributes these

---

[8] Abbas Wilson, personal communication, 6 September 2020.

[9] Robert B. Edgerton, *The Fall of the Asante Empire: The Hundred-Year War for Africa's Gold Coast*. New York: The Free press, 1995.

[10] George P. Hagan, "An Analytical Study of Fantse Kinship," *African Studies Research Review Vol 5* (Accra: University of Ghana Press, 1967), 59.

[11] Emmanuel Osei-Boakye, *Documentation and Dynamics of Oyoko Clan in Asante: Myth, Folklore and Meaning*, Master's Dissertation: University of Ghana, 2013.

[12] Eva L. Meyerowitz, "A Note on the Origins of Ghana," African Affairs 51: 205 (1952), 321.

migrations to drought,[13] while others consider the marauding activities of the Almoravid movement to have been an additional motivation. The Almoravid movement was a militant Islamic religious movement that thrived in north-west Africa in the eleventh century.[14] But the Asante kingdom as presently constituted was carved out by Osei Tutu I, who won independence for the Asante people from the Denkyiras in 1701 after three years of battle.[15] Today, the Asante occupy the entire Asante region of Ghana, which occupies 24,389 km^2 of land, constituting 10.2% of the total area of the country.

The Fantse are also a part of the larger Akan ethnic group. They are said to have migrated from present day Techiman in the Bono East Region and settled in their capital of Mankessim in the Central Region. They are said to be called Fantse from a corruption of the word, *Fa-atsew*, meaning, "half has broken away," referring to the half that moved away from Techiman. Shumway (2011) states that the Fantse migration was led by three great warriors: Obrumankuma, Odapagyan and Oson.[16] On the way, Obrumankuma and Odapagyan died; it was therefore Oson who led them to their present capital of Mankessim. The Fantse are often referred to as a confederacy, because the group's nucleus was created by an alliance of Fantse, Fetu and Assin.[17] Sanders dates the establishment of the Fantse confederacy to 1868.[18]

Both the Asante and Fantse adhere to a matrilineal descent system. I shall quote Owoahene-Acheampong verbatim in order to present a clear concept of how matriliny operates within the Akan setting:

> Among the Akan, succession, inheritance and political allegiance are determined by matrilineal descent. ... And for this reason also, real control and jural rights over the individual come from the head of lineage (Abusua panyin) and the maternal uncle (wofa) respectively. ... A child's genitor is not necessarily his pater ... in terms of social relationship, the child's maternal

---

[13] Edgerton, The Fall of the Asante Empire, 19.

[14] Mervyn Hiskett, *The Development of Islam in West Africa* (London: Longman Group, 1984), 6–8.

[15] Edgerton, *The Fall of the Asante Empire*, 18.

[16] Rebecca Shumway, *The Fante and the Transatlantic Slave Trade*. New York: University of Rochester Press, 2011.

[17] Adu Boahen, "Fantse Origins: The Mankessim Period," in J.F. Ade Ajayi and Ian Espie (eds.), *A Thousand Years of West African History*, Ibadan University Press, 1968.

[18] James Sanders, "The Expansion of the Fantse and the Emergence of Asante in the Eighteenth Century," *Journal of African History 20: 3* (1979), 349–64.

uncle has rights of the socialisation of the child. The father's responsibility to the offspring and thus to the nuclear family (which includes the wife) is the provision of shelter and food. As the children grow older, their father's responsibility to them decreases, but during their childhood, the father is the person upon whom the children may depend.[19]

This is the system of inheritance that binds the *abusua* (lineage) in both Asante and Fantse culture. Yet before we discuss how Asante and Fantse Muslims adhere to this culture, while remaining faithful to their Islamic faith, it is important to understand how Islam was introduced into both Asante and Fantse land.

ISLAM IN ASANTE AND FANTSE LANDS

Contact with Islam dates back to the 1730s for the Asante people, when the Asante kingdom embarked on an expansionist policy by fighting wars of conquest to the north.[20] Key to the Asante policy of expansionism was trade, and they also sought to control the southern section of the trade routes, extending to the Sahel. Indeed, there was an important trading post called Begho situated in today's Bono Region. Begho was not just a trading post but an important Muslim settlement. I have already stated that trade was an important instrument through which Islam was introduced into Ghana and traders also served as itinerant Muslim preachers. The Asante created what was called the *batafekuo* (royal trade corps) whose commercial activities were protected by the state.[21] There was therefore a conscious effort to encourage these Muslim traders to come to the Asante kingdom with their cattle and cola, in exchange for gold and salt. According to Owusu-Ansah, Muslim traders in Asante thus became "an important instrument of the state for the regulation of the commercial and political activities of local subordinate groups."[22]

These Muslims were also recruited by the Asante army to fight in its wars of conquests. In addition to serving as charm and amulet makers for

---

[19] Stephen Owoahene-Acheampong, *Inculturation and African Religion: Indigenous and Western Approaches to Medical Practice* (New York: Peter Lang, 1998), 44.

[20] David Owusu-Ansah, "The State and Islamisation in 19th Century Africa: Buganda Absolutism Versus Asante Constitutionalism," *Journal of Muslim Minority Affairs 8:1* (1987), 140.

[21] Owusu-Ansah, "The State and Islamisation in 19th Century Africa," 140.

[22] Owusu-Ansah, "The State and Islamisation in 19th Century Africa, 140.

Asante warriors. These amulets were talismans which contained Qur'anic writings, which were believed to act as protection against bullets as well as to provide help in many of life's challenges. The Muslim traders in time, were incorporated into the Asante administrative system and became secretaries, scribes and even *gyaasewa* or household servants[23] and many Asante began to convert to the religion of the 'strangers' as a result of intermarriage. The incorporation of Islam into the Asante administrative structure remains evident today; the Suame Imam, for example, also serves as Imam to the Asante king. Suame is a suburb of Kumasi, the capital of the Asante kingdom, and is one of the quarters that the Asante kings gave to the Muslims for habitation.

The introduction and spread of Islam in Fantse land is uniquely different from what took place in the rest of the country. Islam was introduced into all the various parts of Ghana, either through the deliberate efforts of itinerant Muslim preachers as in the case of Asante or through the conversion of the chiefs and kings of kingdoms—such as those of Dagbon and Gonja—who trusted in the efficacy of the intercessory prayers of Muslim clerics. In the case of the Fantse, two prominent indigenous Fantse citizens took the decision to invite Muslim clerics to come to Fantse land to teach them Islam and guide their steps in the Muslim faith. Benjamin Sam was a Wesleyan Methodist and catechist in Ekumfi Ekrawfo near Mankessim. He is said to have dreamt that he was being led in prayer in the fashion of the Muslim ritual *salat* (prayer) by a fair-skinned man. He sought help for the interpretation of his dream from a Nigerian Muslim resident in Ekrawfo at that time called Abdul-Rahman Pedro. Pedro told him that he was being called by Allah to the Islamic faith and told him about fair-skinned people in a country called Pakistan who professed the religion that he dreamt about. With the help of Abdul-Rahman Pedro, Benjamin Sam and his friend Mahdi Appah wrote to the headquarters of the Ahmadiyya Muslim order in Qadian, Pakistan, to send them a missionary to teach them the faith. The Ahmadiyya Movement sent them Maulvi Abdul-Rahman Nayyar, who became the first Ahmadi missionary to Ghana. Maulvi Abdul-Rahman Nayyar came to Ekrawfo, settled among

---

[23] Thomas Edward Bowdich, *Mission from Cape Coast Castle to Ashantee with Statistical Account of that Kingdom and Geographical Notices of other Parts of the Interior of Africa* (London: James Murray, 1819), 308–9.

the people and began propagating the Ahmadi interpretation of Islam. Thus began the spread of Islam in Fantse land.[24]

Because the Ahmadiyya faith was the first form of Islam to be introduced into Fantse land, for a long time, the term Fantse Kramo (Fantse Muslim) referred only to adherents of the Ahmadiyya doctrine. Today, however, a significant number of Fantse belong to the Ahl Sunna (Wahhabi) Muslim denomination, since some men who studied at the Islamic University of Madina returned to spread the Wahhabi interpretation of Islam. So, today, the term Fantse Kramo is applicable to all Fantse who are Muslim and not just those of the Ahmadiyya faith.

Today significant populations of the Asante and Fantse are Muslim. It is important to bear in mind that Islam is more than spirituality. It is also a culture. The Qur'an prescribes a framework that covers all spheres of life—social, political, economic and religious—and when it comes to inheritance, it lays down a comprehensive code for its adherents. As I have already emphasised, this system of inheritance follows largely patrilineal lines. We shall now examine this Islamic system of inheritance and that of the Akan (Asante/Fantse).

ISLAMIC LAW OF INHERITANCE

Islamic laws of inheritance as detailed in the Qur'an generally follow a patrilineal pattern. Patrilineal societies trace succession, descent, and inheritance from the father's line. The system of *asaba* in pre-Islamic Arabia—the male relatives who qualify to inherit—provided the blueprint for the Islamic system of inheritance. The order of inheritance is sons, grandsons, father and brothers, uncles and cousins and then descendants of the grandfather of the deceased. However, provision is also made for female relatives who were completely neglected in the pre-Islamic system of inheritance. The full Qur'anic stipulation on inheritance is as follows:

> Allah commands you with regard to children—for the males, a share equal to that of two females. If there are only females, two or more, two-thirds of what the deceased has left. If there is only one daughter, half goes to her. For the parents—each of them, a sixth of what the deceased has left behind if the deceased had a child. If he had no child and his parents are the only

---

[24] Nathan Samwini, *The Muslim Resurgence in Ghana since 1950: Its Effects Upon Muslims and Muslim-Christian Relations*, Berlin: Lit Verlag, 2006.

heirs, then his mother inherits a third. If the deceased had siblings, the mother only receives a sixth of the estate. All of this after any bequest he may have made or any debt to be paid. Your parents or your children—you do not know which of them is closer to you as regards welfare—an ordinance from Allah! Indeed, Allah is all-knowing and wise.

To you (widowers) belongs a half of what your wives have left, if they have not had children. But if they have had children, then to you goes one-quarter of what they leave after any bequest or any debt to be paid. To them (your widows) belongs one-quarter of what you leave, if you have no children. But if you do have children, then to them (the widows) belongs one-eighth of what you leave after any bequest or debt to be paid.[25]

As is clear from the above, the Qur'an shows a clear sense of preference for patrilineality; children inherit directly from their father, and a son receives twice the inheritance of a daughter. This is because men are expected to bear the burden of earning a livelihood and maintaining their wives, children and parents. A woman is expected to join the economic community of her husband's patrilineage. Another sign of the patriliny of the Qur'anic ideal may be gathered from the fact that widowers inherit half of their wives' property when they predecease their husbands without issue, or a quarter if there have been children between them. Yet widows only receive a quarter of the estate of their late husbands if they have no issue, or an eighth if there are children. This of course appears less unfair when we realise that in the pre-Islamic era, a widow inherited nothing and may, indeed, have been passed to her husband's male heirs with the remainder of his property.

The Akan (Asante/Fantse) System of Inheritance

The Akan system of inheritance is matrilineal. Matriliny implies that the line of inheritance and succession pass down the mother's line. Christensen, writing on the etiology of matriliny among the Fantse, tells the following story:

> Once there was a man who was in debt. It was only four shillings but that was a great amount of money in those days. He wanted to pawn his son to pay the debt, but his wife would not allow it. His sister offered her son as a pawn in order to enable him to secure the money. Out of gratitude to the

[25] Qur'an 4: 11–12.

ASANTE NKRAMO AND FANTSE NKRAMO: UNRAVELLING THE PARADOX...   231

sister and her son, he left his property to the sister's son. That is why we have the sister's son inherit.[26]

In the Akan matrilineal system of inheritance, maternal lines of inheritance take precedence over sons and daughters. Busia details the order of succession in a matrilineal system of inheritance as follows:

A man's potential successors are his brothers in order of age, his mother's sister's son, his sister's son, his mother's sister's daughter's son, his sister's son, his mother's sister's daughter's son, his sister's daughter's son or his mother's sister's daughter's son in that order of preference.[27]

The matrilineal system of inheritance therefore assumes that children belong to their mother's lineage. The Akan attribute this belief to their contention that it is the mother that provides the *mogya* (blood) for the existence of the child and is therefore the essential source of life. The main male responsible for children are therefore the maternal uncles. Assanful, quoting an informant, states that "when you give birth, the children are not for you but for your wife. Since your wife is not a member of your family, you do not belong to the same family with your children since they belong to their mother's family."[28] In the Akan system of inheritance, children therefore have no right to inherit their father's assets when he dies. Wilson quotes a Fantse elder who gives a succinct and clear explanation of how the inheritance system among the Fantse works:

They (children) have no rights to inheritance. A father can give anything to them in his lifetime. However, when he dies, they get nothing, unless the clan of the deceased chooses to give them. In the past, rich men often requested that part of the money that they leave behind be given to their surviving children and spouses. The immovable property on family land and those acquired with the clan's resources reverted to the clan.[29]

---

[26] James Boyd Christensen, *Double Descent Among the Fante* (Ph.D. Dissertation: Northwestern University, 1952), 41.

[27] Kofi Abrefa Busia, *The Position of the Chief in the Modern Political System of Ashanti: A Study of the Influence of Contemporary Social Changes on Ashanti Political Institutions* (Oxford: Oxford University Press, 1968), 1.

[28] Vincent Assanful, *The Role of Indigenous Assin Religion in the Practices of Inheritance and Succession of the Assin.* Ph.D. Dissertation: University of Cape Coast, Ghana, 2017.

[29] Alex J. Wilson, *Mother's Wealth: Matrilineality and Inheritance among the Fantse of Ghana* (Ph.D. Dissertation: University of Ohio, 2011), 194.

232 M. ABDUL HAMID

This demonstrates the contradictions between the inheritance systems of the patriliny of Islam and the matriliny of Akan culture. Yet, there are other matrilineal cultures around the world whose members have embraced Islam; I now turn to review the literature on some of these cultures.

THE AKAN AND FANTSE AND OTHER MATRILINEAL COMMUNITIES

Leela Dube tackles the subject of matriliny and Islam as it pertains in the Laccadive islands, off the south-west coast of India, in her study of the Kalpeni people who reside there. These are an Islamised people with a "duolocal residence pattern," and Dube analyses the social system that has arisen out of the interaction of Islam and the indigenous matrilineal culture.[30] This study is particularly relevant since it employs inculturation theory, which is particularly relevant to the hybrid of Akan and Islamic cultures found in Asante and Fantse society. Dube comes to the same conclusion that there has been a process of "compromise and accommodation between the two apparently incompatible systems," in the case of the Kalpeni people.[31]

Manaf Kottakkunnummal discusses a 'clash' of three cultures among the Mappilar Muslims of Malabar; Islam, the local matrilineal culture and the British legal system imposed by the colonial rulers.[32] Malabar is a region around the southwestern coastline of the mainland Indian subcontinent. Kottakkunnummal's paper looks at "the contesting articulations of gender, family and religion in colonial South India," and is relevant to this study because of the centrality of Islam and matriliny in the analysis.[33] The Mappilar Muslims moved from rejection to accommodation, and Kottakkunnummal avers that "in the 1920s, matriliny was referred to as 'unIslamic' in the discourses of the courts, reform movements and Mappilar youngsters who received Western education."[34] Subsequently, however, "the Mappilars of Malabar retained matrilineal customs rather intact, though the gender relations and religious practices were re-

---

[30] Dube, *Matriliny and Islam*, 3.

[31] Dube, *Matriliny and Islam*, 6–7.

[32] Manaf Kottakkunnummal, "Indigenous Customs and Colonial Law: Contestations in Religion, Gender and Family Among Matrilineal Mappila Muslims in Colonial Malabar, c. 1910–1928," *Sage Open 4*, January–March 2014.

[33] Kottakkunnummal, "*Indigenous Customs and Colonial Law*," 1.

[34] Kottakkunnummal, "*Indigenous Customs and Colonial Law*," 2.

articulated in the idioms of patriarchy and textuality."[35] We shall see similar patterns of re-articulation among the Asante and Fantse Muslims of Ghana.

Sophie Blanchy also examines the 'clash' of Islam and matriliny in the Comoros. The purpose of her paper was to examine how such matrilineal societies "integrate the patriarchal type of normative framework that Islam introduced during its historical expansion from Arabia."[36] She examines the negotiations of gender and family relations amongst the Muslims of the Comoros, who are both matrilineal and matrilocal, and her findings also show a synthesis of matriliny and Islamic patriliny. She contends that "marriage is ruled by Islamic law, but alliances between matrilineal descent groups follow other rationales,"[37] a conclusion that mirrors the situation of the Asante and Fantse Muslims.

Patrick Ryan's paper, *Islam and Matrilineality in West Africa,* is directly relevant. Ryan discusses matrilineal Muslims in West Africa dating from the eleventh century to the present day—a laborious task—and as a result, he does not give detailed attention to all the matrilineal Muslim groups he mentions. However, he does mention the Asante Muslims of Ghana and how the incompatibility of their matrilineal culture with the patriliny of Islam remains a major stumbling block to mass conversions among the Asante. Ryan's paper mentions an important historical event that shows the clear paradox of being both Muslim and Asante; in 1798, the ruler of the Asante kingdom, Osei Kwame, was deposed because it was suspected that he was secretly a Muslim.[38] Since it is difficult to tell what beliefs humans avow in their hearts, it would seem that Osei Kwame showed open likeness and admiration for the Muslims who served in the Asante army and court and gave them prominence within the governance structure of the kingdom. This must have been a source of worry for the custodians of the Asante culture, who feared that the king would "contaminate" the matriliny of the Asante culture with the patriliny of Islam and thus deposed him.

Yet, although Dube, Kottakkunnummal, Blanchy and Ryan all examine groups of matrilineal Muslims and how they combine Islam and matriliny

[35] Kottakkunnummal, "Indigenous Customs and Colonial Law, 2.
[36] Sophie Blanchy, "A Matrilineal Matrilocal Muslim Society in Flux: Negotiating Gender and Family Relations in the Comoros," *Africa* 89:1 (2019), 21.
[37] Blanchy, "A Matrilineal Matrilocal Muslim Society in Flux," 21.
[38] Ivor Wilks, *Asante in the Nineteenth Century: The Structure and Evolution of a Political Order* (Cambridge: Cambridge University Press, 1975), 256.

in their everyday lives, none of them discuss the Asante and Fantse Muslims. Dube only mentions the Asante in passing as a matrilineal Muslim group. There is therefore a lacuna in the scholarship and it is to this problem that I now turn.

Matriliny is central to both Asante and Fantse culture. Islamic laws of inheritance, on the other hand, basically follow patrilineal patterns. To be Asante or Fantse and Muslim at the same time, therefore, presents a 'paradox' of some sort, since matriliny and patriliny are in essence irreconcilable. Even so, Asante and Fantse Muslims are managing to live their lives fully both within the Asante and Fantse cultural milieu and the prescriptions of the Islamic faith. This chapter unravels this 'paradox' as it unfolds in the real lives of Muslim Asante and Fantse, in order to show the vitality and dynamism of culture. It is a qualitative study and as such, it aims at investigating the how and why of human behaviour and the reasons behind it.[39] Creswell posits five designs for qualitative research: ethnographies, grounded theory, case studies, phenomenological research and narrative research.[40] This paper combines the phenomenological and case study research designs. Phenomenology deals with the experiences of people as they live their lives; this study focuses on how Asante and Fantse Muslims, in their everyday lives, demonstrate the dynamism of culture. As a case study, it deals with the phenomenon of inheritance.

Data was gathered from twenty key informant interviews and two focus group discussions as well as drawing on the available academic and popular literature on the subject. Interviews and focus group discussions took place over a period of three months (July–September) followed by further interviews with two key informants in the first week of November 2020. The geographical areas under consideration were Kumasi—the capital of the Asante kingdom, where a large number of Asante Muslims reside— and Saltpond in the Central Region, home to a similarly large number of Fantse Muslims. One focus group discussion was held in Kumasi and one in Saltpond, each consisting of seven participants: family elders, married men and women and also young unmarried men and women. Of the twenty interviewees, ten were in Kumasi and ten in Saltpond. All the interviewees were also part of the focus group discussions in order to validate what they had told me earlier as individuals. Participants were identified through snowball sampling where participants told me of other Asante

---

[39] David Silverman, *Doing Qualitative Research*, London: Sage Publications, 2013.
[40] John W. Creswell, *Research Design*, London: Sage Publications, 2009.

and Fantse *Nkramo* that they knew. Of the twenty interviewees, eight were male heads of families and married and eight were married women. Two were young unmarried men and two were young unmarried women. Ragin states that "in qualitative research, the issue is how many cases are needed to secure statistically significant findings or more broadly, to secure assurance that an observed pattern is not mere happenstance."[41] I am therefore confident that the twenty interviewees and the results presented in this chapter represent the true nature of the dynamics of how Asante and Fantse *Nkramo* live the matriliny of their culture, while remaining faithful to the tenets and dictates of the patriliny of Islam.

Key questions focused on issues that arise for all matrilineal Muslims: do they find that their Asante/Fantse culture contradicts their Muslim faith? Are their families entirely Muslim, or are there other family members who are non-Muslim? Are they accepted by non-Muslim family members? How do they rank their Asante/Fantse culture, vis-vis their Islamic faith? How are the inheritances of the Muslim members of their families shared when they die? Do they follow strictly Islamic rules of inheritance or the Asante/Fantse rules of inheritance? If they use a combination of both systems of inheritance, how do they ensure that conflicts do not arise as a result of such combination of two distinct cultures?

From the research, we discerned two levels of commitment to Islam among Asante and Fantse Muslims, reflecting two different expressions of the compatibility of Islam and matriliny. First of all, there are those whose commitment to Islam is absolute and will not countenance a hybridisation of the two values. They give up their rights to any family or matrilineal inheritance and will their own property wholly to their children and other heirs who qualify according to Islamic edict. These are in the minority and are mostly Wahhabi and Ahmadi—both purist ideologies that tend to frown on any forms of mixing of Islam with other cultural beliefs. Shaykh Ishaq Nuamah, for example, is an Asante and a prominent Wahhabi Muslim cleric in Ghana. He tells us that his father gave up his right to inherit his uncle's properties and decreed that after his death, his property should be shared between his children and other heirs according to Islamic custom.[42] Abbas Wilson, a Fantse Muslim, who is also the Deputy Ameer and head of the Ahmadiyya Muslim Mission in Ghana, is another purist

---

[41] Ragin, Charles C., and Howard S. Becker (eds.) *What Is a Case? Exploring the Foundations of Social Inquiry* (Cambridge: Cambridge University Press, 1992), 10.

[42] Personal Communication from Shaykh Ishaq Nuamah, 25 November 2020.

who believes that once a person embraces Islam, all other identities must be subsumed under the Islamic identity. Ethnicity, he believes, is distinct from religion. Abbas was born to Muslim parents, although his family included non-Muslim members; his father, now deceased, was the head of the family. Abbas said that whenever a family member died, his estate was divided according to his faith. If Muslim, the estate would be shared according to Islamic inheritance laws, while non-Muslim family members' property would be divided in accordance with their religious or cultural system.[43]

Purists like Shaykh Ishaq Nuamah and Abbas Wilson are in the minority, however. The majority of Asante and Fantse Muslims practice what I call "accommodative Islam." Accommodative Islam is the Islam that allows the mixing of Islamic tenets with the cultural tenets of its host community. Those who subscribe to accommodative Islam are most of the Tijaniyya Sufi brotherhood, who comprise the majority of Muslims in Ghana. Imam Abdul-Razak Awal of Kumasi, a Tijaniyya, argues that Islam did not come to obliterate people's cultures and asserts that there is no fundamental contradiction between being Asante/Fantse and being Muslim. He quotes the Quranic verse that states that "humans have been created into tribes and nations, so that they may know one another."[44] Islam according to him is a universal religion, suitable for every culture and tradition around the world, although he believes that the socio-cultural context in which Islam was introduced has been an important factor in shaping its historical development. To him, Asante/Fantse culture can only be enriched by the practice of Islam, and he insists that this is indeed the case.

While the Asante and Fantse cultures remain matrilineal, the key ingredients that accompany the matrilineal system of inheritance have been eroded with the passage of time and as a result of the conversion of some Asante and Fantse to Islam. For example, Dube, quoting Fortes, states that "among the Ashanti(sic) of the Gold Coast in Africa, a form of duolocal residence in which the wife visits the husband is found as one of the alternative residential patterns."[45] In the course of the field work for this chapter, many of the elderly people in Asante confirmed that this duolocal pattern of residence was once practised by the Asante people. However,

---

[43] Personal Communication from Abbas Wilson, 6 July 2020.
[44] Qur'an 49:13.
[45] Dube, *Matriliny and Islam*, 2.

that is no longer the case. They attribute the erosion of the duolocal residence pattern to the influence of three factors: modernity, Christianity and Islam. Musah Ishaq, an Asante Muslim, told us that "Islam and Christianity have diluted and almost rendered extinct, many of our cultural practices as Asantes."[46] Traditionally, wives would continue to live with their birth families and visit their husbands only to perform tasks such as fetching water for them to bathe, bringing food or performing their conjugal duties. In one interview, Opanyin Kofi Agyekum told us that he remembers that wives used to pound fufu[47] in the family homes before carrying it to their husbands' homes so that their husbands could eat.[48]

Today, this practice has changed, and all the male Asante Muslims interviewed said that they lived with their wives in the same house. While some of them say that they were not brought up to expect a duolocal system of residence, some also assert that they live with their wives because they are Muslims and Islam requires them to be the maintainers of their wives. They interpret "maintenance" to include personal care and attention requiring that they share a home with their wives. It is also important to note that while both Asante and Fantse are matrilineal, they are not matrifocal societies: fathers are still considered the heads of families. This understanding syncs easily with Islam and enables Asante and Fantse Muslims to live a double-consciousness that blends Islam and matriliny.

The Fantse Muslims make a distinction between property that belongs to the family and property that belongs to the individual; in most cases, property that belongs to the family refers to landed property and farmlands. Value is placed more on landed property than on other forms of acquisition. The Fantse proverb, *wobisa wo fie, wonbisa wo sika* means, "one is asked about his house; one is not asked about his money," testimony to the value that landed property has within Fantse consciousness. On the death of the head of the family, even if he is Muslim, this landed property is shared according to the matrilineal system of inheritance and the brother of the deceased assumes the headship of the family, giving him principal right to inheritance.

However, they acknowledge that people may have worked to acquire their own personal property which does not belong to the entire family,

---

[46] Personal Communication from Musah Ishaq, 6 July 2020.
[47] Fufu is the staple food of the Asante people. It is made from cassava and/or plantain, which is boiled, pounded, and molded into a ball and eaten with soup.
[48] Personal Communication from Opanyin Kofi Agyekum, 6 November, 2020.

and a Muslim is allowed to will part of the property acquired by his own labour to his children. In other words, both patrilineal and matrilineal systems of inheritance exact some rights over property. While the matrilineal system of inheritance does not dictate the percentage of property that should go to one's own children if the deceased is a Muslim, the Muslims say that they bequeath no more than 5% of their personal property to other members of the matrilineal hierarchy of inheritance, while their own children inherit the remaining 95% according to the Islamic system of inheritance.

This Islamic practice of bequeathing 5% of one's property to people who would not ordinarily qualify to inherit is also in accordance with Fantse inheritance practices. One informant, Opanyin Ato Quansah told us that a person can transfer property he has acquired privately to other people who fall outside the matrilineal inheritance structure without any problem. However, this needs to be done in one's lifetime with the elders of the family present as witnesses that the property has been so transferred.

Professor Gyan Baffour, who is an Asante Christian, tells me that his late uncle, who was once the head of their family, was Muslim. This uncle told his family that since he was Muslim, his children had rights to his property just as Gyan and his siblings as children of his sister could also claim inheritance rights. He therefore devolved part of his estate to them as children of his sister before his death and told them that upon his death, the rest of his estate would be shared according to the Islamic system of inheritance.[49] This is a clear example of how the majority of Asante and Fantse Muslims live a double-consciousness or double heritage, combining the Islamic ideal while at the same time upholding the Asante/Fantse matrilineal heritage. Dube's finding in her study of the Kerala people is thus also applicable in the case of the Asante and Fantse. She states that "the acceptance of sharia has not circumscribed the principle of matrilineal inheritance to the extent of any structural disruption."[50] In both Asante and Fantse lands, the patrilineal lines of authority and coordination as well as close cooperation of the matrilineal kin remains a distinctive feature of the social structure.

In both Asante and Fantse lands, the Muslims marry according to a combination of both the traditional Akan marriage forms and the Islamic marriage. Indeed, in Ghana more generally, all Muslims marry in

---

[49] Personal Communication from Gyan Baffour, 10 July 2020.
[50] Dube, *Matriliny and Islam*, 78.

accordance with both the Islam and the traditions of the area. Paternity is established through *nikah* (marriage), but the children do not belong to the father; they belong to their mother's kin. They are therefore unable to marry their mother's close kin, but can marry their father's close kin since they do not belong to their father's families.

In Islam, non-Muslims cannot inherit the property of Muslims, meaning that if one's child were to apostasise, that child is disqualified from inheriting his or her father's property. However, in the case of the majority of Asante and Fantse Muslims, this Islamic edict does not seem functional. As already stated, an Asante or Fantse Muslim bequeaths his property to his children—as well as to his wives and parents, if still living—according to the Islamic laws of inheritance. However, he also bequeaths some of the property to non-Muslim members of his family according to the matrilineal inheritance system of Asante and Fantse. Asante and Fantse Muslims have thus found an ingenious way of marrying the Islamic system of inheritance with their traditional matrilineal system of inheritance without seriously disrupting either system.

By and large, Islam has not made a significant incursion into Asante and Fantse land as it has among the people of northern Ghana, meaning that the matrilineal system of inheritance is an important aspect affecting in the way Islam is practised. The dethroning of ruler Asantehene Osei Kwame by the Asante kingmakers when they realised that he had sympathies for Islam shows the ingrained Asante belief that Islam and Asante culture are fundamentally at odds. Even so, Asantes and Fantses who have converted to Islam manage to live a double-consciousness that makes them Asante/Fantse without diminishing the value of their adherence to the Islamic faith. It is to the theories that explain this phenomenon that I now turn.

Theories are used as broad explanations for the behaviour and attitudes of people and provide a lens for conducting studies such as this one. As a basis for this research, I have used inculturation theory and have come to believe that W.E.B Du Bois' theory of double-consciousness also helps to explain the hybridisation of the Akan and Islamic systems of inheritance.[51] In the context of southern Africa, Eugene Laponte defines inculturation as "a process through which the gospel penetrates the culture of the evangelised people, becomes one with it and eventually provokes a new cultural

---

[51] W.E.B Du Bois, *The Souls of Black Folk*, New York: New American Library, 1969.

synthesis."[52] In the same context, Crollius defines it as "the integration of the Christian experience of a local church into the culture of its people, in such a way that this experience not only expresses itself in elements of this culture, but becomes a force that animates, orients and innovates this culture so as to create a new unity and communion, not only within the culture in question but also as enrichment of the church universal."[53] When religious cultures are transplanted from their original environments into new ones, there is a tendency for the first culture to influence the host culture in such a way as to give the latter a new meaning and outlook.

From the way that Asante and Fantse Muslims negotiate inheritance, it is clear that the influence of Islam has triggered a process of inculturation, that has resulted in a hybrid system of inheritance, accommodating both the patrilineal inclinations of Islam and the matriliny of Asante and Fantse culture. Leela Dube discovered the same phenomenon among the Kalpeni people, noting that, "for the inheritance of property, two entirely different sets of rules are in operation: the traditional matrilineal rules and the Islamic law of inheritance."[54]

The negotiation of inheritance among Asante and Fantse Muslims reflects Du Bois' theory of double-consciousness. Double-consciousness refers to the inherent 'two-ness' that people experience when their natural selves are confronted with an impinging culture. Du Bois discussed this in relation to African-Americans arguing that because of racialised oppression in white-dominated society, blacks basically led double lives which eroded their identity as black, but at the same time, it did not make them white.[55] It is this double-consciousness that dictates the Asante/Fantse psyche and how inheritances are shared among Asante/Fantse Muslims. Indeed, all the interviewees told us that they live both the worlds of their Asante and Fantse culture and the Islamic culture.

[52] Eugene Laponte, *An Experience of Pastoral Theology in Southern Africa: Inculturated and Committed Christian Communities* (Rome: Urbaniana University Press, 1985), 6.

[53] Ary Roest Crollius, "Inculturation: Newness and Ongoing Process, in John Mary Waliggo, Ary Roest Crollius, Theoneste Nkeramihigo and John Mutiso-Mbinda (eds.), *Inculturation: Its meaning and Urgency* (Nairobi: St Paul Publications, 1986), 16.

[54] Dube, *Matriliny and Islam*, 36.

[55] Du Bois, *The Souls of Black Folk*.

Conclusion

At the beginning of this chapter, I set out to unravel the 'paradox' of Islam and matriliny among Asante and Fantse Muslims. In doing so, I posed the following questions: Do Asante/Fantse Muslims find that their culture contradicts their Muslim faith? Are their families entirely Muslim, or are there other members of their families who are non-Muslim? How are they accepted by other members of their families who are not Muslims? How do they rank their Asante/Fantse culture vis-à-vis their Islamic faith? How are inheritances of the Muslim members of their families shared when they die? Do they follow strictly Islamic rules of inheritance or Asante/Fantse rules of inheritance? If they use a combination of both systems of inheritance, how do they ensure that conflicts do not arise as a result of such combination of two distinct cultures?

During the process of the research, I found that Asante and Fantse Muslims live both the matriliny of the Asante/Fantse culture and the patriliny of Islam. They are able to do this without much difficulty and without much conflict with other non-Muslim members of the extended family. There is general recognition that people belong to different faiths. Muslims are therefore granted their wish for their property is distributed according to the matrilineal system. Family property mostly refers to houses and farmlands, which pass from generation to generation. Even with property that was personally acquired by the deceased, some percentage of it is reserved for inheritance according to the Akan matrilineal system of inheritance. In studying the Kalpeni people, Dube states that they distinguish between 'Friday property' and 'Monday property:' 'Friday property is the property that should be passed on matrilineally, while 'Monday property' should be governed by the Islamic law of inheritance.[56]

Among Asante and Fantse Muslims, the process of inculturation is complete and the people live a double-consciousness. This double-consciousness allows them to be fully Muslim, while at the same time, participating in the culture and law of their kin group.

[56] Dube, Matriliny and Islam, 36.

BIBLIOGRAPHY

Appleby, R. Scott, *The Ambivalence of the sacred.* Lanham, MA: Rowman & Littlefield Publishers, 2000

Assanful, Vincent, *The Role of Indigenous Assin Religion in the Practices of Inheritance and Succession of the Assin.* Ph.D. dissertation: University of Cape Coast, Ghana.

Blanchy, Sophie, A Matrilineal Matrilocal Muslim Society in Flux: Negotiating Gender and Family Relations in the Comoros. *Africa*, 89 (1) (2019), 21–39

Boahen, Adu, "Fante Origins: The Mankessim Period," in J.F Ade Ajayi and Ian Espie (eds.), *A Thousand Years of West African History*, Ibadan: Ibadan University Press, 1968

Bowdich, Thomas Edward, *Mission from Cape Coast Castle to Ashantee with Statistical Account of that Kingdom, and Geographical Notices of other Parts of the Interior of Africa.* London: James Murray, 1819.

Busia, Kofi Abrefa, *The Position of the Chief in the Modern Political System of Ashanti: A Study of the Influence of Contemporary Social Changes on Ashanti Political Institutions*, Oxford: Oxford University Press, 1968.

Christensen, James Boyd, *Double Descent among the Fante.* Ph.D. Dissertation: Northwestern University, 1952.

Clarke, Peter B., *West Africa and Islam.* London, UK: Edward Arnold, 1982.

Creswell, John W., *Research Design*, London: Sage Publications, 2009.

Crollius, Ary Roest, "Inculturation: Newness and Ongoing Process," in John Mary Walligo, Ary Roest Crollius, Theoneste Nkeramihigo and John Mutiso-Mbinda (eds.), Inculturation: *Its Meaning and Urgency*, Nairobi: St Paul Publications, 1986.

Dube, Leela, *Matriliny and Islam: Religion and Society in the Laccadives*, Delhi: India: National Publishing House, 1969.

Du Bois, W.E.B., *The Souls of Black Folk.* New York: USA: New American Library, 1969.

Edgerton, Robert B, *The Fall of the Asante Empire: The Hundred-Year War for Africa's Gold Coast*, New York: The Free Press, 1995.

Ghana statistical service, 2021 Population and Housing Census, 2021.

Hiskett, Mervyn, *The Development of Islam in West Africa*, London: UK: Longman Group, 1984.

Hagan, George P., An Analytical Study of Fante Kinship. *African Studies Research Review*, Vol 5. Accra: University of Ghana Press, 1967.

Kottakkunnummal, Manaf, "Indigenous Customs and Colonial Law: Contestations in Religion, Gender and Family among Matrilineal Mappila Muslims in Colonial Malabar, Kerala, c. 1910–1928," *Sage Open* 4, January-March, 2014.

Laponte, Eugene, *An Experience of Pastoral Theology in Southern Africa: Inculturated and Committed Christian Communities*, Rome: Urbaniana University Press, 1985.

Meyerowitz, Eva L.R., A Note on the Origins of Ghana. *African Affairs*, Vol 51; 205 (1952), 319–23

Osei-Boakye, Emmanuel, *Documentation and Dynamics of Oyoko Clan in Asante: Myth, Folklore and Meaning*, Masters Dissertation: University of Ghana, 2013.

Owoahene-Acheampong, Stephen, *Inculturation and African Religion: Indigenous and Western Approaches to Medical Practice*. New York: Peter Lang, 1998.

Owusu-Ansah, David, "The State and Islamisation in the 19th Century Africa: Buganda Absolutism versus Asante Constitutionalism," *Journal of Muslim Minority Affairs*, Vol 8:1 (1987), 132–43

Ragin, Charles C., and Howard S. Becker (eds.), *What Is a Case? Exploring the Foundations of Social Inquiry*, Cambridge: Cambridge University Press, 1992.

Ryan, Patrick J., "Islam and Matrilineality in West Africa," Conference of Islamic Identities in Africa, School of Oriental and African Studies, London, April, 1991.

Samwini, Nathan, The *Muslim Resurgence in Ghana since 1950: Its Effects upon Muslims and Muslim-Christian Relations*, Berlin: Lit Verlag

Sanneh, Lamin, West *African Islam*, Maryknoll, NY: Orbis Books, 1983.

Sanders, James, "The Expansion of the Fante and the Emergence of Asante in the Eighteenth Century," *Journal of African History*, 20:3 (1979), 349–64

Shumway, Rebecca, *The Fante and the Transatlantic Slave Trade*. New York: University of Rochester Press, 2011.

Silverman, David, *Doing Qualitative Research*, London: Sage Publications, 2013.

Sujimon, Mohamad Som, "Implications and Consequences of Illegitimate Child (walad al-zina) in Islamic Law: A Classical View," *Jurnal Syariah*, 7:1, 1999

Wilks, Ivor, *Asante in the Nineteenth Century: The Structure and Evolution of a Political Order*, Cambridge: Cambridge University Press, 1975.

Wilson, Alex J., A.J., *Mother's Wealth: Matrilineality and Inheritance among the Fantse of Ghana*, Ph.D. Dissertation: University of Ohio, 2011.

INTERVIEWS

Comfort Asante (Linguist), 20 October 2020.

Abdul-Razak Awal, 26 November 2020.

Gyan Baffour, Asante Christian, 10 July 2020.

Musah Ishaq, Asante Muslim, 6 July 2020.

Nuamah Ishaq, Wahhabi Cleric, 25 November 2020

Abbas Wilson, Deputy Ameer of the Ahmadiyya Mission in Ghana, 6 September 2020.

PART IV

Andalusia and Americas

The Tuareg, from Arabia to Americas

Samira Benturki Saïdi

INTRODUCTION: A WIDER VIEW OF ARAB CIVILISATION

In my book *The Arab and Muslim Identity of Native American Peoples and Tribes,* I followed the migrations of Arab and African navigators from the sub-Saharan region of the 'Old World' to what Europeans called the 'New World,' and argued that it is necessary to reject preconceived ideas about history.[1] There is now ample evidence to show that Arab and African ships reached the coast of the Americas long before Columbus, as I shall outline in this chapter, and that they brought with them their languages, traditions, and beliefs—including matrilineal social systems. Yet before any meaningful discussion of the historical narrative, it is important to reclaim some specific terminology: we must be clear that the terms 'Arab' and

[1] Samira Benturki Saïdi, *L'Identité Arabo-Islamique de Peuples et Tribus Indiennes d'Amérique,* London: The Fountain of e-Knowledge & e-Productions Ltd., 2017.

S. B. Saïdi (✉)
Paris, France

© The Author(s), under exclusive license to Springer Nature Switzerland AG 2024
A. Panakkal, N. M. Arif (eds.), *Matrilineal, Matriarchal, and Matrifocal Islam,* Palgrave Series in Islamic Theology, Law, and History, https://doi.org/10.1007/978-3-031-51749-5_9

247

'Arabian' are used when referring to the peoples of the ancient Near East and North Africa, rather than 'Semite' and 'Semetic.' This is, fortunately, becoming more widely accepted, and prominent academics are finally ridding history of the ideological dimensions that have stripped the Arab-Muslim civilisation of its rich, multi-millennial past. The implications are not merely historical or archaeological; they are also epistemological, since they have affected the knowledge that we have of Arab and Muslim civilisation and its global expansion, as well as its geographical extent.

Earlier understanding of history dated the beginning of Arab-Muslim civilisation to 622 C.E., the year of the *hijra*—the Prophet Muhammad's journey from Mecca to Medina. Yet this is to disregard many centuries of Arab history and culture. As Christian Robin noted: "This date of 622 is often given as the entry of the Arabs into history. It ignores the important role they played in the Near East during the millennium that preceded Islam, with brilliant states like Palmyra and the Nabateans of Petra and even a Roman emperor, Philip the Arab (244–249)."[2] These ancient Arab states provide examples of strong female leaders: the Assyrian queens, who led their armies into battle; the queen of Sheba, Bilqis, whose wisdom is mentioned in the Qur'ān and whose government is an illustration of early democracy; Zenobia, queen of Palmyra, whose courage, intelligence, and political judgement enabled her to out-manoeuvre Roman armies; and Queen Mawiya, who defied Rome and personally led her troops into battle. Such leaders demonstrate the profound effect of women in the development of Arab societies, and show that pre-Islamic Arab women—like later generations of Muslim women—were held in high esteem. As Jacques Hureiki observed in his discussion on the origin of the Tuaregs, "[T]here was a pre-Islamic Arab culture in which the status of the female ancestor could sometimes be more important than the status of the male ancestor."[3] He goes on to underline the matriarchal system evidenced among great Arab tribes:

> There were also several fractions of Arab Christian tribes of Kalb, Kinda, and others, who had female ancestor names. Even princes from these tribes, and especially from the Gasssane, had names that referred to their mothers and not to their fathers. Thus the matrilineal character of the Sinhaja (Sanhadja),

[2] Christian Robin, *Les Langues de la Péninsule Arabique*, in Christian Robin (ed.), *L'Arabie antique de Karib'îl à Mahomet. Nouvelles données sur l'histoire des Arabes grâce aux inscriptions* (Aix-en-Provence: Édisud, 1992), 89–111.

[3] Jacques Hureiki, *Essai sur les origines des Touaregs,* Paris: Éditions Karthala, 2003.

THE TUAREG, FROM ARABIA TO AMERICAS   249

who claim Yemeni origin, finds Arab origins and is even in favor of an Arab emigration to North Africa before the appearance of Islam.[4]

The Arab peoples were, by their nature, migratory, and there can be little doubt that pre-Islamic migrations brought entire social structures from Arabia to North Africa—along with cultures, languages, arts, and customs. Firas Alkhateeb states:

> Due to the desert's inability to support settled civilization, the Arabs were constantly on the move in search of fertile land for their flocks. One theory of the etymology of the label "Arab" even posits that the word itself comes from a Semitic root meaning "wandering" or "nomadic."[5]

To limit the Arab civilisation to a simple word or definition is as inadequate as to limit Arab geography to the Arabian Peninsula or to stereotype Arab women as passive. Nevertheless, migration was an essential aspect of Arab history and led to early expansions into North Africa. We shall now turn to their descendants there—the Tuareg peoples.

THE ORIGINS OF THE TUAREG

The widespread rejection of the Arab origins of the Tuareg peoples—also known as Berbers and Songhay—has led to serious distortions of history and fostered misapprehensions about the North African past as a whole. Eminent anthropologists such as André Bourgeot, Jaques Hureiki, and Muhammad Said al-Qashat have underlined the problem of linking the Tuareg to certain linguistic groups while knowingly ignoring their linguistic and cultural heritage that is shared with the Arab people.[6] But where did they come from? Who are the Tuareg? Henri Duveyrier, a nineteenth-century scholar, reports the answer that one Tuareg gave to these questions:

> If you ask us to better characterise the origins of each tribe and to distinguish the nobles from the serfs, we will tell you that our company is mixed

---

[4] Hureiki, *Essai sur les origines des Touaregs*, 667.

[5] Firas Alkhateeb, *Lost Islamic History* (London: Hurst & Company, 2014), 9.

[6] Al-Qashat lived for a long period among the Tuareg while studying their customs; the title of his book is particularly revealing. Muhammed Said al-Qashat, *The Tuareg: the Arabs of the Desert*, Cairo: Markaz Dirāsāt wa Abhāth, 2001.

and intertwined like the fabric of a tent in which the camel's hair joins the sheep's wool. It takes skill to distinguish between the hair and the wool. We know, however, that each of our many tribes came from a different country.[7]

Anthropologists agree that the Tuareg do not form a homogeneous ethnic group, although all seem to have their origins in Arabia or the Near East. The term 'Berber'—meaning in Arabic "to rattle, make noise, chatter, grumble, mumble, utter unintelligible cries"—refers to a number of etymological origins that gave birth to a people who emerged in North Africa long before the Muslim conquest. Yet the 'unintelligible' character of the language present in North Africa and spoken by a so-called Berber tribe has a twin sister in southern Arabia: that of the Himyar.[8] As-Saʿdi, a seventeenth-century chronicler from Timbuku, confirms this in his *Taʾrīkh al-Sūdān*: "The Tuareg are the Masufah who trace their genealogy to the Senhadja, who themselves trace their origin to Himyar."[9] According to as-Saʿdi's account, a powerful king of southern Arabia called Tobbaʾ heard a prophecy concerning the coming of the Prophet Muhammad and invited his people to embrace monotheism. After his death, the pagans regained the upper hand and drove the believers out of the region; these tribes then scattered, some of them crossing the Gulf of Aden to Africa—they then continued to move north and west, some settling in the region of the Sahara desert.

Given the linguistic and historical evidence supporting the case for the Tuareg's Arabian origins, it is surprising that this was so long neglected by scholars. In order to understand this aspect of North African history, it is important to put the work of these earlier scholars in context and understand the political objectives of their work. Historians, anthropologists, and those who have been dispatched by their governments to analyse the political and economic situation have often reported their own views rather than historical facts. They not only had a limited knowledge of Arab civilisation, but, preparing the ground for military invasions, disseminated all kinds of superficial or implausible data: working on the past to review the present and control the future. The exploration carried out by Henri Duveyrier, for example, author of *The Tuareg of the North*, was financed by

---

[7] Henri Duveyrier, *Les Touareg du Nord*, (Paris: Challamel Ainé, 1864), 319.

[8] Robin, *Les Langues de la Péninsule Arabique,* 108.

[9] As-Saʿdi, Abderrahman ben Abdallah ben Imran ben Amir, *Tarikh as-Sudan*, trans. Octave Victor Houdas (Paris: Ernest Leroux, 1900), 42–3.

the French government and obtained support from the Emperor Napoleon III.[10] Like numerous other orientalist or neo-orientalist historians, his descriptions of the Tuareg serve ideological purposes and political aspirations. Other groups of scholars are over-zealous in denying the Arab origins of the Tuareg, believing that it suggests a contempt for Black African traditions. Yet these beliefs, rooted in ideologies rather than historical research, merely distort the truth.

Recent linguistic analysis provides reliable data allowing us to trace the journeys of Arab and African peoples, and see the connections between the languages spoken from Arabia to the Western Sahara which were long ignored by historians. In the 1970s, for example, Professor Barry Fell was able to decrypt inscriptions on ancient Numidian stelae from North Africa with the help of Arabic specialists, proving that the Arabic language was present in Africa long before the Muslim conquest; it was found that royal scribes had used the language in official documents more than eight hundred years before the seventh century C.E.[11] The dialects spoken today in North Africa leave no doubt about their ancient Arabic origins:

The ancient Berber language is derived from the Phoenician language, the Tifinagh (التيفناغ) dialect itself is written with the Phoenician Arabic alphabet. The language of the Tuareg, which they call "Tamachaq" (تاماشاق) or "Tamachak" (تاماشاك) is in fact one of the ancient Arabic dialects that was annihilated by Islam when it unified the language of the Arabs by the language of the Qureïch, through which Allah revealed the Holy Quran.[12]

The Tifiniagh or Tafinagh dialect is still spoken nowadays in the Dhofar region of Oman as well as in Yemen, while Phoenician script was discovered on petroglyphs in these regions as well as in North Africa and America. Phoenician cities bearing the same names are found in Oman and Lebanon, illustrating that, contrary to preconceived ideas, ancient Phoenicia was not limited to the borders of modern-day Lebanon. Such evidence supports the traditional beliefs among the people of North Africa about their own origins, as related by the tenth-century geographer Ibn Hauqal:

Among the Berber tribes, one of the most famous was that of the Sanhadja. An ancient tradition preserved among them made them descend from the

---

[10] Duveyrier, *Les Touareg du Nord.*
[11] Barry Fell, *Saga America*, New York: Times Books, 1980.
[12] al-Qashat, *The Tuareg*, 30.

252   S. B. SAÏDI

Arabs of Yemen, and a prophecy that had been made to their forefather, starting in Arabia, assured his descendants of a powerful empire in a country of the West. It was in the person of Zirir that the prediction was fulfilled, and the tribe of Sanhadja was elevated to the status of a nation.[13]

The Tuareg have long been aware of their own origins; now that there is ample archaeological and linguistic evidence to prove their connection with the Arabian Peninsula, this should also be accepted more widely.

MATRILINEAL PRACTICES AMONG THE TUAREG AND IN THE ANCIENT NEAR EAST

This brings us to the question of the prevalence of matriarchal cultures among the Arabs in the ancient Near East, and among the Tuareg in North Africa. Matriarchy is an anthropological term describing a mother-centred society in which descent and lineage are traced through the mother rather than the father. It is around the woman that the members of the family rotate, and she is their gravitational force. Heidi Goettner-Abendroth, a German philosopher and researcher on matriarchal societies, pointed out that the Greek word *arche* has the double meaning of 'beginning' and 'domination,' concluding that one can translate matriarchy accurately as "mother from the beginning." Matriarchy is present in numerous regions of the globe and is not necessarily opposed to patriarchy; within the same society, the mother may assume partial authority while the father controls other spheres of life. As Mary Evans notes:

> [T]here were some societies (for example in regions of West Africa) where kinship was inherited through the mother. These societies, undeniably matriarchal in their patterns of inheritance, nevertheless invested other forms of social power in the mother's brother, ensuring that even in apparently matriarchal societies it would be wrong to conclude that social relations were represented and ordered as the reverse of patriarchy.[14]

Matriarchy therefore should not always be understood as female 'domination.' Some scholars argue that the patriarchal family, though

---

[13] Ibn Hauqal, *Description de l'Afrique*, ed. Baron de Slane (Paris: Journal Asiatique, Extrait n°5, 1842), 5.

[14] Mary Evans, "Patriarchy", in Bryan S. Turner (ed.) *The Cambridge Dictionary of Sociology* (Cambridge: Cambridge University Press, 2006), 433–4.

THE TUAREG, FROM ARABIA TO AMERICAS   253

representing the majority of human societies, was preceded by the matriarchal family, which caused certain anthropologists to affirm that descent
through the female line was a natural institution belonging to the very first
stages of societal development.

It is also important to understand matrilineal societies on their own
terms, rather than in the context of contemporary feminism. The Western
feminist approach is founded on the belief that men hold the power in
family structures and gender relations need to be changed in order to
improve the status of women in society.[15] This approach is clearly linked to
the fact that Western societies historically ill-treated women, whose position was not an enviable one compared to their sisters on other continents.
As Marsha Robinson points out: "Around 1900, there were still areas of
the world that had not been incorporated into the European gathering
systems as colonies. Some of these unincorporated nations gave women
more rights and higher status than European women had."[16] Many cultures in the Near East, Africa, and the Americas accorded women centre-
stage; for example, as we shall see later, the Cherokee wondered why
European women did not accompany men to political meetings as
Cherokee women did.

Though limited to a few regions of Arabia, the regime of maternal law
existed among the Arabs of the ancient Near East and spread with them to
North Africa. Certain matrilineal communities lived in the midst of predominantly patriarchal ones, including the ancestors of the Tuareg, whose
customs reflect this ancient system. One of the major branches of the
Qahtan tribe, for example, the Sanhān, was matrilineal, as well as the Tayy
and Djuf tribes. The fourteenth-century traveller Ibn Battuta indicated
that a matrilineal system existed in sub-Saharan Africa among the Masufah,
one of the descendants of the Sanhadja after their migration from the
Arabian Peninsula:

> Though Mohammedans, they had a law of succession resembling that of the
> pagans of Malabar. Their women, handsome and finely-formed, went
> unveiled, and conversed with the men on terms of freedom and equality.[17]

---

[15] Jennifer Ithany, *Milieu insulaire tropical: dynamiques de développement, société, patrimoine et culture dans l'espace Caraïbe Amérique,* Ph.D. thesis: Université des Antilles, 2017.

[16] Marsha R. Robinson, *Matriarchy, Patriarchy and Imperial Security in Africa,* Lanham,
MD: Lexington Books, 2012.

[17] Ibn Battuta, *The travels of Ibn Battuta in Asia and Africa,* Cambridge: Cambridge
University Press, 1962.

Since the tribes of the Tuareg are so numerous, their customs and practices have evolved differently. Some follow the order of maternal succession, known as Beni-Oumia, while others have adopted paternal succession, or Ebna-Sid. Henri Duveyrier collected detailed information on the matriarchal customs of the Azdjer and Ahaggar tribes in southern Algeria, noting that these two distinct systems were both in use. Among those who followed the matrilineal Beni-Oumia pattern, it was believed that this form of succession best ensures the transmission of the bloodline. Duveyrier added that there are particular restrictions placed around marriage in matrilineal tribes: marriage with strangers was prohibited, and permitted only when families were dying out. If the only family survivors were women, they could seek husbands from outside the family.[18] Status is passed down through the mother; regardless of the father's status, if the mother is not free her child is not considered a citizen. The Tuareg therefore value their mother's relatives highly and consider their maternal cousins as brothers and sisters.

Even tribes that are predominantly patrilineal, such as the Ouelleminden, involve women in decision-making; Kélétigui observes, for example, that "although the Ouelleminden are predominantly patrilineal, women are always consulted on all important issues."[19] Bourgeot has argued that there is a possible bilinear structure, or a system that retains matrilineal traits after adopting a largely patrilineal form.[20]

In most Tuareg clans, however, the family name continues to be passed down the female line, while the feminine names of some clans suggest a matriarchal heritage.[21] Tuareg women enjoy privileges that are not found in the majority of Muslim societies, nor among other tribes of West Africa, and a man is responsible for his sister's children rather than his own. According to Duveyrier, women "are in no way inferior to men in management and commerce. The elder sister's son inherits the rights of command over serfs and fees paid by travellers." Hubertine Auclert, writing in 1900, also noted that "it is not the chief's son who succeeds his father, but

---

[18] Duveyrier, *Les Touareg du Nord*.

[19] Kélétigui Abdourahmane Mariko, *Les Touareg Ouelleminden: les fils des grandes tentes* (Paris, Éditions Karthala, 1984), 45.

[20] André Bourgeot, "Contribution à l'étude de la parenté touarègue", *Revue des mondes musulmans et de la Méditerranée* 21 (1976), 9–31.

[21] Ahmeth Diouf, *La gens de droit maternel ou la famille matriarcale*, Dakar: L'Harmattan Sénégal, 2016; Philip K. Hitti, *History of the Arabs*, London: Macmillan Education, 1970.

his elder sister's son." She went on to detail matrilineal inheritance practices:

> At the death of the head of the family, his possessions are divided in two parts, the "possessions of justice" acquired by his labour and the "possessions of injustice" acquired with weapons; travellers report that the first are equally divided between all children without distinction of gender, and that all the "possessions of injustice" go to the elder sister's older son.[22]

Tuareg women's dress and ornaments reflect the Arabian origins of their culture; like Yemeni women, they wear necklaces of blue and red stones most likely believed to offer protection from the evil eye.[23] Even more striking is the sexual freedom enjoyed by women in the region, both recently and in antiquity. This freedom directly mirrors that of the Humūm tribal confederation in Yemen, where women were allowed to take a temporary husband if theirs was away, and men were not permitted to retaliate if their wives were unfaithful. There was no social stigma attached to bearing children out of wedlock. Indeed, illegitimate children were permitted to take the name of their mother or maternal uncle—even the tribal chief—and, if she chose, a pregnant woman was allowed to choose a husband who would act as a father to the child. This practice—still in existence, though disappearing—is known as *kasb* (gain) or *iktisāb* (benefit), and dates from pre-Islamic times.[24]

According to some scholars, Tuareg customs are a continuation of the regime of maternal law that originated in Arabia.[25] Jacques Hureiki—one of the few French-speaking academics to have observed the similarities between Tuareg culture and their Arab origins—suggests that some cultural features make this a strong possibility: "Isn't the specific status of the Tuareg women a survival, even a well-preserved copy of the status of Arab Christian women of the pre-Islamic period, and even of the first two centuries of the Hegira?"[26] There is increasing archaeological evidence that at least some societies in ancient Arabia were matrilineal. Inscriptions

---

[22] Hubertine Auclert, *Les Femmes Arabes en Algérie* (Paris: Société d'Éditions littéraires, 1900), 34.

[23] Hureiki, *Essai sur les origines des Touaregs,* 472.

[24] Joseph Chelhod, "Du Nouveau À Propos Du 'Matriarcat' Arabe," *Arabica,* 28:1 (1981), 76–106.

[25] Stéphane Gnessl, *Histoire ancienne de l'Afrique du Nord,* Paris: Librairie Hachette, 1920.

[26] Hureiki, *Essai sur les origines des Touaregs,* 31.

256   S. B. SAÏDI

discovered in the Sabaean capital, Ma'rib, led Korotayev to assert that we can "suppose, with a degree of confidence, that in the third century A.D. a few distinctly matrilineal descent groups existed in south Arabia."[27] Other pre-Islamic religions and societies were more patriarchal, and differed greatly in the rights accorded to women. According to the code of Hammurabi, for example, a widow could inherit from her husband provided the property was passed on to the couple's children, thus remaining in the male lineage:

> The wife shall receive her dowry and the gift which her husband gave and deeded to her on a tablet, and she may dwell in the house of her husband and enjoy (the property) as long as she lives. She cannot sell it, however, for after her (death) it belongs to her children.[28]

In Jewish tradition, the mother confers religious identity to her children, but as soon as a woman marries she becomes the property of her husband, and her assets become his.[29] Daughters could inherit, but only if there were no sons. Christian laws of succession also deprived women of any inheritance rights. In most Arab tribes in pre-Islamic Arabia, too, women were barred from inheriting, and younger children had no rights to claim their share.

Did Islam lead to a decline in status for Tuareg women and a partial shift from matrilineality to a more patriarchal culture? Unlike the Jewish and Christian traditions, Islamic law does not deprive women of their right to inherit and to own property; it affected traditional matrilineal patterns of inheritance among the Tuareg, however, and reinforced the role of the father to the detriment of uncles. While a man's property used to go to his nephews, according to the Islamic system it was divided between his children with sons receiving twice the amount of daughters. According to Erik Guignard, who studied the Udalen Tuareg of the Upper Volta, in contemporary Burkina Faso, this change in inheritance practice undermined traditional concepts of property, reinforcing "the economic flows that are linked to private property and direct inheritance at the expense of

---

[27] Andrey Korotayev, *Matrilineal lineages in the Arabian Peninsula* (Oxford: Archeopress 1994), 92.

[28] Robert Francis Harper (trans.), *The Code of Hammurabi*, London: The Lawbook Exchange, 2010.

[29] Louis M. Epstein, *The Jewish Marriage Contract: A Study in the Status of the Woman in Jewish Law*, Clark, NJ: The Lawbook Exchange, 2004.

collective property that is always transmitted collaterally."[30] Yet despite the changes that came with the new religion, Tuareg women retained their status and their societies remained predominantly matrilineal:

> Although the generally unveiled Tuareg women lost some of their power after their conversion to Islam in the eleventh century, they still retain more economic and social power than most of their present urban counterparts. They live in a completely matrilineal society. Tuareg women regard themselves as men's equals, marry at will, speak in council, and serve as heads of encampments. Wives go where they please, hold property, teach, and govern the home.[31]

This does not mean that Tuareg society is matriarchal, however. Tuareg women had never had direct access to power, unlike the women of ancient Arabia; they were never 'queens,' although they were generally consulted and wielded real influence in matters of politics. Instead, power was transferred from family to family, leading Andre Bourgeot to emphasise that traditional Tuareg society was matrilineal in succession alone; in other areas it was "strongly patrilineal," a situation that was "further consolidated by the intervention of Islam."[32] When it came to politics, the level of women's participation varied from tribe to tribe, but it was always men who took the leading role. Kélétigui Abdourahmane Mariko describes the negotiations between the French government and one Tuareg tribe:

> For three days, the delegates […] continued to arrive in Haria. There were only men, no women, although Tuareg society reserves for women a predominant place in the politics of the country. Women could trigger war or lead to peace. In relations with the (French) Administration, they were not consulted, but only informed of decisions taken.[33]

This blend of matrilineality and male authority, where women took part in tribal decision-making without being leaders, has parallels in a number of Native American cultures. We now turn to the connection between these two geographically distant but culturally similar peoples.

---

[30] Erik Guignard, *Faits et modèles de parenté chez les Touareg Udalen de Haute-Volta* (Paris: Éditions L'Harmattan, 2000), 14.

[31] Ogbonnaya Oko Elechi, *Doing Justice Without the State: The Afikpo (Ehugbo) Nigeria Model*, (New York: Routledge, 2006), 173.

[32] Bourgeot, *Contribution à l'étude de la parenté touarègue*, 9.

[33] Mariko, *Les Touareg Ouelleminden*, 19.

Arab and African Journeys to the Americas

The idea of Columbus 'discovering' the Americas in 1492 remains prevalent in popular understandings of history, despite the wealth of historical evidence that shows that Arab and African sailors had contact with the continent long before. Spanish conquistadores in the Coclé region of modern Panama, for example, met Black Africans there at the beginning of the sixteenth century. These Africans were present on the American continent long before the European slave trade. Their presence, and the influence of Arab and African cultures on those of the Americas, is clearly discernible if we can break out of our intellectual rigidity and acknowledge their heritage.

As Alice Beck Kehoe argues, "Postcolonial anthropology cannot accept either the myth of Columbus as the discoverer of a hidden new world, nor the myth of progress." This mythology was created for political and religious purposes, generated by European settlers to legitimise their taking possession of the Native American territories. In this context, unlike later colonial settlement, the self-proclaimed 'civilising mission' of the European colonists was understood as 'Manifest Destiny.' Kehoe continues to stress the impact this ideology has had on our understanding of earlier maritime history: "Denying non-Western societies' achievements in sea-faring to justify taking over their 'newly discovered' territories, like denying their achievements in 'civilization,' has been part of the ideology of Manifest Destiny."[34]

There is no doubt that crossings of the Atlantic were possible long before the voyage of Columbus. Indeed, it would have happened unintentionally; as nineteenth-century scholar Josiah Priest noted, "[I]f a vessel were lost, or if an eastern storm had driven it far into the ocean or South Atlantic, it would naturally arrive at last on the American coast."[35] In 1970, Norwegian ethnologist Thor Heyerdahl demonstrated that the crossing was feasible for mariners of the past, building a replica of an old reed ship and crossing the Atlantic Ocean from the coast of North Africa to the American continent. Following the winds and the currents, his journey from the famous Moroccan port of Safi to Barbados in the Caribbean took less than two months. We have ample evidence that

---

[34] Alice Beck Kehoe, *Traveling Prehistoric Seas: Critical Thinking on Ancient Transoceanic Voyages* (London: Routledge, 2016), 32.

[35] Josiah Priest, *American Antiquities and discoveries in the West* (Albany, NY: Hoffman and White, 1835), 117.

medieval sailors made the same journey: in approximately 1350 C.E., from the same port of Safi, a Franciscan monk journeyed across the Atlantic Ocean with Arab sailors and visited various Caribbean islands. Once back in Spain, at the monastery of La Rabida in Palos de la Frontera, he wrote a book titled *El Libro del Descubrimiento* ("The Book of Discovery") which became part of the monastery's library—where Christopher Columbus began working on his maritime project nearly a century and a half later. Other expeditions have followed Heyerdahl's; in February 2020 the replica of a Phoenician boat reached Florida after a five-month journey of over six thousand miles, from Carthage in Tunisia to Fort Lauderdale in Florida, via Cadiz, Essaouira, the Canary Islands, and the Dominican Republic. The expedition's aim was to show that long before Columbus, Phoenician navigators could have crossed the ocean and discovered the American continent.

Written sources from ancient history confirm this theory. In *De Mirabilis*, a work in classical Greek attributed to Aristotle, it was documented that the Carthaginians had discovered a new 'island'—a word that was also used to refer to a continent.

> In the sea outside the Pillars of Hercules they say that an island was discovered by the Carthaginians, desolate, having wood of every kind, and navigable rivers, and admirable for its fruits besides, but distant several days' voyage from them. But, when the Carthaginians often came to this island because of its fertility, and some even dwelt there, the magistrates of the Carthaginians gave notice that they would punish with death those who should sail to it, and destroyed all the inhabitants, lest they should spread a report about it, or a large number might gather together to the island in their time, get possession of the authority, and destroy the prosperity of the Carthaginians.[36]

Later historical sources from as far as China also provide clear evidence of a knowledge of the Americas. In 1178 and 1225 C.E., geographers of the Sung Dynasty documented the voyages of Arab sailors from the shores of Morocco to unknown lands in the west, deriving their information from Arab merchants who visited the ports of China. The description they

---

[36] Aristotle, *De Mirabilus*, (Oxford: Clarendon Press, 1953), paragraph 84.

give of the continent, including its flora and fauna, could only refer to America.[37]

Arab geographers, too, confirm that Arab and African sailors had set out for the Americas—in particular the fleet of Abu Bakr, Emperor of Mali. Ibn Fadl Allāh al-ʿUmari recounted that Abu Bakr sent two hundred ships across the Atlantic, of which one returned; the others, according to the captain's account, had vanished after meeting "in the open sea, a river with a violent current"—what we now know to be the Gulf Stream. The emperor did not give up, however: "He ordered two thousand boats to be equipped for him and for his men, one thousand more for water and provisions." Abu Bakr set off and was never seen again, leaving the empire of Mali in the hands of his successor, Mansu Musa.[38] European historians considered Arabs and Africans to be freshwater sailors afraid to stray too far from the coast, who reached other territories only by accident, and concluded that this fleet had sunk to the depths of the Atlantic. Yet this is a conclusion based on prejudice, and there is considerable likelihood that at least some ships in the Malian reached the further shore. Evidence of the presence of Black Africans on the South American continent—particularly traces of Mandingo language and culture in Brazil—supports this theory.[39] Similarly, an ancient Black African tribe named Saramaka lives on in contemporary French Guyana.

With continuing migrations from the East, it is unsurprising that pressure grew to explore the West. It would thus be extraordinary if the peoples of the Western coast of Africa had made no attempt to cross the ocean. As Leo Frobenius wrote, "[C]ivilization was compelled to put to sea. [...] A littoral civilization simultaneously effective in Gaul, in Spain, and in Libya, will always be forced to aim at the dominion of naval power in the West and to bring home the riches gathered out yonder from the other littoral regions of the Atlantic Ocean."[40] If this is little discussed in academia, it is only because historians refuse to see and acknowledge that America has been a destination for Arab and African ships for millennia.

---

[37] Hui-Lin Li, "Mu-Lan-P'i: a Case for Pre-Columbian Transatlantic Travel by Arab Ships", *Harvard Journal of Asiatic Studies* 23 (1960), 114–26.

[38] Ibn Faḍl Allah Al-ʿUmarī, *Masàlik el Absar fi Mamālik el Amsār,* French trans. Maurice Gaudefroy-Demombynes (Paris: P. Geuthner, 1927), 74.

[39] Leo Wiener, *Africa and the Discovery of America*, Philadelphia: Innes and Sons, 1922.

[40] Leo Frobenius, *The Voice of Africa, vol. 1,* (London, Hutchinson & Co., 1913), 344.

Evidence of Arab and African Heritage on the American Continent

Evidence for these voyages can also be found in North and South America, in the fields of linguistics, archaeology, and anthropology. One clear example is the etymological evidence from Colombia. According to Charles Hippolyte de Paravey, writing in the nineteenth century, the peoples of Bogota, particularly the Muyscas—sometimes known as the Chibchas—could be traced back to the Sabaeans and Phoenicians. The area contains linguistic fragments resembling their place of origin: Saba, the ancient kingdom of Sheba in southern Arabia. "Seba or Chiba is also found in the name of the language spoken by the Muyscas ... and it is also found in the place names of Suba and Zipaquire."[41] Their market was known as Tur-Meque, which de Paravey associates with Mecca—already a sacred place in Arabia before the advent of Islam. The famous German explorer Humboldt also described the traditions of the Muyscas, whose legends tell of an old man named Bochica who introduced them to the cult of the sun and taught them to build cities. The name 'Bochica' may be a corruption of the Arabic *shaykh*. The legend continues that Bochica retired to the sacred valley of 'Iraca'—an obvious reference to the historical region of Iraq in ancient Mesopotamia. The Muyscas, it appears, also practised matrilineal descent:

> As was the rule with the Aztecs the eldest brother of the regent, or if there was no brother the eldest nephew succeeded to the throne, instead of the son of the ruler himself. This rule would indicate that the descent was by the matrilineal line, as is the case with many American Indian tribes of the past and present.[42]

A few decades later, in the early twentieth century, the French researcher and officer Commandant Cauvet wrote a remarkable book titled *The Berbers in America*, in which he analysed a vast number of names from America and Africa to highlight their similarities. While some of his arguments are unconvincing, there are others that deserve serious consideration. He points out, for example, that the word 'Almamy'—used in some

---

[41] Charles Hippolyte de Paravey, *Mémoire sur l'origine japonaise, arabe et basque de la civilisation des Peuples de Bogota* (Paris: Dondey-Dupré, 1835), 8–9.

[42] Hyatt and Ruth Verrill, *America's Ancient Civilizations* (New York: G. P. Putman's Sons, 1953), 144.

areas of West Africa to designate a ruler—is likely to be a corruption of the Arabic *al-imām*, resulting from Arab migrations to the west. Furthermore, the same word is found across the Atlantic, alongside examples of a derivation of *al-Murābiṭūn*—the Tuareg or Almoravids:

> I find, in fact, in the American nomenclature a tribe of Alamamys, living in Honduras, that is to say the middle of the Central American isthmus, and the Morabitanas or Marivittinas of Portuguese Guyana. This second name is still used by a whole series of tribes in the same region, Maribios and Maribichicoas from Nicaragua, Marivigena and Marivisana from Venezuela, etc. If I am not mistaken, these names are not ancient ethnicities and reveal the arrival of Muslim Negroes.[43]

Another linguistic link between the Tuareg and the Americas is the connection between the Huari tribe of Peru and the Aït Uari or Huari, an important Tuareg clan found in Niger and Algeria. Muhammed al-Qashat, in his study of the Tuareg, lists the occurrence of similar words in the region:

> Among the Tuareg the proper name Aouari is used and in Algeria we find that of Haouari (Haouaria in the feminine). Finally in Morocco there are Haouara in Guercif, Agadir, and Taroudant, which are the link with the Bene Hoare of the Canary Islands.[44]

He then goes on to stress the similarity between these African tribal names and those of the Huares tribe in Mexico, the Huayairas of the Ghaco of Argentina, and the Huetares of Nicaragua, and concludes: "It does not seem to me possible to give another origin to the American Huares." Further etymological evidence suggests that the very word 'Brazil' may derive from the other side of the Atlantic, referring to the Birzālah tribe, or Banu Birzāl, found in Muslim Spain and Syria as well as North Africa.[45]

More similarities are found further north: Barry Fell notes the likeness between a Hohokam couple from the Mimbres Valley in New Mexico, depicted on a bowl painting dating between the late tenth and early twelfth

---

[43] Commandant Gaston Cauvet, *Les Berbères en Amérique* (Algiers: J. Bringau, 1930), 98.
[44] al-Qashat, *The Tuareg*, 19.
[45] Mohammed Hamidullah.

century C.E., and a North African couple from the Atlas Mountains.[46] In both cases the women have their faces unveiled and their chins tattooed, while the men are veiled and without visible tattoos. This style of tattoo is not limited to North Africa; it is also found in many tribes in the Arabian Peninsula, for example among the women of the nomadic al-Murrah, whose facial tattoos resemble zips.[47] Commandant Cauvet noted other aesthetic elements that suggest connections between the Sioux tribes of North America and the Tuareg: "The Osages (Sioux) had a shaved head with a crest of hair identical to that which Herodotus reported among the Maces and which is still worn by the Tuareg."[48]

MATRILINEAL PRACTICES AMONG NATIVE AMERICAN SOCIETIES

The peoples of the Americas are extraordinarily diverse in their cultural practices; for the purposes of this study we shall focus on some of those that have matrilineal customs. Contrary to many preconceived ideas, women played a powerful political role in Native American societies. Within the Iroquois confederacy, for example, it was women who selected the tribe's representatives at their main council:

> They chose the delegates to the central council from the 49 lineages of the five nations, a lineage which was hereditary through the mother's line. Women held their own councils and advised the central council. They had the power to veto war or to modify decisions about relations with other nations.[49]

Unsurprisingly, the way the European colonists relegated women to the domestic sphere was puzzling to them. Carolyn Ross Johnston relates that the Cherokee leader Attakullakulla arrived in South Carolina to negotiate trade agreements in 1757 and was shocked that there were no women present at the discussions. "Since the white man as well as the red was born of women, did not the white man admit women to their councils?"

---

[46] Fell, Saga America, 249.
[47] Thierry Mauger, *Hereux Bédouins d'Arabie*, Paris: Souffles, 1987.
[48] Cauvet, *Les Berbères en Amérique*, 104.
[49] Judith Nies, *Native American History* (London: Penguin Random House, 1996), 54.

he asked. In Cherokee society, women contributed their advice to the council.[50]

The Cherokee were traditionally matrilineal, even in cases when a Cherokee woman married a white man. While the woman and the couple's children would take the man's surname, according to the patrilineal European custom, the children were still considered to belong to the clan of the mother. Thus "the father's surname and possessions descended patrilineally while clan affiliation and property belonging to lineages continued to descend matrilineally."[51] This difference in the status of women would have been clear to those of both cultures. As Marsha M. Robinson points out:

> This relative imbalance of power between white women and some women of color was a source of embarrassment for many European women and a threat to European patriarchy. In other words, European patriarchy was neither universal nor absolute and it was vulnerable.[52]

It seems likely that more matrilineal kinship systems existed among certain tribes, such as the Choctaw, Cherokee, and Creek, but became weaker after the spread of European influence.[53] In other cases, matrilineal inheritance traditions persisted; Matilda Stevenson praised the humanity displayed by the Zuni people, for example:

> Much generosity is exhibited by these people regarding property left to them. According to the law the landed property of a married man or woman goes after death to the daughters. The sons are supposed to be able to acquire their own fields, but if there are no girls the sons are the next heirs. In case a man has sisters or brothers, especially sisters who are poor, his children are apt to give them part of their property or permit them to enjoy some of the benefits received therefrom. ... The child is always referred to as belonging to the mother's clan and as being the "child" of the father's clan.[54]

---

[50] Carolyn Ross Johnston, *Cherokee Women in Crisis,* Tuscaloosa, AL: University of Alabama Press, 2003.

[51] Theda Perdue, *Slavery and the evolution of Cherokee Society* (Knoxville, TN: The University of Tennessee Press, 1979), 50–51.

[52] Robinson, *Matriarchy, Patriarchy and Imperial Security in Africa*, 26.

[53] David. F. Eggan Hicks, *The American Indian. Perspectives for the Study of Social Change* (Cambridge: Cambridge University Press, 1980), 162.

[54] Matilda Coxe Stevenson, *The Zuni Indians,* Bureau of American Ethnology Report (Washington: Government Printing Office, 1905), 291.

She continued that, among the Zuni, the house and property all belonged to the woman, and was passed down the female line. The husband, therefore, was simply a 'permanent guest' of his wife, although couples were very close—both to each other and to their children. Stevenson concluded, "Their domestic life might well serve as an example for the civilised world."[55]

Could the Cherokee Indians Have a Muslim Heritage?

While the origins of Native American peoples have been lost to history, their traditions give some clue to their trail: "Long ago the Indians travelled a great distance and came to a great water. On arriving at this water, or after crossing [...] they divided; a part went to the North, a part went to the South."[56] It is well within the bounds of possibility that these 'Indians' were, in fact, migrants from the Near East and North Africa. There is certainly linguistic evidence to support this theory: the Arabic word *sharqī*, meaning 'eastern,' may be the origin of the word Cherokee. Commandant Cauvet observed that a similar word was found in tribal names elsewhere on the continent: "Chiri: Chiriguanos or Chihuanas (or Guarayos) of South America, Chiriquis of Panama, Cheroques or Cherokies of the United States, etc."[57]

What do Native Americans today believe regarding their own identities? One key thinker in this field is Professor Robert D. Crane, a member of the Ani Waya (Wolf) clan of the Cherokee Nation, raised in part by his great-grandmother who spoke Cherokee as her native language. Dr. Crane served as the first ombudsman in the Bureau of Indian Affairs, charged with complex problem resolution, and from 1963 to 1968 acted as President Nixon's principal advisor on foreign policy and the role of religion in countering totalitarianism. In a 2004 article, Crane emphasises the links between the Cherokee Nation and the Tuareg, citing the traditional belief that "the Cherokee religion came from a great fleet of ships that

---

[55] Stevenson, *The Zuni Indians*, 291.

[56] Payne, John Howard, *Indian Antiquities* (John Howard Payne Papers, vol. 3, 1814–1841), 10.

[57] Cauvet, *Les Berbères en Amérique*, 76.

brought 'The Book' out of 'The East.'"[58] He goes on to suggest that this could refer to the fleet of the Emperor of Mali, Abu Bakr, sent across the Atlantic in 1310 C.E., or one of the two earlier confirmed Muslim expeditions to America—the first from Africa in 1100 C.E. and the second from China in 1178 C.E. Yet whatever their exact origins, he believes the Cherokee have an Islamic heritage.

During the 1830s, tens of thousands of Native Americans were forced to leave their homelands and walk thousands of miles to the territories the US government had decreed as their new home, leaving their ancient lands for white settlers. During the Cherokees' deadly forced march in the winter of 1839, known as the Trail of Tears, official accounts state one-third of the Cherokees died. Crane takes issue with this official history, however, and states that three groups broke away from the march, going to Ohio and Indiana following the path of the underground railway used by people who had been enslaved to escape to Canada. His own ancestors were part of the group that settled in Hillsboro, Indiana.

Crane asserts that earlier written traditions of the Cherokee were lost, but oral history continued to be passed down the tribe to his own great-uncle, Joseph Franklin Bever.

> He was one of the last formally trained Cherokee imams. He called the *athan* every morning, but when challenged he replied simply that he was calling the hogs. Like all Cherokees, he started every prayer with "Ya Allah." All the prophets, starting with Abraham, are honored in the tradition. Until 1895, the Cherokees held the *hajj*, with *tawaf*, on the land of Uncle Henry Bever (spelled Beaver among the Oklahoma Ani Waya) three miles southwest of Hillsboro, Indiana, on the border with Veedersberg to the west where the other group from the Trail of Tears settled.[59]

Further linguistic evidence supports Crane's belief in the Islamic origins of the Cherokee. In addition to the annual *hajj*, and beginning prayers with "Ya Allah," some Cherokee names show clear Arab-Muslim origins. It seems astonishing that the name of the eighteenth-century Cherokee leader Attakullakulla, for example, did not trigger earlier investigation on the subject. My own study of Muslim names among communities across the world gave rise to a dictionary of 10,000 first names, and was followed

---

[58] Robert Dickson Crane, "Reviving the Classical Wisdom of Islam in the Cherokee Tradition," *The American Muslim* (online), 2004.

[59] Crane, *Reviving the Classical Wisdom of Islam in the Cherokee Tradition*.

by an analysis of American names with probable Arabic and Muslim origins.[60] These years of research have left me with an eye accustomed to the etymological examination of words that are unmistakably Arab-Muslim, wherever they may be, making the similarity of 'Attakullakulla' with the Muslim name 'Attā'ullāh'—meaning 'the gift of God'—strikingly obvious. There are further examples of Muslim names among the Cherokee: according to one source, the last Cherokee chief to surrender to Abraham Lincoln after supporting the South in America's civil war was named Ramadan ibn Wati.[61]

The inheritance system in Cherokee culture also has similarities to Islamic inheritance. As previously mentioned, according to the matrilineal system property would be passed on through the female line in Cherokee society, and a woman had the right to own property—a clear contrast to European traditions, in which a woman's property transferred to her husband upon marriage, or the Jewish tradition in which the woman herself became her husband's property. A number of books have been written on the possible link between the Cherokees and Judaism, based on accounts by men such as James Adair and John Howard Payne, both of whom lived for many years among the Cherokee, yet the difference in the inheritance system is just one of numerous inconsistencies that leave the reader doubtful. It is unsurprising that Adair and Payne were unable to reach any real understanding of these matters, since it was very difficult for any white Americans to learn much about the religious traditions of Native people, who believed that such knowledge was sacred and should be revealed only to the chosen members of the tribe.[62] The aspects of Cherokee culture that were thought to link them to Judaism, however, could equally be a sign of Islamic heritage, while in some areas—such as the inheritance system—there is a much clearer connection. For the Cherokee, the property of husband and wife remains separate; a woman retains control of her own land and possessions after marriage. Likewise, while many Muslim

---

[60] Samira Benturki Saïdi, *Dictionnaire des prénoms musulmans*, Paris: Éditions Universel, 2015.

[61] Letter from Mahir Abdur-Razzaaq to "The Message", first published July 1996. Available online: https://www.islamweb.net/prophet/index.php?page=showarticle&id=16090, The Prophet, accessed 12 January 2022.

[62] John Howard Payne, *Letters to John Howard Payne: Cherokee ethnology, missions and government relations*, letter written by D. S. Batruck, Dec. 291,840 (John Howard Payne Papers, 1814–1841), 99.

societies are patriarchal, the *sharīʿa* gives women the right to freely dispose of their wealth and land, and their husbands have no right to it.

As Crane argues, "Some Western anthropologists have speculated that the Cherokee religion with its emphasis on a sophisticated divine law and system of government may derive from a lost Jewish tribe, but this may be merely an attempt by Christian missionaries to hide the Cherokees' true Islamic identity."

CONCLUSION

When Muslims expanded into North Africa in the early decades after the advent of Islam, they encountered populations whose beliefs were off-shoots of Christianity and were persecuted by the Byzantine Empire. These populations frequently had different names, depending on political events, specific ancestors, and the period of migration. If the term 'Arab' seems at first glance to have appeared relatively recently, it is not because they were absent from the ancient historical landscape, but because, as linguist and archaeologist Christian Robin observes, because they were generally called by names specific to a particular tribe.[63] Yet they shared an ethnic background and spoke dialects of Arabic that were found in both the Middle East and North Africa.

It should now be clear that maritime caravans played a significant part in Arab history, just as the caravans crossing the desert did, and maritime history highlights the exchanges that took place between nations whenever people travelled and learned from each other. These exchanges took the form of knowledge, including knowledge of the sea and navigation; ancient sea charts are evidence that information was accurately passed from people to people, as Hapgood notes: "It appears that the charts must have originated with a people unknown, and they were passed on, perhaps by the Minoans and the Phoenicians, who were for a thousand years and more the greatest sailors of the ancient world."[64] It is therefore through the study of the history of navigation that we can learn much about the common past of humanity. "The sea forms the great highway of the world," wrote anthropologist Cyril Daryll Forde, who continued:

---

[63] Robin, *Nouvelles données sur l'histoire des Arabes grâce aux inscriptions.*

[64] Charles Hapgood, *Maps of the Ancient Sea Kings* (Kempton, IL: Adventures Unlimited Press, 1996), preface.

THE TUAREG, FROM ARABIA TO AMERICAS   269

A far more potent influence has been exerted by seamen than merely transferring people from one country to another. They have carried the gems of civilization and planted them on hitherto uncultivated coastlines, and they have brought to the centers of progress new materials and new ideas for the further development of arts and crafts and of customs and beliefs.[65]

We should not be surprised, therefore, to find so much evidence of Arab culture in the Americas; the transmission of the Arab and Muslim legacy to mankind did not stop on the shores of Africa, or the Iberian Peninsula. As Lin points out, during the eleventh, twelfth, and thirteenth centuries Arab expansion was at its peak, and the Arabs were the leading seafarers of their age with ships more than ten times larger than those of Columbus on his voyage to America two centuries later. He concludes: "That such ships could cross the Atlantic to the Americas seems well within reason."[66]

Arab matrilineal customs were part of the baggage brought by travellers who journeyed from Arabia to Africa—and then to the Americas. It is clear that numerous societies throughout history have had matrilineal or matriarchal social structures, among them the civilisations of the ancient Near East, the Tuareg, and many Native American tribes. This chapter has attempted, in a scientific spirit, to take up the history of these peoples without the burden of preconceived ideas, committed to the pursuit of truth and open to the possibilities of connections between peoples who appear so geographically distant. This, in itself, is a way of recognising the Qur'ānic verse: "O mankind! We have created you from a male and a female, and made you into nations and tribes, that you may know one another."[67]

BIBLIOGRAPHY

Alkhateeb, Firas, *Lost Islamic History,* London: Hurst & Company, 2014.
Aristotle, *De Mirabilus,* Oxford: Clarendon Press, 1953.
Auclert, Hubertine, *Les Femmes Arabes en Algérie,* Paris: Société d'Éditions littéraires, 1900.

[65] C. Daryll Forde, *Ancient Mariners* (New York: William Morrow & Company, 1928), 1–2.
[66] Lin, *Mu-Lan-P'i: a Case for Pre-Columbian Transatlantic Travel by Arab Ships,* 125.
[67] Qur'ān 49:13

Bourgeot, André, "Contribution à l'étude de la parenté touarègue", *Revue des mondes musulmans et de la Méditerranée* 21 (1976), 9-31.

Cauvet, Commandant Gaston, *Les Berbères en Amérique,* Algiers: J. Bringau, 1930.

Chelhod, Joseph, "Du Nouveau À Propos Du 'Matriarcat' Arabe," *Arabica*, 28:1 (1981), 76–106.

Crane, Robert Dickson, "Reviving the Classical Wisdom of Islam in the Cherokee Tradition," *The American Muslim* (online), 2004.

Diouf, Ahmeth, *La gens de droit maternel ou la famille matriarcale*, Dakar: L'Harmattan Sénégal, 2016.

Duveyrier, Henri, *Les Touareg du Nord*, Paris: Challamel Ainé, 1864.

Epstein, Louis M., *The Jewish Marriage Contract: A Study in the Status of the Woman in Jewish Law*, Clark, NJ: The Lawbook Exchange, 2004.

Evans, Mary, "Patriarchy", in Bryan S. Turner (ed.) *The Cambridge Dictionary of Sociology* (Cambridge: Cambridge University Press, 2006), 433-4.

Fell, Barry, *Saga America*, New York: Times Books, 1980.

Forde, C. Daryll, *Ancient Mariners*, New York: William Morrow & Company, 1928

Frobenius, Leo, *The Voice of Africa, vol. 1*, London, Hutchinson & Co., 1913.

Gnessl, Stéphane, *Histoire ancienne de l'Afrique du Nord*, Paris: Librairie Hachette, 1920.

Guignard, Erik, *Faits et modèles de parenté chez les Touareg Udalen de Haute-Volta*, Paris: Éditions L'Harmattan, 2000.

Hapgood, Charles, *Maps of the Ancient Sea Kings*, Kempton, IL: Adventures Unlimited Press, 1996.

Harper, Robert Francis (trans.), *The Code of Hammurabi*, London: The Lawbook Exchange, 2010.

Hicks, David. F. Eggan, *The American Indian. Perspectives for the Study of Social Change* (Cambridge: Cambridge University Press, 1980), 162.

Hitti, Philip K., *History of the Arabs*, London: Macmillan Education, 1970.

Hureiki, Jacques, *Essai sur les origines des Touaregs*, Paris: Éditions Karthala, 2003

Ibn Battuta, *The travels of Ibn Battuta in Asia and Africa*, Cambridge: Cambridge University Press, 1962.

Ibn Faḍl Allah Al-ʿUmarī, *Masàlik el Absar fi Mamālik el Amsār,* French trans. Maurice Gaudefroy-Demombynes, Paris: P. Geuthner, 1927.

Ibn Hauqal, *Description de l'Afrique*, ed. Baron de Slane, Paris: Journal Asiatique, Extrait n°5, 1842.

Ithany, Jennifer, *Milieu insulaire tropical: dynamiques de développement, société, patrimoine et culture dans l'espace Caraïbe Amérique*, Ph.D. thesis: Université des Antilles, 2017.

Johnston, Carolyn Ross, *Cherokee Women in Crisis*, Tuscaloosa, AL: University of Alabama Press, 2003.

Kehoe, Alice Beck, *Traveling Prehistoric Seas: Critical Thinking on Ancient Transoceanic Voyages*, London: Routledge, 2016.

Korotayev, Andrey, *Matrilineal lineages in the Arabian Peninsula*, Oxford: Archeopress 1994.

Li, Hui-Lin, "Mu-Lan-P'i: a Case for Pre-Columbian Transatlantic Travel by Arab Ships", *Harvard Journal of Asiatic Studies* 23 (1960), 114–26.

Mariko, Kélétigui Abdourahmane, *Les Touareg Ouelleminden: les fils des grandes tentes*, Paris, Éditions Karthala, 1984.

Mauger, Thierry, *Hereux Bédouins d'Arabie*, Paris: Souffles, 1987.

Nies, Judith, *Native American History*, London: Penguin Random House, 1996.

Oko Elechi, Ogbonnaya, *Doing Justice Without the State: The Afikpo (Ehugbo) Nigeria Model*, New York: Routledge, 2006.

de Paravey, Charles Hippolyte, *Mémoire sur l'origine japonaise, arabe et basque de la civilisation des Peuples de Bogota*, Paris: Dondey-Dupré, 1835.

Payne, John Howard, *Indian Antiquities*, John Howard Payne Papers, vol. 3, 1814a–1841.

Payne, John Howard, *Letters to John Howard Payne: Cherokee ethnology, missions and government relations*, John Howard Payne Papers, 1814b–1841.

Perdue, Theda, *Slavery and the evolution of Cherokee Society*, Knoxville, TN: The University of Tennessee Press, 1979.

Priest, Josiah, *American Antiquities and discoveries in the West*, Albany, NY: Hoffman and White, 1835.

al-Qashat, Muhammed Said, *The Tuareg: the Arabs of the Desert*, Cairo: Markaz Dirāsāt wa Abhāth, 2001.

Robin, Christian, *Les Langues de la Péninsule Arabique*, in Christian Robin (ed.), *L'Arabie antique de Karib'il à Mahomet. Nouvelles données sur l'histoire des Arabes grâce aux inscriptions* (Aix-en-Provence: Édisud, 1992), 89-111

Robinson, Marsha R., *Matriarchy, Patriarchy and Imperial Security in Africa*, Lanham, MD: Lexington Books, 2012.

As-Sa'di, Abderrahman ben Abdallah ben Imran ben Amir, *Tarikh as-Sudan*, trans. Octave Victor Houdas, Paris: Ernest Leroux, 1900.

Saïdi, Samira Benturki, *Dictionnaire des prénoms musulmans*, Paris: Éditions Universel, 2015.

Saïdi, Samira Benturki, *L'Identité Arabo-Islamique de Peuples et Tribus Indiennes d'Amérique*, London: The Fountain of e-Knowledge & e-Productions Ltd., 2017.

Stevenson, Matilda Coxe, *The Zuni Indians*, Bureau of American Ethnology Report, Washington: Government Printing Office, 1905.

Verrill, Hyatt and Ruth, *America's Ancient Civilizations*, New York: G. P. Putman's Sons, 1953.

Wiener, Leo, *Africa and the Discovery of America*, Philadelphia: Innes and Sons, 1922.

The Origins of Andalusian Muslim Matrilineal Systems

Alfred G. Kavanagh

MATRILINEARITY AND MATRIFOCALITY IN SPAIN

Historically, matrilineal kinship systems are correlated with other cultural traits, including not only economic cooperation but also bride price, residence after marriage, jurisdictional hierarchy, plough use, and presence of animal husbandry. Most anthropologists define matrilinearity as existing when kinship systems of lineage and inheritance are traced through women. However, as noted by Sarah Lowes, matrilineal systems are not symmetrical with patrilineal systems.[1] In order to discuss matrilinearity in Spain, it is important to take into account the country's unique position as

[1] Sarah Lowes, Sarah, "Matrilineal Kinship and Spousal Cooperation: Evidence from the Matrilineal Belt", Stanford University, King Center on Global Development and CIFAR, 2020. Working paper available at: https://cega.berkeley.edu/wp-content/uploads/2020/03/Lowes_PacDev2020.pdf.

A. G. Kavanagh (✉)
Universidad Pontificia de Comillas, Madrid, Spain
e-mail: alfredkavanagh@akkam-es.com

© The Author(s), under exclusive license to Springer Nature Switzerland AG 2024
A. Panakkal, N. M. Arif (eds.), *Matrilineal, Matriarchal, and Matrifocal Islam*, Palgrave Series in Islamic Theology, Law, and History, https://doi.org/10.1007/978-3-031-51749-5_10

a bridge between Europe and Africa, separated by the Strait of Gibraltar—only fourteen kilometres away from Morocco, at its narrowest point off the Spanish city of Tarifa. As the only natural link between the Atlantic Ocean and the Mediterranean Sea, it may be described as the meeting point of different cultures, civilisations, and linguistic families.

Professors Candela L. Hernandez and Rosario Calderón have established that high levels of genetic diversity have been systematically associated with the Andalusian maternal heritage. Andalusia, or al-Andalus, which accounts for about 20% of Spanish territory, has been in continuous interaction with other cultures throughout its history and is also the sole region with a coastline on two seas: the Mediterranean and the Atlantic. For their study, Hernandez and Calderón resorted to the analysis of mitochondrial DNA (mtDNA) and the non-recombining region of the Y chromosome (NRY), a technique used since the 1980s and a useful tool for reconstructing phylogenetic relations between different mitochondrial lineages.[2] According to their study, "[M]atrilineal legacy in the western extremes of the Mediterranean has shown that Iberia should not be only considered as a sink but also as a source population".[3]

The province of Cadiz, located at the tip of Spain, was once the ancient colony of Gadir, established by the Phoenicians of Tyre around 900 B.C.E. According to ancient historians, the columns of Hercules were located in the Straits of Gibraltar, which were sometimes also referred to as the Tartessian or Gadirian straits during the Hellenistic period—probably due to confusion among late Roman historians who equated the toponyms of Gadir and Tartessos, although historians such as Strabo or Scymnus of Chios differentiated between the two, describing Tartessos as an illustrious city where there was gold and copper in abundance.

In his compelling work *Prisoners of Geography*, Tim Marshall notes that "[t]raders from the Middle East and the Mediterranean had been doing business in the Sahara after the introduction of camels, from about 2,000 years ago, and notably trading the vast resources of salt there".[4] Yet it was not until the Arab conquest of the seventh century that the scene was set for a push southward. Contact between the Iberian Peninsula and Africa

---

[2] Candela L. Hernández et al., "Human maternal heritage in Andalusia (Spain): its composition reveals high internal complexity and distinctive influences of mtDNA haplogroups U6 and L in the western and eastern side of region," *BMC Genetics* 15:11 (2014).

[3] Hernández et al., "Human maternal heritage in Andalusia," 4.

[4] Tim Marshall, *Prisoners of Geography, Ten Maps that tell you everything you need to know about global politics,* (London: Elliot & Thompson Limited, 2015), 124.

THE ORIGINS OF ANDALUSIAN MUSLIM MATRILINEAL SYSTEMS   275

can be traced almost one thousand years back, however, and not only referred to trade but also to customs and ways of life that were brought from Saharan and sub-Saharan Africa. If we examine the Ethnographic Atlas,[5] we may observe that 15% of the 527 societies considered in sub-Saharan Africa are matrilineal.

Berber cultures, as modern research has pointed out, display a wide range of institutions which relate to matriarchal social structures and matrilineal descent. The Berbers played an important part in the Muslim conquest of the Iberian Peninsula; a large part of the troops that participated in the military campaigns of 711–50 were recruited from Berber tribes of North Africa on the basis of promises of large booty and lands.[6] A high record of maternal African lineages have been detected in western Andalusia, and scientific research on mitochondrial diversity in the last decade generally agrees that the Iberian Peninsula is the territory that displays the most intense African traces, with a stronger influence on its southern side.[7] "Amazigh" is the correct term for the major linguistic minority of North Africa, but "Berber" remains the more widely used ethno-linguistic word. In antiquity, the Romans and Byzantines used this term to refer to those who did not speak the region's lingua franca, Greek. During and after the arrival of Islam in the seventh century, the Arabs followed this Greco-Roman practice and referred to the indigenous peoples they encountered as "barbar".[8]

As animists, and possibly worshipers of the goddess Isis, some scholars note that the Amazigh are likely to have lived within a matriarchal social structure in which females held essential roles and power within the tribe. For instance, historians have looked to a specific Amazigh tribe, the Tuareg, and noted that women within these tribes have control over their marriages and economic resources, which provide them a level of power;

---

[5] George Murdock, *Ethnographic Atlas*, Pittsburgh: Pittsburgh University Press, 1967.

[6] Ibn Khaldun, *Histoire des Berbères et des dynasties Musulmanes de l'Afrique septentrionale*, French trans. Baron de Slane, Paris: Librarie Orientaliste Paul Geuthner, 1925.

[7] L. R. Botigue et al., "*Gene flow from North Africa contributes to differential human genetic diversity in southern Europe*," Proceedings of the National Academy of Sciences of the United States of America 110 (2013), 11,791–6; N. Harich, N. et al., "*The trans-Saharan slave trade—clues from interpolation analyses and high-resolution characterization of mitochondrial DNA lineages*," BMC Evolutionary Biology 10: 138 (2010).

[8] For a full discussion on whether the term "Berber" in Roman sources may be equated to the use of the word after the Islamisation and Arabisation of Berber populations: Ramzi Rouighi, "The Berber of the Arabs", *Studia* Islamica 106 (2011), 49–76.

they have the right to divorce; they own their own livestock, tents, and utensils; and they have considerable influence over their households.[9] In addition, the Tuareg follow matrilineal descent.

Matrilineal descent is also encouraged through the production of language. Becker explains that the Amazigh language is one "of cultural identity, home, the family, village affiliation, intimacy, traditions, orality, and nostalgia to a remote past" and as such it "perpetuates attributes that are considered female in the Moroccan culture".[10] Further, Amazigh women teach children the language and are thus the guardians and carriers of their cultural identities and traditions. Amazigh women are also weavers and artists within their communities. Within their art they represent the power of femininity through symbology related to birthing (e.g., triangles and diamonds that represent the vulva and uterus). These women also see weaving as a process that reflects the life stages, with a beginning and end, although the end returns them back to birth.

As early as 1100 B.C.E., the Amazigh encountered the Phoenicians who were seeking new trade opportunities in Northern Africa. The Phoenicians developed trade centres in Tangier, Asilah, Salé, and Essaouira, perfect zones for trade and transport, but also perfect for group interactions with the Amazigh. By 146 B.C.E., the Romans had moved to Phoenician lands in northern Africa with the goal of controlling these territories. Specifically, they colonised and built an empire near Fez called Volubilis.[11]

The attractive prehistory and history of Andalusia, the largest and most populated region of Spain, makes its present-day human population a prominent subject of research to analyse the population substructure and to examine the expected impact of African and other Mediterranean populations on the Iberian gene pool. Consistent with the geographical proximity of southern Spain and Africa, previous published studies have obtained results that show evidence of African-linked mtDNA lineages among Andalusians as well as high levels of diversity.[12] The composition of

---

[9] Cynthia Becker, *Arts in Morocco: Women shaping Berber identity* (Austin: University of Texas Press, 2006), 5–9.

[10] Becker, *Arts in Morocco*, 209.

[11] Malika Hachid, *Les Premiers Berbères: entre Méditerranée, Tassili et Nil*, Paris: Edisud, 2000.

[12] H. B. Côrte-Real et al., "Genetic diversity in the Iberian Peninsula determined from mitochondrial sequence analysis", *Annuals of Human Genetics* 60 (1996), 331–50. Also Hernández et al., "Human maternal heritage in Andalusia", 3.

THE ORIGINS OF ANDALUSIAN MUSLIM MATRILINEAL SYSTEMS   277

human maternal heritage in Andalusia reveals high internal complexity and distinctive influences of mtDNA haplogroups U6 and L in the western and eastern side of the region. Western Andalusians (from the province of Huelva) register the highest frequencies (14.6%) of African lineages reported in the Iberian Peninsula and throughout the European continent. The corresponding proportion in eastern Andalusians (Granada sample) was much lower (3.3%).

Human maternal heritage in Andalusia reveals high internal complexity and distinctive influences of mtDNA haplogroups U6 and L in the western and eastern side of the region. It must not be assumed, however, that every primitive society can be easily classified as "cognatic", "patrilineal", or "matrilineal". Patrilineal and matrilineal inheritance are really matters of degree; they may be expressed in many different forms and most societies give some recognition to both principles. Conflicting interests lead to all sorts of compromises in social structure between emphasis on matrilineal and patrilineal relations. There may even be a full and simultaneous development of both patrilineal and matrilineal kin groups, with both groups corporately organised.

Another important issue when it comes to understanding the diversity of narratives surrounding al-Andalus is the unique role played by Berber cultures both before and during the Muslim conquest of the Iberian Peninsula, as well as the Peninsula's underlying complexity before that date; it was composed of an extremely rich and complex social tissue which did not disappear during the period of Islamic rule but rather interacted with the new arrivals and created unique social structures of intersection.[13] By way of example, the two great attempts to restore the original purity of Islam were carried out by Berber tribal confederations: the Almoravids and the Almohads. The former group began as a group of nomadic Berber tribes of the Sahara, occupying the territory between the Draa, Niger, and Senegal rivers, and eventually controlled large areas of the south of Spain and North Africa from 1062 to 1147. One of its most noted leaders, Abu

---

[13] María Elena Díez Jorge, *Mujeres y arquitectura: Mudéjares y cristianas en la construcción*, Granada: Universidad de Granada, 2011. The author discusses one of these intersections related to the role of Christian and Muslim women in the creation of what may be considered as one of the most original architectural styles in Spanish art, Mudéjar Style (mudajan, or *ahl al-dajn*), which strongly reveals the culture of syncretism of the Iberian Peninsula by combining technical, ornamental, and decorative elements originating in Islamic art with Romanesque, Gothic, and Renaissance architectural styles that were current in the Christian kingdoms of Iberia.

278 A. G. KAVANAGH

Bakr ibn Umar, had married a wealthy and noble Berber woman, Zaynab an-Nafzawiyyat, who would become very influential in the development of the dynasty.

II. The Origins of Matrilinearity in Spain Before Islam

Methodological Issues

When it comes to reconstructing the universe of matrilinear and matrifocal structures in the Iberian Peninsula, it seems inevitable to resort to a wide approach from experts of different fields: archaeology, anthropology, epigraphy, literature, arts, women's studies, and history understood in a wider sense. Chronology and historical periods are useful as reference points, but the cultural influences of many societies, civilisations, creeds, and religions continued exerting an influence in the social life after they had been historically replaced by other groups. Particularly relevant is the period from the fall of the Roman Empire of the West to the arrival of Islam in Spain, as the Visigoth Empire was unable to fully replace Roman institutions with Germanic ones, meaning that many pre-Roman traditions continued displaying their efficacy in local regions remote from the main centres of power.[14] The official dates of Christian or Islamic rule over certain territories are in many cases merely nominal, and pagan symbols were simply clothed or veiled by the acculturation efforts of Christian and Muslim rulers. The study of social customs, rites, traditions, and legal institutions in the Iberian Peninsula is therefore one of the major sources that can help trace the influence of past matrilinear systems.

(a) Iberians and North African Influences

A complex issue—one that has not yet been satisfactorily explained by experts of different disciplines such an epigraphy, anthropology, or history—is the role played by the so-called Iberians,[15] who settled in the

---

[14] Peter Brown, *The World of Late Antiquity: AD 150–750,* New York: W. W. Norton and Company, 1989.

[15] Quesada Sanz, Fernando, "Los Iberos y la cultura Ibérica", in Sebastian Celestino Pérez (ed.) *La Protohistoria en la Península Ibérica* (Madrid: Ediciones Akal, 2017), 441–62. As Professor Quesada Sanz points out: "After more than one century of archaeological research, what we know on an intuitive basis about 'Iberian culture, the culture of the ancient Iberians', in fact, is an equivocal and confusing intellectual construct". However, Greek historians such as Dionysius of Halicarnassus or Herodotus referred in their writings to Spain and Portugal as the Iberian Peninsula. It is worth noting that the Kingdom of Colchis and the Iberians (subsequently, the Kingdom of Iberia) located in present-day Eastern Georgia are mentioned in *The Histories* of Herodotus.

south-east of Spain during the Iron Age. It must be borne in mind that Spain as a cultural concept is the result of the intermingling of many different groups, cultures, and civilisations. There is evidence that it was inhabited in the Palaeolithic period, as proven by the hominid remains of the Atapuerca Mountains which can be dated to one million years ago. Megalithic cultures were present during the Neolithic in different areas of Spain, and Phoenician traders settled in coastal areas around 1000–800 B.C.E. The mythical kingdom of Tartessos, allegedly located in a region close to the mouth of the Guadalquivir River and referred to in the Hebrew Bible as Tarshish, sheds new light on the discussion of Phoenician and Greek colonisation in the Iberian Peninsula.[16]

According to Bachofen, the Iberian peoples[17] settled in the North of Spain were a clear example of cultures with a strong presence of women in public and private life, although Bachofen's seminal work, *Das Mutterrecht*, published in 1861 does not use the term "matriarchy"; this term appeared later, in the context of intense debate on the three stages or cycles from a chaotic-undifferentiated state of promiscuity between males and females, symbolised by Aphrodite, to an agricultural order which venerated the Mother-Goddess.[18] Freedom in sexual relations, which some anthropologists call the prehistoric human sexual promiscuity of both sexes, did not allow people to be certain of the identity of a child's father; this was the basis from which anthropologists such as Bachofen, Morgan, and Briffault developed the theory of matrilinear kinship. From the perspective of Engels, the suppression of women came when private property was imposed, giving rise to the traditional family and, therefore, the patriarchal social system.

---

[16] Carolina López-Ruiz, "Tarshish and Tartessos Revisited: Textual Problems and Historical Implications" in: *Colonial Encounters in Ancient Iberia: Phoenician, Greek, and Indigenous Relations* (Chicago: The University of Chicago Press, 2009), 255–80.

[17] Adolf Schulten, *Hispania: Geografía, Etnología e Historia,* Seville: Editorial Renacimiento, 2017.

[18] Charles Malamoud, *Féminité de la parole, études sur l'Inde ancienne* (Paris: Albin Michel, 2005), 264: "ce qui importe dans le mariage sine manu ou par inclination mutuelle, c'est que la femme est libre. S'il existe un espace où la femme est livre, c'est celui ou l'entraîne le guerrier (...); le mariage gāndharva des textes indiens, mariage d'amour et de libre choix mutuel est, en fait rémplacé, dans le récits qui concernent les hommes pour le svayamvara, qui permet à la femme non pas de choisir mais de prendre pour époux l'homme qui sortira vainqueur d'une série d'épreuves sportives et martials." The works of Dumézil on the nature of Indo-European sovereignty also cited by the author and the major research conducted by Benveniste in his seminal work, *Vocabulary of Indoeuropean Institutions,* provide valuable insight into many legal rites and customs inherited from the Indo-European tradition which may be traced to Pre-Roman settlements in Spain.

280   A. G. KAVANAGH

However, some modern anthropologists have refuted the ethnographic evidence on which Bachofen and Engels based their arguments. This evidence, as presented, became proof not of matriarchy, but of matrilocality and matrilinearity. Contrary to what was previously believed, a connection between kinship structure and the social position of women cannot always be established. In many matrilineal societies it is a male relative—usually the woman's brother or uncle—who controls economic and family decisions.

From a religious perspective, this concept also means that women hold effective power in terms of leadership, moral authority, and control of property and lineage; at a later stage, matriarchies were replaced by a Greco-Roman-Christian model based on patriarchal structures that impose their authority resorting to the use of force supported by statutory and codified law. It must be noted that Bachofen makes numerous references to certain Iberian peoples in order to support his gynaecocracy theories:

> The indubitable the origin of the Iberian fabric of customs and of Cantabrian family law appears, therefore, the more surprising for being preserved, although modified over the centuries, in the Basque countries of France and Spain. In particular they have been preserved in the Barège valley, whose customs law, which was created relatively late, shows a singular similarity with Cantabrian practices, and which can be considered as the perfect and finished model of the Basque distinction of women. (…) In contrast to the feudal German legal system, the right of the firstborn is not limited in these cases to the son, but significantly includes the daughters,[19] with whom the younger siblings establish a dependency relationship that we have already analysed. In customs and law, the woman appears as the sole representative of the family, and her name is also given to the chosen husband and all his descendants.[20]

---

[19] Julio Caro Baroja, *Los Pueblos de España* (Madrid: Ediciones Istmo, 1976), 34: "[A]ccording to the legal practitioner of the seventeenth century, Jacques de Bela (1585–1667), the fact that women could inherit with the same legal rights as men must be traced to the agricultural conditions of the Basque people of his time. The strict law of the first born right to inheritance, or the freedom by the parents to choose an heir, whether male or female, is explained because any of them is capable of managing the family home and estate, considering that men and women share all tasks equally."

[20] Johann Jakob Bachofen, *Mitología arcaica y derecho materno,* Spanish trans. Begoña Ariño (Barcelona: Editorial Anthropos, 1988), 170–1.

THE ORIGINS OF ANDALUSIAN MUSLIM MATRILINEAL SYSTEMS   281

Modern historiography is divided as to the scope of the term "Iberians" used by Bachofen and other nineteenth-century writers, and many references to the Iberian matriarchal system probably in fact refer to later institutions or customs related to the Celtiberic period. In fact, the knowledge we have from the so-called Iberians derives from the writings of Greek and Roman historians, and from expert reconstructions of a diverse group of tribes and settlements generally termed Iberian.

The admixture of Indo-European with proto–Indo-European Iberian groups led to the creation of the Celtiberi ethnic groups mentioned by Roman historians, a result of intermarriage between Celts and Iberians after a period of continuous warfare. In addition, the origin of the Vascones, referred to as *ouáskones* by Strabo, is still under discussion.

Apart from the Greek historians such as Strabo or Polybius, other Roman authors such as Sallust, Livy, or Appian include references, albeit disparaging, to the barbarous tribes located in the north of Hispania in which women—particularly among the Cantabri and the Basque peoples—held a prominent position, revealing a number of customs: that a dowry was paid by a suitor to his future wife, that women could own and inherit land, and that inheritance took place through the female line. As Professor Llinares García points out:[21]

> The case that a matrilineal filiation system could have existed in the north of Spain at the time of the Roman conquest is based fundamentally on epigraphic inscriptions, some of them contested. (...) According to Barbero y Vigil in a now classical work (1974, pp. 141 and ff), in the area where the famous Vadinian stellae were found (North and South area of the Cantabrian mountain range, lower and upper basin of river Sella and the Pisuerga river), a pre-Roman system of kinship would have survived until the High Middle Ages.

The later period, in which Iberian tribes came into contact with the Phoenicians, provides evidence of women who had prominent roles as priestesses and were considered mediators between men and the pantheon of Iberian gods, which included many female divinities. Ceremonies were carried out in natural spaces such as caves or chasms, and in temples. In many shrines there were votive offerings in the shape of a woman, and archaeologists have traced the influence of Greek and Phoenician culture

---

[21] Mar Llinares García, *Los lenguajes del silencio. Arqueologías de la religión* (Madrid: Ediciones Akal, 2012), 80 and ff.

in the cult of goddesses of nature and fertility. Although we have passing references from Roman historians regarding Phoenician laws, the Carthaginians who rose to prominence after the fall of Phoenicia in 575 B.C.E. established colonies in the coastal areas of Spain, eventually clashing with Rome for control of the Mediterranean. An international treaty was concluded between Carthage and Rome in the year 508 B.C.E. in order to settle their differences. The outcome of the Second Punic War and the defeat of the Carthaginians in Zama led to Roman penetration of the Iberian Peninsula with a gradual implementation of Roman law by means of decrees and provincial laws, but it was only with Vespasian that all the territory of Hispania became nominally subject to Roman law. The strong role of Celtic women in public life is also evidenced in the treaty signed between the Carthaginian general Hannibal and the Celtic ruler Volcae during a march against Rome, which was concluded with the assistance of a female ambassador.[22]

However, the pre-Roman peoples settled in the Iberian Peninsula still retained many of their laws and customs, particularly in the rugged areas of the North of Spain, and for centuries before and after the Roman conquest they continued to follow their traditions; it is in these areas that matrilinear institutions flourished. In particular, these groups included the Callaici or Gallaecians, who inhabited the territory of Galicia in north-east of Spain, and which would be roughly equivalent to the Autonomous Community of Galicia following the territorial division enshrined by the Spanish Constitution of 1978; the Astures, who lived in the region known as Asturias, now the Principality of Asturias; the Cantabri, in the area at present belonging to the Autonomous Community of Cantabria; and the Vascones,[23] who had settled in the upper course of the Ebro river and the southern basin of the western Pyrenees in the Basque region, currently the Autonomous Basque Community; in addition to smaller tribal confederations such as the Iacetani, the Ilergetae, and the Ilercavones.

---

[22] Lyn Webster Wilde, *Celtic women in legend, myth and history*, New York: Sterling Publishing Co., 1997.

[23] Caro Baroja, *Los Pueblos de España*, 25: "While in the cities of the Ebro Christianity soon dislodged the previous religions, the mountain Basques insistently maintained their pagan beliefs, so that it can be said that even in the ninth century, there were probably very few Christians in Guipúzcoa, Vizcaya and the extreme north of Navarre".

THE ORIGINS OF ANDALUSIAN MUSLIM MATRILINEAL SYSTEMS   283

(b) Indo-European Influences in Pre-Roman Spain

One of the early works by Bachofen, *Versuch über die Gräbersymbolik der Alten*[24] ("Essay on the Grave Symbolism of the Ancients"), shows that he advocated for a symbolic-mythological interpretation of his theories, in which cultural, religious, and mythical elements are present as archetypes of the universal unconscious; this area was developed much later by Jung and other members of the Eranos circle, such as Karl Kerényi, Erich Neumann, Gilbert Durant, and Joseph Campbell, among others.[25] This approach affords a valuable hermeneutical tool to elucidate the presence of matrifocal structures in different societies by means of cultural and linguistic studies.

Nuptial formalities, probably from pre-Roman traditions, found their way into the Visigothic compilations of laws. As mentioned by Professor Rafael Gibert, "A constitution issued by Constantin to Tiberianus, count of the Spains (AD 322), [the plural is significant, as it reveals the diversity of peoples and regions], on the allocation of spousal donations depending on whether the betrothed had kissed each other or not (the 'Osculum Interveniente'), was significantly included in a number of compilations of Visigothic laws and applied even during the period of the Reconquest (*Reconquista*)".[26] Throughout this period many legal institutions and

---

[24] Johann Jakob Bachofen, *Versuch über die Gräbersymbolik der Alten,* Basel: G. Detloff, 1859.

[25] Arturo Sánchez Sanz "The theoretical development of matriarchy in nineteenth century," *Boletín del Museo Arqueológico Nacional* 37 (2018), 221–38. In the conclusions of this interesting paper, which summarises the discussion of matriarchy by different schools of thought from the nineteenth century to the present day, the author points out that "[b]e that as it may, for more than two centuries, the idea of matriarchy in primitive societies has become one of the most important challenges for modern thought, occupying the debates of the most illustrious anthropologists, philosophers, historians, ethnographers, etc. from all over the world".

[26] Kiril Petkov, *The Kiss of Peace: Ritual, Self, and Society in the High and Late Medieval West* (Leiden: Brill, 2003), 82. Also refer to Judith G. Evans "Emperor Constantine" in John Witte Jr. and Gary S. Hauk (eds.) *Christianity and Family Law: An Introduction* (Cambridge: Cambridge University Press, 2017), 36–51. The writings of C.G. Jung regarding the Mother Archetype which resides in every human psyche must be taken from a symbolic perspective and embrace widely varying types of the mother-goddess. One of the major references regarding this symbolic perspective may be found in Erich Neumann, *The Great Mother an analysis of the archetype* (New Jersey: Princeton University Press, 1963), 168: "This matriarchal significance of the Feminine is far older than the 'agricultural phase', from which the sociological school has attempted to derivate the matriarchate. It was not only the agricultural age with its ritual of sacred marriage and rain magic, but also and especially the primordial era and the hunting magic pertaining to it which served to shape the matriarchal world whose later offshoots we encounter in early primitive cultures." See also Carl G. Jung, *Archetypen: Urbilder und Wirkkräfte des kollektiven Unbewussten* (Zürich: Edition C. G. Jung im Patmos Verlag, 2019).

284   A. G. KAVANAGH

social customs that existed before the advent of Islam exercised an influence on Islamic family law and social interactions, particularly due to the existence of matrilinear institutions and practices in certain regions located in the north of Spain, Asturias, and the Basque[27] country, the use of Germanic dowry (*mahr*) regulations, the interpretation made of Islamic law by the jurists (*fuqahā*) of al-Andalus, and the survival of different ancient customs in many areas of Spain which attest to a multi-layered civilisation.

Moreover, evidence suggests that the personal statute of women among the Celtic peoples and tribes who settled on the Atlantic coast entitled them to a greater degree of legal protection than under Roman law. Overall, marriage seems to have been viewed by the ancient Celts as a partnership between men and women. Women could not be married against their will. They may have been allowed to choose their husbands, and it was customary in certain dowry systems that each party would bring an equal sum to the marriage, these assets becoming part of the estate of the spouses to be passed on to their descendants. Within marriage, women were allowed to own and inherit property independently.

In medieval Asturian society, the monarchy descended from Pelagius, who is credited with initiating the Reconquest movement after the battle of Covadonga (c. 718) in which the leader of the Moorish troops, al-Qama, was killed when attempting to conquer the region. According to the *Chronica Rotensis*, he was designated as *princeps* after his appointment in a general council of leaders, reigning over all the Astures. Following the death of Pelagius' son, Faffila, who was the second king of the Asturian kingdom, his children did not inherit the kingdom, but the dynasty continued through the husband of his sister, Alphonsus I.

---

[27] It is worth noting that many parallels have been established between ancient Georgian traditions and Basque customs. Ivane Javakhishvili, Niko Berzenishvili and Simon Janashia, *Saqartvelos istoria udzvebsi droidan XIX saukunis damgedamde (History of Georgia from Antiquity to the nineteenth century)*, (Tbilisi: Soviet Socialist Republic of Georgia Press, 1943), 7–8: "In Neolithic times Georgians lived in separate 'homes'. The 'home' was a large family comprising the relatives belonging to the mother's side of the family who lived all under the same roof. The grouping of different 'homes' constituted an independent community and the grouping of the communities linked by kinship ties was considered a tribe. Their main occupation was agricultural tasks supervised by women. The family was also headed by an older woman, called 'diasaxlisi' (mother of the house). The diasaxlisi also took care of any type of work and tasks inside and outside the home. Matriarchy dominated Georgian society at that time, which is still reflected in words such as 'Gutnisdeda' (mother of the plough). We may infer therefore that ploughing and sowing were tasks conducted by women. There is also an ancient word for woman 'dedakatsi' (male mother), whose origin may be traced to the matriarchal period."

THE ORIGINS OF ANDALUSIAN MUSLIM MATRILINEAL SYSTEMS   285

In the Asturian monarchy we find several cases in which the succession takes place through the children of the king's sister. It was only when Ramiro I was crowned in 842 that the matrilinear system decayed completely and the Gothic element prevailed over the indigenous tradition. From that time onwards the crown was transmitted from father to son, without the right of primogeniture being imposed immediately, yet always within the branch formed by the descendants of Bermudo I of Asturias. Without going into a discussion on whether extant chronicles may have been corrupted or manipulated to conceal such matrilinear structures, we find that the terms used in Latin—for example, in the Chronicle of Alphonsus III—referred to cousins or nephews from the mother's side of the family.[28]

Due to the agricultural and herding activities conducted in the territories of Cantabria and Asturias from ancient times, matrilinear structures survived well after the Roman and Visigoth periods and, as some authors have pointed out, property belonging to each lineage was custody of the women and inherited by their children, while their husbands, in their role as migratory herders, spent a considerable part of the year away from the communal pastures and land held by their wives. Women had economic obligations and social duties, being fully responsible for cultivation, harvesting, and breeding pigs and other animals in the farms which they held jointly with other women who belonged to the same family line. There is therefore evidence to suggest that in the regions designated currently as Cantabria and Asturias, as well as part of Leon, matrilinear structures existed as part of the indigenous heritage that would subsequently become merged with other systems of family law.

The North-West of Spain, in the region of Galicia, appears to reveal a highly matrifocal family structure, and many claims were made by historians and writers like Camilo José Cela regarding a matriarchal society that existed in the remote past, which from the perspective of legal historians

---

[28] Luis Rubio Hernansáez, "Los Astures y los inicios de la monarquía Astur (una aproximación)", *Antigüedad y Cristianismo* 13 (1997), 299–319. For a discussion on the social and economic background of the Astures, Abilio Barbero de Aguilera and Marcelo Vigil, "La organización social de los cántabros y sus transformaciones en relación con los orígenes de la Reconquista" *Hispania Antiqua* 1 (1971), 197–232. For matrilinear traces in the Middle Ages, see also Abilio Barbero, "Pervivencias matrilineales en la Europa medieval: el ejemplo del norte de España" in Yves-René Fonquerne and Alfonso Esteban (eds.) *La condición de la mujer en la Edad Media: Actas del Coloquio de la Casa de Velázquez* (Madrid: Universidad Computense, 1984), 215–22.

286   A. G. KAVANAGH

is attested by the existence of matrilinear institutions regarding inheritance and marriage settlement provisions.[29] If we consider that matrifocality exists when a family structure is centred around the mother and her children, pivoting on the role of a woman as mother, then we may say that even today the area which roughly would be equivalent to the province of Galicia and the North-West of Portugal shows many traits of matrifocality.

The dynamics of interaction between Celtic and Iberian ethnic groups and the influence of other cultures such as Phoenicians, Carthaginians, and Romans over a period of more than one thousand years make it difficult to consider that Spain has a single narrative. This was the view held by classical historians who considered that the history of certain fundamental institutions in Spanish Civil Law—such as marriage, kinship, property statutes, dowry, inheritance, or matrilinear/patrilinear descent—should be reconstructed by resorting to a mere diachronic perspective in which one legal system is merely replaced by the other. On the contrary, a cultural and anthropological approach shows that historical dates, while convenient for framing major events, do not imply that new empires, cultures, or civilisations effectively managed to impose a unified system of law throughout the territory. The laws of the pre-Roman peoples were retained in many cases even after the Carthaginian or Roman conquests. When the Visigoths, a major Germanic people together with the Ostrogoths, settled in the south of France and occupied the former provinces held by the Roman Empire in Spain, their legislation reflects the dynamics of the occupation and of their political decisions, and their legal compilations reflect the progressive influence of Germanic institutions on the Roman Law substratum they inherited.[30]

(c) Basque Culture and Matrifocal Institutions

In the nineteenth century, in the wake of the seminal works published by Bachofen regarding an initial stage of humanity in which matriarchal societies prevailed, a major debate on the subject ensued among scholars from

---

[29] Jan Brøgger and David D. Gilmore, "The Matrifocal Family in Iberia: Spain and Portugal Compared," *Ethnology: An international journal of cultural and social anthropology*, 36: 1 (1997), 13–80. The matrifocal view is also supported by the research of Carmelo Lisón, *Teoría etnográfica de Galicia. Antropología cultural de Galicia*, Madrid: Ediciones Akal, 2018.

[30] Rafael Gibert, *Historia General del Derecho Español* (Madrid: Copigraf, S.L., 1974), 16–17. Also, for an overview of Visigothic Law in Spain, see P.D. King, *Law and Society in the Visigothic Kingdom*, Cambridge: Cambridge University Press, 1972.

THE ORIGINS OF ANDALUSIAN MUSLIM MATRILINEAL SYSTEMS   287

different fields. During that period, studies regarding a proto-Indo-European language common to all Aryan peoples had been sparked by the German philological movement, which would have a great influence on many Spanish philosophers and thinkers.

The discussion on whether matriarchal, matrilinear, or matrifocal societies existed in certain areas of the north of Spain has sparked a considerable amount of controversy among Spanish historians, ethnologists, anthropologists, and linguists.[31] As we have already discussed, there was a considerable corpus of sources from Greek and Roman historians that mentioned the existence of matriarchal societies in the north of Spain, particularly with regard to the Basque region. For Andrés Ortiz-Osés,[32] there is no direct evidence that matriarchate systems existed in the Basque country; he prefers the use of the term "matriarchalism", which he defines as a society in which women have a deep influence on the social tissue. Such systems probably arose from the interaction between different cultural traditions and systems, as pointed out by José Miguel de Barandiaran.[33] Modern linguistic research shows that the Basque language should not be considered as Indo-European, and that its origin can probably be traced to the north Caucasus. The complexity of the Basque language is evidenced by its number of layers; apart from the initial Dene-Caucasian vocabulary, there are also imprints of Middle-Eastern Afroasiatic languages, Egyptian and Semitic languages, and pre-Roman Celtic languages.[34] An analysis of the Basque language in terms of kinship vocabulary reveals the role played by women in the household.

---

[31] Others, such as Dargun and Zmigrodski, decided to focus their research on the linguistic analysis of the Proto-Indo-European language to argue that the Aryan people were initially organised in a matriarchal system. Michal Zmigrodski, *Die Mutter bei den Völkern des arischen Stammes: eine anthropologisch-historische Skizze als Beitrag zur Lösung der Frauenfrage*, Munich: T. Ackermann, 1886.

[32] Andrés Ortiz-Osés, *La Diosa Madre: Interpretación desde la mitología vasca*, Madrid: Trotta, 1996.

[33] José Miguel de Barandiarán et al., *Cultura vasca*, (Donostia: Editorial Erein, 1977), 18–19. "From the available data on the beliefs and rites that remain from that time, we have become convinced that, at that time, the conception of the world and of man was dominated by a kind of animism (...) due to indigenous myths which had a long-standing tradition and different historical factors such as the contacts which, over millennia, the Basque people had held with different peripheral Indo-European groups (...)."

[34] John D. Bengtson, "The Basque language: history and origin", *International Journal of Modern Anthropology* 4 (2011).

288   A. G. KAVANAGH

In one his major works, *Historia y etnografía vasca* ("Basque history and ethnography"), anthropologist Julio Caro Baroja advances the idea that before the Roman invasion there were traits of matrilinear succession with regard to ownership of property and other aspects of social life. It is significant that among the Vascones as well as the Cantabrii, according to Caro Baroja, it was the future husband who provided a dowry to the wife. Also, from a legal perspective, daughters inherited and women chose the future bride for their sons.

Another unique institution, described in detail by Strabo, was known as the *covada*: "[W]hen a child is born they have a strange custom, as they do not take any part in caring for their women at the time of labour, and once she has given birth to the child the husband lies on the bed, as if he were ill, for a number of established days, as if he had given birth to the child".[35] This custom seems to have also existed among the Asturians, the Cantabrii, the *maragatos* and *ibicencos,* and in certain areas of the Pyrenees. Among the nobility, certain matrilinear structures existed up to the High Middle Ages. This is attested in part by the role played by high-ranking women, particularly in Navarre, where the Salic Law drafted by the Frankish King Clovis I did not apply. King Sancho Ramírez (1043–1094) appointed his sister, Sancha Ramírez, as bishop of Iruñea-Pamplona. A detailed study of the Fueros[36] applicable in the Basque region reveals that certain Germanic institutions had mingled with their pre-Roman traditions, such as trial by ordeal, *las arras* (the pre-nuptial agreement), and the joint system of property as the prevailing marriage regime. According to Caro Baroja:

> If we relied on the testimony of Strabo, the Basque region would be one of the most extreme cases of matriarchal cultures, comparable to the Khasi of Assam or the Iroquois, in which not only inheritance but also the creation of the family is governed by matrilinear structures, unlike other matriarchal

[35] Estrabón Libro III, capítulo 4, Spanish trans. M. J. Meana and F. Piñero, Madrid: Gredos, 1998.

[36] The term *Fuero*, plural *Fueros* in Spanish, refers to a charter or body of laws granted by the King to a certain city, area, or region, although at times it could also refer to specific groups of individuals; these local laws, which usually included a number of privileges or exemptions, were a key factor for the reconquest process, because it encouraged the repopulation of areas which had been reconquered from the Muslim sovereigns. With the context of feudalism in Spain, "fueros" could also be granted by the nobility to fiefs in which they exercised sovereign functions. Their study is of particular interest for our subject because they reveal an overlap from different legal traditions.

THE ORIGINS OF ANDALUSIAN MUSLIM MATRILINEAL SYSTEMS   289

communities in which the matrilocal residence merely implies a preponderance of the wife's family more than an effective dominance.[37]

Archaeological, ethnographic, epigraphic, and linguistic evidence from studies carried out by researchers over the past decades reveal that the evolution of matrilinear structures in different regions of northern Spain was different over time, depending on the specific circumstances of each area.[38]

(d) The Influence of Sephardi Jews Settled in Spain

In addition, the uniqueness of the conquest process, which had a fundamental influence on the historical development of Spain, led to the "Islamisation of a very important part of the Hispanic population, mixed marriages, and the restored economic-social balance".[39] Initially, the Mozarabs enjoyed a privileged status as a protected community. In addition to this group, we must add the Muladis, or *muwalladūn*: people who did not have an Arab lineage, but had been brought up as Muslims as a result of marriages between Muslims and Christian or Jewish women. It should not be forgotten that the Jews, who had been subjected to numerous forms of oppression during the Visigothic monarchy, were able to enjoy an atmosphere of greater tolerance as a community belonging to the People of the Book (*ahl al-Kitāb*) during the period of Muslim rule. The great social cohesion of the Jewish community and the protection they received from the Muslim sovereigns allowed them to access numerous positions of responsibility in the Umayyad court. Hispano-Jewish society also presented unique features, due to the interaction of the three cultures in one of the most dynamic periods of the European Middle Ages. As noted by María Ángeles Gallego, "[F]or Spanish-Jewish women, the phenomenon of women becoming protagonists as a consequence of the

---

[37] Caro Baroja, *Los Pueblos de España*, 34.

[38] Hernandez et al., "Human maternal heritage in Andalusia", 2: "The first studies on matrilineal diversity in Iberian populations were performed in northern Spain, and, more specifically in the Basque Country. Mitochondrial DNA variation in Basques has consistently shown low diversity levels and peak frequencies of haplogroup H, the most frequently detected clade in Europe. These findings have allowed the Basque mitochondrial profile to be distinguished from other European populations."

[39] Miguel Cruz Hernández, *El Islam de al-Andalus. Historia y estructura de su realidad social* (Madrid: M.A.E. Agencia Española de Cooperación Internacional, 1992), 73.

290   A. G. KAVANAGH

so-called 'absence of man' was expressed in a very different context: a woman could become the heir of the family patrimony after the male members of the family had converted to Christianity (…)".[40]

In the detailed study by Yov Tom Assis on sexual behaviour in that period, we may infer that Spanish Jews were influenced by the Islamic milieu. Although private life was controlled by Jewish law and traditions, Islamic social patterns had a lasting impact on the Christian and Jewish communities of the Iberian Peninsula to the extent that bigamy was prevalent among Iberian Jews.[41] As Sylvie-Anne Golberg emphasises, Judaism is essentially transmitted by the mother.

> Paradoxically the contemporary platitude according to which Rabbinic Judaism was conceived by men for men is rivalled only by the crucial place occupied by women in the survival and transmission of Jewishness, a place reflected in legal norms, literature and social foundations. Originating in Roman times, the Talmudic phrase informing fathers that their children born of non-Jewish mothers belong to the maternal line [was]—"Your child born of a Gentile is not yours but hers".[42]

Charles Burnett aptly described the influence of Jewish scholars not only as translators but as cultural agents of Islamic science in medieval Spain.[43] Trade relations between different regions subject to Christian and Muslim monarchs were undertaken by Jews, who also acted as de-facto diplomats in the proposal of cultural projects, benefitting from their

[40] María Ángeles Gallego, "Approaches to the study of Muslim and Jewish women in medieval Iberian Peninsula: The poetess Qasmuna Bat Isma'il", *MEAH, sección Hebreo* 48 (1999), 63–75.

[41] Yom Tov Assis, "Sexual Behaviour in Mediaeval Hispano-Jewish Society," in Ada Rapoport-Albert and Steven J. Zipperstein (eds.), *Jewish History: Essays in Honour of Chimen Abramsky* (London: Peter Halban, 1988), 25–59.

[42] Sylvie-Anne Golberg, "Blood ties/social ties. Matrilineality, converts and Apostates from late antiquity to the Middle Ages", *Clio* 44:2 (2016), 171–200.

[43] Fernando Díaz Esteban, *La herencia de Al-Andalus en el mundo antiguo*, in La Herencia de Al-Andalus, Fátima Roldán (ed.) (Sevilla: Fundación El Monte, 2007), 33: "In contact with the Arab-Islamic world, the Jews recovered the interest in philosophy, science, history and secular literature which they had already had in Hellenistic times and in the first centuries of Christianity, when they sometimes wrote in Hebrew, sometimes in Aramaic, and sometimes in Greek (…)".

THE ORIGINS OF ANDALUSIAN MUSLIM MATRILINEAL SYSTEMS 291

fluency in the Arabic language and their close contacts with the Umayyad court.[44]

The Jews, who had been subject to fierce persecution during the Visigoths' rule in Spain, particularly following the alliance between the Church and the Gothic monarchy during the reign of Reccared, settled in the major cities of al-Andalus as traders, skilled artisans, professionals, and cultural intermediaries.[45] It must be remembered that the effective Islamisation of Cordoba took place gradually and the ruling Visigoth families continued wielding considerable power, some of them occupying major positions in the Umayyad court. This also implied that many customs that stemmed from the blending of different legal traditions[46] in existence before the advent of Islam in Spain found their way into the new system insofar as they did not contradict the main tenets of the *sharīʿa*, which at that time was still in the process of formation throughout the different territories under Islamic rule. As Sylvie-Anne Golberg put it:

> Towards the end of the fourth century, this move in the direction of matrilineality was supplemented by the assertion made on behalf of Ravina in the Babylonian Talmud: "The son of your daughter, who was born to a Gentile, is 'your son'".[47]

[44] Charles Burnett, "The Coherence of the Arabic-Latin Translation Program in Toledo in the Twelfth Century", *Science in Context* 14:1/2 (2001), 249–88.

[45] Jerrilynn D. Dodds, *The arts of intimacy: Christians, Jews, and Muslims in the Making of Castilian Culture* (New Haven: Yale University Press, 2009); Jane S. Garber, "Ornament of the World", *Humanities magazine* (online), 2019: "Most of Sephardic Jewry's daring innovations in the manipulation of the Hebrew language in versification or Sephardic interest in philosophy and science flourished while the Caliphate of Córdoba briefly blossomed (929–1031). With the breakup of the Caliphate of Córdoba in the eleventh century, Andalusia was divided into more than two dozen statelets or mini-kingdoms (the Taifa kingdoms 1031–1089), each boasting its own court of poets and scientists and a patronage system that included the talents of the minority populations. Jewish courtiers flourished in Saragossa, Granada, Mérida and elsewhere, sponsoring their own secular salons that mirrored the dominant hybrid culture. Jews branched into astronomy, cartography, medicine and mathematics, philosophy and Hebrew and Arabic philology, and poetry."

[46] Cruz Hernández, *El Islam de al-Andalus,* 171: "[S]ocial relations, especially in the urban environment, led them (the Mozarabs) quickly to the knowledge of the Arabic language and subsequent bilingualism; but apparently, the urban nuclei were deeply Arabized, since Álvaro de Córdoba in the *Indiculus luminosus* complains of the abandonment of Latin and classical humanities, reproaching his co-religionists for preferring the Arabic language and humanities and for following their customs and fashions."

[47] Sylvie-Anne Golberg, "Blood ties/social ties. Matrilineality, converts and Apostates from late antiquity to the Middle Ages", *Clio* 44:2 (2016), 167.

292   A. G. KAVANAGH

Considering that during the time of the Roman Empire, especially after the destruction of the second Temple in 70 C.E. and the ban on Jews residing in Jerusalem following the Great Revolt (Bar Kokhba) of 132–5 C.E., the settlement of Sephardic Jews in Spain increased considerably and preserved their cultural traditions, many of which stressed the importance of women in preserving Judaism, in line with the Talmudic injunction that a person should always be willing to sell all he has in order to marry the daughter of a Torah scholar. If he cannot find the daughter of a Torah scholar, he should marry the daughter of one of the great people of the generation, who are pious although they are not Torah scholars.[48]

Not only did Muslims acculturate, but the dominant Christian society itself had consciously or unconsciously assumed numerous Andalusian cultural uses, as Daniel Gil Benumeya points out; such uses included a considerable number of rituals and traditions from the three cultures that contributed to the making of al-Andalus. The complex social tissue of the Spanish Middle Ages was based on a true culture of coexistence and assimilation of different traditions with numerous local particularities. This had, at times, been deliberately hidden in the official narrative of Spain, a process which involved the concealment or elimination of conflicting sources. As a result, when the Spanish Inquisition was officially abolished in 1834, most textual references to Spanish history and culture had been aligned to an official version which downplayed the role of these three cultures in the construction of Spanish identity.

This rather "naive" approach of attempting to filter the national identity and eliminate alleged perverse or foreign particles to achieve the highest degree of "Spanish-ness" exerted a strong pressure on research regarding the "other" in Spanish history—be it women, mozarabs (*mustʿarab*), "moriscos", mudéjares (*al-mudajjan*), and more generally, as expressed by Menéndez Pelayo, "the Spanish heterodox".[49] It must be considered that until the eighteenth century, when the current paternal-maternal surname combination norm was adopted, matrilineal surname transmission also existed in Spain, meaning that children use their mother's surname or occasionally that of a grandparent, rather than of either parent. Sometimes this was for prestige, since this custom was perceived as

---

[48] William Davidson, *The William Davidson Talmud*, (Jerusalem: Koren Publishers, digital edition available at www.sefaria.com), Peshachim 49b.

[49] Marcelino Menéndez Pelayo, *Historia de los heterodoxos españoles,* Madrid: La Editorial Católica, 1978.

THE ORIGINS OF ANDALUSIAN MUSLIM MATRILINEAL SYSTEMS 293

higher class, or for profit, flattering the matriarch or patriarch in hope of inheriting land.[50]

III. Matrilineal Systems in Al-Andalus

As we have previously discussed, matrilineal structures and systems had existed in different regions of the Iberian Peninsula for centuries before the arrival of Islam, arising from the numerous contacts with North Africa and the Atlantic coast.[51] For many generations of scholars and historians, the confluence of Roman law and Christianity were the pillars of Spanish national identity, at times threatened by unruly tribes or groups located particularly in the north of Spain which had nevertheless left virtually no imprint on Spanish history. In similar terms, the Muslim conquest of Spain—also referred albeit inaccurately as the Arab Conquest—was perceived as an interlude between two major historical periods: the Visigoth Kingdom and the emergence of the nation state of Spain. It must be considered that until the beginning of the sixteenth century the territory of Spain was divided into different Christian kingdoms, while the Emirate of Granada ruled by the Naṣrid dynasty. It was not until the marriage of Queen Isabella I of Castille and King Ferdinand II of Aragon that the seeds of the future nation state of Spain were planted, which would in time lead to the creation of a world empire with the accession of Charles V to the Spanish throne in 1516.

Regardless of the controversial attitudes that have existed since the nineteenth century among Spanish historians regarding the role of al-Andalus in shaping the Spanish nation and *weltanschauung*, the objective fact remains that it represents the longest presence of a Muslim-ruled territory (711–1492) in any European state. This process started with arrival of Ṭāriq ibn Ziyād in Gibraltar, with a small group of Berber troops. One year later, the combined efforts of Ibn Nuṣayr and Ibn Ziyād led to the total defeat of the Visigoth Kingdom and the beginning of the al-Andalus period in Spanish history, which reached its peak with the Caliphate of Cordoba, proclaimed by ʿAbd al-Raḥmān I in 929, then collapsed one

---

[50] Dolores Collado, Ignacio Ortuño Ortín, and Andrés Romeu, "Surnames and social status in Spain," *Investigaciones económicas* 32:3 (2008), 259–87.

[51] For a general overview of this issue, Pierre Guichard, *Al-Andalus: Estructura antropológica de una sociedad islámica en occidente*, Granada: Universidad de Granada, 1998, and Jacinto Bosch-Vilá, "Establecimiento de grupos humanos norteafricanos en la Península Ibérica" *Atti del Iᵉʳ Congresso Internazionale di Studi Norte-Africani*, Cagliari, 1965, 147–65.

century later with the so-called Fitna al-Andalus conflict between the descendants of the last caliph, Hishām II, and the followers of his chamberlain, al-Mansūr.

The territories formerly controlled by the Caliphate of Cordoba and subsequently by the Taifa kingdoms varied in geographical extent as the Reconquista movement—a coalition of different Christian kings and nobles—gradually advanced. Yet, as evidenced in numerous examples, it was also a time of coexistence and tolerance between Christians, Muslims, and Jews; even after the conquest of the city of Toledo in 1085 by Alfonso VI of Castille, Toledo flourished as a major seat of learning thanks to its school of translation. The relations between the three cultures have, at times, simplified the complex process of interaction between them in the different territories of Spain which requires a dynamic approach because the reconquest (Reconquista) started with the Battle of Covadonga (718) seven years later after the group Arab-Berber troops crossed the strait of Gibraltar, lasted almost eight centuries.

As Miguel Cruz points out, although the rapid and glorious expansion of Islam must be considered a certain fact, the situation of the Arabs in the Maghreb was precarious, with strong resistance from the Christianised Berbers.[52] Another form of instability that would have an important influence on the formative process of al-Andalus was the fact that Berbers constituted the majority of the army that crossed the strait under the leadership of Tariq ibn Ziyād. Shortly after, in the year 740, there was a general uprising of the Berbers in North Africa who succeeded in occupying Tangier, leading to uprisings in many regions of Spain. The social structure of al-Andalus at the time of the founding of the Umayyad monarchy indicates that the Arabs, although the architects of the conquest of much of the Iberian Peninsula, were a minority group. On the other hand, the much more numerous Berbers would retain many of their ancestral customs, even if they converted to Islam, showing a deeply rooted tribal sentiment.

Although estimates vary regarding the number of Arab and Berber troops that crossed to the Iberian Peninsula in the first wave of conquest, Pierre Guichard considers that on the basis of the existing evidence it would be reasonable to consider that the armies comprised around 60,000 Berbers and 30,000 Arabs.[53] The conquest was very gradual, and consid-

---

[52] Cruz Hernández, *El Islam de Al-Andalus*, 65.

[53] Pierre Guichard, "Les Arabes ont bien envahi l'Espagne: les structures sociales de l'Espagne musulmane", *Annales, Economies, Sociétés, Civilisations*, 29:6 (1974), 1483–513.

THE ORIGINS OF ANDALUSIAN MUSLIM MATRILINEAL SYSTEMS   295

ering that the combined Arab-Berber troops were small in number compared with the existing indigenous population, many pre-Islamic traditions and customs found their way into the Hispano-Islamic civilisation, particularly through the process of mixed marriages with women from the Visigoth noble families who continued to control substantial parts of the Spanish territory. It is worth noting that the term "Hispano-Muslim", according to Lévy-Provençal,[54] seems to have been forged around the middle of the tenth century when an awareness of such an identity came into existence. Although ethnically the Hispano-Muslim may originate from North Africa (the Maghrib) or from the East, his character is different. The nature of this "Andalusian" prototype is beyond the scope of this chapter, but has led to acrid discussions between experts in different fields of Arab studies in Spain when assessing the contribution of Islam to Spanish identity.[55] If the matter is raised here, it is only as evidence that the social and political changes and interaction triggered by Islam in Spain created unique political, social, cultural, and legal structures and systems as a result of the coexistence of Christians, Muslims, and Jews in many cities of Spain. These communities were not isolated, but lived in enlightened coexistence.

The legal status of women in certain Germanic kingdoms, particularly the Lombards and the Visigoths, influenced the social status and consideration of women in Muslim Spain. The Visigoths, former clients of the Roman Empire, ruled in Spain for two centuries (501–711) through a system of elective monarchy in which prominent members of the aristocratic class forged alliances to appoint a new king. Initially, the Visigothic

---

[54] Evariste Lévi-Provençal, "España Musulmana hasta la caída del Califato de Córdoba, 701–1031 de J.C. (Madrid: Espasa Calpe, S.A., 1982), 117.

[55] José Luis Gómez Martínez, "Américo Castro y Sánchez Albornoz: dos posiciones ante el orden de los españoles," *La Nueva Revista de Filología Hispánica* 11:2 (1972), 300–19. The embittered discussion between these two major Spanish historians of the twentieth century divided the field of Islamic studies in Spain into at least two well-differentiated groups: those who sympathised with the views of Americo Castro and those who sided with Claudio Sánchez Albornoz. Castro's was that: "Islam forced [Spain] to reflect, and opened up a new perspective on the traditional way of life and the social commitments of the inhabitants of the north," (Américo Castro, *España en su historia: cristianos, moros y judíos,* Buenos Aires: Losada, 1948). Sánchez Albornoz, on the other hand, believed that "Islam twisted the fate of Spain. (…) Had Spain followed the same course as France, Germany and England, and based on what, despite Islam, we have done through the centuries, perhaps we would even have been able to take the lead." (Claudio Sánchez Albornoz, "España y el Islam," *Revista de Occidente* 70 (1929), 11–20.)

invasion of Spain relied heavily on Roman provincial traditions and administrative organisation of the territory, but subsequently we find a progressive influence of Germanic law, particularly in the area of criminal law, nuptial contracts, inheritance, dowries, and the economic system of marriage. With the Visigoth law codes, women acquired the legal capacity to inherit land and title over real estate, being able to manage landed property independently from their husbands or male relations, including the disposal of property by means of a will if they had no heirs. From a procedural perspective, women were able to appear in person at the courts to represent their interests if they were above fourteen years of age and arrange their own marriages once they reached the age of twenty. Visigothic law allowed women to prepare the contractual agreements for their daughter's weddings, which no one could revoke. The Visigoths under Flavius Recesvintus allowed a widowed woman to select her own husband as long as he was an older man.

It must be taken into account that Visigoths were more liberal than other Gothic tribes with regard to widows' property rights. As argued by S.P. Scott in his introduction to *The Visigothic Code*:

> While the wife had the right to the use of half of the deceased husband's property during her lifetime, he had a right to the use of only one third of hers, as he has today. The favor generally shown to the wife in the stipulations of the marriage contract is largely the result of the independence enjoyed by the sex under the Teutonic and Scandinavian customs.[56]

The classic work by the Roman historian Tacitus provides us with an interesting insight regarding the position of women under unwritten ancient Germanic law, which was based on tradition:

> The wife does not bring a dowry to the husband, but rather the reverse occurs. (...) In return for these gifts, a wife is obtained, and she in turn brings the man some weapon: they consider this exchange of gifts their greatest bond, these their sacred rites, these their marriage divinities.[57]

[56] S. P. Scott, S. P. (ed. and trans.), *The Visigothic Code*, (Littleton: F.B. Rothman, 1982), 125–6.

[57] Tacitus. Agricola, "Germania, and Dialogues on Orators", ed. and trans. Herbert W. Benario (Norman: University of Oklahoma Press, 1991), 72 and ff.

THE ORIGINS OF ANDALUSIAN MUSLIM MATRILINEAL SYSTEMS 297

The study of the evolution of certain legal institutions in al-Andalus reveals the presence of earlier matrilinear institutions—as, for example, pre-Roman dowry systems that interacted with Germanic law—that were later assimilated by Islamic law. These merit a detailed study which exceeds the scope of this chapter. As pointed out by López Ortiz, the Germanic dowry system is extremely similar to the Islamic one, particularly in reference to notarial documents drafted by Andalusian notaries during the Naṣrid dynasty.[58] In order to understand how the Germanic[59] institution of the *Morgengabe* (morning gift) influenced the Islamic dowry system in al-Andalus, it is essential to take into account that the prior legal systems and traditions existing in Spain before the Muslim invasion permeated certain areas of Islamic law, particularly in the case of the dowry system which had great similarities with the practices of the Mozarabs living in territories under Muslim rule.

Many Islamic marriage contracts from different periods in al-Andalus, particularly Cordoba, Seville, and Murcia, include additional gifts for the bride such as rich clothes, quantities of linen and wool, expensive textiles, gold-embroidered silks, and jewellery; such gifts may have been a standard custom in the community.[60] As Amelia Zomeño notes in her detailed study of Wansharīsī's *Al-Mi'yār*[61]—already been the subject of research by H.R. Idris in the 1970s—in the marriage transfer systems of al-Andalus the *ṣadāq* (the source of the exact equivalent word in Spanish, *acidaque*) was treated as a part of the mandatory monetary gift given by the groom to his future wife, not as a dowry. This gift consisted of two parts, one part (*naqd*) that was delivered to the father of the bride for the purchase of his

---

[58] José López Ortiz "Algunos capítulos del formulario notarial de Abensalmún de Granada," *AHDE* 4 (1927), 319–76.

[59] Simeon L. Guterman, *The Principle of the Personality of Law in the Early Middle Ages: A Chapter in the Evolution of Western Legal Institutions and Ideas, Law Review University of Miami* 21:2 (1966), 263–4. "The establishment of Germanic kingdoms in Italy, Gaul, Spain, and North Africa reduced the law of the Roman population to the status of a tolerated personal legislation. Among the Franks, Burgundians, Visigoths, and even Ostrogoths a dualistic system was established in which Romans retained the privilege of their own private law, but in which the Germanic law undoubtedly enjoyed territorial validity in disputes between Germans and Romans."

[60] Amalia Zomeño Rodriguez, "The Islamic marriage contract in al-Andalus (10th–16th centuries)" in Asifa Quraishi and Frank E. Vogel (eds.) *The Islamic marriage contract: case studies in Islamic family law*, (Cambridge, MA: Harvard University Press, 2008), 136–55.

[61] Vincent Lagardère, *Histoire et société en Occident musulman au Moyen Âge: Analyse du Mi'yar d'al-Wansarisi*, Madrid: Collection de la Casa de Velázquez, 1995.

daughter's trousseau, which could consist of a monetary sum, chattel, or property and that was generally included in the marriage contract. Payment of the second part (*siyāqa*) was deferred and consisted of real estate (land, houses, or holdings) that the husband was obliged to deliver directly to his new wife. Such gifts given by the husband to the bride and by the father to the daughter as part of marriage agreements became customary in many areas of al-Andalus, but their origin must be traced to the legal customs of the Spanish Gothic families, particularly of higher status, and their tradition of the *Morgengabe*.

The presence of Berber/Imazighen tribes in al-Andalus and their settlement in the Iberian Peninsula is only mentioned in a few Islamic historical sources. While there is no consensus among scholars about their origins before their presence in North Africa, it is generally admitted that their presence in the region can be traced more than five thousand years back, with distinctive cultural, language, and matrilinear family institutions. One of the major sources as to the origin and practices of the Berbers who participated in the Muslim conquest of the Iberian Peninsula is the fourteenth-century North African historian and sociologist, Ibn Khaldun.[62] In his major work, *The History of the Berbers*, he identifies different tribes such as the al-Butr, who resisted all attempts of Roman or Byzantium domination, and the Barānis, who had settled in coastal areas and displayed more traces of Romanisation. From an ethnic perspective, they belonged to the Zanata and Maṣmūda branches, although other tribes such as the Miknāsa, Hawwāra, and Nafza also participated in the initial wave of conquest. When the expression "Arab-Berber conquest of Spain" is used, usually the role of the different Berber groups in Spain and the interaction with the local institutions are downplayed. According to Chalmeta,[63] the total number of Arabs in the Iberian Peninsula never exceeded 40,000–50,000 men for the entire period of the existence of al-Andalus, but the waves of Berber tribes that crossed the strait of Gibraltar could amount to several hundred thousand. In fact, the first ruler of the Umayyad dynasty in Spain, ʿAbd al-Raḥmān I, would probably not have been able to consolidate his rule in al-Andalus had it not been for the support of the Berber tribes and clans, his own mother being from the Nafza tribe.

---

[62] Ibn Khaldun, *Histoire des Berbères.*
[63] Pedro Chalmeta, *Invasión e Islamización: la sumisión de Hispania y la formación de al-Andalus*, Madrid: Editorial Mapfre, 1994.

The Origins of Andalusian Muslim Matrilineal Systems   299

The Arabisation of the different Berber tribes in Spain was slow, and revolts—including the revolt of 740–2—attest that relations with the Arab rulers of different principalities were complex. The Caliphate of Cordoba (929–1031) was also a short-lived experience, barely one century, and by the end of the eleventh century was replaced by the Almoravids (al-Murābiṭūn), a dynasty founded by the powerful Ṣanhāja Berber confederation, who had been present in southern Arabia, Africa, and America long before the advent of Islam and had preserved their matrilinear institutions. As suggested by certain scholars, it was probably this matrilineal character that had enabled them to migrate and settle in regions so far from their place of origin, presumably in southern Arabia/Yemen. A branch of the Ṣanhāja, the Masufah tribe, were among the Berber groups that settled in Spain and, according to Ibn Baṭṭūṭa, "though Mohammedans, they had a law of succession resembling that of the pagans of Malabar. Their women, handsome and finely formed, went unveiled and conversed with the men on terms of freedom and equality, which spoke of the dissolute manners of the place."[64]

As Guichard points out, "[I]t is not surprising therefore, that Muslim Spain, with regard to the rest of the Muslim world in the medieval period, displays fully original features".[65] One of the elements of this singularity lies in the matrilineal filiation systems of numerous Berber tribes that settled in the southern half of Spain. This system did not conflict with the kinship systems existing in the Christian West at least until the tenth century, however, that centred on the conjugal couple, being a bilateral and non-patrilinear kinship system.

Even before the Islamic invasion of the Iberian Peninsula in 711, as the historian Ibn ʿAbd al-Ḥakam points out, al-Kāhina, the queen of the Buṭr tribes in the Aurés area, had led a formidable rebellion against the Arab conquerors. Sensing defeat, he entrusted his two sons to the governor Hassān ibn al-Nuʿmān, who offered them command posts among the Berber contingents of his army. The role of women in North African Berber tribes who later migrated to the Iberian Peninsula was not limited to the household, and many also acted as leaders of their community.[66]

---

[64] Ibn Battuta, *The travels of Ibn Battuta in Asia and Africa*, trans. H.A.R. Gibb, Cambridge: Cambridge University Press, 1962.

[65] Pierre Guichard, "Les Arabes ont bien envahi l'Espagne: les structures sociales de l'Espagne musulmane" *op. cit.*, p. 1486.

[66] Ibn ʿAbd al-Hakam, *Conquête de l'Afrique du Nord et de l'Espagne*, [Futūh Ifriqīya wa al-Andalus], ed. and French trans. A. Gateau (Alger: Éditions Carbonel 1948), 77–8. For a general overview of the influence of the Berber tribes in al-Andalus, see Eduardo Manzano, "Bereberes de Al-Andalus: Los factores de una evolución histórica", *Al-qantara: Revista de estudios árabes* 11:2 (1990), 397–428.

300 A. G. KAVANAGH

The swift Arabisation process is more a myth than a historical reality, and until the proclamation of the Caliphate of Cordoba by ʿAbd al-Raḥmān III in 929, the different Berber tribes and groups preserved their own traditions and social structures in al-Andalus. In fact, as pointed out by Christine Mazzoli-Guintard, "in al-Andalus the women from the Umayyad royal family used their position in the court to influence on the appointment of the heir to the throne".[67] Such was the case of Ṣobh, the concubine of the Caliph al-Ḥakam (961–76), originally a Christian from Navarre, who had been brought as a slave (*jāriya*) to the Caliph's harem and, having become his favourite wife, managed through her ambition and political skills to ensure the designation of her son (Caliph Hisham II) as al-Hakam's successor, with the support of the chamberlain al-Manṣūr. During the years of her regency, she undertook considerable reforms in the organisation of the administration and, at the same time, al-Manṣūr reorganised the army to ensure that the tribal structures that existed would become considerably weakened, to the point of almost disappearing at the beginning of the eleventh century.

However, in certain regions, far from the effective control of both the Visigothic nobility and the Arab emirs, there is evidence for the survival of matrilineal systems that already existed in the Iberian Peninsula. One example is the rugged region of Las Alpujarras, a region located south of the Sierra Nevada, that provides a natural division between the provinces of Granada and Almeria. The area had been occupied by the Spanish-Roman and Gothic population under control of the Visigoth count Theodemir, who later took refuge in Orihuela after signing a peace covenant with Mūsa ibn Nuṣayr. The arrival of Berber (Amazigh) and Tuareg groups in the tenth century did not entail a modification of these structures, since they were also matrilineal communities. Centuries later, after the forced conversion process carried out in the sixteenth century that resulted in the resettlement and expulsion of the Moors from that area, we find testimonies from travellers and historians about the prominent role of women in the towns of the Alpujarra, who enjoyed much more freedom than women in other areas of Spain. On a trip to this region in 1896, the physician and anthropologist Federico Olóriz[68] collected valuable data on

---

[67] Christine Mazzoli-Guintard and Almudena Ariza Armada, *Gouverner en terre d'Islam X–XV siècle* (Chevaigné: Presses universitaires de Rennes, 2014), 71.

[68] Fedérico Olóriz Aguilera, *Diario de la expedición antropológica a la Alpujarra en 1894*, ed. Javier Piñar Samos, Granada: Colección Sierra Nevada y la Alpujarra, 1995.

THE ORIGINS OF ANDALUSIAN MUSLIM MATRILINEAL SYSTEMS   301

the family, social, and sexual relationships of women in the area that pointed to the existence of a matriarchy in the past. In the notes he collected for his diary, he showed his surprise at having found such an egalitarian society in terms of women's rights compared to the puritanism that prevailed elsewhere in Spanish society during that period. The women from the villages in Alpujarras enjoyed much more freedom, including sexual freedom; young people of both sexes lived together without segregation, premarital relations being common. This region had been considered by many chroniclers as untameable, on the basis of the numerous riots and rebellions against policies dictated by the central administration. Such notoriety attracted the attention of numerous writers of the Romantic period, as well as the well-known British Hispanist Gerard Brenan, who dedicated numerous stories to the way of life of the inhabitants of the Alpujarras, far removed from the existing conventionality, showing a society characterised by women who had decision-making power over family matters and their own lives.[69]

During the period of consolidation of the Islamic presence in the Iberian Peninsula from 711 to 929, there was considerable influence from the existing social and kinship structures that already were in place in certain regions of the north of Spain, and also from the matrilinear systems of Berber groups that had settled in al-Andalus. It should also be noted that the first migrations of Berber peoples to the Canary Islands possibly occurred at the beginning of the Christian era and their matrilineal systems influenced the cultural traditions of each of the islands, whose population is generically and somewhat imprecisely designated as "Guanche" (from the Berber term *igwanchiyen*). Due to its geographical location close to the Atlantic coast of Africa, it is probable that there would have been navigation between the continent and the islands from ancient historical times. Later, also during the Islamic period, contact with Berber tribes from the Sahara and Mauritania continued. We have scant testimonies from Middle Age chronicles regarding the Canary Islands, but many of the customs collected by ethnologists show the existence of a matriarchy in the past; for example, the marriage rite required the delivery of a gift from the husband, and a man assumed the paternity of his wife's children, who received the name from "zorrocloco"; even after the Spanish invasion, royal descent was passed through the female line, and the woman

---

[69] Gerard Brenan, *South from Granada*, London: Penguin Books, 2008.

transmitted the right to the throne.[70] Certain matrilinear customs were still in place when the Canary Islands became part of Spain in the late fifteenth century, and chroniclers of the time affirm that in Lanzarote "(…) most of the women had three husbands, one of them serving the others for one month, and then the next husband would take on such duties, each of them in turn".[71]

As Franco Moreno points out, in some areas such as Merida there was an important Berber presence that took advantage of the fertile valleys of the Guadiana river, the Alagón valley, and the middle valley of the Tagus for their expansion, introducing numerous cultivation and irrigation techniques from their ancestral traditions that were unknown in the Iberian Peninsula.[72] Women were involved in various agricultural activities, which implied also taking decisions on all issues related to lands held by the extended family and relations with neighbours regarding easements, encumbrances, and use of water rights.

> [This] correlates with many toponyms in Al-Andalus which attest to Berber settlements in view of their etymology, such as Almodóvar, Fates, Guadalmesí (*Wādī al-Mansil*), La Janda (*al-jandaq*), Patalagana (*Bayt al-ᶜayn*, "house of the fountain"), Guadalbacara, (*Wādī al-baqara*), Zahara (*Sajra*), Trafalgar, Zahora, Almarchal (*al-maysar*), Abulagar, Algallarín, Almarache, Bonnet, Xustar, Azaba, Casba, Betix, Alfaneque, (…).
>
> Often, the toponymy coincides with a form of social distribution of water and the application of hydraulic techniques that confirm the link between the settlements, mainly farmhouses and spaces irrigated farms adjacent to them [...].[73]

As pointed out by Soha Abboud:

---

[70] José Juán Jiménez González, "Las fuentes etnohistóricas canarias. Crónicas, historias, memorias y relatos", *Anuario de Estudios Atlánticos* 44 (1999), 199–263.

[71] Antonio Tejera, *La religión de los guanches. Ritos, mitos y leyendas*, Santa Cruz de Tenerife: Asociación Cultural de las Islas Canarias, 1995; Antonio Tejera and Antonio Chausa, "Les nouvelles inscriptions indigènes et les relations entre l'Afrique et les îles Canaries", *Bulletin Archéologique du C.T.H.S.* 25 (1999), 69–74.

[72] Bruno Franco Moreno, "Distribución y asentamientos de tribus bereberes (Imazighen) en el territorio emeritense en época emiral (S. VIII–X)", *Arqueología Y Territorio Medieval* 12:1 (2005), 39–50.

[73] José Beneroso Santos, "Acerca del establecimiento de los grupos bereberes en la zona de Tarifa. Pautas, dinámicas y posibles asentamientos," *Al Qantir* 16 (2014), 150–151.

THE ORIGINS OF ANDALUSIAN MUSLIM MATRILINEAL SYSTEMS   303

As for the Berbers, the data shows that non-Arab Muslim populations had to be dispensed with as regards taxes. Thus, those who had settled in rural areas had to pay *al-ʿushr* on their lands. Those who were incorporated into the Emir's personal guard service and whose relationship with him was that of *istisnaʾ*, that is, "favourable treatment", as in the East, could also have received territorial concessions such as the *jund*, since they were already perceived as "owners" of some areas in al-Andalus.[74]

As Pedro Chalmeta pointed out, "[T]he essential component of Al-Andalus is its people, *ahl al–Andalus*, and not the geography".[75] The fact that so much controversy has existed among Spanish historians regarding its definition and its influence in Spanish culture is not only a result of its complexity due to cultural, linguistic, and religious syncretism, but also because, as discussed above, it is a key issue in defining the identity of Spain. For Claudio Sánchez Albornoz, "Arabs or Syrians [in Spain] notwithstanding their male ancestry were Spanish through their mothers and grandmothers like the grandchildren of Sara la Goda".[76] From her marriage with ʿUmayr b. Saʿīd al-Lajmī, Habīb b. ʿUmayr was born, the common ancestor of the Banū Sayyid, the Banu Hayyāy and the Banu Maslama, according to Ibn al-Qūṭiyya,[77] a reputed Arab historian and philologist whose father had been the last Visigoth King in Spain and whose mother was this same Sara, nicknamed the Goth (*la Goda*).

As we know in Classical Arabic, apart from the given name (*ism*) of an individual, the *nisba*[78]—literally "attribution"—must be considered. This "attribution" is the adjective indicating the place of origin; for example, "al-Samarqandī" meant that the lineage of that person came from the city of Samarkand. As pointed out by Adeel Mohammadi:

> The positive power of the maternal *nasab* is evident in several examples where men are filiated to their mothers because of some exceptional quality.

---

[74] Soha Abboud-Haggar, *Andalusian Precedents for the Taxation of Mudejar Communities*, En la España Medieval, *2008, vol. 31, pp. 475–512.

[75] Chalmeta, *Invasión e Islamización*, 26.

[76] Claudio Sánchez Albornoz, *La España Musulmana según los autores islamitas y cristianos medievales* (Madrid: España Calpe, 1978), 82–3.

[77] Abū Bakr Ibn ʿUmar Ibn al-Qūṭiyya al-Qurtubī, *Taʾrīkh Iftitāh al-Andalūs*, ed. and Spanish trans. Julián Ribera, Madrid, 1926.

[78] Delfina Serrano Ruano, "Paternity and filiation according to the jurists of al-Andalus: legal doctrines on transgression of the Islamic social order," *Imago temporis: medium Aevum* 7 (2013), 59–75.

304   A. G. KAVANAGH

Abū Bakr b. al-Qūṭiyyah (d. 367/977), a prominent Andalusian historian, was filiated to his mother Sārah al-Qūṭiyyah, who was from the royal family of the Visigoths (*Qūṭ*) that ruled parts of Spain before the Muslim conquest. The famous Shāfiʿī jurist Tāj al-Dīn b. Bint al-Aʿazz (d. 665/1267) was named as such because his mother was the daughter of the noted jurist al-Aʿazz Fakhr al-Dīn b. Shukr. The Persian chronicler, Ibn Bībī al-Munajjamah (d. after 684/1285), is referred to by a maternal *nasab* because his mother was a prominent and well-known astronomer. (…) Alternatively, the maternal *nasab* could be used to differentiate between the sons of a prominent man with many children, in which case the maternal *nasab* would be primarily for identification and differentiation.[79]

Among the bibliographic sources that collect not only Arab lineages but also those of the Berbers, we must highlight the work *Jamharat ansāb al-ʿarab*[80] by the prolific writer and philosopher Ibn Hazm of Cordoba, whose works also collect valuable testimonies on the consideration of women in Cordoba society of the time. The well-known poet Abū Bakr Muḥammad ibn ʿAmmār[81] closely attached to al-Muʿtamid, sovereign of Seville, congratulated him on the birth of twins with these verses:

> *I congratulate you for your two children, male and female,*
> *The light of the sun and the light of the moon are the same.*

The reconstruction and survival of matrilinear and matrifocal systems in al-Andalus should not only be carried out on the basis of historical sources, however; in my opinion, a comprehensive approach that takes into account research carried out in the fields of anthropology, ethnology, sociology, linguistics, epigraphy, literature, sociolinguistics, genetics, gender studies, iconography and symbolism,[82] folklore, and music is particularly useful.

---

[79] Adeel Mohammadi, "The Ambiguity of Maternal Filiation (nasab) in Early and Medieval Islam," *The Graduate Journal of Harvard Divinity School*, 2019.

[80] Ibn Hazm, *Jamharat ansāb al-ʿarab*, ed. E. Lévi_Provençal, Cairo: Al Maaref Publishers, 1948.

[81] Claudio Sánchez Albornoz, *Ben Ammar de Sevilla. Una tragedia en la España de las Taifas*, Madrid: Espasa Calpe, 1972.

[82] Ingrid Bergström, "Disguised symbolism in Madonna Pictures and Still Life," *The Burlington Magazine* 631 (1995), 303–8: "The criteria for carrying out an interpretation requires the examination of a wide repertoire of comparative material consisting of works of art, religious ideas, literature and other aspects of social relations. The question is also more complex because the same object can be interpreted in different ways."

THE ORIGINS OF ANDALUSIAN MUSLIM MATRILINEAL SYSTEMS   305

For example, oral traditions and music have not received the attention they merit as an account transmitted down generations that links different periods, styles, and cultures. We find examples of this in the Arab-Andalusian musical tradition that was greatly influenced by Ziryāb, who flourished in the court of ʿAbd al- Raḥmān II.

The anthropologist Manuel Lorente considers that

> matrifocality as a symbolic socio-cultural profile will effect a transfer ana-logue from the processional imagery of Holy Week, to the popular culture of the *Cante Jondo*, especially during the time that goes from the end of the 18th century and first half of the 19th century, and coinciding with the dates of the prohibition of Holy Week brotherhoods between 1771 and 1850 in Jerez. This is the time during which *cante jondo* emerges, especially the musical form known as the *seguiriya*, a form of musical poetry with great expressive intensity.[83]

Notwithstanding the cliché that the South of Spain is a male-orientated society in which "machismo" is prevalent, as Jan Bregger and David Gilmore point out, "(…) everywhere in Spain, north and south, matrifocal family structure is prevalent, despite machismo in the south". However, even this view regarding the south of Spain should be examined in light of evidence that in spite of the traditional boundaries of men and women in that region, women continue exerting a major role in family decisions. In their matrifocal study of the city of Fuenmayor, located in the province of Jaén, they ascertained "that of 416 extended families, 295 show couples living with the wife's family, that is, 71 per cent of extended families are matrilateral".[84]

The matrilinear and matrifocal past permeates Al-Andalus, so that its traces can be evidenced not only from studying certain traditions regarding family or personal law, dowries, donations, inheritances or marriage property systems but also from taking into account the presence of women in arts and architecture. As Luce Lope-Baralt reminds us, "[O]f the unsurpassed aesthetical level achieved by couples that were also poets in Al-Andalus, such as Ibn Zaydūn and Wallāda during the Taifa period, or

---

[83] Manuel Lorente, "Matrifocalidad, Semana Santa y Cante Jondo en Jérez de la Frontera", in *Música Oral del Sur—Papeles del Festival de música española de Cádiz*, Granada: Consejería de Cultura y Deporte, 2012.

[84] Jan Bregger and David D. Gilmore, "The matrifocal family in Iberia: Spain and Portugal compared," *Ethnology* 36:1 (1997), 13–30.

Ibn Saʿīd and Hafṣa during the Almohad Caliphate".[85] These poets, who were couples in real life, also reveal one of the most profound understandings of women in al-Andalus through their poems, which include praise, complaint, disdain, and quarrel: that they saw themselves as having the right to reply.

CONCLUSIONS

1. Matrilineal heritage and matrifocal institutions have existed in different forms almost from the dawn of history in various regions in the Iberian Peninsula. The matrifocal family structure may be traced to both the north and the south of Spain.
2. The numerous contacts between North Africa and the Atlantic coast reveal high levels of genetic diversity and maternal heritage as far back as Neolithic times due to the strategic geographic position of Spain and its close link to Africa through the Strait of Gibraltar.
3. As discussed in this chapter, matrilineal heritage and matrifocal institutions cannot be traced to just one source; in our study we have discussed four potential sources that have contributed to such heritage. Each of them, due to specific regional developments and interaction between Indo-European and Semitic groups, has given rise to kinship structures, traditions, rites, and institutions which attest to the diversity of Spanish cultural and historical interaction.
4. The traditional focus and bias on the influence of Roman law in other legal systems does not take into consideration the influence of matrilinear institutions that already existed among the Celtiberian peoples before the Roman invasion of Hispania. Such institutions—which are traditionally focused on marriage customs, inheritance, and dowry provisions—survived and merged with other social and legal systems that arrived to the Iberian Peninsula at a later period.
5. One of the elements of the singular nature of al-Andalus lies in the influence of the numerous Berber tribes, groups, and confederations that arrived in Spain at the beginning of the Muslim conquest and settled in different areas, particularly in the southern half of Spain. Many of these tribes had matrilinear systems or matrifocal institutions

---

[85] Luce Lope-Baralt, *Huellas del Islam en la literatura española: De Juan Ruiz a Juan Goytisolo*, (Madrid: Libros Hiperión, 1989), 26.

THE ORIGINS OF ANDALUSIAN MUSLIM MATRILINEAL SYSTEMS   307

which did not conflict with the existing bilateral and non-patrilinear kinship systems in the Christian West.

6. The study of the evolution of certain legal institutions in the Iberian Peninsula reveals the presence of former matrilinear institutions, for example, pre-Roman dowry systems that interact with Germanic law, that were later assimilated by Islamic law and were probably influenced by the customs of the Mozarabs living in territories under Muslim rule. For example, gifts given by the new husband to his bride and by the father to the daughter as part of marriage agreements became customary in many areas of al-Andalus, but their origin must be traced to the legal customs of the Spanish Gothic families, particularly of higher status, regarding the *morgengabe* (morning gift).

7. The process of assimilation and interaction between the different Arab-Berber groups and the former Visigoth nobility and the practice of mixed marriages with daughters from the ruling families in Christian principalities or kingdoms are evidenced in the survival of matrifocal practices in al-Andalus.

8. The study of matrilinear and matrifocal institutions before and after the al-Andalus period requires a comprehensive approach that takes into account not only the existing historical records but also the research carried out in other fields such as anthropology, genetics, ethnology, sociology, linguistics, epigraphy, history of law, and legal institutions, as well as iconography and the migration of symbols at different cultural periods and levels.

9. The vast symbolism related to the different roles of women in the Iberian Peninsula (e.g., the extreme devotion, at times described as iconodulism, to the Virgin Mary in many regions of Spain, but particularly in Andalusia, or given names for men in Spain which due to Marian devotion include Mary as the second part of a compound, such as José María, literally Joseph Mary)[86] is an untapped source for the study of matrilinear structures and influences, as I have suggested in this study with some examples. The migration of symbols from different cultures, and from the East to the West, requires an interdisciplinary approach in line with the studies conducted by Fritz Saxl, Jean Seznec, Edgar Wind, Rudolf Wittoker, and René Guénon, among others, in order to analyse our symbolic heritage from a dynamic per-

---

[86] Amy G. Remensnyder, *La Conquistadora: The Virgin Mary at War and Peace in the Old and New Worlds*, Oxford: Oxford University Press, 2004.

spective and to explain numerous interactions and even contradictions arising from the coexistence of matrilinear and patrilinear structures in Iberian societies.

10. The reconstruction of the role of women in the creation of Spanish identity implies understanding the complex cultural interaction that took place between different peoples and groups that were living in the Iberian Peninsula before the arrival of Islam in 711 C.E., and how throughout the Caliphate and until the fall of the Nasrid dynasty in 1492 C.E. women exerted power in private and public.

Bibliography

Abboud-Haggar, Soha, "Andalusian Precedents for the Taxation of Mudejar Communities", *En la España Medieval* 31 (2008), 475–512.

Ángeles Gallego, María, "Approaches to the study of Muslim and Jewish women in medieval Iberian Peninsula: The poetess Qasmuna Bat Isma'il," *MEAH, sección Hebreo* 48 (1999), 63–75.

Bachofen, Johann Jakob, *Versuch über die gräbersymbolik der alten*, Basel: G. Detloff, 1859.

Bachofen, Johann Jakob, *Mitología arcaica y derecho materno*, Spanish trans. Begoña Ariño, Barcelona: Editorial Anthropos, 1988.

de Barandiarán, José Miguel, et al., *Cultura vasca*, Donostia: Editorial Erein, 1977.

Barbero, Abilio and Marcelo Vigil, "La organización social de los cántabros y sus transformaciones en relación con los orígenes de la Reconquista," *Hispania antiqua* 1 (1971), 197–232.

Barbero, Abilio, "Pervivencias matrilineales en la Europa medieval: el ejemplo del norte de España" in Yves-René Fonquerne and Alfonso Esteban (eds.) *La condición de la mujer en la Edad Media: Actas del Coloquio de la Casa de Velázquez* (Madrid: Universidad Computense, 1984), 215–22.

Becker, Cynthia, *Arts in Morocco: Women shaping Berber identity*, Austin: University of Texas Press, 2006.

Beneroso Santos, José, "Acerca del establecimiento de los grupos bereberes en la zona de Tarifa. Pautas, dinámicas y posibles asentamientos", *Al Qantir*, 16 (2014), 150–151.

Bengtson, John D., "The Basque language: history and origin", *International Journal of Modern Anthropology* 4 (2011).

Bergström, Ingrid, "Disguised symbolism in Madonna Pictures and Still Life," *The Burlington Magazine* 631 (1995), 303–8.

Bosch-Vilá, Jacinto, "Establecimiento de grupos humanos norteafricanos en la Península Ibérica", *Atti del 1er Congreso Internazionale di Studi Norte-Africani*, Cagliari, 1965, 147–65.

THE ORIGINS OF ANDALUSIAN MUSLIM MATRILINEAL SYSTEMS 309

Botigue, L. R. et al., "*Gene flow from North Africa contributes to differential human genetic diversity in southern Europe,*" Proceedings of the National Academy of Sciences of the United States of America 110 (2013), 11791–6.

Bregger, Jan, and David D. Gilmore, "The matrifocal family in Iberia: Spain and Portugal compared," *Ethnology* 36:1 (1997), 13–30.

Brenan, Gerard, *South from Granada*, London: Penguin Books, 2008.

Brøgger, Jan and David D. Gilmore, "The Matrifocal Family in Iberia: Spain and Portugal Compared," *Ethnology: An international journal of cultural and social anthropology*, 36: 1 (1997), 13–80.

Brown, Peter, *The World of Late Antiquity: AD 150–750*, New York: W. W. Norton and Company, 1989.

Burnett, Charles, "The Coherence of the Arabic-Latin Translation Program in Toledo in the Twelfth Century", *Science in Context* 14:1/2 (2001), 249–88.

Caro Baroja, Julio, *Los Pueblos de España*, Madrid: Ediciones Istmo, 1976.

Castro, Américo, *España en su historia: cristianos, moros y judíos*, Buenos Aires: Losada, 1948.

Chalmeta, Pedro, *Invasión e Islamización: la sumisión de Hispania y la formación de al-Andalus*, Madrid: Editorial Mapfre, 1994.

Collado, María Dolores, Ignacio Ortuño Ortín, and Andrés Romeu, "Surnames and social status in Spain," *Investigaciones económicas* 32:3 (2008), 259–87.

Cruz Hernández, Miguel, *El Islam de al-Andalus. Historia y estructura de su realidad social*, Madrid: M.A.E. Agencia Española de Cooperación Internacional, 1992.

Davidson, William, *The William Davidson Talmud*, Jerusalem: Koren Publishers, digital edition available at www.sefaria.com.

Díaz Esteban, Fernando, "La herencia de Al-Andalus en el mundo antiguo", in Fátima Roldán (ed.), *La Herencia de Al-Andalus*, Sevilla: Fundación El Monte, 2007.

Díez Jorge, María Elena, *Mujeres y arquitectura: Mudéjares y cristianas en la construcción*, Granada: Universidad de Granada, 2011.

Dodds, Jerrilynn D., *The arts of intimacy: Christians, Jews, and Muslims in the Making of Castilian Culture*, New Haven: Yale University Press, 2009.

Evans, Judith G., "Emperor Constantinte" in John Witte Jr. and Gary S. Hauk (eds.) *Christianity and Family Law: An Introduction*, Cambridge: Cambridge University Press, 2017.

Franco Moreno, Bruno, "Distribución y asentamientos de tribus bereberes (Imazighen) en el territorio emeritense en época emiral (S. VIII–X)", *Arqueología Y Territorio Medieval* 12:1 (2005), 39–50.

Garber, Jane S., "'Ornament of the World' and the Jews of Spain," *Humanities magazine* (online), 2019.

Gibert, Rafael, *Historia General del Derecho Español*, Madrid: *Copigraf*, S.L., 1974.

310   A. G. KAVANAGH

Golberg, Sylvie-Anne, "Blood ties / social ties. Matrilineality, converts and Apostates from late antiquity to the Middle Ages", *Clio* 44:2 (2016), 171–200.

Gómez Martínez, José Luís, "Américo Castro y Sánchez Albornoz: dos posiciones ante el orden de los españoles," *La Nueva Revista de Filología Hispánica* 11:2 (1972), 300–19.

Guichard, Pierre, "Les Arabes ont bien envahi l'Espagne: les structures sociales de l'Espagne musulmane", *Annales, Economies, Sociétés, Civilisations*, 29:6 (1974), 1483–513.

Guichard, Pierre, *Al-Andalus: Estructura antropológica de una sociedad islámica en occidente*, Granada: Universidad de Granada, 1998.

Guterman, Simon L., "The principle of the personality of law in the early Middle Ages: a chapter in the evolution of Western legal institutions and ideas," *Law Review University of Miami* 21:2 (1966).

Hachid, Malika, *Les Premiers Berbères: entre Méditerranée, Tassili et Nil*, Paris: Edisud, 2000.

Harich, N. et al., "*The trans-Saharan slave trade—clues from interpolation analyses and h*igh-resolution characterization of mitochondrial DNA lineages," BMC Evolutionary Biology 10: 138 (2010).

Helfferich, Adolf, *Entstehung und Geschichte des Westgoten-Rechts*, Paderborn: Salzwasser-Verlag GmbH, 2013.

Hernández, Candela L. et al., "Human maternal heritage in Andalusia (Spain): its composition reveals high internal complexity and distinctive influences of mtDNA haplogroups U6 and L in the western and eastern side of region," *BMC Genetics* 15:11 (2014).

Ibn ʿAbd al-Hakam, *Conquête de l'Afrique du Nord et de l'Espagne*, [Futūh Ifrīqīya wa al-Andalus], ed. and French trans. A. Gateau, Alger: Éditions Carbonel 1948.

Ibn Battuta, *The travels of Ibn Battuta in Asia and Africa*, trans. H.A.R. Gibb, Cambridge: Cambridge University Press, 1962.

Ibn Hazm, *Jamharat ansāb al-ʿarab*, ed. E. Lévi_Provençal, Cairo: Al Maaref Publishers, 1948.

Ibn Khaldun, *Histoire des Berbères et des dynasties Musulmanes de l'Afrique septentrionale*, French trans. Baron de Slane, Paris : Librarie Orientaliste Paul Geuthner, 1925.

Javakhishvili, Ivane, Niko Berdzenishvili, and Simon Janashia, *Saqartvelos istoria udzvelesi droidan XIX saukunis damgedamde (History of Georgia from Antiquity to the 19[b] century")*, Tbilisi: Soviet Socialist Republic of Georgia Press, 1943.

Jiménez González, José Juán, "Las fuentes etnohistóricas canarias. Crónicas, historias, memorias y relatos", *Anuario de Estudios Atlánticos* 44 (1999), 199-263.

Jung, Carl G. *Archetypen: Urbilder und Wirkkräfte del kollektiven Unbewussten*, Zürich: Edition C. G. Jung im Patmos Verlag, 2019.

King, P. D., *Law and Society in the Visigothic Kingdom*, Cambridge: Cambridge University Press, 1972.

THE ORIGINS OF ANDALUSIAN MUSLIM MATRILINEAL SYSTEMS 311

Lagardère, Vincent, *Histoire et société en Occident musulman au Moyen Âge: Analyse du Mi'yar d'al-Wansarisi*, Madrid: Collection de la Casa de Velázquez, 1995.

Lévi-Provençal, Évariste, *España Musulmana hasta la caída del Califato de Córdoba (701–1031 de J. C.)*, Madrid: Espasa Calpe, S.A., 1982.

Lisón, Carmelo, *Teoría etnográfica de Galicia. Antropología cultural de Galicia*, Madrid: Ediciones Akal, 2018.

Llinares García, Mar, *Los lenguajes del silencio. Arqueologías de la religión*, Madrid: Ediciones Akal, 2012.

Lope-Baralt, Luce, *Huellas del Islam en la literatura española: De Juan Ruiz a Juan Goytisolo*, Madrid: Libros Hiperión, 1989.

López Ortiz, José, "Algunos capítulos del formulario notarial de Abensalmún de Granada" in *AHDE* 4 (1927), 319–76.

López-Ruiz, Carolina, "Tarshish and Tartessos Revisited: Textual Problems and Historical Implications" in Michael Dietler and Carolina López-Ruiz, *Colonial Encounters in Ancient Iberia: Phoenician, Greek, and Indigenous Relations* (Chicago: The University of Chicago Press, 2009), 255–80.

Lorente, Manuel, "Matrifocalidad, Semana Santa y Cante Jondo en Jérez de la Frontera", in *Música Oral del Sur—Papeles del Festival de música española de Cádiz*, Granada: Consejería de Cultura y Deporte, 2012.

Lowes, Sarah, "Matrilineal Kinship and Spousal Cooperation: Evidence from the Matrilineal Belt", Stanford University, King Center on Global Development and CIFAR, 2020. Working paper available at: https://cega.berkeley.edu/wpcontent/uploads/2020/03/Lowes_PacDev2020.pdf.

Malamoud, Charles, *Féminité de la parole. Etudes sur l'Inde ancienne*, Paris: Éditions Albin Michel, 2005.

Manzano, Eduardo, "Bereberes de Al-Andalus: Los factores de una evolución histórica", *Al-qantara: Revista de estudios árabes* 11:2 (1990), 397–428.

Marshall, Tim, *Prisoners of Geography, Ten Maps that tell you everything you need to know about global politics*, London: Elliot & Thompson Limited, 2015.

Mazzoli-Guintard, Christine and Almudena Ariza Armada, *Gouverner en terre d'Islam X-XV siècle*, Chevaigné: Presses universitaires de Rennes, 2014.

Menéndez Pelayo, Marcelino, *Historia de los heterodoxos españoles*, Madrid: La Editorial Católica, 1978.

Mohammadi, Adeel, "The Ambiguity of Maternal Filiation (nasab) in Early and Medieval Islam," *The Graduate Journal of Harvard Divinity School*, 2019.

Murdock, George, *Ethnographic Atlas*, Pittsburgh: Pittsburgh University Press, 1967.

Neumann, Erich, *The Great Mother an analysis of the archetype*, New Jersey: Princeton University Press, 1963.

Olóriz Aguilera, Federico, *Diario de la expedición antropológica a la Alpujarra en 1894*, ed. Javier Piñar Samos, Granada: Colección Sierra Nevada y la Alpujarra, 1995.

312   A. G. KAVANAGH

Ortiz-Osés, Andrés, *La Diosa Madre: Interpretación desde la mitología vasca*, Madrid: Trotta, 1996.

Petkov, Kiril, *The Kiss of Peace: Ritual, Self, and Society in the High and Late Medieval West*, Leiden: Brill, 2003.

Quesada Sanz, Fernando, "Los Iberos y la cultura Ibérica", in Sebastian Celestino Pérez (ed.) *La Protohistoria en la Península Ibérica*, Madrid: Ediciones Akal, 2017.

al-Qurtubī, Abū Bakr Ibn ʿUmar Ibn al-Qūṭiyya, *Taʾrīkh Iftitāh al-Andalūs*, ed. and Spanish trans. Julián Ribera, Madrid, 1926.

Remensnyder, Amy G., *La Conquistadora: The Virgin Mary at War and Peace in the Old and New Worlds*, Oxford: Oxford University Press, 2004.

Rouighi, Ramzi, "The Berber of the Arabs", *Studia* Islamica 106 (2011), 49–76.

Rubio Hernansáez, Luis, "Los Astures y los inicios de la monarquía Astur (una aproximación)," *Antigüedad y Cristianismo* 13 (1997), 299–319.

Runciman, Steven, *The Medieval Manichee. A Study of the Christian Dualist Heresy*, Cambridge: Cambridge University Press, 1991)

Sánchez Albornoz, Claudio, "España y el Islam," *Revista de Occidente* 70 (1929), 11–20.

Sánchez Albornoz, Claudio, *Ben Ammar de Sevilla. Una tragedia en la España de las Taifas*, Madrid: Espasa Calpe, 1972.

Sánchez Albornoz, Claudio, *De la Andalucía islámica a la de hoy*, Madrid: Ediciones Rialp, 2007.

Sánchez Albornoz, Claudio, *La España musulmana según los autores islamitas y cristianos medievales*, Madrid: Espasa-Calpe, 1978.

Sánchez Sanz, Arturo, "The theoretical development of matriarchy in 19th century," *Boletín del Museo Arqueológico Nacional* 37 (2018), 221–38.

Schulten, Adolf, *Hispania: Geografía, Etnología e Historia*, Sevilla: Editorial Renacimiento, 2017.

Scott, S. P. (ed. and trans.), *The Visigothic Code*, Littleton: F.B. Rothman, 1982.

Serrano Ruano, Delfina, "Paternity and filiation according to the jurists of al-Andalus: legal doctrines on transgression of the Islamic social order," *Imago temporis: medium Aevum* 7 (2013), 59–75.

Tacitus, *Agricola, Germania, and Dialogues on Orators*, ed. and trans. Herbert W. Benario, Norman: University of Oklahoma Press, 1991.

Tejera, Antonio, *La religión de los guanches. Ritos, mitos y leyendas*, Santa Cruz de Tenerife: Asociación Cultural de las Islas Canarias, 1995.

Tejera, Antonio and Antonio Chausa, "Les nouvelles inscriptions indigènes et les relations entre l'Afrique et les îles Canaries", *Bulletin Archéologique du C.T.H.S.* 25 (1999), 69–74.

Tov Assis, Yom, "Sexual Behaviour in Mediaeval Hispano-Jewish Society," in Ada Rapoport-Albert and Steven J. Zipperstein (eds.), *Jewish History: Essays in Honour of Chimen Abramsky* (London: Peter Halban, 1988), 25–59.

Webster Wilde, Lyn, *Celtic women in legend, myth and history*, New York: Sterling Publishing Co., 1997.

Zmigrodski, Michal, *Die Mutter bei den Völkern des arischen Stammes: eine anthropologisch-historische Skizze als Beitrag zur Lösung der Frauenfrage*, Munich: T. Ackermann, 1886.

Zomeño Rodríguez, Amalia, "The Islamic marriage contract in al-Andalus (10th-16th centuries)" in Asifa Quraishi and Frank E. Vogel (eds.) *The Islamic marriage contract: case studies in Islamic family law*, (Cambridge, MA: Harvard University Press, 2008), 136–55.

Index[1]

A
Abu Bakr, 260, 266
Aceh, 173
Adat, 4, 5, 11–17, 22, 23,
  26, 27, 34–37,
  173, 205–207
Adat Perpatih, 43–72
African, 194, 202–206, 208–210,
  214, 215
Akan, 221–226, 229–241
Al-Andalus, 274, 277, 284, 291–307
Algeria, 199, 205, 208
Allah, 225, 228–230
Amazigh, 275, 276, 300
American, 258, 259, 261–263, 267
Amini Island, 77, 80
Andalusian, 273–308
Arabia, 247–269
Arabs, 222, 247–253, 255, 256,
  258–263, 268, 269, 274, 275,
289, 294, 295, 298–300,
  303, 304
Asante, 221–241
Asturian, 284, 285, 288

B
Bao'an, 116, 139
Basque, 280–282, 280n19, 282n23,
  284, 284n27, 286–289,
  287n33, 289n38
Berber, 275, 275n8, 277, 278,
  293–295, 298–304, 299n66,
  306, 307
Bugis, 23

C
Cadiz, 274
Cherokee, 253, 263–268

[1] Note: Page numbers followed by 'n' refer to notes.

© The Author(s), under exclusive license to Springer Nature
Switzerland AG 2024
A. Panakkal, N. M. Arif (eds.), *Matrilineal, Matriarchal, and
Matrifocal Islam*, Palgrave Series in Islamic Theology, Law, and
History, https://doi.org/10.1007/978-3-031-51749-5

315

316 INDEX

China, 113–140
Christian, 224, 238, 240
Colonialism, 195, 210, 214
Confucian, 146, 148, 152–154, 160
Cordoba, 291, 297, 304
Culture, 169, 170, 184–186
Customs, 169, 185, 193–215

D
Divorce, 194, 210–213
Dongxiang, 116, 139

E
East Africa, 194, 204
Ethnic, 222, 223, 225–227

F
Family, 193–215
Fantse, 221–241
Fiqh, 194, 198–206, 211, 213, 214
French, 194, 198, 198n15, 199, 202, 204, 205, 207, 209, 214
Futūhāt al-Jazā'ir, 77, 78n2, 80–85, 87, 100, 101

G
Gedimu, 139
Gender, 113, 114, 116–121, 125–139
Geography, 303
Germanic, 278, 284, 286, 288, 295–297, 297n59, 307
Ghana, 221–241
Goryeo period, 145, 147
Greek, 275, 278n15, 279, 281, 287, 290n43

H
Hadīth, 146, 163, 200, 205
Hadramī, 195
Haenyeo, 150–155
Al-Hakam, Caliph, 300
Hanaf/Hanafī, 139, 140, 198, 200
Hijra, 248
Hikayat Raja Pasai, 47
Hispania, 281, 282, 306
Hong Kong, 169
Huihui, 116, 117
Huijiaotu, 116
Hui Muslims, 114–127, 129–132, 134, 138, 139

I
Iberian, xxiv, 276, 278–282, 286, 289n38, 290, 308n9
Ibn 'Abd al-Hakam, 299
Ibn Fadl Allāh al-'Umari, 260
Ikhwani, 139
Indiana, 266
Indians, 265–268
Indigenous, 275, 285, 287n33, 295
Indo-European, 279n18, 281, 283–287, 287n33, 306
Indonesia, 44, 71
Inheritance, 4–6, 22–23, 25–30, 35, 37, 44, 55, 64–68, 71, 72, 145–147, 160, 162, 164, 165, 171–174, 179, 194, 195, 203, 207, 210, 213, 221, 222, 224, 226, 227, 229–232, 234–236, 238–241
Integrations, 77–107

INDEX 317

Islam, 5, 7, 11–17, 22, 34, 35, 37,
46, 49, 57–61, 66, 67, 72,
114–117, 119, 123, 125, 126,
128, 131, 132, 135, 136,
138–140, 176, 184–188,
221–241, 248, 249, 251, 256,
257, 261, 268, 275, 277, 278,
284, 291, 293–295, 295n55,
299, 308
Islamic law, 194, 198, 199, 201,
204–208, 214, 221, 229–230,
233, 234, 239–241
Islamisation, 12–15
Island, 145–165

J
Japan, 169–188
Jeju, 145–165
Jilbab, 14, 16, 21, 32
Jindeok, 147
Joseon Dynasty, 146, 148,
156, 157

K
Karanavar, 88
Karanavathi, 89
Kaum Muda, 13
Kaum Tua, 13
Kazakh, 116, 139
Kim Man-Deok, 151, 154
Kingdom of Silla, 145
Kinship, 4, 6, 7, 16, 18, 22, 23, 28,
29, 30n87, 33, 79, 80, 82–86,
88–96, 88n37, 103, 105, 194,
205, 207
Korea, 145–165
Kyrgyz, 116, 139

L
Lahu, 114
Lakshadweep, 77, 78, 81, 84, 87–89,
88n37, 100, 106, 107
Lineage, 252, 256, 263, 264

M
Ma'bar, 83, 84
Madhāhib, 200
Makkathayam, 86
Malabar, 78, 82–88, 88n37, 90–94,
94n63, 96–99, 101, 103,
105–107, 253
Malaysia, 43–72
Mali, 260
Manqūs Mawlid, 82, 82n16
Mansu Musa, 260
Marumakkathayam, 88–90, 102,
105, 106
Maternal, 169–188
Matriarchal, 3–37, 77–107,
145–165
Matrifocal, 3–37, 77–107, 278, 283,
285–289, 304–307
Matrilineal, 3–37, 77–107, 193–215,
247, 248, 252–257, 261,
263–265, 267, 269, 273–308
Matriliny, 221–241
Matrivocality, 113–140
Ma Xiuzhen, 128
Mediator, 169–188
Medina, 80, 84, 85
Melaka, 48–50
Merantau, 5, 21–23, 24n71,
25, 31–33
Minangkabau, 3–37, 44, 45n4, 47–51,
47n13, 47n15, 48n16, 53n31,
61–63, 71, 172, 173

318 INDEX

Morgengabe, 297, 298, 307
Mosques, 175, 182, 186, 187
Mosuo, 114
Mozambique, 193–215
Muafakat, 46, 47, 54, 71
Muhiyudheen, 82
Muladis, 289
Mumb Maulā, 78, 78n2, 82
Murābitūn, 262
Muslims, 77–107, 113–140, 145–165,
    169–188, 193–215, 221–225,
    227–229, 232–241, 248, 250,
    251, 254, 265–269, 273–308
Muwalladūn, 289

N

Nagari, 4, 16, 17n50, 26, 29,
    33, 34, 36
Near East, 248, 250, 252–257,
    265, 269
Negeri Sembilan, 4
Negotiator, 188
Negri Sembilan, 68
Nkramo, 223, 224
North Africa, 248–253, 258, 262,
    263, 265, 268
North African, 278–282, 298

O

Orientalism, 198–204

P

Padang Panjang, 13
Padri Wars, 12, 27
Pancarian, 26, 27
Paternal, 146, 164
Patriarchal, 146, 148,
    153, 154

Patriliny, 222, 224, 225,
    230, 232–235
Periangan, 47, 47n15
Polygamy, 212
Portuguese, 193–215

Q

Qadiriyya, 129n62, 140
Qiṣṣat Shakarwatī Farmāḍ,
    79n8, 83–87
Qur'ān, 11, 15, 16, 86, 146, 156,
    163, 164, 194, 200, 205

R

Ratheeb, 82
Resilience, 3–37
Roman law, 282, 284, 286, 293, 306

S

Safina Pattu, 81
Salar, 116, 139
Sendeok, 147
Seolmundae Halmang, 151
Sephardi Jews, 289–293
Shāfiʿī, 173, 199, 200,
    204, 212,
    214, 215
Sharīʿa, 193–215
Sharīfs, 195, 195n2
Shawwāl, 80
Southeast Asia, 172–174
South India, 77–107
South Korea, 169
South Sulawesi, 23
Spain, 273–307, 278n15, 288n36,
    289n38, 295n55, 297n59
Suarang, 26
Sultanate, 173

INDEX 319

Sultan Muzaffar Shah, 49
Sumatra, 11–13, 47, 48, 51, 173
Sumatra Thawalib school, 13
Swahili, 194–196, 204

T
Taiwan, 169
Tajik, 116, 139
Tartar, 116, 139
Translator, 188
Tribes, 248–254, 256, 257,
    260–264, 266–269
Tuareg, 247–269, 275,
    276, 300

U
Ulamā', 198, 200
Umayyads, 289, 291, 294,
    298, 300

Uyghur, 116, 139
Uzbek, 116, 139

V
Visigothic law, 283, 296
Vulnerability, 3–37

W
Waqf al-Aulād, 87–88
Women's Voices, 113–140
Writers, 113–140

Y
Yemen, 251, 252, 255

Z
Zuni, 264, 265

Printed in the United States
by Baker & Taylor Publisher Services